FOOD LAW

This book provides a broad conspectus on the application of EU and international regulation of the food sector on English law. It is aimed at practitioners and students of this vital and emerging branch of law, which has become an important part of current political and legal debate. It is written not just for lawyers as a statement of current law, but is also aimed at all those involved or interested in the food industry who wish to familiarise themselves with how the law is applied practically in this jurisdiction.

The book commences with a short conceptual framework for the study of food law. It then provides a comprehensive and up-to-date account of current English law, explaining fully the detailed processes by which both international and national law and EU decision making have impacted upon most aspects of the production, sale and consumption of food in England.

The book explains and assesses the operation of the current law by describing in detail the roles of Government, the Food Standards Agency and local enforcement authorities in the making and enforcing of laws concerning food.

The work contains full outlines of the developments in the most significant areas of food law. It concentrates specifically on topics such as food labelling and advertising, quality and compositional requirements, geographical food names, genetic modification, organic production, animal welfare and also the role of law in tackling poor health, obesity, and diet-related disease.

The book, though primarily designed as a law text, goes beyond the usual confines of such works. It sets out to explain and describe the impact of successive food crises, such as BSE and the use of horsemeat in beef products, on food safety and transparency requirements. The book considers and assesses how the existing rules on the chemical and biological safety of food impact on our law, and concludes with a review of the developing legal issues concerning the environmental impacts of current and proposed food law, in particular the relationship between food law, climate change and food security.

D1427287

Food Law

European, Domestic and International Frameworks

Caoimhín MacMaoláin

·HART·
PUBLISHING
OXFORD AND PORTLAND OREGON
2015

Published in the United Kingdom by Hart Publishing Ltd
16C Worcester Place, Oxford,OX1 2JW
Telephone: +44 (0)1865 517530
Fax: +44 (0)1865 510710
E-mail: mail@hartpub.co.uk
Website: http://www.hartpub.co.uk

Published in North America (US and Canada) by
Hart Publishing
c/o International Specialized Book Services
920 NE 58th Avenue, Suite 300
Portland, OR 97213-3786
USA
Tel: +1 503 287 3093 or toll-free: (1) 800 944 6190
Fax: +1 503 280 8832
E-mail: orders@isbs.com
Website: http://www.isbs.com

Hart Publishing is an imprint of Bloomsbury Publishing plc.

British Library Cataloguing in Publication Data
Data Available

ISBN: 978-1-84946-670-7

Typeset by Compuscript Ltd, Shannon
Printed and bound in Great Britain by
CPI Group (UK) Ltd, Croydon CR0 4YY

CONTENTS

TABLE OF CASES

TABLE OF LEGISLATION

UNITED KINGDOM

Acts of Parliament

Statutory Instruments

Treaty on European Union (TEU)

Charter of Fundamental Rights

Regulations

Directives

1

History and Development
of Food Law

1.1 Introduction

Food law first emerged as an identifiable strand of academic legal inquiry in the United Kingdom in the late 1990s. Prior to this, there had been some literature in this part of the world related to aspects of the subject.[1] Most of it tended to be based on articles on the law of the European Union on the free movement of goods.[2] Some books had been published. They tended to be guides for practitioners on EU rules, with no significant contextual analysis of the application of these laws at national level, the political environment, social considerations or judicial decision making. 'Mad cow disease' changed all of this.

While food laws have existed since ancient times, and were well developed by the nineteenth century, it was really accession to the EU that most significantly affected English law in this area. When the UK joined the European Economic Community (EEC), as it then was, in 1973, many of the EEC food laws that were transposed into domestic law by the *acquis communautaire* tended to be very general in nature and poorly implemented (by many Member States, not just by the UK). They dealt with a range of disparate, unrelated and often relatively unimportant issues. It was difficult to identify a coherent body of rules regulating the production and marketing of food at this time. Food law was not really a subject yet in its own right.

A series of well-publicised issues on the relationship between food regulation and human health led to a vastly increased impetus for the creation of a new, more reasoned way of controlling how the food sector operates. The first of these was the crisis involving BSE (bovine spongiform encephalopathy, or 'mad cow disease') in the mid to late 1990s. There were two issues here. The first was that

---

[1] It should be noted that food law had already emerged as a subject for examination in the United States of America, where the *Food and Drug Law Journal* (formerly the *Food, Drug and Cosmetic Law Journal*) was first published in 1946.
[2] Eg O Brouwer, 'Free Movement of Foodstuffs and Quality Requirements: Has the Commission Got it Wrong?' (1988) 25 *CML Rev* 237; and H von Heydebrand, 'Free Movement of Foodstuffs, Consumer Protection and Food Standards in the European Community: Has the Court of Justice Got it Wrong?' (1991) 16 *EL Rev* 391.

a possible link between beef consumption and the human form of BSE (variant Creutzfeldt-Jakob disease (vCJD)) was suggested by scientists. The claim was that people could contract this deadly disease just by eating meat, or even beef products, such as gelatine. People now believed that the consumption of burgers, steaks, prepared puddings and children's sweets, such as jellies, could all kill them. The second issue was that existing laws were shown to be hopelessly inadequate in dealing with a crisis such as this. Because of EU membership, many of the decisions on how to control the spread of the disease were outside national control. It would be up to the EU institutions to reassure the public that all necessary steps were being taken to safeguard their health. On this, they failed.

The second 'headline-grabbing' issue that acted as a catalyst in the creation of increased interest in the study of food law was the initial regulation of genetically modified organisms (GMOs). Again, it was scientists who sparked public controversy here by making suggestions that the use of genetic modification techniques in food production could damage the intestines of rats, and therefore presumably those of humans as well. Outrage ensued, fostered by the fact that the presence of a GMO in food did not have to be stated on the label. Consumer groups protested that the law was again failing to protect them from the potential, or unknown, harms of food consumption.

They were right. A series of loopholes in the legislation allowed genetically modified foods onto the market without adequate disclosure that the foods were in fact genetically modified. The resultant pressure on politicians led to a ban on the approval of new GMOs across the EU. This in turn created difficulties for the EU at the international level, when the World Trade Organization called into question the legality of this prohibition.

These two sagas, and other incidents, really brought the way in which the law regulates the food sector into public, and consequently increased academic, focus. A plethora of articles and a series of books were published, not just on general issues of food law, but also detailed works on more specific areas, such as genetic modification, food safety, labelling and the precautionary principle. Subject-specific journals such as the *European Food and Feed Law Review* have come into existence and are published several times per year. There have been special issues of the *European Law Journal* and the *European Journal of Consumer Law* dealing exclusively with food law. University students have organised successful postgraduate research conferences where all of the sessions over an entire weekend had aspects of this newly discovered subject alone as their central focus. There are academies of food law run every summer across Europe, there are firms that specialise or deal exclusively with food law matters and there are now multiple annual food law conferences organised by a range of bodies across many EU Member States. Food law is taught at undergraduate and postgraduate levels in the UK and throughout the EU. Food law has become an established, stand-alone subject, supported by a wealth of peer-reviewed articles, journals and books. Food laws have significant implications for human health, the environment, animal welfare, consumer satisfaction, sectoral employment and the wider economy. While 'mad cows' and 'Frankenstein foods' may have been responsible for bringing increased attention to the study of food law, its growth and further establishment as a topic of student, academic and practitioner inquiry is perhaps sustained by the fact that many of the issues assessed are not just interesting to those professionally engaged in the food industry, but also concern matters of fundamental personal importance.

1.2 History of Food Laws

Laws controlling the production and marketing of food have existed since ancient times. The Code of Hammurabi makes several references to grain and cattle stocks, the former often being used as the currency of fines. Ancient Egypt carried laws on the labelling of wines, similar to those in existence today. Details would have to be provided of the name and the location of the producer and the estate, the type of wine, its vintage, and an assessment of its quality. Consumer protection laws were introduced in Ancient Rome to minimise fraud and the sale of poor-quality food.[3]

The Bible makes many references to which foods should and should not be eaten. Leviticus 11:3 permits the eating of 'clean' animals: 'Whatsoever parteth the hoof, and is clovenfooted, and cheweth the cud … that shall ye eat.' Pigs, hares and camels are specifically excluded from this category. They are all deemed 'unclean'. Fish that have fins and scales may be eaten. Others, such as shellfish, may not. There follows a long list of birds which may not be eaten. These include storks, owls, eagles and vultures. Similar references are made in Deuteronomy 14.

Most ancient laws on food dealt with requirements for specific, rather than for all, foodstuffs—also known as 'vertical' legislation.[4] They were general in nature and usually prescribed that a substance could, or could not, be eaten, or that it had to be labelled in a particular way. Another feature of early food laws was that they sought to prevent the adulteration of products, which were often laced with cheap ingredients, many of which could be very harmful to human health.

1.2.1 Aspects of Early Food Law

The earliest English food laws included the Assize of Bread and Ale, introduced during the reign of Henry III in 1266.[5] It, too, was specific in its content, regulating

---

[3] FAO and WHO, 'Origins of the Codex Alimentarius' in *Understanding the Codex Alimentarius* (1999), ISBN 92-5-104248-9.

[4] As opposed to 'horizontal' legislation, which deals with one aspect, or aspects, of food law but across all foodstuffs. An example of a 'horizontal' provision might be food labelling requirements, applicable to all foods. A 'vertical' provision, on the other hand, might set labelling requirements, but just for one type of food, such as beef or chocolate.

[5] 51 Hen 3 Stat 1.

the quality, weight and price of bread and beer. The price of beer, for example, was to be set according to the price of the raw materials used in its production. Harsh penalties were set to deter bakers from short-changing their customers—often resulting in the inclusion of an extra portion of bread in the customer's order to ensure compliance with minimum weight requirements, hence the expression 'a baker's dozen' referring to the number 13. Acts of Parliament were later introduced to set specific requirements designed to maintain the quality and safety of certain foods and drinks. These included the Adulteration of Tea and Coffee Act 1724, and later the Adulteration of Tea Acts of 1730 and 1776. The latter prohibited the inclusion of sloe, liquorice, or previously used leaves in retailed tea. More of this vertical legislation was introduced through the Bread Acts of 1822 and 1836, which stipulated that bread now had to be sold by the pound or a multiple thereof, and the Corn, Peas, Beans or Parsnips and Cocoa Act 1822, which established a licensing system for the sale of these foodstuffs. Much of this early legislation continued along these vertical lines. The first really significant statutes to set legal requirements for the manufacture and/or sale of food more generally, or 'horizontal' legislation, were the Adulteration of Food or Drink Act 1860 and, perhaps more importantly, the Sale of Food and Drugs Act 1875.

The 1860 Act made it an offence to knowingly sell any foodstuff which endangered health, or which had been adulterated in any way.[6] Adulteration, in this context, has come to mean, quite simply, 'the mixing of other substances with food', but it was not defined in the 1860 Act—one of several reasons underlying its lack of effectiveness in achieving the stated aim. More recently, the Food Act 1984 provided that it was an offence to add any substance to food that would render it 'injurious to health'.[7] As discussed in chapter five, this term 'injurious to health' is problematic. The 1984 Act states that

> [i]n determining for the purposes of this Act whether an article of food is injurious to health, regard shall be had not only to the probable effect of that article on the health of a person consuming it, but also to the probable cumulative effect of articles of substantially the same composition on the health of a person consuming such articles in ordinary quantities.[8]

The test of whether an offence has been committed is therefore to be based on both immediate and longer-term risks of consumption at ordinary levels. This has the potential to include foods that are both 'dangerous' and 'harmful', if we define the former as being those foods which contain something that can make the person unwell in the short term, such as a non-fatal amount of contaminant or toxic substance, and if we define the latter as including those foods which are more likely to have an effect on health over the long term, such as foods of poor nutritional quality. It is not usual to query whether the lawfulness of manufacturing and/or selling the latter is contrary to the test of being 'injurious to health'.

[6] Section 1.
[7] Section 1(1) of the Food Act 1984.
[8] Section 1(4).

This important, yet insufficiently considered, distinction between 'dangerous' and 'harmful' foods will be returned to later in this book. This distinction highlights how food law has developed in a way that deals with 'dangerous' foods, but which, it will be argued, has been negligent in its treatment of 'harmful' foods.

The 1860 Act did contain some provisions on the analysis of food for indications of adulteration,[9] as well as setting a legal definition for 'food and drink' for the first time in English law. Section 14 provided that this included

> not only all alimentary substances, whether solids or liquids, but also all eatables or drinkables whatsoever not being medical drugs or articles usually taken or sold as medicines.

As stated, the 1860 Act was largely ineffective and was supplemented by two further adulteration acts, in 1862 and 1872. These facilitated the appointment of inspectors who could take food samples for analysis. They also provided a more developed definition of 'adulteration', making it illegal to 'admix, with any article of food or drink any injurious or poisonous ingredient or material to adulterate the same for sale'. Problems persisted. In particular, some producers were prosecuted under the 1872 Act for merely changing foods from their original form by adding non-injurious ingredients. A Government Select Committee, charged with reviewing the Adulteration Acts, heard that there had been cases of prosecution for selling mustard which contained not only mustard seed, but also turmeric and chillies. Over-zealous, and often erroneous, interpretations of the new legislation led to accusations that the mere addition of other ingredients to food was 'adulteration'. Difficulties were also reported with the sale of cocoa, when it was mixed with sugar and starches. The Select Committee reported that consumers were being 'cheated rather than poisoned' by adulteration, and that most food manufacturing was perfectly safe. The focus of regulation should therefore, it was stated, be on retailers who tampered with goods in an active attempt to mislead or deceive consumers.[10] The Licensing Act 1872, for example, prohibited the addition of salt to beer, which had been used to induce additional thirst in consumers.[11]

Since the eighteenth century, it has also been an indictable offence at common law to provide someone with food that is not fit for human consumption, regardless of whether this was done out of malice or profit-seeking.[12] Selling, or being in possession with intent to sell, diseased or unwholesome food is a common law nuisance.[13] A supplier can be indicted for manslaughter if someone dies from

---

[9] Sections 3–5.

[10] For further discussion on the proceedings before the Select Committee see J Phillips and M French, 'Adulteration and Food Law, 1899–1939' (1998) 9 *Twentieth Century British History* 350, esp pp 354–356.

[11] Schedule 1 to the Licensing Act 1872. Other substances which could no longer be added to beer under the Act included opium, hemp and tobacco.

[12] *R v Treeve* (1796) 2 East PC 821.

[13] *Shillito v Thompson* (1875) 1 QBD 12.

eating diseased meat or contaminated food that he has provided. There can be a conviction on these charges if the evidence shows that it was provided in the knowledge that it was unfit for consumption, or if the supplier was guilty of gross negligence in this regard.[14]

The recognised need for a change in the Adulteration of Food Acts later materialised through the introduction of the Sale of Food and Drugs Act 1875, which consolidated the more progressive provisions introduced since 1860, along with clearer legal definitions and enforcement mechanisms for those given responsibility for ensuring compliance with the law.

1.2.2 Sale of Food and Drugs Act 1875

The Sale of Food and Drugs Act 1875 repealed the Act of 1860,[15] simplifying many of the provisions that had been introduced in this area in the earlier Victorian period. 'Food' was defined simply as including 'every article used for food and drink by man, other than drugs or water'.[16] The Act also separated the provisions on adulteration, categorising them according to whether the addition of other substances to food was of a nature that was either (i) injurious to health; or (ii) affected the quality of the food concerned. Section 3 provided that

> [no] person shall mix, colour, stain, or powder, or order or permit any other person to mix, colour, stain, or powder, any article of food with any ingredient or material so as to render the article injurious to health, with intent that the same may be sold in that state, and no person shall sell any such article so mixed [etc] under a penalty in each case.

Conviction under this provision of the Act was punishable by a fine or up to six months' imprisonment, with hard labour. Section 6 further provided that

> [no] person shall sell to the prejudice of the purchaser any article of food ... which is not of the nature, substance, and quality of the article demanded by such purchaser.

This was qualified by the fact that ingredients that were not harmful to health, and the inclusion of which was necessary to actually make the product, could be added. This would not now be considered 'adulteration'—provided that this was not done 'fraudulently to increase the bulk, weight, or measure of the food ... or conceal the inferior quality thereof'.[17] The inclusion of ingredients would now, under the 1875 Act, have to be stated on a label. This would have to be 'distinctly and legibly written or printed on [the packaging of the food]'.[18]

---

[14] *R v Kempson* (1893) 28 L Jo 477.

[15] Section 1 of the Sale of Food and Drugs Act 1875.

[16] Section 2.

[17] In *Hotchin v Hindmarsh* [1891] 2 KB 181, the appellant, a foreman of a dairy company, was prosecuted and convicted under section 6 of the Sale of Food and Drugs Act 1875 for supplying milk to which water had been added. It was a clear dilution of the 'quality of the article demanded by [the] purchaser'.

[18] Section 8.

The Sale of Food and Drugs Act 1875 also set out a range of provisions on the role of analysts in certifying the safety and quality of food. These analysts, who were appointed at local authority level,[19] could, for a fee, be called upon by any purchaser of food to analyse and certify the safety or otherwise of a product.[20] Analysts were also obliged to report quarterly to their appointing authority on the number and outcome of their investigations.[21] The analyst's report was also deemed to be the most significant piece of evidence in any resulting prosecution under the Act, although the analyst himself could be cross-examined in court on this.[22] Those convicted of an offence under the Act could appeal, subject to the satisfaction of certain conditions.[23] The main defence available to those charged under the Act was a satisfactory demonstration that they could not have been aware that what they were selling was adulterated, in particular where it could be shown that the offending article had been purchased by them in the same condition as that in which it was subsequently sold.[24] Figures published in the Annual Reports of the Local Government Boards in England and Wales show that between 5 and 10 per cent of purchased food samples were usually found to have been adulterated. In 1899 the figure stood at around 9.4 per cent, dropping pretty consistently to closer to the 5 per cent mark by the 1930s. The figures for adulteration levels tended to be higher in Scotland, ranging from 6.5 per cent (1926) to 14.4 per cent (1899).

Finally, the 1875 Act also included special provisions on tea. All imported tea was to be subjected to an examination by the customs authorities. This was to be done to ensure that the tea had not been mixed with other, usually cheaper, substances, or that the leaves had not already been used to make tea.[25] All products that were deemed after analysis to be unfit for sale as tea were to be forfeited and destroyed.

1.2.3 Food and Drugs Act 1955

In the first half of the twentieth century it was widely believed, amongst those charged with regulating the food sector, that the law was not in need of further reform. It was felt that 'the processes and ingredients of production were essentially sound and in little need of regulation'.[26] There was little consideration for consumers' concerns. The only body which was dedicated to the support of

---

[19] Section 10.
[20] Section 12.
[21] Section 19.
[22] Section 21.
[23] Section 23.
[24] Section 25.
[25] Section 30.
[26] J Phillips and M French, 'Adulteration and Food Law, 1899–1939' (1998) 9 *Twentieth Century British History* 350, which provides a more comprehensive account of the history of English food law during this period than can be here attempted.

consumers' interests in Britain before the Second World War was the Consumer Council, and it 'was unable to exert significant influence on the nature or detail of regulation'.[27] The use of chemicals and pesticides was becoming more common in food production, but these were mostly unregulated until the 1920s. Deliberate adulteration still occurred. It may have been more likely to be in a form that posed less of an immediate danger to human health, but, as the data presented above shows, there was clearly still deliberate deception of the purchasing public going on. Some ad hoc vertical legislation was introduced, setting compositional and labelling requirements for specific foodstuffs, such as milk, butter and meat. A rather piecemeal body of rules was developing, resulting in the need for some consolidation through the introduction of the Food and Drugs (Adulteration) Act 1928 and later the Food and Drugs Act 1938.

The more significant Food and Drugs Act 1955 was designed to further consolidate English food law at this time. It replaced the 1938 Act, as well as the Food and Drugs (Milk, Dairies and Artificial Cream) Act 1950 and the Food and Drugs Amendment Act 1954. It also introduced new provisions on the regulation of abattoirs. Part I of the 1955 Act set out a series of general provisions on labelling, inspections, transport, hygiene and sanctions to be imposed for breach of the Act. It set the definition of adulteration that was carried through to the Food Safety Act 1990.[28] Authorised officers were given wide-ranging powers under the 1955 Act, including the ability to

> at all reasonable times examine any food intended for human consumption which has been sold, or is offered or exposed for sale, or is in the possession of, or has been deposited with or consigned to, any person for the purpose of sale or of preparation for sale, and, if it appears to him to be unfit for human consumption [and to] seize it and remove it in order to have it dealt with by a justice of the peace.[29]

These powers were extended to include food in transit, with the ability to both inspect and detain any vehicle if necessary.[30] Other provisions of the 1955 Act included a ban on the sale of any product derived, in whole or in part, from an animal that was slaughtered in a knacker's yard,[31] and more detailed provisions and empowerments on the hygienic production and sale of food.[32]

1.2.4 Food Act 1984

While the 1955 Act continued to be supplemented by statutory instruments dealing with more specific areas in need of regulation, such as the Arsenic in Food

---

[27] ibid, p 360.
[28] Section 1(1) of the Food and Drugs Act 1955.
[29] Section 9(1).
[30] Section 11.
[31] Section 12(1).
[32] Section 13.

Regulations 1959,[33] and several relating to the manufacture of ice cream,[34] it needed to be replaced. The Food Act 1984 was passed to do so.

The 1984 Act was the most comprehensive set of food regulations ever introduced into English law by that time. It covered a whole range of areas, both through consolidation and new legislative initiatives. It was also the first general food act introduced after accession to the European Economic Community, meaning that some new rules in some areas had to be created, while others had to be modified to reflect harmonised European standards, in particular in relation to hygiene and labelling. A much more significant alignment with Community rules takes place with the introduction of the Food Safety Act 1990.

The Act follows familiar lines at the outset, dealing with the old issue of adulteration. It states that

> [a] person is guilty of an offence who adds any substance to food, uses any substance as an ingredient in the preparation of food, abstracts any constituent from food, or subjects food to any other process or treatment so as ... to render the food injurious to health, with intent that the food shall be sold for human consumption in that state.[35]

This definition marked a clear departure from that contained in the earlier Acts already discussed in this chapter, in particular those of the mid-nineteenth century. Section 1 referred to abstractions from food, as well as additions to it. It also created a clear link between adulteration, in whatever form, and injury to health. The mere addition of sugar to cocoa, for example, would no longer therefore be considered adulteration of food. Finally, there was recognition of the more widespread use of chemicals and technology in food production, reflected in the inclusion of provision for processes and treatments in the list of ways in which food could become 'injurious'.[36] These provisions of the 1984 Act move the key offence in food law from being one of adulteration to 'offences as to preparation and sale of injurious foods'. In this way, at least, the Food Act 1984 addresses the primary shortcoming of the Victorian legislation. The 1984 Act has now also been mostly replaced by the Food Safety Act 1990.[37] This is discussed in more detail in chapter five.

---

[33] SI No 831/1959. These Regulations stipulated the quantity of arsenic that could be lawfully present in specified foodstuffs, as set out in the Schedule. The Regulations also provided that fish, edible seaweed and hops were not subject to these maximum permitted levels (usually one part per million on a per weight basis) where the arsenic was naturally present in those higher quantities. Anything exceeding these permitted levels was deemed 'unfit for human consumption' and had to be seized and destroyed (reg 4). The maximum sentence that could be imposed for contravention of the Act was a fine of £100, three months' imprisonment, or both (reg 5(1)).

[34] Such as the Ice-cream (Heat Treatment) Regulations 1959 (SI No 734/1959) and 1963 (SI No 1083/1963).

[35] Section 1(1).

[36] Specific provision is also made in section 36 of the Act for those acts which could adulterate milk.

[37] Parts III (Markets) and V (Sugar Beet and Cold Storage) of the Food Act 1984 have not been replaced.

1.3 European Integration

As has already been stated, it is membership of the EU which has led to the vast majority of food laws as they stand in England to take their current format and content. This, of course, presupposes a complex relationship between the two systems. Some EU rules have direct applicability. Regulations automatically become part of English law on the date stated in the legislation. Significantly, the use of this format for introducing new EU requirements has become more commonplace since the turn of the millennium, meaning there is little room for derogation at national level from the rules set out in the regulations. Directives, which had previously been the traditional format for many of the EU rules on food, do require some further implementation by the Member States and will not always, therefore, have 'direct effect'—meaning that individuals may not always be able to rely on their provisions until after they have been formally and effectively transposed into English law. This is discussed in more detail below. Despite this, it can usually be accepted that secondary legislation adopted by the EU legislative institutions must also be adopted and applied by English institutions. As a result, it is European obligations, and some international requirements arising out of this, which now account for the introduction of almost all of the laws in England which apply specifically to food.

1.3.1 Supremacy of European Union Food Law

The European Communities Act 1972, which gives internal legal effect to EU law, provides that

> [a]ll such rights, powers, liabilities, obligations and restrictions from time to time cre-
> ated or arising by or under the Treaties, and all such remedies and procedures from time
> to time provided for by or under the Treaties, as in accordance with the Treaties are
> without further enactment to be given legal effect or used in the United Kingdom shall
> be recognised and available in law, and be enforced, allowed and followed accordingly;
> and the expression 'enforceable EU right' and similar expressions shall be read as refer-
> ring to one to which this subsection applies.[38]

This effectively means that any EU legislation which is designed to become part of domestic law must be applied at national level. Directly effective provisions of EU law are thus, under the terms of the European Communities Act 1972, incorporated into English law. This includes all Treaty on the Functioning of the European Union (TFEU) provisions, regulations and directives that together form the body of EU food law. The Act further states that

---

[38] Section 2(i).

any designated minister or department may by regulations, make provision for the purpose of implementing any Community obligation of the United Kingdom, or enabling any rights enjoyed or to be enjoyed by the United Kingdom under or by virtue of the Treaties to be exercised [or] for the purpose of dealing with matters arising out of or related to any such obligation or rights [and] in the exercise of any statutory power or duty, including any power to give directions or to legislate by means of orders, rules or regulations or other subordinate instrument, the person entrusted with the power or duty may have regard to the objects of the Communities and to any such obligation or rights.[39]

Secondary legislation, such as statutory instruments, can thus be used to give effect to the many EU food directives and to provide the necessary detail and administrative requirements for the practical application of EU regulations. It may also be used, for similar purposes, for any provision of food law that may be made by Act of Parliament.[40] Finally, the Act states that

[f]or the purposes of all legal proceedings any question as to the meaning or effect of any of the Treaties, or as to the validity, meaning or effect of any Community instrument, shall be treated as a question of law and, if not referred to the European Court, be for determination as such in accordance with the principles laid down by and any relevant decision of the European Court or any court attached thereto.[41]

This makes decisions of the Court of Justice applicable in English law and binding on the English courts. This supremacy of EU law, requiring that it take precedence over domestic law, was further supported by the House of Lords in *Factortame*.[42] This is, of course, subject to the EU acting within the scope of its authority. Any legal instrument introduced in a manner that is contrary to the procedural and competence requirements set out in the TFEU does not have supremacy in English law, and is also open to an application for annulment, which can be brought before the European courts.[43] Parliament can also revoke the supremacy of EU law by modifying the European Communities Act 1972 through the application of the European Union Act 2011. Article 18 provides that

[d]irectly applicable or directly effective EU Law (that is, the rights, powers, liabilities, obligations, restrictions, remedies and procedures referred to in section 2(1) of the European Communities Act 1972) falls to be recognised and available in law in the United Kingdom only by virtue of that Act or where it is required to be recognised and available in law by virtue of any other Act.

In other words, it restates the constitutional principle of parliamentary sovereignty—that future parliaments cannot be bound by the Acts of previous ones. Having said all of this, we can normally presume that EU directives, regulations

---

[39] Section 2(2).
[40] Section 2(4).
[41] Section 3(1).
[42] *Factortame Ltd v Secretary of State for Transport (No 2)* [1991] 1 AC 603.
[43] For further discussion see ch 2.

and Court decisions will be applied, in one way or another, at national level. However, it can, of course, be more complicated than this.[44]

Significance of 'Metric Martyrs'

The nature of the relationship between English law and EU law was most famously scrutinised by the domestic courts in what has become known as the 'metric martyrs' case.[45] Appeals were brought by greengrocers and market traders against their convictions for operating contrary to the Weights and Measures Act 1985 by selling and advertising their wares using imperial rather than metric units of measurement. The EU Metrification Directive had been introduced in 1979 in a bid to impose the use of the same units of measurement across all Member States.[46] Annex 1 to this Directive set the standardised unit of mass as the kilogram and the unit of volume as the litre. The 1985 Act, used to transpose this Directive into English law, prescribed that

> [no] person shall use for trade any unit of measurement which is not included in ... this Act, or use for trade, or have in his possession for use for trade, any linear, square, cubic or capacity measure which is not included in ... this Act, or any weight which is not so included.[47]

Prices must be advertised in metric units. The Price Marking Order 1999 provides that the 'unit price' is

> the final price, including VAT and all other taxes, for one kilogram, one litre, one metre, one square metre or one cubic metre of a product.[48]

Traders are obliged, under the terms of the Order, to indicate the unit price to their customers.[49] Breach of this requirement is a criminal offence.[50] One of the defendants used weighing machines calibrated in pounds and ounces. Another displayed unit prices by weight in pounds, and not kilograms.

The case makes interesting reading for constitutional lawyers. Specifically, Laws LJ highlighted that rights and obligations created by EU law are, by virtue of the European Communities Act 1972, incorporated into English law and are supreme over national law. Where there is an inconsistency between EU law and national law, the latter must be modified or repealed, even where originally contained in an Act of Parliament. However, where an EU measure is contrary to a fundamental

---

[44] For discussion on the difficulties that EU supremacy can create for the preservation of food culture and tradition see D Chalmers, 'Food for thought: reconciling European risks and traditional ways of life' (2003) 66 *MLR* 532.

[45] *Thoburn and others v Sunderland City Council and others* [2003] QB 151.

[46] Council Directive 1980/181/EEC of 20 December 1979 on the approximation of the laws of the Member States relating to units of measurement and on the repeal of Directive 1971/354/EEC [1980] OJ L 39/40.

[47] Section 8(1) of the Weights and Measures Act 1985.

[48] Para 1(2).

[49] Para 5(1).

[50] Para 5 of the Schedule to the Prices Act 1974.

right or constitutional guarantee provided by English law, the question arises as to whether the European Communities Act 1972 was sufficient to incorporate that contravening measure into English law. This, he considered, 'gives full weight both to the proper supremacy of [EU] law and to the proper supremacy of the United Kingdom Parliament'. For the purposes of this book, the case identifies a series of examples of the difficulties that can arise when a supranational body seeks to harmonise existing food laws across a number of Member States.

The Court in *Thoburn* found that the Weights and Measures Act 1985 presented an incorrect transposition of EU directives on the use of weights and measures. It is clear that imperial measurements were not prohibited outright at the time. Dual measurement systems could be used until the expiration of a transitional period, which had not yet passed. The Court also considered itself 'dismay[ed]' at the fact that criminal offences had been created in the first place. The over-zealous application of incorrectly interpreted EU legislation had led to convictions for what were, at worst, minor offences.

The facts that led to the convictions, and the subsequent appeals, and all of the campaigning on behalf of the defendants that went with this, shows how politically and socially sensitive the transposition of EU law into domestic legal systems can be. Resistance to a whole range of EU food laws that seek to change local traditional and cultural practice has remained commonplace since the harmonisation programme commenced in the 1960s. The use of unpasteurised milk in cheese production, the labelling of chocolate, and the 'metric martyrs' case offer three clear examples of this continuing confrontation. It is also worth noting that in 2009, the EU Commission abandoned its time limits for full transfer to the metric system. An awareness of the problems that a more literal application of these legislative acts can pose at local level has thus led to a decision that dual-measurement can continue indefinitely.

1.3.2 Free Movement and Food Law

It is difficult to understate the impact that EU rules on the free movement of goods have on English food law. They are significant in three main ways. First, the creation of an internal market in goods means that almost all standards related to the production and marketing of food are set at EU level, through the adoption of harmonised rules that are then applied in the Member States. Free movement is facilitated by the application of the same or similar rules in all EU States. This is usually done by the introduction of regulations and directives. Second, Treaty provisions prohibiting the application of charges equivalent to customs duties on imported food, as well as those on ensuring that domestic systems of taxation do not directly or indirectly discriminate against non-national food producers, ensure that imported products from other EU Member States can compete more fairly with domestic produce. This is discussed in more detail in chapter four. Finally, and perhaps most significantly, the Treaty prohibition on the application of measures equivalent to quantitative restrictions on traded goods ensures that no Member State can maintain any national law which has the effect, whether direct or indirect, of inhibiting to any degree the importation of food from elsewhere in the EU. This has hugely significant consequences for English law. It has dictated that certain laws, such as those on the composition of foodstuffs, will not be introduced, and that others cannot be introduced, such as those designed to deal with rising rates of obesity.

1.4 Conclusion

This book is designed to provide a broad conspectus of English food law. This involves a lot of references to EU law, as it is from this source that almost all domestic legal requirements are now created. As this chapter has identified, this new influence has created a whole series of requirements for the State, for producers and for retailers, as well as introducing additional ways of protecting consumers. However, it is also pointed out that in some areas the EU's laws provide insufficient protection, yet the system prevents Member States from initiating local laws to protect their population. EU law prescribes that free movement requirements usually take precedence over domestic initiatives designed to improve or maintain the value, integrity or quality of food.

In its assessment of food law, this book deals with the relevant legislation in a variety of ways. Where EU regulations or directives have been introduced, their key provisions are identified and analysed. In addition to this, the book also indicates the national implementation of these EU legislative requirements, identifying any shortcomings in the domestic transposition. This usually takes place through the use of statutory instruments. Directives will always require national application through the introduction of a national legislative measure such as this. Regulations, which are directly applicable in English law, do not require any implementing measures but usually carry some corresponding national legislation to give full and proper meaning to these, identifying national competent authorities or domestic remedies for example, as they are required to do by the terms of the EU legislation. Interpretation of these measures, both the original EU versions and the domestic implementations, is usually done by the Court of Justice. Relevant English cases are also identified where they show some additional point of interpretation on the provisions under review. To summarise, the book identifies the relevant EU legislation, Court of Justice case law on this, national implementing measures and domestic case law where appropriate. It also discusses related policy documents, legislative proposals, codes of conduct, national standards and international conventions where these identify a policy direction or a method of interpretation for existing measures.

The book chapters deal with four key aspects of, or influences on, English food law. The first of these, including chapters two, three and four, outline and discuss the main sources of food law and the role of those charged with developing and applying legal requirements in this area. This involves an examination of the relationship between national, EU and international law, with specific focus on how this relates to regulation of the food sector. It includes an assessment of the roles of the institutions of the EU in this regard, as well as that of international organisations such as the World Trade Organization, the Codex Alimentarius Commission and the United Nations. At national level, the roles of the main actors in the devising and implementation of food law and policy are all addressed, including the relevant government departments, national competent authorities and important State agencies, such as the Food Standards Agency and the Health Protection Agency, as well as others. This first part of the book concludes with a discussion on the significant influence that EU rules on the free movement of goods exercise on the content and application of both national and EU legal requirements and responsibilities and the restrictions that this can then place on national policy. This is the single biggest influence on national food law.

The next part of the book looks at the important issue of food safety. It was concerns over the spread of disease through the consumption of contaminated beef that really set much of the agenda for EU food law makers over the past couple of decades. It is contended in this book that there has been an overemphasis on safety since the BSE crisis, possibly at the expense of other, often more problematic considerations, such as nutrition and quality. Chapter five includes a comprehensive assessment of the key provisions of the Food Safety Act and the directly applicable EU General Food Law Regulation, which together provide the template for all national controls in this area. It includes an examination of the role of the European Food Safety Authority in preventing the spread of contamination and disease through the production and consumption of food, as well as looking at its other functions and responsibilities. This part concludes with a chapter on the chemical and biological safety of food, which mostly involves an identification of the main provisions related to hygienic production, as well as the controls which have been placed over the use of hormones, pesticides and radiation in the preparation of food.

Food labelling is the main line of communication between producer and consumer. It can be used to clarify details about the content, quality, value or origin of food. It is a key marketing tool, enabling differentiation between products and the palatability, or otherwise, of their characteristics or quality. It can also be manipulated to deceive consumers into believing that a product is better, more wholesome, more local, more environmentally friendly or more welfare-friendly than is really the case. Chapter seven identifies existing laws in this area, with a strong emphasis on changes that are being made by EU regulation from 2014 onwards. It addresses the increasingly important, and somewhat controversial, issues surrounding the use of nutrition labelling and the making of nutrition and health claims. It also makes an assessment of quality requirements that have been introduced for specific foodstuffs. The next chapter focuses on the protection of food names for quality products or for those possessing identifiable characteristics. There has also been new EU legislation introduced in this area that will take full effect over future years.

The book concludes with two chapters on the most pressing concerns for many food lawyers. The first of these provides an examination of how the legal regulation of food affects the health and well-being of those that consume it. This involves an assessment of the interplay between national policy on obesity prevention and health protection on the one hand, and harmonising EU legislation and free movement of food requirements on the other. It shows how efforts made at national level to deal with a national health crisis are mostly in vain due to the application of the TFEU. It argues that this will continue to be the case until there is a reassessment of some of the most established rules in this area. Finally, some of the ethical and environmental aspects of food production and marketing are considered, including an assessment of existing rules on organic production, genetic modification and animal welfare, as well as a discussion on the relationship, both existing and potential, between food law and climate change.

2

Domestic, European Union and International Food Law

2.1 Introduction

English food law is tied up in a complex relationship with EU rules and international laws, policies and recommendations. There are a vast range of influences on the content and application of food law at national level. These are introduced in this chapter, and are discussed in more detail, in the domestic context, in chapter three. If we take as a starting point the fact that almost all English food law now comes directly from EU initiatives, then we can say that the very first place to look for a source of this is the Treaty on the Functioning of the European Union (TFEU). This includes a range of provisions, such as those on the free movement of goods, the protection of consumers and the protection of human health, which are the basis for the development of new EU laws in a range of areas. Many of the English statutory instruments that give effect to the EU legislation started life as proposals from the European Commission, based on one or more of these TFEU provisions. Following the exhaustion of the relevant legislative process, either a directive or a regulation is published, instructing Member States as to how they are to go about making this part of their national law.

Many of the directives and regulations that become part of English law will be designed to 'harmonise' or 'approximate' the laws of all of the Member States. The ideas behind EU legislative initiatives often arise because similar provisions exist within some of the Member States already. The EU legislation is designed to ensure that the same rules exist in all of the Member States. In some cases, therefore, English food law will not be changed at all by the introduction of new EU legislation as the same provisions already exist at national level.

International codes and guidelines for food, such as those of the Codex Alimentarius, can also have a cross-influence on the provisions of EU and national laws. While the international standards are often developed out of laws that already exist amongst many Codex members, a Codex standard can be used as a template in the drafting of new EU requirements, ultimately becoming part of the national laws of EU Member States. Codex standards can also be of persuasive authority in cases before the European Court of Justice. The World Trade

Organization (WTO) Agreements set parameters within which new EU, and consequently national, legislation must be created. Any measures operating outside these limits are open to challenge before the WTO's Dispute Settlement Body and, if found to contravene these Agreements, may either need to be amended accordingly or result in the imposition of fines or the suspension of international trade concessions. International policy recommendations and guidelines can also be used as the basis for the development of codes at national level. Advice on best practice from bodies such as the World Health Organization (WHO) often underlies the publication of non-binding standards for both the corporate sector and for individuals, such as was the case in the issue of guidance by the Scientific Advisory Committee on Nutrition (SACN) on sugar intake in June 2014.

2.2 TFEU Obligations

The TFEU permits the EU institutions to create legislation in many areas that affect the food sector. Several key provisions transfer power away from the Member States and towards the Commission.

Article 30 TFEU prohibits Member States from imposing customs duties, or any charges of equivalent effect, on the importation or exportation of food. Articles 34 and 35 TFEU also require that no quantitative restrictions, or measures of equivalent effect, are placed on food traded within the Union. The limits placed on both customs duties and quantitative restrictions, and measures deemed equivalent to them, are discussed in much more detail in chapter four.

Article 43 TFEU stipulates that secondary legislation may be introduced, via the consultation procedure, to support the Common Agricultural Policy (CAP). Article 114 TFEU facilitates the introduction of legislation designed to support free movement objectives. It states that the ordinary legislative procedure, involving full parliamentary participation, is to be used to harmonise national laws in a manner that enhances the internal market. There should be consultation with the Economic and Social Committee during this process. Paragraph 3 makes specific reference to health and consumer protection forming the basis for legislative initiatives. The Commission is to 'take as a base a high level of protection, taking account in particular of any new development based on scientific facts' when drafting proposals for new legislation.[1] Where legislation is adopted under Article 114 TFEU, Member States may make a plea to the Commission that national laws contrary to these new EU laws should be allowed to continue in force to fulfil some specific health or intellectual property protection policy objective.[2] The Commission then has six months to decide whether or not, on the basis of the

---

[1] Art 114(3) TFEU.
[2] Para 4.

supporting evidence submitted, it approves of the Member State's action.[3] The Commission's failure to make a decision constitutes approval.[4] Authorisation of the Member State's request can be used to trigger a re-examination of the content of the legislation.[5] All harmonising measures introduced under Article 114 TFEU are to include, where appropriate, a safeguard clause authorising Member States to take provisional measures, such as a ban on the importation of certain goods from other Member States, when this is deemed necessary for health protection reasons.[6]

Article 4 TFEU provides that the EU and its Member States share competence to act in a range of areas, including consumer protection and common safety concerns in public health matters. Article 168 TFEU, originally introduced by the Maastricht Treaty in 1993, provides that '[a] high level of human health protection shall be ensured in the definition and implementation of all Community policies and activities'. EU strategy is to complement, rather than replace, national policy in this area. The ordinary legislative procedure is to be used for the introduction of veterinary and phytosanitary measures which are designed to protect human health, even where the scope of the legislation might suggest that the subject matter is directly related to the Common Agricultural Policy.[7]

The protection of consumers is first mentioned in the Treaty in Article 12 TFEU. Here it is listed as one of the 'provisions having general application', alongside other important areas such as the promotion of equality, protecting employment and combating discrimination on a range of grounds. It states that

[c]onsumer protection requirements shall be taken into account in defining and implementing other Union policies and activities.

A more specific Treaty provision on the protection of consumers, again first introduced by Maastricht, is set out in Article 169 TFEU. It states that

[i]n order to promote the interests of consumers and to ensure a high level of consumer protection, the Union shall contribute to protecting the health, safety and economic interests of consumers, as well as to promoting their right to information, education and to organise themselves in order to safeguard their interests.

This is to be achieved by using harmonising legislation designed to support the internal market, introduced under Article 114 TFEU, as well as other measures which 'support, supplement and monitor the policy pursued by the Member States'. Again, the ordinary legislative procedure is to be used.[8] According to

---

[3] Para 6.

[4] ibid.

[5] Para 7.

[6] Art 114(10) TFEU. The use of these 'safeguard clauses' is now widespread in food law. For further discussion on this see G Berends and I Carreno, 'Safeguards in food: ensuring food scares are scarce' (2005) 30 *EL Rev* 386.

[7] Art 168(4) TFEU.

[8] Art 169(3) TFEU. The ordinary legislative procedure, by which most new EU food laws are now introduced, is discussed in more detail later in this chapter.

Article 169(4) TFEU, Member States may maintain or introduce more stringent protective measures, provided these are compatible with other Treaty provisions, primarily the free movement of goods. The Commission must be notified where a Member State introduces any such domestic measure.

Finally, most of the EU legislation referred to throughout this book is either in the form of a regulation or a directive. To summarise the previous discussion, the key difference between the two is that regulations are 'directly applicable', meaning that they automatically become part of the national laws of the EU Member States on the date(s) set out in the terms of the legislation. Directives, on the other hand, usually require some implementing or transposing action at national level. Article 288 TFEU provides that

> [a] regulation shall have general application ... be binding in its entirety and directly applicable in all Member States [but] a directive shall be binding, as to the result to be achieved, upon each Member State to which it is addressed, but shall leave to the national authorities the choice of form and methods.

Directives can have 'direct effect' in some circumstances, meaning that they create rights for individuals enforceable before national courts. This is a complicated area, and a full discussion of it is beyond the scope of this book. However, it can be pointed out at this stage that most EU legislation, be it regulations or directives, is enforceable at national level after the date has passed for implementation, as set out in the legislation. Most EU food legislation becomes part of English law after the introduction of a statutory instrument, where this is necessary. Regulations, of course, will be part of national law regardless, but they are often accompanied by statutory instruments designed to give them proper meaning and clarification as to the implementation of their provisions at national level.

2.2.1 Role of the Commission

As mentioned already, most new food laws enter into the English legal system as either a transposition or direct application of EU directives and regulations, or as a consequence of judgments delivered by the European Court of Justice. The EU is responsible for the introduction of legislative initiatives on a whole range of issues related to the production and marketing of food, many of which are explored in this book. Initially, much of this EU legislation was designed to harmonise the laws of the Member States on, for example, preservative use[9] and antioxidant authorisation.[10] They also served to harmonise standards designed to minimise

---

[9] Council Directive 1964/54/EEC of 5 November 1963 on the approximation of the laws of the Member States concerning the preservatives authorised for use in foodstuffs intended for human consumption [1964] OJ L 12/161. English Special Edition Series I, Chapter 1963–1964, p 99.
[10] Council Directive 1970/357/EEC of 13 July 1970 on the approximation of the laws of the Member States concerning the antioxidants authorised for use in foodstuffs intended for human consumption [1970] OJ L 157/31. English Special Edition Series I, Chapter 1970 (II), p 429.

the potential impact of disease on trade in animals and meat,[11] as well as facilitating the free movement of food by setting standardised compositional requirements for a range of specified products, such as honey,[12] coffee[13] and chocolate.[14]

The Commission plays a central role in the development and application of food laws. There are three aspects to this. First, the Commission, in particular through the Directorate-General for Health and Consumers (DG SANCO), proposes new or amending legislation in a range of areas, such as labelling, nutrition and safety. Second, following the 1987 Council Decision to delegate to committees the power to make legislation,[15] the Commission has the most significant role to play in the introduction of regulations through what is known as 'comitology'. Third, under the terms of Article 258 TFEU, the Commission brings proceedings against Member States where it considers that there has been a failure to fulfil Treaty obligations. Much of the jurisprudence of the Court of Justice on many areas of food law has developed out of these 'enforcement actions'.

Directorate-General for Health and Consumers

The bureaucracy of the Commission is made up of Directorates-General (DGs). Each DG has responsibility for an area of Commission competence, such as agriculture, competition, employment and regional policy. DG SANCO (*Santé et Consommateurs*) deals with health and consumer protection matters. It was founded in October 1999.

The primary role of DG SANCO is to draft and propose EU laws on food and product safety, consumer rights and health protection. Of course, these laws are then applied at a local or national level in the Member States, observed by this Directorate-General. DG SANCO reports to the EU Commissioner for Health and Food Safety, an office which was rebranded in 2014. Having said that, duty is owed to the Commission as an institution, rather than to the individual commissioner.

The Directorate-General for Health and Consumers is headed at bureaucratic level by the Director-General, assisted by two deputies. Beneath this, DG SANCO is split into six areas: general affairs; consumer affairs; public health and risk assessment; animal health and welfare; safety of the food chain; and food and veterinary office. Staff are based in Brussels, Luxembourg and Ireland. The Directorate-General is assisted in the development of legislative proposals by the

---

[11] Council Directive 1964/432/EEC of 26 June 1964 on animal health problems affecting intra-Community trade in bovine animals and swine [1964] OJ L 121/1977. English Special Edition Series I, Chapter 1963–1964, p 164.

[12] Council Directive 1974/409/EEC of 22 July 1974 on the harmonisation of the laws of the Member States relating to honey [1974] OJ L 221/10.

[13] Council Directive 1977/436/EEC of 27 June 1977 on the approximation of the laws of the Member States relating to coffee extracts and chicory extracts [1977] OJ L 172/20.

[14] Council Directive 1973/241/EEC of 24 July 1973 on the approximation of the laws of the Member States relating to cocoa and chocolate products intended for human consumption [1973] OJ L 228/23.

[15] Council Decision 1987/373/EEC of 13 July 1987 laying down the procedures for the exercise of implementing powers conferred on the Commission [1987] OJ L 197/33.

Standing Committee on the Food Chain and Animal Health, established by the General Food Law Regulation.[16] This committee is composed of representatives of the Member States. It is chaired by a representative of the Commission.[17] The Committee is organised into eight sections, dealing with general food law; biological safety of the food chain, toxicological safety of the food chain; controls and import conditions; animal nutrition; genetically modified food and feed and environment risk; animal health and animal welfare; and phytopharmaceuticals. The Standing Committee replaced the former Standing Veterinary Committee, the former Standing Committee on Foodstuffs, and the former Standing Committee on Animal Nutrition. It also took over the Standing Committee on Plant Health's responsibility for plant protection products and pesticides residues. The Standing Committee on the Food Chain and Animal Health plays a key role in the EU decision-making process on food matters, especially through the comitology procedure. This is discussed in more detail in the next section. The European Commission has also established the Advisory Group on the Food Chain and Animal and Plant Health, another key contributor to policy and legislation development and application, also discussed below.

Creating Ordinary Legislation

Since the introduction of the TFEU, the vast majority of new EU rules are to be introduced under what is now called the ordinary legislative procedure. This was previously known as 'co-decision', and the method to be used was set out in Article 251 EC. Article 294(2) TFEU now states that '[t]he Commission shall submit a proposal to the European Parliament and the Council'. There then follows the procedure that is to be employed to bring this proposal to fruition as legislation. There are first and second readings for the Parliament and for the Council, where amendments can be proposed and accepted or rejected. When agreement cannot be reached between these two institutions, a Conciliation Committee can be formed, comprising representatives of both. This Committee is then charged with producing a compromise text, which can then be sent back to the Parliament and the Council for a third reading.

The Commission plays a very prominent role in the ordinary legislative procedure. Despite the level of participation of the other two institutions in this, it is clearly the Commission which exerts the most influence over the content of new EU legislation. First, it produces the proposal on which the parliamentary and Council readings are based. Second, it is very difficult for amendments to be carried during the first two readings without the Commission's acceptance of this. Finally, while the Commission is not directly involved in the conciliatory stage,

---

[16] Art 58 of Regulation (EC) No 178/2002 of the European Parliament and of the Council of 28 January 2002 laying down the general principles and requirements of food law, establishing the European Food Safety Authority and laying down procedures in matters of food safety [2002] OJ L 31/1.
[17] ibid.

other than as a conciliator between the Council and Parliament positions, most texts are adopted prior to this and therefore never require a third reading. Most legislation related to the food sector has traditionally been introduced via the ordinary legislative procedure. Agriculture and fisheries were previously outside those areas where new legislation was introduced following co-decision. However, the amendments made by the Lisbon Treaty have changed this. Measures designed to implement or alter aspects of both the Common Agricultural Policy and the Common Fisheries Policy are now subject to the ordinary procedure.[18] Having said that, some significant aspects of fisheries policy, such as the setting of annual catch limits and quotas, are to be decided by the Council, acting on a Commission proposal.[19] Legislation on animal and plant health, zootechnics and animal welfare are now also to be introduced by way of the ordinary legislative procedure, having previously required mere consultation with the Parliament.

To summarise, legislation is usually introduced using the ordinary procedure outlined above or, in some circumstances, by a special legislative procedure— set out on a provision-by-provision basis in the Treaty. Special procedures used include the consultation procedure. This is also initiated by the submission of a proposal from the Commission to the Council. The Council then consults on its content with the Parliament, before deciding on the adoption of the measure. There is a duty to consult with the Parliament,[20] but it is not required to take account of the Parliament's views.

The other main special procedure used is assent. This procedure differs from the others in that the Commission is not the only institution that can introduce the initial proposal. Depending on the issue, and subject to what is stated in the Treaty, proposals can also be made by either the Parliament, the Member States or by the European Council. Key to the assent procedure is that no matter who initiates the legislation, the Parliament must consent to what is proposed before it can become law. In addition, depending on the circumstances, the Council or the European Council may also have to consent to the measure. While the Parliament may use its powers of veto under the ordinary legislative procedure (although it rarely does) it must actively consent to legislation under the assent procedure. There are no time limits placed on the Parliament in this regard. It can delay the introduction of such proposals for as long as it likes. It can also prevent them from ever reaching the statute books.

Little detail is provided on how the special legislative procedures are to operate, which is why we have to look to individual provisions of the TFEU to see which course is to be followed and which institutions are to be involved. Special procedures have less relevance for food law than the ordinary procedure, in any case. They are mainly used to introduce legislative initiatives in other areas of Union competence, such as anti-discrimination measures (Article 19 TFEU), aspects

---

[18] Art 43(2) TFEU.
[19] Art 43(3) TFEU.
[20] Case 138/1979, *Roquette Frères v Council* [1980] ECR 3333.

of citizenship (Article 21 TFEU), capital movement (Article 64 TFEU), taxation harmonisation (Article 113 TFEU), the tasks of the European Central Bank (Article 127 TFEU), the management of natural resources, including water (Article 192 TFEU), and the EU's own resources (Article 311 TFEU).

Comitology

Law making in the EU can be in either the 'ordinary' format, discussed above, where institutions draft, propose, consult and consent to legislation, in the form of directives and regulations, or it can be introduced by the Commission, using powers delegated to it by the 'ordinary' type—the enabling act. The use of delegation powers has become relatively commonplace since the introduction of the comitology procedure in 1987, being contained in around one in every four or five pieces of legislation. Measures introduced using comitology are known as 'delegated acts'.[21] The TFEU describes ordinary legislation, introduced by either the ordinary legislative procedure or a special legislative procedure, as 'legislative acts',[22] whereas the delegated and implementing legislation are deemed to be 'non-legislative acts'.[23]

The comitology procedure works on the basis that committees should provide the Commission with expert advice during the course of the development of policy and legislation. These committees are made up of national representatives of the Member States and are chaired by the Commission. They provide advice during the policy development phase, identifying emerging issues in need of attention and contributing to proposal drafting; the legislation implementation phase; and on policy monitoring and evaluation, assessing the enforcement of legislative measures by national authorities and the efficacy of the legislation introduced.

The nature of the comitological relationship between the committees and the Commission is now set out in the 2011 Comitology Regulation.[24] Most of the delegated acts referred to in this book were introduced under the old system, established by the original Comitology Decision.[25] The 2011 Regulation establishes a more streamlined set of procedures than that which previously existed under the old Decision. There are now only two ways in which comitology can be used—either the 'examination procedure' or the 'advisory procedure' should be employed. Article 2 of the Regulation states that the basic legislation may provide for the application of the advisory procedure or the examination procedure,

---

[21] Art 290 TFEU.

[22] Art 289 TFEU.

[23] Arts 290 and 291 TFEU.

[24] Regulation (EU) No 182/2011 of the European Parliament and of the Council of 16 February 2011 laying down the rules and general principles concerning mechanisms for control by Member States of the Commission's exercise of implementing powers [2011] OJ L 55/13.

[25] The original Comitology Decision was introduced in 1987, Decision 1987/373/EEC of 13 July 1987 laying down the procedures for the exercise of implementing powers conferred on the Commission [1987] OJ L 197/33. This was later replaced by Decision 1999/468/EC [1999] OJ L 184/23, which was itself amended by Council Decision 2006/512/EC [2006] OJ L 200/11. All have since been repealed by Reg 182/2011, n 24 above.

taking into account the nature or the impact of the implementing act required. The examination procedure applies, in particular, for the adoption of implementing legislation relating to the common agricultural and fisheries policies; the environment, security and safety, or protection of the health or safety of humans, animals or plants; the common commercial policy; and taxation.[26]

The advisory procedure is to be used for the adoption of other legislation which does not come within the scope of those types listed above. It may, however, be used in some of those areas which are usually subject to the examination procedure, where deemed appropriate.[27] Whichever of the two procedures applies, the Commission is assisted in its decision making by a committee, composed in the usual manner—representatives of the Member States and chaired by a representative of the Commission.[28] The Commission submits a draft proposal to the committee, which then delivers its opinion on the document to the Commission, subject to whichever procedure is to be used. The opinion of the committee carries a different authority, depending on the procedure. If the advisory procedure is being used, the Commission is only obliged to take 'the utmost account of the conclusions drawn from the discussions within the committee and of the opinion delivered'.[29] If, however, it is the examination procedure that has been used to introduce the implementing legislation, the committee delivers either a 'positive', 'negative' or no opinion, based on qualified majority voting, weighted according to the size of the Member State represented.[30] A positive opinion should lead to the adoption of the legislation.[31] The legislation should not, however, be adopted in its proposed form if the committee has issued a negative opinion. An amended version may be submitted back to the committee for reconsideration,[32] or its introduction may be referred to an appeal committee.[33] The Commission may usually go ahead and adopt its proposal where no opinion has been delivered.[34] The Commission must ensure that there is transparency in the procedures and committee proceedings.[35] Both the European Parliament and the Council must be properly and continuously informed of committee proceedings through the Comitology Register. The Commission must also publish an annual report on the work of the committees.[36] This report noted in 2012 that 268 comitology committees existed, issuing nearly 2,000 separate opinions.[37] Fourteen of these dealt with agriculture and rural development. A further 24 committees were dealing with health and consumer affairs.

[26] Art 2(2) of Reg 182/2011, n 24 above.
[27] Art 2(3).
[28] Art 3(2).
[29] Art 4(2).
[30] Art 5(1).
[31] Art 5(2).
[32] Art 5(3).
[33] The appeal procedure is set out in Art 6 of the Regulation.
[34] Art 5(4).
[35] Art 10(1).
[36] Art 10(2).
[37] Report from the Commission on the Working of the Committees During 2011, COM (2012) 685.

Advisory Group on the Food Chain

Distinction should be drawn between the committees that are involved in the comitology procedure and the expert groups, created by the Commission and used to provide expertise in the preparation and implementation of law and policy. One such expert group is the Advisory Group on the Food Chain and Animal and Plant Health, which was established in 2004.[38] In its 2001 White Paper on European governance,[39] the Commission committed itself to opening up the policy-making process in the EU, involving more people and organisations in the development and implementation of policies. The General Food Law Regulation also provides for 'open and transparent public consultation, directly or through representative bodies, during the preparation, evaluation and revision of food law'.[40] It was felt that this consultation system requires the support of structured meetings in the context of an advisory group, facilitating direct dialogue between the Commission and interested parties, such as consumer associations.[41] The Advisory Group on the Food Chain was thus established.[42]

Under the terms of the Decision, the Commission consults with the Advisory Group on matters related to safety, labelling, nutrition, animal welfare and crop protection.[43] The group itself is made up of no more than 45 representatives of relevant interest groups, who are required to express an interest in participation in the Advisory Group.[44] The Commission then chooses from these applicants on the basis of their suitability. The Group should meet at least twice yearly, and working groups may be established to examine more specific matters.[45] Experts or observers may also be invited to participate in the work of the Group.[46] It should be noted that consultation with the Advisory Group may not always be possible, nor is it always required, in emergency situations.[47]

Enforcement Actions

The Commission is entitled to bring an action before the Court of Justice where it considers that a Member State has breached its Treaty obligations. Article 258 TFEU states that

---

[38] By Commission Decision 2004/613/EC of 6 August 2004 concerning the creation of an advisory group on the food chain and animal and plant health [2004] OJ L 275/17.

[39] COM (2001) 428 final.

[40] Art 9 of Reg 178/2002.

[41] Preamble to Decision 2004/613.

[42] Commission Decision 1980/1073/EEC establishing a new statute of the Advisory Committee on Foodstuffs [1980] OJ L 318/28 was repealed. Art 6 of Decision 2004/613.

[43] Art 2(1).

[44] Art 3.

[45] Art 4.

[46] Art 4(3).

[47] Art 9 of Reg 178/2002.

[i]f the Commission considers that a Member State has failed to fulfil an obligation under the Treaties, it shall deliver a reasoned opinion on the matter after giving the State concerned the opportunity to submit its observations.

It further states that

[i]f the State concerned does not comply with the opinion within the period laid down by the Commission, the latter may bring the matter before the Court of Justice of the European Union.

It is clear that two things must happen before the failure to observe Treaty obligations ends up in the Court. First, an issue related to non-compliance has to be identified. This can occur when a complaint is made to the Commission that a Member State is acting inappropriately. Over half of enforcement actions commence as a result of a complaint.[48] These can come from a variety of sources, including private citizens or petitions made to the European Parliament by individuals, businesses or other interested parties. The remainder of the proceedings are those initiated by the Commission. Decisions on whether or not to investigate a complaint remain at the discretion of the Commission. However, this mechanism has been affected by the introduction of a standardised complaint form, which may be used to report grievances or issues relating to a Member State's failure to adhere to its obligations.[49] Alternatively, an ordinary letter may be used. Whichever mode is employed, it can be submitted to the Commission headquarters in Brussels, or to any of the Commission's offices in any of the Member States. It must relate to an infringement of EU law by a Member State.

Second, a set procedure must be followed before the matter can be dealt with by the Court. When the Commission is alerted to a possible breach of Treaty obligations, it should negotiate with the Member State concerned, affording it the opportunity to explain its position and to remedy the situation. If the matter is not resolved at this initial stage, the Member State must be formally notified of the alleged infringement in a letter from the Commission. The State then usually has two months to reply, at which stage the Commission can decide whether or not to proceed with its investigation of the complaint. Should the matter remain unresolved at this stage, the Commission can then issue a reasoned opinion, setting out the grounds on which the alleged infringement rests. The matter is then referred to the Court, if the Member State still refuses to comply. The hope is that most initial notifications of non-compliance with Treaty obligations will never make it as far as court referral. Over two-thirds of complaints are closed before the first formal step in infringement proceedings; 84 per cent are closed before any reasoned opinion is issued; and only 6 per cent ever make it as far as the Court of

[48] The Commission has reported that complaints account for the initiation of 54% of all enforcement proceedings, or 64% of all cases on issues other than the late transposition of directives: 26th Annual Report on Monitoring the Application of Community Law (2008), COM (2009) 675.
[49] Failure by a member State to comply with Community law: Standard form for complaints to be submitted to the European Commission [1999] OJ C 119/5. The form is available at: http://ec.europa.eu/community_law/docs/docs_your_rights/complaint_form_en.rtf.

Justice. The average time taken to process infringements, from opening the file to court application, is around two years.[50]

Many of the most significant decisions on principles of EU food law have come about as a result of an infringement proceeding. Examples include key cases related to the taxation of imported food and drink,[51] the free movement of food,[52] and labelling and health claims.[53] Roles may also be reversed and cases can be brought against the Commission by the Member States. This most famously happened, for example, when the UK took action in objection to the measures that were adopted at EU level in efforts to avoid the further spread of BSE amongst cattle,[54] and also where several other EU Member States objected to the registration of 'feta' cheese as a protected geographical food name.[55] All of these cases, and many others, are discussed in more detail in the relevant sections of this book.

2.2.2 European Union Courts and English Food Law

The Treaty on European Union (TEU) sets out that the EU is to have its own court structure, charged with ensuring that the law is observed in the interpretation and application of the Treaties. Article 19(1) TEU provides that

> [t]he Court of Justice of the European Union shall include the Court of Justice, the General Court and specialised courts. It shall ensure that in the interpretation and application of the Treaties the law is observed. Member States shall provide remedies sufficient to ensure effective legal protection in the fields covered by Union law.

Article 19(3) further provides that the Court of Justice is to

> rule on actions brought by a Member State, an institution or a natural or legal person; give preliminary rulings, at the request of courts or tribunals of the Member States, on the interpretation of Union law or the validity of acts adopted by the institutions; rule in other cases provided for in the Treaties.

The first two categories stated above are of particular significance to the development of food law. The former of these, actions brought by a Member State or an institution, relate to food law in that this includes the enforcement actions taken by the Commission where it considers that a Member State has breached its Treaty obligations, discussed above, as well as reviews of the legality of EU acts. The second of

---

[50] 26th Annual Report on Monitoring the Application of Community Law (2008), COM (2009) 675.

[51] Case 168/1978 *Commission v France* (spirit tax) [1980] ECR 347; Case 170/1978 *Commission v UK* (wine and beer tax) [1983] ECR 2265; and Case 184/1985 *Commission v Italy* (banana consumption tax) [1987] ECR 2013.

[52] eg Case 178/1984 *Commission v Germany* (beer) [1987] ECR 1227; Case 216/1984 *Commission v France* (milk substitutes) [1988] ECR 793; Case 274/1987 *Commission v Germany* (meat products) [1989] ECR 229; and Case C-24/2000 *Commission v France* (fortified foods) [2004] ECR I-1277.

[53] Case C-221/2000 *Commission v Austria* (health claims) [2003] ECR I-1007.

[54] Case C-180/1996 *United Kingdom v Commission* (BSE) [1998] ECR I-2265.

[55] Joined Cases C-465/2002 and 466/2002 *Germany and Denmark v Commission* [2005] ECR I-9115.

these categories set out in Article 19(3) TEU, preliminary rulings, is looked at in more detail below. Most cases concerning aspects of food law have come before the Court of Justice in one of these ways—they usually involve action taken by the Commission against Member States; applications for the annulment of EU legislation; or referrals from national courts or tribunals for clarification on points of EU law.

As Article 19 TEU also states, the Court of Justice of the European Union is made up of three layers—the Court of Justice, the General Court and specialised courts. The Court of Justice consists of judges from each of the Member States, assisted by eight Advocates General.[56] The Advocate General is required to issue an opinion on a case where the Statute of the Court of Justice requires this. These opinions, which set out the facts, reasoning and findings of the Advocate General, are adopted prior to the Court's judgment on a case. They are not binding on the Court, but they are usually a good indication of what it is likely to decide. The Court of Justice has a broad jurisdiction. The only exceptions to this are cases concerning matters related to the Common Foreign and Security Policy,[57] aspects of judicial co-operation in criminal and policing matters,[58] and the grounds for expelling a Member State from the Union.[59]

The General Court, formerly known as the Court of First Instance, also comprises at least one judge from each of the Member States.[60] The jurisdiction of the General Court is more limited than that of the Court of Justice, although it has expanded over the course of time. It can review the legality of EU activities, such as the introduction of new food laws, and its decisions may be subject to an appeal to the Court of Justice on points of law.[61] It can also deal with actions initiated by Member States against the Commission.[62] Perhaps most significantly, it can also 'hear and determine questions referred for a preliminary ruling under Article 267, in specific areas laid down by the statute'.[63] However, '[w]here the General Court considers that the case requires a decision of principle likely to affect the unity or consistency of Union law, it may refer the case to the Court of Justice for a ruling'.[64] The Parliament and the Council can also establish specialised courts, which are attached to the general court, to hear and determine proceedings brought in specific areas.[65]

Preliminary References

English courts can refer questions on points of EU law to the EU courts under what is know as the preliminary reference procedure. Article 267 TFEU states that

[56] Art 252 TFEU.
[57] Art 275 TFEU.
[58] Art 276 TFEU.
[59] Art 269 TFEU in conjunction with Art 7 TEU.
[60] Art 19(2) TEU.
[61] Art 256 TFEU.
[62] Art 263(2) TFEU.
[63] Art 256(3) TFEU.
[64] ibid.
[65] Art 257 TFEU.

> [t]he Court of Justice of the European Union shall have jurisdiction to give preliminary rulings concerning the interpretation of the Treaties [and] the validity and interpretation of acts of the institutions, bodies, offices or agencies of the Union.

It further states that

> [w]here such a question is raised before any court or tribunal of a Member State, that court or tribunal may, if it considers that a decision on the question is necessary to enable it to give judgement, request the Court to give a ruling thereon.

The English courts establish the facts and then identify whether any issues related to the interpretation of EU law arise. Where it is deemed that they do, the English courts make a reference to the European Court of Justice—asking it to determine how EU law should be applied in the case. It is up to the national court to decide what gets referred. Private parties do not get any direct access to the European courts. Nor can they appeal national decisions to the courts of the EU. Representations by private parties before the Court of Justice are also limited. Essentially, it is the national court which makes the necessary submissions. It outlines the subject matter of the dispute, any applicable national provisions and case law, relevant EU law provisions, the reasons that prompted the referral, and summaries of the main arguments of the parties to the case. It is this submission upon which the Court of Justice's determination will be based.

The preliminary reference procedure has been, and continues to be, vital to the development of food law. Many of the key principles that now underpin aspects of food law stem directly from decisions taken by the Court of Justice after a referral by a national court or tribunal. The Annual Reports of the Court of Justice show that usually over half of cases heard are preliminary references. They are discussed throughout this book.

Reviewing the Legality of EU Acts

The Treaty provides that the legality of EU legislation or acts can be challenged before the Court. Many pieces of food legislation have been subject to this sort of review. Article 263 TFEU states that

> [t]he Court of Justice of the European Union shall review the legality of legislative acts, of acts of the Council, of the Commission and of ... the European Parliament and of the European Council intended to produce legal effects vis-à-vis third parties.

While this provision clearly facilitates the challenging of EU food legislation, the legal standing to bring such an appeal is rather limited. Article 263(2) TFEU states that the Court has jurisdiction

> in actions brought by a Member State, the European Parliament, the Council or the Commission on grounds of lack of competence, infringement of an essential procedural requirement, infringement of the Treaties or of any rule of law relating to their application, or misuse of powers.

This grants these named institutions the status of 'privileged applicant', meaning that they all have the legal standing to bring an application for the review of Union legislation before the Court. In many cases, however, those affected by the legislation at issue are likely to be private individuals, who have also had no formal role to play in the introduction of these contentious new rules in the first place. This category of applicant has 'non-privileged' status. This is set out in Article 263(4) TFEU, which states that

> [a]ny natural or legal person may ... institute proceedings against an act addressed to that person or which is of direct and individual concern to them, and against a regulatory act which is of direct concern to them and does not entail implementing measures.

This is problematic. An applicant must demonstrate that they are directly and individually concerned by an act which is not specifically addressed to them. Establishing direct and individual concern is very difficult to do.[66] A regulation, for example, may prohibit commercial fishing for mackerel in the English Channel. At the time of the introduction of this (fictional) legislation there may be only one trawler actively engaged in fishing for mackerel in the Channel. However, the regulation is not addressed to the skipper of that trawler; it deals more generally with fishing for a certain species in a designated body of water. It is clear in our example that it could be that only one trawler is really affected by the regulation. Owing to previous court determinations on the matter, this potential applicant, who may seek to challenge the legality of the regulation, cannot do so as the regulation is not addressed to him. He cannot even demonstrate that the regulation is of 'direct and individual concern' to him.

This difficult situation arises out of the decision of the Court in *Plaumann*.[67] Here, the applicant sought the partial suspension of duty payable on the importation of mandarins and clementines imported from third countries. A Commission decision, addressed to the German Government, declined this request.[68] An application was brought to have this decision annulled. This application could only proceed, under the terms of the Treaty, if it could be shown that Plaumann was 'individually concerned' by the decision. It was made clear that this could only be deemed to be so where the decision affects the applicant 'by reason of certain attributes which are peculiar to them or by reasons of circumstances in which they are differentiated from all other persons'. Whether or not there was only one importer of clementines into Germany was not relevant. The fact that the applicant was involved in 'a commercial activity which may at any time be practised by any person' meant that they were not distinguishable. They were not, therefore, 'individually concerned'.

---

[66] For further discussion on this see A Arnull, 'Private applicants and the action for annulment since *Codorniu*' (2001) 38 *CML Rev* 7.

[67] Case 25/1962 *Plaumann & Co v Commission* [1963] ECR 95.

[68] Decision No SIII 03079; 22/05/1962.

As stated, it is difficult for a private individual, or non-privileged applicant, to demonstrate that they have the legal standing required to challenge EU acts. Almost all commercial activities can be entered into by new operators at any time. Being the only, or the major, player in a particular market that is affected by new EU legislation does not indicate that one is individually concerned—and the test for standing cannot therefore be satisfied. It is only where those who are, or who in the future may be, affected by the legislation are a 'closed' group, identifiable and distinguishable from all other current or potential operators, that the required 'individual concern' may be established. In *Codorniu*,[69] for example, the fact that the applicant had held a trademark for use of the sales name Cremant in Spain since 1924 was held to distinguish that operator from all others, as no new wine producer could potentially be affected by a regulation limiting the use of this name.[70] There could only be one trademark holder. No other operator could have their intellectual property rights affected by the regulation in the same way.

If legal standing is established, the grounds upon which the challenge is based can be reviewed. For an EU act to be deemed illegal, it must be shown that the act was entered into when the institutions responsible did not have the competence to do so; or that there had been an infringement of an essential procedural requirement; or that there had been an infringement of the Treaty; or that there had been a misuse of power.[71]

It is generally very difficult for non-privileged applicants to establish that they have the standing required to proceed with a challenge to the legality of a Union act. Hence most of the examples of food-related cases that have tested whether one of these four grounds listed has been breached involve privileged applicants—usually either inter-institutional contentions or applications brought by Member States. For example, one of the more significant food-related challenges brought under the Article 263 TFEU procedure centred on the inclusion of genetically modified organisms in the list of non-organic components that could be present in products lawfully labelled as 'organic'.

In *Parliament v Commission*,[72] the applicant sought the annulment of aspects of the Commission Regulation that facilitated this.[73] The Parliament pleaded that its prerogatives had been infringed and contested the validity of that inclusion of genetically modified micro-organisms as a substance permitted for inclusion in organic foodstuffs. Its action was based on three pleas: that the Commission had exceeded its powers; that the Commission had misused its powers; and that the statement of reasons for introducing the contested provision was insufficient. The action was dismissed, the Court finding that the relevant legislative procedures had been complied with. EU law was, however, later amended to remove

---

[69] Case C-309/1989 *Codorniu v Council* [1994] ECR I-1853.

[70] Council Regulation (EEC) No 2045/1989 of 19 June 1989 amending Regulation (EEC) No 3309/1985 laying down general rules for the description and presentation of sparkling wines and aerated sparkling wines [1989] OJ L 202/12.

[71] Art 263(2) TFEU.

[72] Case C-156/1993 *Parliament v Commission* [1995] ECR I-2019.

genetically modified organisms from the list of permitted ingredients in organic foods, the Council stating that

> [g]enetically modified organisms and products derived therefrom are not compatible with the organic production method; in order to maintain consumer confidence in organic production, genetically modified organisms, parts thereof and products derived therefrom should not be used in products labelled as from organic production.[74]

GMOs can no longer be used in organic products.

As mentioned earlier, the Article 263 TFEU procedure was, perhaps, most famously used by the UK when seeking to annul the Commission's ban on the export of cattle during the BSE crisis.[75] The focus of this particular challenge to EU law arose out of the Commission's adoption of a Decision banning the export of cattle, beef and beef derivatives from the UK to all EU Member States and to third countries.[76] The UK sought the annulment of the Decision on several grounds, including that the Commission had acted beyond its powers, that there had been a misuse of powers and that there was a failure to comply with the principle of the free movement of goods. According to the Court, EU law at the time did facilitate the taking of safeguard measures, such as this ban, where there was an outbreak of a disease that was likely to pose a serious risk to animal or human health.[77] The UK's Spongiform Encephalopathy Advisory Committee (SEAC) had stated in March 1996 that BSE was 'the most likely explanation' for the outbreak of the human variant, Creutzfeldt-Jakob disease. This, it was argued, could be used to justify the adoption of safeguard measures. One of the objectives of EU law, to enable the Commission to take swift action where necessary to prevent the spread of disease, would be stifled if it were to be prevented from taking the sort of action that it had, in circumstances such as these. The Court was of the opinion that the SEAC statement contained new information which significantly altered the existing perception of the risk posed.[78] The immobilisation of animals was deemed a proportionate and lawful response to this.[79] Although the Commission

---

[73] Commission Regulation (EEC) No 207/1993 of 29 January 1993 defining the content of Annex VI to Regulation (EEC) No 2092/1991 on organic production of agricultural products and indications referring thereto on agricultural products and foodstuffs and laying down detailed rules for implementing the provisions of Art 5 (4) thereto [1993] OJ L 25/5.

[74] Preamble to Council Regulation (EC) No 1804/1999 of 19 July 1999 supplementing Regulation (EEC) No 2092/1991 on organic production of agricultural products and indications referring thereto on agricultural products and foodstuffs to include livestock production [1999] OJ L 222/1.

[75] The crisis itself, and the new direction in which it has subsequently led the development of food law, is discussed in much more detail in ch 5.

[76] Commission Decision 1996/239 of 27 March 1996 on emergency measures to protect against bovine spongiform encephalopathy [1996] OJ L 78/47.

[77] Art 10(1) of Council Directive 1990/425/EEC of 26 June 1990 concerning veterinary and zootechnical checks applicable in intra-Community trade in certain live animals and products with a view to the completion of the internal market [1990] OJ L 224/29, and Art 9(1) of Council Directive 1989/662/EEC of 11 December 1989 concerning veterinary checks in intra-Community trade with a view to the completion of the internal market [1989] OJ L 395/13.

[78] Para 52.

[79] Para 57.

Decision clearly affected the free movement of goods, it was found that this did not automatically render it contrary to EU law as it was adopted in accordance with the terms of free movement promoting directives, such as those on compulsory veterinary inspections.[80] Finally, it was held that the Commission had not misused its powers. The Court noted that this would only be the case where an EU institution adopted a measure designed to achieve a result contrary to that stated in the Preamble.[81] Looking at the recitals in the Preamble to the Decision, the Court found that the Commission had introduced the contested measure in order to protect human health from the potential risk of BSE transmission, and not, as was contested, for any economic reason, such as protecting the beef industry or maintaining consumer confidence in beef production. The action was dismissed.

2.3 International Obligations

2.3.1 World Trade Organization Agreements

International trade agreements have had more of an impact on domestic food law since the establishment of the World Trade Organization (WTO) in 1995. As we have earlier explained, practically all new and existing food law comes from EU legislation. It will now be demonstrated that it is also the influence that international trade law has on EU law that in turn impacts on the scope of national legislation and measures.

WTO agreements can affect the nature and content of EU rules in a number of ways. The most significant of these is where EU legislation or action is found to be contrary to one, or several, of the individual WTO agreements. These include, in particular, the Agreement on the Application of Sanitary and Phytosanitary Measures (SPS Agreement), the Agreement on Technical Barriers to Trade (TBT Agreement), the Agreement on Trade-Related Aspects of Intellectual Property Rights (TRIPs Agreement) and the Agreement on Agriculture, as well as the General Agreement on Tariffs and Trade (GATT). Each of these, and their impact on EU food law, and consequently domestic food law, is examined below. These agreements also carry the general principles of international trade law that oblige Members to act on the basis of (i) most favoured nation; and (ii) national treatment. 'Most favoured nation' works on the basis that Members should, where

---

[80] Para 63. The Directives concerned are Directive 1990/425 and 1989/662, n 77 above. The principle of Directive conformity being espoused by the Court here was first proclaimed in Case 37/1983 *Rewe-Zentrale v Landwirtschaftskammer Rheinland* [1984] ECR 1229, para 19.

[81] See Case C-84/1994 *United Kingdom v Council* [1996] ECR I-5755, para 69; Case C-156/1993 *Parliament v Commission* [1995] ECR I-2019, para 31; and Case C-248/1989 *Cargill v Commission* [1991] ECR I-2987, para 26.

possible, treat their trade relations and conditions with all other Members in the same way that they treat the most favourable of these. This can be problematic when a Member enters into a bilateral agreement because, by definition, the States involved should then extend the concessions of this agreement to all other WTO Members.[82] The principle of 'national treatment' provides that Members should provide the same advantages for traders from other States as they provide to their own. In both cases, there is a general exemption for regional trading blocs such as the EU. This means that the same treatment and advantages that are provided between EU Member States do not have to be extended to all WTO Members. They should, however, provide the same treatment and advantages in their dealings with all other WTO Members.

Individual WTO agreements, and WTO rules or principles more generally, can also be used to challenge the legality of EU law, in a similar manner to that examined above in relation to Article 263 TFEU. Applications can be brought to annul Union legislation based on a claim that it does not adhere to international trade law requirements. While such applications are possible, it should be noted at this stage that this is a very difficult claim to make successfully. The Court of Justice has consistently held that the nature of the international trade law system dictates that the criteria for establishing the legal effect of WTO rules cannot be met—nullifying the possibility of using these rules to challenge EU law. Essentially, the Court states that the WTO does not oblige its Member States to adhere directly to the Agreements, therefore the ECJ will not tie the EU institutions to them either. This is explained below.

Effect of World Trade Organization Rules on English Law

According to the Court of Justice, neither the provisions of GATT, nor WTO rules, create rights for individuals. Their existence cannot be used to challenge the validity of EU law. EU legislation that is contrary to WTO obligations therefore remains valid and applicable. It cannot be deemed unlawful on the ground that it runs contrary to international legal obligations. This reduces the significance of GATT and the WTO Agreements on the development of EU, and consequently English, food law.

The principle that GATT would not have legal effect in EU law was first established in *International Fruit Company*.[83] Here, the applicant queried the validity of three EU regulations that placed restrictions on the importation of apples from third countries, on the grounds that they were contrary to Article XI of GATT. Article XI states that

---

[82] For further discussion on the complications that can be created when such agreements are entered into, see P Benyon, 'Community mutual recognition agreements, technical barriers to trade and the WTO's most favoured nation principle' (2003) 28 *EL Rev* 231.

[83] Cases 21-24/1972 *International Fruit Company NV and others v Produktschap voor Groenten en Fruit* [1972] ECR 1219.

[n]o prohibitions or restrictions other than duties, taxes or other charges, whether made effective through quotas, import or export licences or other measures, shall be instituted or maintained by any contracting party on the importation of any product of the territory of any other contracting party or on the exportation or sale for export of any product destined for the territory of any other contracting party.

In other words, quantitative restrictions on trade between GATT contracting parties should be abolished. The three regulations at issue placed a quantitative restriction on such trade in apples.

The Court found that international law must be binding on the EU before it can be used to test the validity of EU law. International law must also confer rights on individuals before it can be relied upon before a national court. Therefore, if GATT did not create rights for individuals it could not be used by those same individuals to demonstrate that some provision of EU law was invalid. Looking at the wording of GATT, and in particular the references in the preamble to 'the principle of negotiations undertaken on the basis of reciprocal and mutually advantageous arrangements, the Court found that it was a document 'characterised by the great flexibility of its provisions, in particular those conferring the possibility of derogation, the measures to be taken when confronted with exceptional difficulties and the settlement of conflicts between the contracting parties'.[84] It was further noted that the settlement of disputes involved consultation and the issuing of recommendations, with the possibility of suspending concessions granted under GATT in some circumstances. States could withdraw from GATT if dissatisfied with any recommendations made or concessions suspended.[85] These factors combined demonstrated to the Court that Article XI of GATT could not confer rights on individuals. It could not therefore be used to test the validity of the three 'apple regulations' either.[86]

Agriculture

The WTO Agreement on Agriculture is designed to facilitate market access for agricultural products amongst Member States. It is hoped that, through a combination of this and the provision of supports for domestic production, as well as enabling further competition between products, the Agreement will improve the prospects of achieving international food security. There is also provision

---

[84] Para 21.

[85] It should be noted that at the time of the decision in *International Fruit Company* no procedure existed for a Member State to similarly withdraw from its membership of the EU. This has now changed with the introduction of Art 50 TEU by the Treaty of Lisbon. It states that '[a]ny Member State may decide to withdraw from the Union in accordance with its own constitutional requirements', suggesting that the validity of this line of reasoning by the Court here is no longer effective.

[86] The same principles, on the effect of international trade agreements in the legal systems of members, that were devised by the Court in Cases 21-24/1972 *International Fruit Company*, n 83 above, continue to apply since the establishment of the WTO, even in circumstances where the WTO's Dispute Settlement Body has specifically found that the EU legislation under examination is contrary to WTO obligations. See Case C-377/2002 *Van Parys* [2005] ECR I-1465.

within the terms of the Agreement for giving special and preferential treatment to producers in developing countries, to further their prospects of achieving access to markets elsewhere, and to limiting competition from imports.[87] This is to be done by, amongst other things, liberalising trade in tropical agricultural products and for those who diversify their activities away from the illicit production of narcotics.

Agriculture has really only achieved significant coverage in international trade law and regulation since the GATT Uruguay Round Negotiations of 1986–1992. Articles 3–10 of the Agreement call for Members to limit the use of export subsidies for certain agricultural products in order to reduce protectionism and improve competition. These provisions also call for Members to commit to reducing tariffs on international trade in food, as well as providing for more access to their markets for goods produced elsewhere. Article 9 of the Agreement specifically calls for reducing the use of direct subsidies provided to and through firms, producers, co-operative societies and national marketing boards. Indirect subsidies can also sometimes be provided through reducing transportation costs, for example, for exporters. This should be minimised. Article 12, in accordance with Article XI of GATT, does permit the placing of prohibitions or restrictions on the exportation of food, but only where there has been due consideration taken for the food security of the importing state. One of main reasons as to why agriculture received relatively little coverage during the GATT years 1947–1994 was that the Contracting Parties could not agree on many aspects of international trade regulation for this sector, such as the use of tariffs, quotas and subsidies. In order to reach a compromise on this, the WTO Agreement on Agriculture contains a 'peace clause' in Article 13, which provides that States should refrain from raising disputes on subsidies and similar issues for an initial period of nine years. They should also exercise 'due restraint' on actions relating to such support measures indefinitely. One of the key criticisms of the Agreement on Agriculture is that it is incomprehensible in places, and is consequently difficult to implement properly.[88]

Technical Barriers to Trade

The WTO Agreement on Technical Barriers to Trade (TBT) covers all products, including agricultural products.[89] Article 2 of the Agreement provides that WTO Members must take a series of considerations into account when drafting national technical standards, designed to minimise the impact that these requirements can have on the free flow of international trade in goods. Members are obliged to refrain from creating unnecessary obstacles to trade, except where this may be required to protect national security, prevent deception or protect health or the

---

[87] Through the use of Art 15 of the Agreement on Agriculture in particular.

[88] For further discussion on this point, and for more analysis on the Agreement on Agriculture more generally, see B O'Connor, 'A note on the need for more clarity in the World Trade Organization Agreement on Agriculture' (2003) 37 *Journal of World Trade* 839.

[89] Art 1(3).

environment. Technical standards should only be introduced by Members where these are shown to be necessary, and they should be withdrawn when no longer required. Members must be able to justify the existence of a national standard where this is requested by another Member. When standards are introduced, they should be based on the performance of the product rather than its design or description. Members are also obliged to recognise that similar standards of other Members are equivalent to their own, where both sets achieve the same objective. Most significantly for the liberalisation of international trade in food, the TBT Agreement makes it clear that internationally set standards should be deemed to be the norm where these exist or where their completion is imminent. If a national standard is equivalent to a set international standard, it is to be presumed that it is in compliance with TBT obligations. The codes and guidelines for food which are set by the Codex Alimentarius Commission, which are discussed in more detail below, are recognised as a relevant international standard for this purpose.[90]

WTO Members are obliged to adhere to a notification procedure when introducing a new national technical standard that both differs from the international norm and is likely to affect international trade in some way. The new technical standard should be publicised or published in an appropriate place, preferably prior to introduction. The Member State should also provide others with copies of the new technical standard when requested, as well as clearly identifying those parts of the standard which are different from international guidelines. Other Members should also be facilitated in making comments on the proposed new national standard.

Article 4 of the TBT Agreement requires Members to comply with the Code of Good Practice when preparing, adopting and applying national standards. The Code itself is set out in Annex 3 to the Agreement. The Code mostly reiterates the points made in Article 2 of the Agreement on technical regulations, such as those referring to using internationally set requirements as the basis for national standards. It also sets out further stipulations on the notification procedure and acceptance of comments from other Members on proposed new standards. As with other WTO Agreements, there is special provision for the position of developing and least-developed WTO Members, such as allowing these States to deviate from international norms when necessary for the protection of their own domestic production.[91]

Sanitary and Phytosanitary Measures

The WTO Agreement on the Application of Sanitary and Phytosanitary Measures enables Members to adopt and implement provisions for the protection of the

---

[90] This was certified to be the case by the Dispute Panel and Appellate Body in DS 231, *European Communities—Trade Description of Sardines*.

[91] Art 12 of the TBT Agreement.

health of humans, animals and plants. It has become an increasingly significant agreement for EU Member States, such as the UK, since the White Paper on Food Safety brought about significant change in policy direction after its publication in 2000. The increased use of the precautionary principle and the impact of scientific developments have added to this significance. The terms of the SPS Agreement must be considered before science-based or precautionary measures are introduced in the interests of food safety.

SPS measures are an impediment to international trade. However, they are even more restrictive as such when introduced in an arbitrary way that offers little or no meaningful benefit for health protection. As a result, the Agreement is set out in a way that permits these trade-restricting measures to be introduced, but within tight parameters that oblige those introducing them to only do so on the basis of scientific evaluation of probable risk to human, animal or plant health. As with other WTO Agreements, such as that on Technical Barriers to Trade, there is a general acceptance within the terms of the SPS Agreement that existing international standards on safety or risk minimisation should be deemed the norm. Compliance, therefore, with the standards of bodies such as the Codex Alimentarius Commission, the World Organisation for Animal Health (formerly the International Office of Epizootics) or the Food and Agriculture Organization (FAO) run International Plant Protection Convention is usually deemed to be compliance with SPS obligations as well. The primary obligation set out in the SPS Agreement is that Members should base their own food safety measures on appropriate risk assessments.

As stated, WTO Members have the right to adopt SPS measures. However, this is limited to those measures which are consistent with the other parts of the Agreement and only to the extent that is absolutely necessary to protect health.[92] These other provisions that must be complied with include basing domestic requirements on international standards and guidelines where appropriate,[93] accepting the standards of other States as being equivalent to domestic requirements where an appropriate level of protection has been demonstrated,[94] basing measures on an appropriate risk assessment that minimises the negative effects of this on trade,[95] and providing prompt notification of any new measures introduced to all other Members through the appropriate channels.[96] The Agreement also permits the introduction of precautionary measures where the scientific evidence concerning a potential risk is inconclusive, but sufficient.

---

[92] Art 2.

[93] Art 3.

[94] Art 4. However, the European Court of Justice held in Case C-432/1992 *R v Minister of Agriculture, Fisheries and Food, ex parte Anastasiou* [1994] ECR I-3087 that this demonstration must be made by the presentation of certificates issued exclusively by national competent authorities. For further discussion on this, see M Cremona, 'Case C-432/92 *R v Minister of Agriculture*' (1996) 33 *CML Rev* 125.

[95] Art 5.

[96] Art 7.

The SPS Agreement can impact upon English and European food law in a number of ways. The most obvious of these is the general obligation that new measures introduced should be based on international guidelines. Individual Members, such as the UK, or free trade areas, such as the EU, must provide reasons for the taking of any action or the introduction of any measures that are not based on such international standards.[97] Where national or EU SPS measures are introduced or applied they are also, of course, subject to the scrutiny of the Dispute Settlement Body of the WTO where another Member raises a complaint. This has most famously happened in both the *Hormones Dispute*,[98] and later in the *GMO Dispute*.[99] In the former, the United States and Canada claimed that the EU had failed to comply with its SPS obligations, amongst other complaints, by the introduction of a directive which banned the use of hormones in meat production.[100] In particular, it was argued that the introduction of this legislation was contrary to Articles 3 and 5 of the Agreement in that the content of the directive was not in accordance with existing international guidelines, nor was its introduction supported by an appropriate scientific risk assessment. Both the Panel and the Appellate Body of the WTO's Dispute Settlement Body found that the risk assessment was inadequate and that the measures adopted deviated from internationally accepted standards. The introduction of this directive by the EU was thus deemed to be action that was contrary to SPS Agreement obligations. Compensation was offered by the EU as a resolution to the dispute as it did not believe that it would be in the interests of its Member States to repeal the ban on hormone use. Ultimately, however, concessions were suspended to the tune of nearly $130 million. The EU responded by introducing a new directive on the matter in 2003,[101] which it claimed was based on a full and appropriate risk assessment.[102] The *GMOs Dispute*, which also deals with the application of the SPS Agreement at EU and national level, is discussed in more detail in chapter ten. In both cases, action taken at EU, and consequently Member State, level had to be reversed or modified to bring it into compliance with SPS obligations. There has

---

[97] Art 5.

[98] DS 26 and DS 48, *European Communities—Measures Concerning Meat and Meat Products*. For an early critique on the *Hormones Dispute* see R Quick and A Blüthner, 'Has the Appellate Body erred? An appraisal and criticism of the ruling in the WTO *Hormones Case*' (1999) 2 *Journal of International Economic Law* 603.

[99] DS 291, 292 and 293, *Measures Affecting the Approval and Marketing of Biotech Products*.

[100] Directive 1996/22/EC concerning the prohibition on the use in stockfarming of certain substances having a hormonal or thyrostatic action [1996] OJ L 125/3, transposed into English law by the Animals and Animal Products (Examination for Residues and Maximum Residue Limits) Regulations 1997, SI No 1729/1997. Originally prohibited by the introduction of Council Directive 1981/602/EEC of 31 July 1981 concerning the prohibition of certain substances having a hormonal action and of any substances having a thyrostatic action [1981] OJ L 222/32. This ban is discussed in more detail in ch 6.

[101] Directive 2003/74/EC of the European Parliament and of the Council of 22 September 2003 amending Council Directive 1996/22/EC concerning the prohibition on the use in stockfarming of certain substances having a hormonal or thyrostatic action and of beta-agonists [2003] OJ L 262/17.

[102] The complainants disagreed with this, however, resulting in another dispute process being initiated, DS 320 and DS 321, *Continued Suspension of Obligations in the EC – Hormones Dispute*. This was ultimately resolved in November 2008.

traditionally been widespread objection at EU Member State level, including in the UK, to the use of both hormones and genetic modification in food production. However, international obligations, such as those arising out of the application of the WTO SPS Agreement, means that individual States, and regional blocs, are limited in the action that they can take to satisfy the objectors in such circumstances. Public or political objection to the use of certain practices in agriculture is not enough to warrant the implementation of any trade-restricting national measures designed to appease this. Any such measures must be based on scientific evidence indicating that there is a real or potential risk to health.[103]

Intellectual Property Protection

The WTO Agreement on Trade-Related Aspects of Intellectual Property Rights (TRIPs) has also been used to call into question the validity of EU and national law, ultimately compelling the EU to modify its existing legislation to bring it into line with the obligations set out in TRIPs. Articles 22–24 of the TRIPs Agreement are of particular relevance for food law. Article 22(2) provides that

> [i]n respect of geographical indications, members shall provide the legal means for interested parties to prevent … the use of any means in the designation or presentation of a good that indicates or suggests that the good in question originates in a geographical area other than the true place of origin in a manner which misleads the public as to the geographical origin of the good.

'Geographical indications' are defined in the TRIPs Agreement as being those which 'identify a good as originating in the territory of a Member … where a given quality, reputation or other characteristic of the good is essentially attributable to its geographical origin'.[104] WTO Members are obliged, under the terms of Article 22(3) of the TRIPs Agreement, to refuse or invalidate the registration of a trademark which uses a geographical indication for goods that have not originated in the place suggested by this. Article 23 provides additional protection for geographical indications used for wines or spirits. Members should provide legal protection for interested parties who seek to prevent the use of a geographical indication for wines that do not originate in the place that their name suggests. The application of these provisions has been problematic. WTO Members have proved reluctant to de-register trademarks containing geographical indications for those goods which have traditionally used them, despite their lack of association with the place used in their name. Article 24 is significant in this regard. It provides the possibility for further negotiations in this area, on both a bilateral and a multilateral basis, with a view to establishing lists of protected names that could be applied internationally.

---

[103] For more detailed discussion on the relationship between the SPS Agreement and regulation of the food sector see A Alemanno, *Trade in Food: Regulatory and Judicial Approaches in the EC and the WTO* (London, Cameron May, 2007) 239–290.

[104] Art 22(1).

As is discussed in more detail in chapter eight, the EU originally developed a system for the registration of protected geographical indications and protected designations of origin in 1992.[105] Both the USA and Australia took issue with the fact that the EU Regulation did not offer protection for non-EU registered geographical indications and trademarks.[106] It was also very difficult, under the terms of the Regulation, for non-EU applicants to access the protection process established. Complaints were brought under Articles 22 and 24 of the TRIPs Agreement. It was also claimed that the perceived shortcomings with the EU Regulation contravened the general principles set out in Articles I–III of GATT, designed to ensure 'most-favoured nation' and 'national treatment' status for producers or their representatives from third countries. These two important principles of international trade law are explained further below.

It was accepted by the parties to the *Geographical Indications Dispute* that the 1992 Regulation, and the procedures that it established, were designed to fulfil a legitimate objective of the EU. It was felt, however, that the failure to facilitate applicants from third countries made the Regulation more restrictive on international trade than that which was necessary to achieve the stated aim. The Dispute Settlement Body Panel found that the EU had failed to provide for national treatment in that it had provided a privileged status for applicants from within its own Member States. Two problems with the original geographical indications regulation were identified. The first was that geographical indications originating in a third country could only be registered for protected status in the EU if the law of the third country provided equivalent protection for its own products there, and also gave reciprocal protection for EU foodstuffs traded in that State. This was very limiting. It essentially meant that there would only be protection available for products in the EU where the State in which the food was produced had a system for registering food names that was as well developed as that established by the 1992 Regulation.[107] The second problem identified by the Panel was that even where access was provided to applicants from third countries, it was further restricted by another requirement set out in the Regulation. This provided that the State must have inspection systems in place that were at least equivalent to those operating in the EU Member States, before any applications for protection, or objections to the registration of EU names, would even be considered. It was agreed that the EU would modify its legislation to reflect these findings.[108] It did

---

[105] Regulation 2081/1992 of 14 July 1992 on the protection of geographical indications and designations of origin for agricultural products and foodstuffs [1992] OJ L 208/1.

[106] DS 174 and DS 290, *EC Protection of Trademarks and Geographical Indications for Agricultural Products and Foodstuffs*. For further discussion on the Dispute see M Handler, 'The WTO Geographical Indications Dispute' (2006) 69 *MLR* 70.

[107] Reg 2081/1992, n 105 above.

[108] Under the terms of Art 21(3)(b) of the WTO Dispute Settlement Understanding, which provides that the parties to a dispute must find a resolution within 45 days of the adoption of recommendations by the DSB, it was agreed that the EU would have 11½ months to amend the 1992 Regulations to avoid the need for concessions to be suspended or compensation to be paid.

this through the introduction of two new regulations in 2006.[109] The Preamble to the revised Protected Food Names Regulation recognised the significance of the TRIPs Agreement for the content and application of EU food laws. It was accepted that the obligations set out in this Agreement would require that EU law would facilitate the protection of geographical indications from third countries where they were also protected in their country of origin. It also meant that the EU registration process would have to operate in a manner that would enable those with legitimate interests from third countries to object to the registration of a name in the EU. These recognitions were reflected in the introduction of a new Article 5 (registration open to applicants from third countries) and a new Article 7 (objections to registrations possible for interested parties from third countries who lodge a duly substantiated claim with the Commission) into the Protected Food Names Regulation. The PDO/PGI registration system was thus properly opened up to applicants and objectors from third countries for the first time. This was as a direct result of the proper application of the TRIPs Agreement to the provisions of EU law.

General Agreement on Tariffs and Trade

There are several provisions of the General Agreement on Tariffs and Trade (GATT) that should be mentioned at this point. The two most obvious are the general principles of most favoured nation and national treatment, set out in Articles I and II and III respectively, and which have been outlined above. These form the basis for all of the WTO Agreements discussed above. Article 2 of the TBT Agreement, for example, provides that

> [m]embers shall ensure that in respect of technical regulations, products imported from the territory of any Member shall be accorded treatment no less favourable than that accorded to like products of national origin and to like products originating in any other country.

Other specific provisions of GATT which are potentially significant for international traders in food include Article XI on quantitative restrictions. This provides that

> [n]o prohibitions or restrictions other than duties, taxes or other charges, whether made effective through quotas, import or export licences or other measures, shall be instituted or maintained by any contracting party on the importation of any product of the territory of any other contracting party or the exportation or sale for export of any product destined for the territory of any other contracting party.

---

[109] Council Regulation 509/2006 of 20 March 2006 on agricultural products and foodstuffs as traditional specialities guaranteed [2006] OJ L 93/1, and Council Regulation (EC) No 510/2006 of 20 March 2006 on the protection of geographical indications and designations of origin for agricultural products and foodstuffs [2006] OJ L 93/12. These Regulations have since been replaced by Regulation (EU) No 1151/2012 of the European Parliament and of the Council of 21 November 2012 on quality schemes for agricultural products and foodstuffs [2012] OJ L 343/1.

There are some exceptions to this general obligation to eliminate quantitative restrictions on international trade, such as where this is necessary for the temporary prevention or relief of shortages of foodstuffs, or where used to deal with a surplus of domestically produced agricultural or fisheries products. However, where any contracting party to GATT uses one of these, or any other permitted exemptions, it must first provide public notice of the details of any quantitative restriction imposed. Other States will then, of course, have an opportunity to object to such action being taken.

Article IX of GATT also provides for the application of the principle of most favoured nation in the setting of national requirements on origin markings. It states that where domestic regulation on the use of origin marks is applied, this should only be done with full consideration of 'the difficulties and inconveniences which such measures may cause to the commerce and industry of exporting countries'. The provision accepts that while labelling disclosures on the origin of products may be required in some circumstances to protect consumers against fraudulent or misleading indications, the inconvenience that this may cause to importers should be kept to a minimum. There is also a call in Article XI of GATT for the Contracting Parties to co-operate with each other with a view to preventing the use of trade names that may misrepresent the true origin of a product to the detriment of distinctive regional or geographical names. This has obvious implications for international trade in food, where producers are often willing to use names for their products which indicate an association with another that is recognised for its quality or distinguishing characteristics, such as has been the case with American 'Champagne' or Canadian 'Parma' ham.

Other provisions of GATT which have the potential to impact upon international trade in food include Article V. This provides for freedom of transit for importers, with access to the most convenient transportation routes to be provided. Article VI of GATT is designed to limit the use of 'dumping', or the sale of imported goods at less than their normal value, in international trade. Article VII of GATT sets out how goods are to be valued for customs purposes when traded internationally, which can, of course, have an impact on the level of import duties payable, and the consequent effect that this can then have on the ability of imports to compete with domestic foodstuffs. Finally, Article XXIV deals with the application of GATT to free trade areas, such as the EU. It states that nothing in GATT should prevent the formation of customs unions and free trade areas.

2.3.2 Codex Alimentarius Commission

The United Nations Food and Agriculture Organization and the World Health Organization have combined to run the Codex Alimentarius Commission. This organisation, which was formed in 1963, exists to devise international standards and guidelines for food. These can be both horizontal, applying to all foods across a set theme, for example nutrition labelling, or they can be vertical, applying to a specific food or food type, such as canned fruits, desiccated coconut, frog legs or cheese.[110] Codex Standards are international, but they can influence both national and EU food laws where they are used as the basis for legally binding compositional or safety requirements, or where they are considered to be the recognised benchmark in international trade regulation. As was noted above, Codex standards are directly referred to in the WTO Agreement on Sanitary and Phytosanitary Measures as setting the basis by which the validity of all national food safety stipulations will be judged. Compliance with Codex usually infers compliance with SPS obligations. Membership of the Codex Alimentarius Commission now covers 99 per cent of the world's population.

Codex Standards have had a direct bearing in several important free movement of food cases that have come before the European Court of Justice.[111] They have been used to gauge whether EU Member States could potentially continue to apply national compositional requirements by making a demonstration that they were in accordance with those set by Codex. They have also formed the basis for new EU legislation, directly applicable at national level. A good example of this can be seen in the introduction of the EU Nutrition and Health Claims Regulation in 2006.[112] This is discussed in more detail in chapter seven.

2.3.3 Other International Organisations

There are really two different categories of international organisation that can have a bearing on national food law. The first of these is the organisation which deals specifically, and almost exclusively, with food, such as the Codex Alimentarius Commission. This type of organisation drafts codes and guidelines which may be used as a template for EU and subsequently national law. This is a two-way relationship. Existing EU and national requirements can also have an influence on the content of international standards, as many of these are drawn from what is already common practice amongst Members. The second category of international organisation is the generic one. They do not deal specifically or exclusively with food, but this does come within their remit, either directly or indirectly. This second group includes inter-state organisations such as the World Health Organization and the World Intellectual Property Organization. They issue generic guidelines and advice, which may relate to food on occasions. They can have an influence on national law, and particularly on national policy. This is discussed in more detail below.

---

[110] For more on Codex standards see C Downes, 'Only a footnote? The curious Codex battle for control of additive regulations' (2012) 7 *European Food and Feed Law Review* 232.

[111] Such as Case 298/1987 *Proceedings for compulsory reconstruction against Smanor SA* [1988] ECR 4489 and Case 286/1986, *Ministère Public v Gérard Deserbais* [1988] ECR 4907.

[112] Regulation (EC) No 1924/2006 of the European Parliament and of the Council of 20 December 2006 on nutrition and health claims made on foods [2007] OJ L 12/3.

United Nations Agencies: World Health Organization and Food and Agriculture Organization

The World Health Organization co-ordinates and directs health policy within the United Nations. It does this by setting guidelines, standards and policies in a range of areas, including those aspects of health protection that relate to food. This can include preventing the emergence or spread of disease, as well as the formulation of guidance on good dietary practice. Many WHO reports on the latter are subsequently used, at least in a persuasive way, in the adoption of national policies and guidance. This has been the case, for example, in relation to WHO advice on the prevention of overweight and obesity. The WHO has issued a series of guidelines in this area, including those on sugar intake for adults and children in 2014. This document and related consultation process has suggested that people are consuming too much sugar in their diet, and that this should usually be halved, reducing it to 5 per cent of daily total calorie intake, or roughly 25 g per day for an adult.

By 2014, there were 196 WHO members. Since 2007, all members of the WHO have been bound by the revised International Health Regulations. These Regulations are designed to assist the international community, including the UK, to prevent and respond to public health risks that could potentially cross borders, such as the outbreak of food-borne illness and disease. The Regulations oblige the WHO Members to report and respond to such disease outbreaks and public health events. The Agreement is legally binding, and was to be implemented by June 2012, although most States agreed a two-year extension to this deadline. Some, albeit limited, further extensions may also be granted. While the Regulations do apply to public health emergencies in general, there is specific reference to food-related issues in their terms. The Regulations also designate the Food and Agriculture Organization as the competent inter-governmental organisation with which the WHO must co-operate and co-ordinate its activities where appropriate.

The Food and Agriculture Organization (FAO) is also a United Nations body, established between 1943 and 1945 towards the end, and in the immediate aftermath of, World War II. It was designed initially to deal with ongoing food shortages which had become a feature of the preceding war years. The achievement of food security is still the key objective of the FAO. 'Food security' was defined at the World Food Summit 1996 as existing 'when all people at all times have access to sufficient, safe, nutritious food to maintain a healthy and active life'. The FAO does now also have a broader remit, which extends its activities to include the sustainable management and utilisation of natural resources, including land, water, air and climate. The FAO is driven by five stated strategic objectives. These are: helping to eliminate hunger, food insecurity and malnutrition; making agriculture, forestry and fisheries more productive and sustainable; reducing rural poverty; enabling inclusive and efficient agricultural and food systems; and increasing the resilience of food and agricultural systems to natural disasters. These objectives are to be achieved through the implementation of action plans, involving the devising of agreements, codes and standards with States, the collection, analysing and sharing of agricultural data and facilitating policy dialogue at global, regional and State levels. The FAO regularly publishes the results of its expertise and findings on a range of issues, such as the use of additives in food production, approaches to sustainable fishing and making adaptations to agriculture in response to climate change.

As discussed above, the WHO and the FAO share responsibility for the operation of the Codex Alimentarius Commission. They also jointly operate the International Food Safety Authorities Network (INFOSAN). This network is designed to link national food safety authorities across UN Member States in order to bring about the best possible responses to food safety emergencies. This alert and emergency response system has been used, for example, in the recall of products, such as milk whey protein concentrate, which were found to be contaminated with potentially dangerous bacteria. It was also engaged in the aftermath of the Great East Japan earthquake and tsunami in 2011. It provided an assessment of the potential for this natural disaster and related nuclear fallout to present risks to human health, were the food supply to be contaminated. The network, which originated out of the Codex Alimentarius *Principles and Guidelines for the Exchange of Information in Food Control Emergency Situations,* and which has been in existence since 2004, has over 180 Member States. Each has a designated contact point for communication between the national food safety authorities and the INFOSAN secretariat in cases of emergency. The contact point depends on the nature of the emergency. Each Member can nominate several. INFOSAN is alerted to potential emergencies in a number of ways. This can be done by reference from either the national contact points of the Member States, its own monitoring in conjunction with the WHO Alert and Response Operations Programme, or by working with the Global Outbreak Alert and Response Network and the Global Early Warning System for Major Animal Diseases, including zoonotic diseases.

World Intellectual Property Organization

The World Intellectual Property Organization (WIPO) provides a global forum for dealing with the international protection of rights attached to copyright, trademarks, patents and, most importantly from a food law perspective, geographical names. WIPO, which was established in 1967, has 187 member states, with a headquarters in Geneva and external offices in New York, Tokyo, Singapore and Rio de Janeiro. Around 250 non-governmental organisations and intergovernmental organisations also have official observer status at WIPO meetings. The work of WIPO is shaped by nine strategic goals, developed by the members in 2009. These include the co-ordination and development of global intellectual property infrastructure, providing a world reference source for intellectual property information and analysis, building respect for intellectual property protection, and the operation of a responsive communications interface between WIPO, its member states and all stakeholders.

The protection of geographical food names takes place at both EU level, through the application of the relevant regulations,[113] and at international level, through the application of the WTO TRIPs Agreement, as discussed above. WIPO does not have any direct control over the protection of these protected indications and designations of origin. It does, however, have a direct role to play in the protection of geographical names in other ways. First, WIPO operates the Standing Committee on the Law of Trademarks, Industrial Designs and Geographical Indications. This provides a forum for WIPO Member States to discuss policy and legal issues relating to the development of the law in this area, at both regional and global levels. Second, WIPO organises a biennial international symposium on geographical indications, bringing together governments, producer representatives and legal specialists for discussion on the development of national and international law in this area.

The third way in which WIPO has a direct role to play in the protection of geographical names is through the administration of the Lisbon Agreement for the Protection of Appellations of Origin and their International Registration. This Agreement was devised in 1958, and later revised and amended in 1967, and again in 1979. These establish the International Register of Appellations of Origin. Any country which is party to the Paris Convention for the Protection of Industrial Property can accede to the Lisbon Agreement. Those countries which adhere to the provisions of the Lisbon Agreement are also members of the Lisbon Union Assembly. There are, however, only 28 contracting parties to the Lisbon Agreement. These include France, Italy and Portugal. Other states which are party to the Agreement include Bulgaria, Burkina Faso, Costa Rica, South Korea and Macedonia.

The Lisbon Agreement provides that all parties to it must undertake to protect the appellations of origin of the other Assembly countries which have been registered at the International Bureau of Intellectual Property.[114] An 'appellation of origin' is defined in the Agreement as

> the geographical denomination of a country, region or locality, which serves to designate a product originating therein, the quality or characteristics of which are due exclusively or essentially to the geographical environment, including natural or human factors.[115]

Protection of these appellations of origin is to be ensured 'against any usurpation or imitation, even if the true origin of the product is indicated [or is] accompanied by terms such as kind, type, make [or] imitation'.[116] One of the major difficulties with the operation of the Lisbon Agreement system is that States can make a declaration that they are unable to protect an appellation of origin, a

---

[113] Reg 1151/2012, n 109 above.

[114] Art 1(2) of the Lisbon Agreement. The International Bureau is listed in the Convention establishing the World Intellectual Property Organization.

[115] Art 2(1) of the Lisbon Agreement.

[116] Art 3.

so-called 'declaration of refusal'.[117] Another problem with the system is that the name must first have been formally registered for protection in the country of origin. This means that the system is really only open to applicants from those States where such a formalised legal procedure is in place. The main difficulty with the system, however, is how few States have signed up to its commitments. Neither the USA, China, Canada, Australia or Japan are members. The UK is not a member, although, as noted above, some other EU Member States are. Protected appellations of origin cannot become legally generic in the country of origin.[118] They can also only remain protected internationally, amongst Lisbon signatories, for as long as they are similarly protected in the country of origin. Examples of appellations of origin registered under the Lisbon system include tequila, limiting the area of production for this to the territory of Jalisco in Mexico, Costa Rican bananas, Parmigiano-Reggiano and certain types of regionally produced olive oil. Around 900 products, many of which are foodstuffs, have been registered under the Lisbon Agreement. It has not, however, been as influential at international level as was intended. As will be discussed later in this book, this is really due to the fact the different systems for protection now operate at EU and national levels. This has significantly reduced the need for an international protection system like the WIPO-operated Lisbon Agreement.

National Non-Governmental Organisations

There are a number of non-governmental organisations and umbrella bodies operating in the UK which can influence the application of food law and the development of policy. These include the UK Food Group, which is a network of NGOs, including over 30 development, farming, consumer and environment interest groups. Its primary concern is the attainment of food security, and it represents the UK at international and European levels on matters relevant to its remit. While the primary interest of the UK Food Group relates to issues in developing countries, it also sees that the activities of consumers in the UK can have a bearing on what happens elsewhere, in a number of ways, including climate change and global food security. It has therefore also lent its support, for example, to the Eating Better Alliance, which is a campaign designed to encourage people in the UK to consume less meat and more of the types of food that are better for health and which can be produced with lower carbon emission and pollutant levels. The Alliance has also backed a campaign for food sovereignty in the UK which advocates putting producers, distributors and consumers at the centre of the decision-making processes on food systems and policies. It is based on the belief that the demands of markets and corporations have come to dominate the global food system, at the expense of those who actually produce and eat the food. The legal system should therefore provide for a right to food that is healthy

---

[117] Art 5(3).
[118] Art 6.

and culturally appropriate, where local and regional provision take precedence over the supply of distant markets, and production and distribution systems are designed to protect natural resources and reduce greenhouse gas emissions, avoiding energy-intensive industrial methods that damage the environment and health. The Alliance seeks tougher rules on 'food speculation', reducing its use as a commodity to be traded rather than a source of sustenance for the population. Lobbying has been done on this at EU level.

The Food and Drink Federation exists to represent the industry to government, regulators, consumers and the media. The Food and Drink Federation, which has offices in London and Edinburgh, is made up of a series of divisions including an Economics and Commercial Services Division, a Regulatory, Science and Health Division and a Sustainability Division. The Federation regularly issues its policy positions on a range of issues related to its priority areas: food safety and science; health and wellbeing; sustainability; and competitiveness. The Federation has produced position papers on topics such as genetic modification, additive use, food labelling, nanotechnology, the Public Health Responsibility Deal, trans-fats, carbon emissions and reform of the EU Common Agricultural Policy (CAP). Many of these are direct responses to government consultation processes.

There are many other organisations in operation in the UK which represent various elements of the food sector. Two have been mentioned briefly here. Their aims and objectives often come into conflict as they seek different outcomes from the same regulatory processes. Many more exist, each with their own interests. These can be foodstuff-specific organisations, established to promote their producers' wares, such as the British Cheese Board or the British Potato Council, they can have membership from a broader base, such as is the case for the British Beer and Pub Association, or they can be designed to promote a particular cause, such as Slow Food UK or Drinkaware. A vast range of interests may therefore have to be accommodated in the creation and application of new food laws.

3

Key Actors in Food Law

3.1 Introduction

Several government departments have a role to play in the devising, implementation and enforcement of food law and policy. The most significant of these is the Department for the Environment, Food and Rural Affairs (DEFRA). As will be seen throughout this book, DEFRA has a crucial role to play in most areas of food law, and is the responsible national authority for overseeing the majority of the EU legislative initiatives that must be applied at national level. The Departments of Health and Energy and Climate Change also have key roles to play.[1]

Most of the significant enforcement of food law comes at the local level, through the operations of the designated competent authorities. It is the individual units and officers of these authorities that interact directly with the food business operators, ensuring compliance with the regulatory requirements and taking action where these standards have not been met. State agencies, most notably the Food Standards Agency (FSA), also have a crucial practical role to play in protecting the public from risks to their health which may arise from the consumption of unsafe food. They carry out this function through the provision of advice and recommendations and the taking of action, based on the findings of others or arising out of their own risk assessments or investigations. The Food Standards Agency also has an increasing role to play in the development of national policy, including through its representation of the government on food safety and standards issues in the EU and its working relationship with the European Food Safety Authority (EFSA).

3.2 Government Departments

3.2.1 Department for the Environment, Food and Rural Affairs

As mentioned, DEFRA has most of the responsibility for the oversight of law and policy on food and related environmental and rural issues. This includes

[1] For discussion on some of the historical problems with the way in which the food sector has been regulated in the UK see C Yapp, 'Food safety regulation in the UK' in E Vos and F Wendler (eds), *Food Safety Regulation in Europe* (Antwerp/Oxford, Intersentia, 2006).

ensuring the proper implementation of EU food-related legislation on sustainable development, farming, fisheries, animal health and welfare and environmental protection. DEFRA only has direct responsibility for this in England, although it does work with the devolved administrations in other parts of the UK. It also usually represents the State in EU and international negotiations on food matters. DEFRA consists of approximately 10,000 staff, including those who work for its executive agencies, some of which are discussed further below. Its headquarters are in London, but it also has offices in York, Bristol and Alnwick, amongst others.

The key roles of DEFRA are discussed in more detail, as and when appropriate, throughout this book. It should also be noted at this stage that DEFRA is assisted in its work by 36 agencies and public bodies, including the Animal Health and Veterinary Laboratories Agency, the Food and Environment Research Agency, the Agriculture and Horticulture Development Board, the Consumer Council for Water and the Sea Fish Industry Authority. This figure also includes a range of advisory public bodies, such as the Advisory Committee on Pesticides, the Advisory Committee on Releases to the Environment, the Science Advisory Council and the Veterinary Products Committee. Expert Committees, such as the Farm Animal Welfare Committee (FAWC), also provide DEFRA with expertise on specific matters. FAWC regularly publishes its position on matters related to the keeping of animals on farms, during transit and at the time and place of slaughter, including, for example, a proposal in 2014 on the development of an Animal Health and Welfare Stewardship Programme and a consultation on Farmer Wellbeing and Farm Animal Welfare, also launched in 2014.

3.2.2 Department of Health

Other government departments have a less obvious, but significant role to play in the formulation and application of food policy and law. The Department of Health, for example, is active in promoting good public health, in particular through the development of strategies on countering overweightness, obesity and nutrition-related disease. The Public Health Responsibility Deal, initially launched in 2011 and an initiative at the Department of Health, is designed to get commitments in a number of areas from businesses and other organisations on the things that they can do to promote good health. Organisations can become national responsibility deal partners by signing up to the core commitments and supporting pledges set out and registering this promise with the Department of Health. Registered partners must also provide annual updates on their progress in the delivery of their pledges. The core commitments include a recognition by the organisation that it has a key role to play in improving people's health; an undertaking to encourage and enable people to adopt a healthier diet; fostering a culture of responsible drinking, which will help people to drink alcohol only within recommended guidelines; encouraging and assisting people to become more physically active; and actively supporting employees to lead healthier lives. The

Department of Health claims that this programme 'embodies the Government's ambition for a more collaborative approach to tackling the challenges caused by our lifestyle choices'.

There are supporting pledges to these core commitments for both food and alcohol. For food, the pledges include providing calorie information, committing to targets on the reduction of salt in food, avoiding the use of artificial trans-fatty acids in production, recognising the 'Call to Action on Obesity in England' challenges of overall calorie consumption reduction rates, by creating a positive environment that supports and enables people to increase their consumption of fruit and vegetables, reviewing portion sizes and menu options where appropriate and providing education and information on lower calorie options and reduced salt intakes. The pledges on food also include more specific undertakings on the adoption and implementation of the Government's 2013 recommended front-of-pack nutrition labelling scheme, which is discussed in detail in chapter nine, including the promotion and explanation to consumers on how to use this format. Also included is a pledge to recognise and act upon the fact that the over-consumption of saturated fat can result in higher mortality rates from cardiovascular and coronary heart disease. Progress on this final point must be monitored and reported by registered partners on an annual basis. Nationally, the National Diet and Nutrition Survey fulfils a similar function.

The Public Health Responsibility Deal sets out a series of pledges for those involved in the production, marketing and retail of alcoholic drinks. These include an undertaking to ensure that the vast majority of products will carry information on the label about alcoholic unit consumption and details of National Health Service guidelines about drinking alcohol when pregnant.[2] Similar information should be carried, where possible, in licensed premises to raise awareness about the unit content of alcoholic drinks. The Deal also contains commitments to providing simple and consistent information across the off-licence trade on consumption units, calories content, NHS drinking guidelines and the harms that could be caused to health by exceeding these. There is a reiteration of the position established in the Memoranda of Understanding between Industry, Government and Drinkaware about publicising a responsible drinking culture, as well as a commitment to ensuring that effective action is taken in the sector to reduce and prevent the sale of alcohol to those who are under the legal minimum age requirements.[3]

---

[2] Available at: https://responsibilitydeal.dh.gov.uk/pledges/.

[3] Under section 146 of the Licensing Act 2003, it is illegal to sell alcohol to anyone under the age of 18. However, section 150(4) also provides that it is not an offence for a 16 or 17 year old to consume alcohol, in the form of beer, wine or cider, on a licensed premises, provided that this is consumed with a meal and the individual is accompanied by an adult. Section 5 of the Children and Young Persons Act 1933 makes it an offence for anyone to give alcohol to someone under the age of five except where this is under the order of a qualified medical practitioner in an emergency.

3.2.3 Department of Energy and Climate Change

Agriculture and the production of food are significant contributors to UK carbon emissions. As will be discussed in chapter ten, the growing, treatment, manufacture, transportation and consumption of food all have energy costs. While the Department of Energy and Climate Change has no direct role to play in regulating the food sector, there is at least an indirect influence over the production and transportation of food in particular. The Department has identified nine general policies where it seeks to bring about change that results in lower energy use, carbon emissions and pollution levels. This includes four areas which can impact on policy and regulation related to food. It also shares responsibility in these four areas with DEFRA due to overlap between these departments in interest in the issues concerned. Policy areas where there is an indirect, and potentially more direct, influence over food regulation include (i) adapting to climate change; (ii) supporting international action on climate change; (iii) reducing demand for energy from industry, business and the public sector; and (iv) reducing the UK's greenhouse gas emissions by 80 per cent by 2050. Steps that can be taken by regulators to bring about change in producer and consumer behaviour in support of these polices are dealt with in more detail later in this book, but it should be noted at this stage that the Department of Energy and Climate Change has a relatively limited direct influence over the food sector at present. It is likely to become much more influential in this area in future years as the impact of, and the impact on, agriculture of high carbon emissions and the decreasing availability of natural resources become a more pressing concern.

3.3 Enforcing Food Law

Determining which food authority has specific responsibility for the enforcement and oversight of any particular aspect of English food law depends on which legislative act applies in the circumstances. In general, however, the designated food authority is the local borough, district or county council. The Food Safety Act 1990, for example, prescribes that

> the food authorities in England and Wales are (a) as respects each London borough, district or non-metropolitan county, the council of that borough, district or county; (b) as respects the City of London (including the Temples), the Common Council; (c) as respects the Inner Temple or the Middle Temple, the appropriate Treasurer.[4]

It is more complicated than this, however. The Food Safety Act 1990 goes on to state that

---

[4] Section 5(1).

[w]here any functions under this Act are assigned (a) by an order under section 2 or 7 of the Public Health (Control of Disease) Act 1984, to a port health authority ... (b) by an order under section 6 of the Public Health Act 1936, to a joint board for a united district; or (c) by an order under paragraph 15(6) of Schedule 8 to the Local Government Act 1985, to a single authority for a metropolitan county, any reference in this Act to a food authority shall be construed, so far as relating to those functions, as a reference to the authority to whom they are so assigned.[5]

The Public Health (Control of Disease) Act 1984 assigns these responsibilities to port health authorities when there is a possibility of a food-borne illness or disease entering the State and the appropriate port authority would be best placed to deal with the control of this. Various bodies, therefore, have responsibility for enforcing food law at local level. However, much of the EU legislation which brings these national laws into existence also requires the designation of a national or local competent authority to oversee proper implementation.

3.3.1 National Competent Authorities

In some circumstances the designated competent authority may be either the local authority, as discussed above, or the Food Standards Agency.[6] The latter has a major responsibility for the enforcement of the Hygiene Regulations, for example. This is discussed in more detail in chapter six. Other legislation, such as the Official Feed and Food Controls (England) Regulations 2006, have designated a degree of competence to the Food Standards Agency in a range of areas.[7] The way in which there must be oversight of the domestic application of EU food regulations is set out in the Official Controls Regulation.[8] This Regulation provides that these official controls are necessary to ensure that EU Member States enforce feed and food law, and monitor and verify that the relevant requirements are fulfilled by business operators at all stages of production, processing and distribution.[9] In order to properly achieve this, controls should be exerted regularly and proportionately to the potential risk involved in the activities of the operator concerned. There should also be ad hoc checks where there is any suspicion of non-compliance.[10] Overall, official controls that are implemented at national level must be designed to prevent, eliminate or reduce risks to human health to acceptably low levels.[11]

---

[5] Section 5(3).

[6] For further discussion on this see ch 5.

[7] SI No 15/2006.

[8] Regulation (EC) No 882/2004 of the European Parliament and of the Council of 29 April 2004 on official controls performed to ensure the verification of compliance with feed and food law, animal health and animal welfare rules [2004] OJ L 191/1.

[9] Preamble Recital 6 to Reg 882/2004, n 8 above.

[10] Preamble Recital 13 to Reg 882/2004, n 8 above.

[11] Art 1(1).

It must be understood at this stage that where EU rules are introduced, either by way of regulation or directive, they will be virtually meaningless if there is inadequate enforcement at both local and national levels. While the EU Commission does take some responsibility for overseeing the uniform application of legislation in the Member States, it is the domestic transposition of the EU rules that is so vital to ensuring that they are effective at achieving the aim pursued. This is particularly so in the case of EU regulations. They do not require any further implementing measures to be adopted at national level before they are applicable in the English legal system. However, they will usually require some form of domestic legislation to provide for their practical application. This is why we usually see statutory instruments introduced to provide for the proper functioning of EU regulations. One of the key roles of these statutory instruments is to set out who will have responsibility at local level for ensuring that the terms of the EU regulation are met by food business operators, and how they are to go about ensuring that this happens. The Official Controls Regulation sets out the general obligations for Member States to ensure that this is done in the appropriate manner.

Regulation 882/2004 provides that Member States must ensure that official controls are carried out with some degree of regularity, the frequency of this being directly associated with the level of risk involved with the activity concerned.[12] So, for example, we are likely to see higher levels of monitoring of those businesses which are involved in the production of food from animals than for those which process non-animal-based raw materials. The frequency of monitoring the compliance of an individual food business operator is then to be determined on the basis of the nature of any risk identified, the past record of compliance by the business with relevant food laws, any information that indicates non-compliance and the reliability of any previous checks carried out by the business itself. It is usual for official controls to be carried out without prior warning.[13] They can, of course, be carried out at any stage of production, processing or distribution of food.[14]

The EU Official Controls Regulation provides that it is for the individual Member States to designate who is to be the competent authority in each case.[15] These designated authorities are then charged with ensuring that the controls they employ over the operation of food law are effective and appropriate; that staff carrying out their tasks are free from any conflict of interests; that they have access to adequate laboratory facilities for testing food samples; that they have the appropriate facilities and equipment for carrying out their tasks; that they have the legal powers to carry out their tasks; and that they have contingency plans in place in the event of an emergency.[16] Member States must ensure that they place

---

[12] Art 3(1).
[13] Art 3(2).
[14] Art 3(3).
[15] Art 4(1).
[16] Art 4(2).

a binding obligation on the food business operators to undergo inspections and assist the designated authority's staff in the carrying out of their functions.[17]

Local authorities and/or the Food Standards Agency can, in some circumstances, delegate specific controls to other bodies.[18] The comitology procedure is used at EU level to determine when this can happen.[19] Tasks can only be delegated where certain conditions are met, such as ensuring that the control body has the staffing levels, expertise, equipment and infrastructure required to carry out the activities assigned to it.[20] These organisations must also be accredited according to set EU standards.[21] They should also be audited and inspected as necessary by the competent authority,[22] and their appointment should always be notified to the European Commission.[23]

National authorities charged with overseeing the implementation and enforcement of EU legislation must do so in accordance with documented procedures, which indicate instructions for their staff on what needs to be done.[24] As will be seen throughout this book, each individual regulation and directive clearly sets out what the designated competent authorities, and those bodies to which their tasks have been delegated, must do in order to ensure that the provisions of the EU legislation are properly applied at national level. Member States must support this work by ensuring that they have legal procedures in place that secure access for the competent authorities to the premises and documentation of food business operators within their jurisdiction.[25]

The methods that can be used by designated authorities to monitor compliance with food law include inspections, audits, sampling and analysis. The techniques to be employed vary, according to the area of food law that is being surveyed. This will usually be specified in the relevant specific EU and/or English legislation. Examples of this can be seen throughout this book. Laboratories used for sampling and analysis must, however, always be designated by the national authorities in accordance with specific EU standards, such as the 'General requirements for the competence of testing and calibration laboratories' or the 'General criteria for the assessment of testing laboratories'.[26] EU Commission experts can also carry out audits in the Member States on a regular basis.[27] Reports issued on the basis of these audits can then be used to make recommendations to the

---

[17] Art 4(2)(g).
[18] Art 5(1).
[19] Art 5(1) in conjunction with Art 62(3).
[20] Art 5(2)(b).
[21] Art 5(2)(c).
[22] Art 5(3).
[23] Art 5(4).
[24] Art 8(1).
[25] Art 8(2).
[26] Art 12.
[27] Art 45(1).

national authorities on how to go about improving compliance with food law.[28] The national authorities must then take appropriate follow-up action on this.[29]

In a measure designed to standardise the implementation of EU legislation at national level across all of the Member States, the Official Controls Regulation provides that the Commission can organise training courses for competent authority staff on food law, systems of control and production methods.[30] The Regulation also provides that designated national authorities are obliged to take action where they identify instances of non-compliance with food law.[31] This action can include the imposition of sanitation procedures, marketing restrictions, product recalls and/or business closures.[32] The imposition of sanctions on operators for breaches of food law is left up to the Member States;[33] however, any sanction that is imposed must be 'effective, proportionate and dissuasive'.[34] The State must also inform the Commission about the nature and level of sanctions it intends to impose, as well as details of any subsequent amendments that are made to this.[35]

3.3.2 Official Feed and Food Controls Regulations

As discussed above, the 2004 EU Official Controls Regulation stipulates that all Member States must designate national competent authorities to oversee the implementation of food law.[36] This designation is carried out at national level through the application of the Official Feed and Food Controls (England) Regulations 2009.[37] These Regulations provide that this competence at national level is to be divided between the Food Standards Agency and local authorities, depending on the circumstances.[38] Local 'food authorities' and 'authorised

---

[28] Art 45(3).

[29] Art 45(5).

[30] Art 51. The Regulation provides that there must be adequate training for all designated authority staff charged with performing official controls, at both national and EU level. Annex II to Reg 882/2004 sets out the areas in which these staff must be trained, including control techniques and procedures, food law, production methods, health risks, HACCP, contingency arrangements during emergencies and examining records and documentation.

[31] Art 54(1).

[32] Art 54(2).

[33] This is a common principle in EU law known as 'national procedural autonomy'. For further discussion see, amongst others, P Craig and G de Búrca, *EU Law: Text, Cases and Materials*, 5th edn (Oxford, OUP, 2011) 219–241; and D Chalmers, G Davies and G Monti, *European Union Law*, 3rd edn (Cambridge, CUP, 2014), ch 7.

[34] Art 55(1).

[35] Art 55(2).

[36] Reg 882/2004, n 8 above.

[37] SI No 3255/2009.

[38] A 'feed authority' is as stipulated in s 67(1) of the Agriculture Act 1970 which states that '[i]n England it shall be the duty of a county, metropolitan district or London borough … to enforce this part of the Act within their respective areas'.

officers' are as set out in the Food Safety Act 1990.[39] Determining whether it is the Agency or an Authority which has the competence can only be identified by looking at the relevant provisions of the Regulations. Most of the time, the competence is actually shared between the two. Schedules 4 and 5 to the Regulations set out which body is responsible for which provisions for feed and food matters respectively, as set out in the EU Official Controls Regulation.[40] For example, Schedule 5 provides that the Food Standards Agency is charged with dealing with notifying the European Commission and the other EU Member States where a decision has been taken to refuse the importation of feed or food into the country from a third country. It is really in this sort of area, liaising with the appropriate EU institutions, where the FSA has exclusive responsibility for food law enforcement matters.[41] Designated local authorities are charged with the collection of the costs of investigating the compliance with food law of suspected consignments of food from third countries. These expenses are to be taken from the feed or food business operators responsible for the importation of the suspected batch of feed or food.[42]

3.4 State Agencies

The use of state agencies, instead of government departments, to oversee the proper implementation of food law has become much more commonplace since the BSE crisis of the 1990s. Bodies such as the Food Standards Agency, the Health Protection Agency, the Environment Agency and the Intellectual Property Office all have a significant role to play in the development of policy, and the application of the relevant legal requirements, throughout the State. In addition to this, other more specific groups, in particular advisory committees, can be established to deal with more targeted concerns. For example, with the abolition of the Spongiform Encephalopathy Advisory Committee (SEAC) in March 2011, a new Transmissible Spongiform Encephalopathy (TSE) Risk Assessment Subgroup was established to assist the Advisory Committee on Dangerous Pathogens (ACDP). The terms of reference for this group are

---

[39] In particular section 5, which provides that 'the food authorities in England are the council of [the] borough, district or county'. An 'authorised officer' is 'any person (whether or not an officer of the authority) who is authorised by them in writing, either generally or specially, to act in matters arising under [the Acts]; but if regulations made by the Secretary of State so provide, no person shall be so authorised unless he has such qualifications as may be prescribed by the regulations'.

[40] Reg 882/2004, n 8 above.

[41] For another example of this see Art 52 of Reg 882/2004, n 8 above, which provides for the making of requests by Member States for assistance from the Commission when exercising controls in third countries.

[42] As set out in Art 22 of Reg 882/2004.

[t]o provide ACDP as requested with scientifically based assessment of risk from [TSEs] in relation to food safety, public and animal health issues, taking appropriate account of scientific uncertainty and assumptions in formulating advice.

The ACDP advises the Health and Safety Executive, as well as the Department of Health and the Department for the Environment, Food and Rural Affairs on all aspects of hazards and risks from exposure to pathogens. The most significant of all of these agencies, committees and subgroups, however, is the Food Standards Agency. It has a key role to play in a number of areas.

3.4.1 Food Standards Agency

The Food Standards Agency (FSA), which was of the first of its kind in Europe at the time of its establishment, is responsible for overseeing a wide range of food safety related matters across the UK. The FSA rarely has sole responsibility for many of the matters that are within its remit. It shares the oversight of labelling matters with both DEFRA and the Department of Health, the latter in relation to nutrition labelling issues in particular. Animal welfare concerns are also shared with DEFRA. As will be seen throughout this book, the FSA has a role to play in many aspects of the regulation of the food sector, but it is usually just one part of the process, albeit a very important one. The main idea behind the establishment of the Food Standards Agency is to have a body in place which can connect the producing, scientific and regulating sectors to the public. The hope has always been that much of the public confidence in the safety of food which was lost during the BSE crisis would be restored by having a public, yet independent body in place which can direct industry, advise consumers and interject where necessary to prevent future concerns arising, or at least minimise the potential risks to health by taking immediate and decisive action when they do. While the FSA may lack the power to make laws, it does possess a significant degree of persuasive power, both in relation to its dealings with Government and with the general public. The FSA can order food authorities to act to ensure compliance with codes of practice, enforceable by mandamus.[43] This includes enforcing the duty to appoint a public analyst.[44] The FSA also represents the State on food safety and standards matters at EU level.

The FSA was established by the Food Standards Act 1999. The main objective of the Agency, set out in section 1 of the Act, is to 'protect public health from risks which may arise in connection with the consumption of food … and otherwise to protect the interests of consumers in relation to food'.[45] For administrative

[43] Section 40(3) of the Food Safety Act 1990, as amended.

[44] *R v Leicester Union* [1899] 2 QB 632.

[45] Summarised by the Court of Appeal in *National Association of Health Stores v Department of Health* [2005] EWCA Civ 154 as 'protecting public health from risks carried by foodstuffs'. It was also stated by the High Court in *Friends of the Earth v Food Standards Agency* [2007] EWCH 558 that the formation of the Food Standards Agency, and presumably the interpretation of its functions, should be considered in light of its creation in the wake of the 'BSE problem'.

purposes, the Agency is led by a board, which consists of a chairman and up to 12 members who are appointed in a variety of ways, including by the National Assembly for Wales, as well as representation from Scotland and Northern Ireland. Others can be appointed by the Secretary of State.[46] Having said that, the Agency must act independently of Government, and is free to advise in any way that it deems appropriate.[47] The legislation also establishes that the FSA is to be assisted by Advisory Committees who are charged with giving advice or information to the Agency about any matters connected with its functions.[48]

Functions of the Food Standards Agency

The primary functions of the Food Standards Agency are assisting in the development of policies relating to matters connected with food safety or other interests of consumers in relation to food; and the provision of advice, information or assistance in respect of any of these matters to any other public authority.[49] Any government minister can request that the FSA exercise its powers in relation to the carrying out of these functions,[50] and it is the duty of the Agency to comply with any such request where this is reasonably practicable.[51]

The FSA also has the function of providing advice and information to the general public in respect of matters connected with food safety or other relevant interests.[52] This function must be carried out with a view to ensuring that members of the public are kept adequately aware of, and advised in relation to, any matters which the Agency considers might affect their capacity to make informed decisions about the purchase and consumption of food.[53] Another of the FSA's functions is the compilation and review of information and studies about food safety and related consumer interests.[54] This includes monitoring scientific and technological developments within the food sector. The FSA should also carry out and commission its own research on these matters.[55] The hope is that the collection and commissioning of information and data will be sufficient to provide the Agency with the knowledge required to make the most informed decisions in relation to its other functions, such as providing the public with sound advice on food safety matters.[56] The FSA has the same general functions in relation

---

[46] Section 2(1).

[47] Section 19. The exercise of this power granted to the FSA to publish advice and information is subject to the requirements of the Data Protection Act 1998. This power is also limited where such publication is expressly prohibited or is deemed incompatible with an EU obligation or where it would be considered as a contempt of court.

[48] Section 5.

[49] Section 6(1).

[50] Section 6(2).

[51] Section 6(3).

[52] Section 7(1).

[53] Section 7(2).

[54] Section 8(1).

[55] Section 8(2).

[56] Section 8(3).

to animal feed.[57] The Agency is entitled to observe practices and procedures at food premises or businesses to assist it in gathering data and information.[58] This includes the power to enter premises, take samples and inspect records.[59]

As was discussed above, local authorities, and others, have a very significant role to play in the enforcement of most aspects of food law. Under the terms of the Food Standards Act 1999, the FSA is charged with monitoring the performance of these authorities in enforcing the legislative requirements.[60] This function includes setting standards in relation to this enforcement. The FSA's Annual Reports should contain details on its activities in monitoring the enforcement authorities in the carrying out of their tasks.

Other functions of the Food Standards Agency include the potential to have the power to make emergency orders under the Food and Environment Protection Act 1985,[61] and the power to make emergency control orders under the Food Safety Act 1990.[62] This power may be granted by the Secretary of State, and is subject to possible limitations and conditions prescribed.[63] However, it should be noted that even where this power is granted to the FSA, the Act reserves the right of the Secretary of State to issue his own emergency orders or emergency control orders where required.[64] The Agency can also issue general guidance, as it thinks fit, to local authorities or other public authorities on matters connected with the management of outbreaks or suspected outbreaks of food-borne disease.[65] Finally, the Act provides that the FSA should publish a statement of general objectives that it intends to pursue.[66] In 2014, these objectives included ensuring that food produced or sold in the UK is safe to eat; that imported food is also safe to eat; that food producers and caterers give priority to consumer interests in relation to food; that consumers have the information and understanding they need to make informed choices about where and what they eat; and that business compliance with their food safety and related obligations is effectively

---

[57] Section 9.

[58] Section 10.

[59] Section 11. Section 11(4) provides that this entry can take place 'at any reasonable hour'. Reasonable hours are usually presumed to be the opening times of a business, although this could include other times in the case of an emergency: *Small v Bickley* (1875) 32 LT 726; and *Davies v Winstanley* (1930) 144 LT 433.

[60] Section 12.

[61] In particular section 1(1) thereof, which provides that an Emergency Order can be issued where the designating authority is of the opinion that 'there has been or may have been an escape of substances of such descriptions and in such quantities and such circumstances as are likely to create a hazard to human health through human consumption of food'.

[62] In particular section 13(1) thereof, which provides that '[i]f it appears to [the Agency] that the carrying out of commercial operations with respect to food, food sources or contact materials of any class or description involves or may involve imminent risk of injury to health, [it] may, by an [emergency control order] prohibit the carrying out of such operations with respect to food, food sources or contact materials of that class or description'.

[63] Sections 17(1) and 17(2) of the Food Standards Act 1999.

[64] Section 17(4).

[65] Section 20.

[66] Section 22.

supported where it delivers consumer protection. The final objective listed here is, according to the FSA, to be achieved by focusing on an effective, risk-based and proportionate approach to regulation and enforcement. These objectives are to be used to inform and direct the way in which the FSA carries out its functions, as listed above.[67] The Secretary of State can intervene where this does not happen effectively.[68] The Secretary of State may also give the Agency directions on how to act where this is deemed necessary for the proper implementation of the State's obligations under EU or international law.[69] While the Secretary of State retains significant control over the operations of the Food Standards Agency, and also reserves the power to issue enforcement functions set out in other legislative acts, such as the Food Safety Act 1990, many of the functions of the Minister set out in this legislation are transferred to the FSA.[70] So while the FSA is given the flexibility to operate independently, it remains a State Agency over which the Government has retained, through the provisions of the Food Standards Act 1999, a significant degree of control. There is also an obligation placed on the Secretary of State to consult the Food Standards Agency on some matters.[71]

3.4.2 Health Protection Agency and Public Health England

The Health Protection Agency, which has become part of Public Health England, is an executive agency of the Department of Health. Public Health England was established to provide a body having as its key aim and objective the protection and improvement of the nation's health and well-being. This includes providing support to local authorities to deliver improvements in public health. It came into existence in April 2013.

A range of responsibilities have been set for Public Health England. These include advising Government on policy that will encourage the provision of support for the public in a manner that facilitates them in protecting and improving their own health. The Public Health Responsibility Deal offers a good example of this in practice. Other responsibilities include researching and analysing data to improve understanding on health and then sharing this information and other expertise with local authorities and industry to assist them in making decisions designed to improve public health. The stated priorities of Public Health England are reducing preventable deaths and the burden of ill-health arising out of, amongst other things, poor diet, obesity and alcohol consumption. The

---

[67] Section 23.
[68] Section 24(1).
[69] Section 24(4).
[70] Section 26(1) of the Food Standards Act 1999.
[71] Section 29(1). It was stated by the High Court in *Bapio Action Limited and Yousaf v Secretary of State for the Home Department and Secretary of State for Health* [2007] EWHC 199, that this provision 'expressly [imposes] on an executive authority an obligation to consult before exercising a statutory power'.

combined organisations that make up Public Health England employ around 5,500 staff, a figure which is mostly made up of scientists, researchers and public health professionals.

The Health Protection Agency has a range of functions directly related to the prevention of ill-health arising out of the production and consumption of food. These include setting guidelines for some types of food sampling and analysis, such as those which are to be used to assess the microbiological safety of ready-to-eat foods. These guidelines do not take precedence over EU or national legislation on this, but they do complement the legally enforceable standards and they provide an indication of the microbiological safety of foods where relevant standards do not exist. The Health Protection Agency, in association with Local Government Regulation, implements a national programme of studies on foods which have been identified by environmental health officers and HPA public health microbiologists as possibly giving cause for concern from a safety perspective. The studies are designed to provide national data on the safety of ready-to-eat and raw food samples examined within the UK, as well as providing national information on areas where there may be specific high-level risks, such as butcher's shop hygiene, salads, vegetables, eggs and spices. The purpose of these surveillance studies is to assist in the development of systems for monitoring and improving targeted food hygiene problems.

The Health Protection Agency has also operated a system for the surveillance of infectious intestinal disease in England and Wales since 1992. This includes monitoring foodborne gastrointestinal outbreaks of these illnesses. An 'outbreak' is defined as being

> an incident in which two or more people, thought to have a common exposure, experience a similar illness or proven infection, at least one of them having been ill.

Finally, the Agency provides support to a number of national (Department of Health) scientific advisory committees, including the Advisory Committee on Dangerous Pathogens, the Committee on the Carcinogenicity of Chemicals in Food, Consumer Products and the Environment, the Committee on the Mutagenicity of Chemicals in Food, Consumer Products and the Environment and the Committee on Toxicity. The operations of the final three of these committees listed are contributed to jointly with the Food Standards Agency.

3.4.3 Environment Agency

The Environment Agency has a range of roles, including the organisation of responses to emergencies in England. Its also has a range of responsibilities that relate more specifically to the food sector, such as dealing with waste regulation, water quality and fisheries. In particular, the Environment Agency includes amongst its priorities the protection and improvement of water and land quality through tackling pollution, as well as acting to reduce climate change and its consequences. As is discussed in chapter ten of this book, the regulation of the food sector has the potential to play a meaningful role in reducing carbon emissions and the possible consequences of this on climate change and pollution.

The Environment Agency, which has over 11,000 employees, is directly responsible to the Secretary of State for the Environment, Food and Rural Affairs. With its head office in Bristol, the Agency is divided into six regions—the South East, the South West, the Midlands, Anglia, the North West and Yorkshire and the North East. It has a direct responsibility towards ensuring that its priorities are achieved through the monitoring of, and intervening in, the food sector. It must be remembered that the food and drink manufacturing sector is the largest industrial manufacturing sector in the UK. Consequently, it uses large volumes of water and energy and it produces a lot of waste.[72] This can, and does, have a significant impact on the environment and pollution levels. The Environment Agency is charged with providing environmental permits to food companies of a certain size for the carrying out of certain activities. This is a key part of regulating the activities of these companies where they have the potential to affect the environment, water quality, pollution, waste levels and carbon emission levels.

3.4.4 Intellectual Property Office

The Intellectual Property Office, which deals with all aspects of intellectual property protection, such as copyright, trademarks and patents, also has a key role to play in the application of the WTO Agreement on Trade Related Aspects of Intellectual Property Rights (TRIPs) in the UK. The Office is responsible for the formulation and delivery of UK policy on TRIPs topics, including the protection of geographical food names. As discussed in chapter two, this Agreement provides a degree of international protection for protected designations of origin and protected geographical indications. The TRIPs Agreement provides that WTO members should provide the legal means for parties to prevent the use of geographical names that indicate or suggest that a good originates in a geographical area other than its true place of origin, in a manner that misleads consumers or which constitutes unfair competition. It also provides for an enhanced level of protection for the geographical names of wines and spirits, subject to the exception set out in Article 24 of TRIPs, which facilitates the continued use of previously registered trademarks. The Intellectual Property Office oversees the implementation of all

---

[72] K Bromley-Challenor, M Kowalski, R Barnard and S Lynn, for the Waste and Resources Action Programme (WRAP), have calculated that the food and drink sector in the UK was using between 347 million metres cubed and 366 million metres cubed of water per year. This actually showed a reduction of around 15% on the figures for 2007. Almost 270 million metres cubed of this usage was in England, with a further nearly 14 million metres cubed in Wales. Almost all of this was in manufacturing and hospitality services combined. Report available at: www.wrap.org.uk. According to a DEFRA report entitled 'Food industry sustainability strategy', the food industry was also estimated to account for around 14% of the total energy consumption of businesses by 2006, involving 7 million tonnes of carbon emissions. The report is available at: www.gov.uk/government/publications.

this, as well as ensuring that other aspects of English law, such as the Trade Marks Act 1994, which provides that trademarks which consist of signs which serve to indicate geographical origin should not be registered as such.[73] UK practice on the registration of geographical designations and indications is set out in the IPO Trade Marks Work Manual.[74] However, it is the Food Composition and Standards Team at DEFRA that has responsibility for overseeing applications for registration as a protected designation of origin or geographical indication. It is also DEFRA which acts as the national competent authority for PDO/PGI applications, sending applications on to the EU Commission once complete and valid.

3.5 Conclusion

There are many national bodies with responsibility for different aspects of the implementation of food law. Much of the time, however, their roles are limited to (i) the enforcement of EU-derived legislative requirements; and (ii) the setting of policies and guidelines. The latter, however, is often further limited to the creation of non-binding measures and advice. As is discussed in chapter four, EU rules on the free movement of food prevent Member States from either maintaining or creating national rules that create any sort of barrier to importation, no matter how small or significant. Such rules may be deemed contrary to the TFEU prohibitions on measures equivalent to quantitative restrictions on trade or to that on charges of equivalent effect to customs duties. In some circumstances, national fiscal measures may be deemed unlawful where they discriminate, directly or indirectly, against non-national produce. Almost all 'national' food law is now therefore about the enforcement and implementation of EU requirements. There is very little scope left for national legislative initiative designed to regulate the food sector. This is also discussed in more detail in chapter four, where it is shown that EU rules on the free movement of food preclude Member States from adopting their own binding measures that are designed to protect their people in some way. Member States can be the subject of a Commission enforcement action before the European Court of Justice where they introduce a law to protect human health or consumers.

---

[73] Section 3(1)(c).
[74] Available at: www.ipo.gov.uk.

4

EU Rules on the Free Movement of Food

4.1 Introduction

There are four ways in which EU rules on the free movement of goods impact on English food law. The first of these is the prohibition on measures equivalent to quantitative restrictions on trade. This has come to mean that any national measure that has the potential to restrict the movement of goods either into or out of a Member State should be discontinued. There are some circumstances where the Member State can justify the maintenance of such a national measure. The point is usually made that a compositional requirement or an outright prohibition on the sale of a good may be necessary to protect consumers from deception or to protect human health. The case law of the Court of Justice shows us that this is usually a difficult argument to make successfully.

The second way in which EU rules impact on English food law relates to the prohibition on charges of equivalent effect to customs duties. These charges must be set at 0 per cent on all goods traded between Member States. However, the Treaty extends this to any national measure that imposes an additional financial burden on the importer or exporter that the national producer operating in the national market does not have to face. Charges for inspections of imported animal produce offer an example of the type prohibited by this provision. Again, there are some exceptions to the rule, but they are hard for Member States to successfully establish, and it is usually only where EU law has prescribed a particular activity that Member States will be permitted to pass on the costs of this to the food business operator.

Third, while the majority of taxation decisions remain at the discretion of the Member States, the Treaty on the Functioning of the European Union does not allow national taxes to discriminate against non-national produce. Ad valorem taxes, in particular, can be shown to contravene this provision if they place a higher rate of tax on produce that is mostly made in other EU Member States. Any such tax must be modified where it is found to be contrary to these equality requirements, in order to reduce or eliminate the discriminatory element.

Finally, the harmonisation of food laws can have a very significant impact on national measures by obliging Member States to alter their rules so that they become the same, or at least very close to the same, as similar rules operating across the EU. Most of the rest of this book deals with these harmonised requirements.

4.2 Measures Equivalent to Quantitative Restrictions on Trade in Food

The prohibition set out in Article 34 TFEU is the single most important, and far-reaching, element of EU law and policy on the free movement of goods. It states that '[q]uantitative restrictions on imports and all measures having equivalent effect shall be prohibited between Member States'. This provision of the Treaty has significant implications. It is designed to ensure that there are no unnecessary impediments set or applied in the domestic laws of EU Member States which restrict intra-Union trade in any way. The European Court of Justice defined these 'measures equivalent to quantitative restrictions' on trade in the broadest sense possible in *Dassonville*.[1] There it stated that '[a]ll trading rules enacted by Member States which are capable of hindering, directly or indirectly, actually or potentially, intra-Community trade are to be considered as measures having an effect equivalent to quantitative restrictions'.[2] Any national law setting a compositional or labelling requirement for food would thus be deemed to be within the scope of this provision, requiring an Article 34 TFEU compatibility examination. Unless this national law could be justified, and it has become clear that this is a difficult justification to make, then it would be contrary to Article 34 TFEU, and consequently to the Treaty obligations of the imposing Member State. National law would have to be repealed or significantly modified to bring it back into line with EU requirements on the free movement of goods. It also prevents Member States from introducing new measures where these have the potential to 'directly or indirectly' affect trade, even where this is considered necessary to protect consumers or human health.

4.2.1 Restricting the Free Movement of Food

EU Member States may have national laws in place that stipulate the inclusion or exclusion of certain ingredients from a particular type of food. Only products that are manufactured in accordance with these rules are permitted to use a specified

---

[1] Case 8/1974 *Procureur du Roi v Benoît and Gustave Dassonville* [1974] ECR 837.
[2] Para 5.

name, set out in the same legislation. For example, English law could prescribe that digestive biscuits can only be called 'digestive biscuits' where they contain wheat flour (at least 70 per cent), sugar (no more than 15 per cent), malt extract, vegetable oil and raising agents. However, a French producer who markets his 'digestive biscuits' in England could not, because of EU rules on the free movement of food, be required to comply with this (fictional) English law. He would have to be allowed to market his product as 'digestive biscuits' in England even if they were made with only 60 per cent flour and over 20 per cent sugar. This is because of a principle developed by the European Court of Justice known as 'mutual recognition'. It means that once a product is lawfully marketed in one EU Member State, it must be lawfully marketable in all EU Member States. There are some exceptions to this rule, but it remains difficult for Member States, such as the UK, to argue that any national law that operates contrary to the principle of mutual recognition is necessary and should be able to persist.

Suppose, however, the French producer of 'digestive biscuits' adds hazelnuts to his ingredients. The flour content remains at 60 per cent, the sugar 20 per cent, but in addition, 15 per cent is made up of nuts. There is now the potential for the English authorities to make the case that this biscuit is not lawfully marketable as a 'digestive biscuit'. The reason for this is that the European Court of Justice has found that where there is a 'substantial difference' between a product entering the market (the French digestive biscuit) and the product normally known by that name (the existing English digestive biscuit) then it may be necessary to allow some form of restriction to be placed on the sales name that is used when marketing the former. It may be accepted that the need to protect consumers facilitates the imposition of national laws that impede free movement in such circumstances. However, it should be noted that this is also a difficult position for a Member State to successfully argue as the Court of Justice often holds that a prohibition on the use of a particular name, even when describing what is essentially a different product, may go beyond what is necessary in the circumstances. They usually decide that a more proportionate response in these situations is to oblige the producer of the different product to give a clear indication of this difference on the labelling. This 'principle of proportionality' is one of the general principles of EU law. As will be seen in the discussion below, there can also be difficulties when determining what may constitute a 'substantial' difference between products.

Finally, if the French biscuit producer does not include hazelnuts, but does add a quantity of some other substance such as fructose or salt to the ingredients, then an argument can be put forward by the Member State of sale that the product should not be marketed in their territory, as it poses some sort of danger to human health. If studies show that the consumption of either of these constituents in high amounts can have a negative impact on health, then it may be deemed acceptable for the Member State to prohibit the sale of that foodstuff in that form. However, it should be noted that there must be evidence of the potential risk to health presented in support of any such action. The risk must be a real, and usually immediate, one. It is often also a requirement that the Member State imposing any such restriction does not permit similar quantities of these potentially harmful substances to be present in other foods which are not subjected to similar prohibitions. The case law and legislation that has created each of these positions is discussed in more detail below.

4.2.2 Compositional Requirements and the Principle of Mutual Recognition

If *Dassonville* is to be considered the seminal case in determining what a 'measure equivalent to a quantitative restriction on trade' is to be, then we must also consider that the decision of the Court of Justice in *Cassis* is of similar significance to the application of what is now Article 34 TFEU.[3] It determined that once a product is lawfully marketable in any EU Member State it must be marketable in all. This is known as the principle of 'mutual recognition', briefly mentioned earlier in this chapter. Each Member State must recognise the application of the laws of the others as being adequate for the protection of consumers and health. In some, albeit relatively limited, circumstances there will be permissible exceptions to this rule. It has become the cornerstone of the application of Article 34 TFEU. In summary, it usually means two things. First, food produced anywhere in the EU can be sold anywhere in the EU, without restriction. Second, Member States cannot set or apply compositional, or similar, requirements for food which inhibit, in any way, the sale of products from other Member States. This is particularly significant when we come to consider the limitations placed on States wishing to take measures to counter public health concerns, such as rising rates of obesity.

This section aims to provide an overview of the key issues and principles involved in the application of Article 34 TFEU at national level, as well as their effects on English law and policy. Much more comprehensive assessments of the general prohibition on quantitative restrictions on trade and measures of equivalent effect are provided elsewhere.[4] In *Cassis*, a case was brought against German authorities for refusing to allow the importation of a consignment of the French-produced blackcurrant liqueur, Cassis de Dijon. German law at the time prescribed that liqueurs like this one had to have a minimum alcohol content of 32 per cent in order to be lawfully marketable there. The French product tended to be sold with an alcohol content in the range of 15 to 20 per cent. It was argued that the German law was a measure equivalent to a quantitative restriction on imports. The law did not prohibit the sale of French liqueurs, but it did restrict

---

[3] Case 120/1978 *Rewe-Zentral AG v Bundesmonopolverwaltung für Branntwein* (Cassis) [1979] ECR 649.

[4] eg in C Barnard, *The Substantive Law of the EU*, 4th edn (Oxford, OUP, 2013), chs 4–6; P Oliver, *Free movement of goods in the European Union*, 5th edn (Oxford, Hart, 2010); P Craig and G de Búrca, *EU Law*, 5th edn (Oxford, OUP, 2011), ch 19.

the ability of French producers to sell products in Germany that did not meet the minimum alcohol requirements set there. This is what is meant by a 'compositional requirement'. It is a domestic rule that stipulates compositional considerations that must be met for lawful marketability—in this case a minimum alcohol level requirement. Other obvious examples of these 'compositional requirements' would include stipulations about the inclusion or exclusion of certain ingredients, or the setting of minimum or maximum quantities for these ingredients, before a particular sales name can be used.

Using the formula developed in *Dassonville*, the European Court of Justice found that the German law on minimum alcohol level was a measure equivalent to a quantitative restriction on imports, examinable under Article 34 TFEU (Article 30 EEC at the time). It stated that

> [a]ccording to the settled case law of the Court any measure of such a kind as to hinder, directly or indirectly, actually or potentially, trade between Member States falls under the prohibition contained in [Article 34 TFEU]. To prohibit the marketing of a product from one Member State in another Member State hinders the importation of that product in a direct and immediate manner; it is therefore a measure having an effect equivalent to a quantitative restriction on imports prohibited by [Article 34 TFEU], subject to the exceptions laid down by [Union] law.

These possible exceptions to the rule on limiting trade were listed as the effectiveness of fiscal supervision, the protection of public health, the fairness of commercial transactions and the defence of the consumer.[5] Together, these are known as the 'mandatory requirements'. Unnecessarily, the protection of health was listed here as a possible basis upon which a Member State could maintain a law that was, prima facie, contrary to the application of Article 34 TFEU. It was unnecessary because the protection of health is specifically listed in Article 36 TFEU as providing such an exception. This is discussed further below. However, the protection of consumers is not included in the Article 36 TFEU exceptions, but the Court here added it to the list of possible justifications for the maintenance of national trade-restricting rules.

Having decided that the rule was caught within the scope of Article 34 TFEU, it then had to be determined whether its existence could be justified on any of the grounds set out. Two arguments were put forward here. The first was that the application of the rule was necessary to protect public health. This was rejected. The German Government had claimed that the rule was necessary as it was designed to prevent the proliferation of low-alcohol products on the market. The Court noted that there was a wide range of other low-alcohol beverages freely available in Germany, and that no similar restrictions had been placed on these. The second argument put forward was that the measure was necessary to protect consumer interests. This was also rejected. Here, the case made was that the alcohol level in a product was usually reflected in the price, and that lower-alcohol

---

[5] Para 8 of the judgment.

products would therefore have a competitive advantage over their higher priced rivals. This is a weak point, as it fails to recognise the obvious advantages to the consumer of having both cheaper alternatives and a wider range of products on the market. More sensibly, it was also pointed out that allowing products into lawful free circulation where they comply with the rules laid down in another Member State would lead to standardisation at the lowest level. In other words, if a Member State had no minimum alcohol content requirement, then no other Member State could impose their minimum permitted levels. This could lead to a 'race to the bottom', where there could be no standards at all where even a single Member State had no compositional requirements in a particular area. This would '[render] any requirements in this field inoperative since a lower limit of this nature is foreign to the rules of several Member States'.[6]

The solution presented by the Court continues to be hugely significant in this area. It was presented as 'a simple matter'. Member States could not impose rules like these on imports. The more proportionate response would be 'to ensure that suitable information is conveyed to the purchaser by requiring the display of an indication of origin and of the alcohol content on the packaging of products'.[7] Labelling could be used to relay the details about the nature and composition of a product to consumers. Anything more inhibiting to trade than this would be deemed an unlawful obstacle to trade, prohibited by Article 34 TFEU. Consumers could be adequately protected by the more proportionate response of requiring adequate labelling disclosures.

Finally, the Court encapsulated all of this in the principle of mutual recognition, which is central to understanding EU rules on the free movement of food, and the impact that they have on national laws. It stated that

> [t]here is ... no valid reason why, provided that they have been lawfully produced and marketed in one of the Member States, alcoholic beverages should not be introduced into any other Member State; the sale of such products may not be subject to a legal prohibition on the marketing of beverages with an alcohol content lower than the limits set by the national rules.[8]

Therefore, once a foodstuff is lawfully produced and marketed in one Member State, it must be lawfully marketable in all.

The decision in *Cassis* applied to a set of circumstances where the use of labelling presented an easy remedy to satisfy the test of proportionality. The Court insisted that it was always, where possible, more trade-promoting to insist upon clear indications on the label than it would be to have an outright prohibition in place. However, sometimes, the labelling itself can be the issue. There may be no prohibition on the sale of a particular product, but instead there may be a restriction in place on the use of a particular sales name. Suppose, for example, English law prescribes that rye bread must contain at least 70 per cent rye flour.

---

[6] Para 12.
[7] Para 13.
[8] Para 14.

If it is produced and marketed as rye bread in another Member State, but is made with only 60 per cent rye flour, then it could still be sold in England, but it could not be marketed as rye bread under English law. It could be sold instead as mere 'bread'. English law has not prohibited the sale of the product. It has just prohibited the use of a particular sales name, one that it wishes to preserve for products that meet a minimum standard in relation to the main ingredient of the product concerned. Article 34 TFEU would prevent this. On the application of the principle of mutual recognition developed by the Court of Justice in *Cassis*, it would require that English law was modified to allow the sale of imported rye bread as rye bread in England, even where the 70 per cent flour standard was not met. Other labelling disclosures could be used instead to indicate this difference. A reference in the list of ingredients could be used to indicate that there was only 60 per cent rye flour, and not the usual 70 per cent. Here we see the far-reaching consequences of the decision in *Cassis*. There it applied to an outright prohibition. In our hypothetical situation here, it applies to a labelling indication—one where it would be considered a more proportionate response to indicate the difference between the products concerned by using another labelling disclosure to bring this to the attention of the consumer.

The principle of mutual recognition has been applied by the Court of Justice in a number of free movement of food related cases since its original inception in *Cassis*. Liqueurs were also the subject of the Court's deliberations in *Fietje*, where proceedings had been brought at national level against a trader who was selling alcoholic drinks which did not carry the word 'likeur' on the labelling, as they were obliged to do for this type of drink under Dutch law.[9] It was recognised by the Court of Justice that the national law at issue did not prohibit the importation of the products in question into the State, but it did make their marketing there more difficult. It was thus capable of impeding, directly or indirectly, actually or potentially, interstate trade. As the rule was within the scope of that which was prohibited by the application of Article 34 TFEU, it would have to be justifiable on the grounds of health or consumer protection if it were to be maintained, and if the action against the respondent in this case could proceed. The Court recognised, as it does in these Article 34 TFEU cases, that national rules like this may be deemed necessary where they provide consumers with protection by seeking to minimise confusion. This can be the case even where the rules oblige the importer to alter the labelling of their product in some way, such as the addition of the word 'likeur'. While the Court regularly states this as being its position, it almost always finds that the other disclosures already made on the label are sufficient to prevent such confusion amongst consumers. In *Fietje* it was stated that

> there is no longer any need for such protection if the details given on the original label of the imported product have as their content information on the nature of the product and that content includes at least the same information, and is just as capable of being

[9] Case 27/1980 *Criminal proceedings against Anton Adriaan Fietje* [1980] ECR 3839.

understood by consumers in the importing State, as the description prescribed by the rules of that State.[10]

The Dutch rule on the labelling of these liqueurs was thus found to be in contravention of Article 34 TFEU where sufficient or similar information was still provided to consumers by the labels used on the imported products, including those that did not directly comply with the 'likeur' requirement. The fact that the application of the rule made it necessary for some imported products to have their labels altered made the law a measure equivalent to a quantitative restriction on imports. This could not be justified unless it could be shown that its non-application would be likely to cause confusion amongst consumers. This would be a difficult thing to prove where the labelling disclosures of imported products provided information on the nature of the product. The Court of Justice decided in *Cassis* that additional labelling disclosures are preferable, and more proportionate, than prohibitions. The same court determined in *Fietje* that national obligations to provide additional labelling disclosures on food or drink may also, depending on the circumstances, be contrary to EU rules on free movement.

In similar circumstances to those examined by the Court of Justice in *Cassis*, Dutch rules setting a minimum alcohol requirement for 'jenever' came under scrutiny in *Miro*.[11] An off-licence operator had been prosecuted for selling Belgian jenever, which is a gin-style drink, in the Netherlands which failed to meet the stipulation on alcohol level. The product had been lawfully manufactured and marketed in Belgium for many years. The national court had already found that consumers were adequately protected and informed by the label of the Belgian drink, as it clearly indicated the origin of the product and its alcohol content.

The Dutch authorities argued before the European Court of Justice that this was not sufficient to indicate a significant difference between the varieties as (i) many consumers would not know that jenever 'traditionally' had an alcohol content of 35 per cent, and not 30 per cent as was the case in Belgium; and (ii) the labelling would be completely ineffective where the drink was sold in hotels and restaurants. The Court rejected the Dutch claims, instead accepting that the information provided on the label of the Belgian variety was sufficient to inform consumers and needed no further examination. The Dutch rules were thus deemed contrary to Article 34 TFEU, being unjustifiable on consumer protection grounds.

In *van der Laan* proceedings had been brought in Germany against a meat distributor for selling products that were not in compliance with provisions of German food law.[12] This obliged the producers of cured meats and meat products to be quite explicit with their labelling disclosures. For example, a product that the respondent had called 'Bristol' should, under the terms of the Code, have been labelled as 'formed shoulder ham composed of ham pieces'. In addition to this, the German Code prohibited the addition of water to meat products, and it required

---

[10]   Para 12 of the judgment.
[11]   Case 182/1984 *Criminal proceedings against Miro BV* [1985] ECR 3731.
[12]   Case C-383/1997 *Criminal proceedings against Arnoldus van der Laan* [1999] ECR I-731.

that cured pork products should actually contain 100 per cent pork meat, at least 90 per cent of which should be muscle meat protein. The disputed products did not meet any of these standards, and could not therefore be lawfully marketed in Germany. The Court of Justice was asked whether rules like these were allowable under any of the permitted exceptions to the terms of Article 34 TFEU.

It is clear that German food law, as it applied to these meat products, was a measure equivalent to a quantitative restriction on imports. It was argued that this was justifiable on the ground of consumer protection. In response to this, the Court of Justice stated that consumer protection

> can be guaranteed by means which do not hinder the importation of products which have been lawfully manufactured and marketed in other Member States, in particular by suitable labelling giving the nature of the product sold.[13]

At the time of the decision, the original framework food labelling directive had come into effect.[14] If the labelling of 'Bristol' complied with this, it would have to be lawfully marketable in Germany, regardless of how diluted the meat product had become in its manufacture. The Court found that if the products concerned carried details about both the meat and water content levels, they would be deemed to be in compliance with EU law. A list of ingredients that included water, and whichever other substances had been added to the product, could not be restricted in any other way. It was stated that

> a Member State cannot claim that a list of ingredients which complies with [the framework food labelling] directive none the less constitutes fraud ... justifying the application of non-harmonised rules.[15]

This is a very significant, and unsurprising, statement. Effectively, this is a licence to include any non-dangerous substance in food and allow it to be in free competition with more pure versions of the same product. Rather than protecting consumers, the obligation to present a list of ingredients on all pre-packaged foodstuffs, set out in both EU law and national law, actually provides a means of lawfully reducing the quality of products, and ensuring that they must be allowed to freely circulate between Member States. The Court uses the existence of harmonised labelling requirements to facilitate the marketability of inferior quality products. This presents a problem for the consumer, the producer and for the State. The consumer is presented with a lower quality product as if it is equivalent to the higher-quality variety. The only way of determining this difference is to compare the lists of ingredients. The quantity of water or other substances used may not even be properly disclosed. Their presence should be indicated in the ingredients list, but there will not necessarily be any indication of how much of these have been added. The producer of the higher-quality product, who does not

---

[13] Para 24.
[14] Directive 1979/112, n 29 below.
[15] Para 37.

add water or other substances to his foods, now has to compete in this environment with the cheaper substitute. The State may suffer also.

The quality, and often consequently the nutritional value, of foods deteriorates as other substances can be added to foods. It was noted in chapter one of this book that this was originally prohibited in English law, as it was deemed to be 'adulteration'. This practice, depending on what is added to the food, can result in poorer health, higher rates of obesity and related disease. The cost of this to the National Health Service, and to economic output, is substantial.[16] EU rules on the free movement of food are contributing to the availability of lower-quality and nutritionally inferior foods. Food law, which has done so much to improve the safety and quality of products in the past, is now being destabilised in the interests of free movement. As is clearly demonstrated by the findings of the Court of Justice in cases such as *van der Laan*, national laws designed to maintain quality standards are being undermined, and their application deemed unlawful, by the process of harmonisation at EU level.

Gilli and Andres concerned a more outright prohibition on the sale of certain foods.[17] Here, criminal proceedings had been brought at the national level against both respondents for selling apple vinegar in Italy. Italian law prescribed that only products made through the fermentation of wine could be marketed as vinegar. It was contended that such a rule was in contravention of Article 34 TFEU, the apple vinegar in question being lawfully manufactured and marketed in Germany before importation into Italy. The Court agreed. It found that there were no grounds available for justifying the ban on apple vinegar. It contained no substances that could be harmful to human health. Nor was there the potential for there to be confusion amongst consumers, as the receptacles containing the apple vinegar were clearly labelled as such. The national law at issue served no purpose in the general interest that could take precedence over Union requirements on the free movement of goods.

The Commission later took infringement proceedings against Italy for the maintenance of such compositional requirements for vinegar.[18] Italy had already been issued with two reasoned opinions by the Commission indicating that the rules at issue contravened EU free movement requirements. Italy responded by claiming that Italian consumers considered all vinegar to be made from the fermentation of wine. Consequently, the use of this sales name by vinegars produced in a different manner, or with alternative ingredients, was therefore, in their opinion, liable to confuse Italian consumers. This was again rejected. The Court held that 'vinegar' was a generic term and that

> it would not be compatible with the objectives of the common market and in particular with the fundamental principle of the free movement of goods for national legislation to

---

[16] For more detailed discussion on this see ch 9.
[17] Case 788/1979 *Criminal proceedings against Gilli and Andres* [1980] ECR 2071.
[18] Case 193/1980 *Commission v Italy* [1981] ECR 3019.

be able to restrict a generic term to one national variety alone to the detriment of other varieties produced, in particular, in other Member States.[19]

However, the Court did not completely discard the possibility that there could be confusion amongst consumers in a State where they had become accustomed to the reservation of a particular generic name for a specific product, such as vinegar produced from wine. While the Member State could be permitted to intervene in support of its consumers, it would have to do so in a manner which was more proportionate to the aim being pursued. Labelling disclosures alerting them to the difference would suffice. This would only be acceptable practice, however, where the affixing of labels indicating details about the nature of the product applied to all types of the product concerned. According to the Court of Justice, this would place the importer at no more of a disadvantage than the domestic producer. All would have to comply with the same labelling obligations. However, this is not necessarily the case. The imported product could have to comply with two sets of national labelling requirements—those applicable in the importing State as well as those with which it must comply to be lawfully marketable in the State of production. The Court is therefore clearly differentiating between foods where a failure to provide detailed labelling disclosures could cause confusion, presumably for some factor like the degree to which national consumers associate a particular name with a product possessing specific characteristics.

While the Court demonstrates a degree of flexibility here with the way in which it applies EU rules on the free movement of goods, it is also at odds with its clear statement in *Commission v UK*, albeit in the context of discriminatory domestic taxation on wine and beer, that 'Member State [policies] must not therefore crystallise given consumer habits so as to consolidate an advantage acquired by national industries concerned to comply with them'.[20] Member States should not be able to use their failure to comply with EU free movement requirements to justify their continued flouting of the rules. If the Court were to compel all vinegars to carry clear labelling disclosures, beyond those set by their own national laws, and thereby placing an additional burden on imports which could have to carry two sets of labels, one for their own market and one for the importing State, it would, in effect, be supporting something that was contrary to free movement rules. It would be allowing the fact that Italian consumers, for example, had been underexposed to other types of vinegar, primarily due to the restrictive Italian laws, to justify the need for additional labelling presentations for imported vinegars, which were placing an additional burden on their producers.

One of the most significant cases on national compositional requirements came about when the Commission queried the lawfulness of Germany's centuries-old rules on beer production.[21] At issue was the application of the 'Biersteuergesetz',

---

[19] Para 26.

[20] Para 14 of Case 170/1978 *Commission v UK* [1980] ECR 417. For more on this see S Weatherill, *EU Consumer Law and Policy* (Cheltenham, Edward Elgar, 2005) ch 2.

[21] Case 178/1984 *Commission v Germany* [1987] ECR 1227.

which set manufacturing requirements for breweries established in Germany, as well as conditions attached to the use of the sales name 'Bier' (beer) for all such products sold in Germany, regardless of where they had been manufactured. Under these rules, German Bier had to be made from a combination of malts (usually barley), hops, yeast and water—and nothing else. Imported beers not meeting this compositional requirement could be sold in Germany, but only under a different name. They could not be marketed as 'Bier'. They would also have to be additive-free. German law prescribed that additives could only be used in food production if they had been authorised for this purpose. Beer was, however, subject to special rules, which prescribed that only the specified ingredients listed above could be used in its manufacture. The use of any additional ingredients, including additives, was not allowed.

Germany maintained that the rules were necessary to protect consumers. In their view, there was an inseparable link in the German consumer's mind between the product 'Bier' and the application of the strict compositional requirements. In similar language to that mentioned above on the 'crystallisation' of consumer habits, the Court stated here that

> consumers' conceptions which vary from one Member State to the other are also likely to evolve in the course of time within a Member State. The establishment of the common market is, it should be added, one of the factors that may play a major contributory role in that development. Whereas rules protecting consumers against misleading practices enable such a development to be taken into account, legislation of the kind [at issue here] prevents it from taking place.[22]

The EU's policy in support of the free movement of food is well encapsulated in this statement. It recognises that there are differences between consumer expectations in different Member States; however, the proper promotion of free movement should diminish this. Consumer expectations will evolve, becoming more harmonised. Protecting consumers through trade prohibitions would prevent this from happening. Free movement itself will therefore reduce the need for compositional requirements like those at issue here.

There is a second argument that could be made here. The case law of the Court of Justice makes it clear that labelling disclosures are usually sufficient to inform consumers about the nature or characteristics of a product, even where these differ from what they may be expecting. As a result of the development of this line of reasoning in *Cassis*, the Commission later decided that this removed the need for the introduction of harmonised compositional requirements for most foodstuffs at EU level.[23] There would only be a need for food laws in the future where this was necessary for some obvious health, consumer or environmental protection purpose. It essentially decided that there would be no need for many more 'recipe laws', which set minimum standards for certain foodstuffs. These

---

[22] Para 32.
[23] Commission Communication on the free movement of foodstuffs within the Community [1989] OJ C 271/3.

usually take the form of vertical legislation, applying to one type of food. They are discussed in more detail in chapter seven. At this point, however, it must be remembered from *Cassis* that the German authorities argued that the principle of mutual recognition would lead to a 'race to the bottom', where no Member State could apply its minimum compositional rules if there were no similar rules in any other Member State. That threat remains. 'Recipe laws' offer a potential solution to this problem. Setting harmonised compositional requirements at EU level for certain foodstuffs, which would apply no matter where in the Union the products were made, would at least guarantee that minimum quality standards were being met. What has developed post-*Cassis* is a major drawback of the way in which maximising the potential for the free movement of food is pursued. There is little regard for consumer expectations in different Member States. There is almost no concern about the fact that foods must be allowed to trade freely even where they fail to meet the most basic of minimum quality requirements or characteristics. A return to the development of a body of 'recipe laws' could really assist in this regard. This is also discussed in more detail in chapter seven.

The Court of Justice in *Commission v Germany* found that use of the German designation 'Bier' and its equivalents in other languages could not be restricted to products manufactured according to the purity law requirements.[24] Avoiding confusion and failing to meet consumer expectations could, it was stated, be ensured by other, more proportionate means, in particular labelling. According to the Court, a list of ingredients would achieve this.

Cases on the application of EU rules on measures equivalent to quantitative restrictions on trade often arise when laws are designed to protect, in some way, products that are an important part of national food culture. In *Zoni*, for example, proceedings had been brought before the Italian courts against a wholesaler who had imported pasta from Germany.[25] Italian law at the time provided that dry pasta had to be made from durum wheat only, and that it could not be sold in Italy where it had been mixed with other wheats. Fresh pasta, and that which was made for export, could be made with a mixture of durum and non-durum wheats. The Italian Government claimed that the law was necessary to protect the quality of pasta available to consumers in Italy, and to promote the durum wheat industry. The respondent claimed that this was contrary to EU rules on the free movement of food. The Court of Justice agreed. Noting its earlier decision in *Cassis*, the Court accepted that protecting consumers was a legitimate function of national law, but also that where this happens these laws must be based on the most proportionate response available in the circumstances.[26] Following its earlier decisions in *Commission v Italy*,[27] and the *Beer Purity* case,[28] the Court

---

[24] Case 178/1984, n 21 above.
[25] Case 90/1986 *Criminal proceedings against Zoni* [1988] ECR 4285.
[26] Para 10.
[27] Case 193/1980, n 18 above.
[28] Case 178/1984, n 21 above.

held that the most proportionate response available in circumstances like these was to require that appropriate disclosures should be made on the product's label. This would already happen here due to the fact that the Italian law at issue, and the relevant EU legislation,[29] required the listing of ingredients. This list would disclose the presence of other types of wheat used in the production of the pasta to the consumer. The Court also found that the option of restricting use of the wording 'pasta made from durum wheatmeal' to products which contained no other type of wheat was available to the Italian authorities, thus providing even more clarity for consumers.

While many free movement of food issues have been examined over the years by the European Court of Justice, one issue that has not been satisfactorily resolved is what is to happen in the case of foods served in restaurants and other catering establishments. They are not pre-packaged, and are not therefore subject to the same labelling requirements. The argument was made in *Zoni* that use of the word 'pasta' on a menu, for example, would suggest a product made exclusively from durum wheat. As noted earlier, however, Italian law did permit the use of other types of wheat for other types of pasta, such as that which was to be served fresh or which was manufactured for the export market. Pasta was, therefore, in the opinion of the Court, a generic term. The Italian authorities could not restrict its use, either for pre-packaged dry pasta, or for that which was to be served fresh or exported.

4.2.3 Packaging as an Impediment to the Free Movement of Food

The cases outlined up to this point have all related to national laws designed to regulate the internal compositional requirements of foodstuffs. Those which limit, or compel the use of specified external features, such as packaging, have also faced Court of Justice scrutiny. The shape of margarine tubs, for example, was examined in *Rau*.[30] Here, Belgian law only permitted the sale of margarine if it was packaged in cube-shaped containers. A German seller brought proceedings against a Belgian buyer who refused a consignment of margarine that had been packaged in cone-shaped tubs. It was questioned as to whether this packaging requirement was a measure equivalent to a quantitative restriction on imports of the type prohibited by Article 34 TFEU.

The Court found that there was clearly a restriction on trade, further evidenced by the fact that there was very little foreign margarine available for sale in Belgium, despite the product commanding appreciably higher prices there than

---

[29] The relevant EU legislation in operation at the time was Council Directive 1979/112/EEC of 18 December 1978 on the approximation of the laws of the Member States relating to the labelling, presentation and advertising of foodstuffs for sale to the ultimate consumer [1979] OJ L 33/1. It is discussed in much more detail in ch 7.

[30] Case 261/1981 *Walter Rau Lebensmittelwerke v De Smedt PVBA* [1982] ECR 3961.

in many other Member States. The only justification for this requirement was that it was necessary to prevent consumers from confusing margarine with butter by obliging that it be sold in different-shaped containers. It was accepted that this was a legitimate concern, but also that an outright prohibition on the use of a packaging type that was lawfully used elsewhere in the Union was completely disproportionate. Consumers could, in the opinion of the Court, be protected 'just as effectively by other measures, for example by rules on labelling, which hinder the free movement of goods'.[31]

In *Prantl*, criminal proceedings had been brought against an Italian drinks dealer for persistently importing wine into Germany which was to be sold in bulbous-shaped bottles, or 'Bocksbeutel'. This type of bottle had traditionally been used by a range of quality German wines for centuries. It was also, however, used by wine producers in parts of Italy for more than one hundred years. There were some slight differences between the two varieties of bulbous-shaped bottles used, but they were very similar to each other. National law prescribed that only specified German wines could be marketed in this type of bottle there.

It was queried whether the application of this rule was an unlawful and unjustifiable impediment to the free movement of goods. The German Government argued that the measure at issue was not contrary to EU law as it did not have an appreciable effect on trade between Member States; that it applied to national and imported products alike; that it only made the non-authorised use of the 'Bocksbeutel' an offence and did not therefore usually apply to imported products which were marketed in slightly different bottles; and, finally, that this was justified on grounds of consumer protection. The first point was dismissed on the basis of *Dassonville*.[32] The measure at issue would only have to 'directly or indirectly, actually or potentially' affect inter-State trade to be caught within the scope of Article 34 TFEU as being a measure equivalent to a quantitative restriction on imports. It was not a requirement that any impact on trade would have to be 'appreciable'. The second argument was also dismissed, the Court pointing out that national measures would still be examinable under Article 34 TFEU if they, in practice, gave national products any trading advantage, even where there was detriment to other domestic production. A producer using a bulbous bottle in their own State would be met with an additional cost and burden if required to change the packaging or container shape to meet the marketing conditions of another Member State.

It was not accepted by the Court in *Prantl* that the application of law on bottle shape was necessary to protect consumers. Other legislation existed at Union level to ensure that such confusion would not arise. Provision was contained in the 1979 Wines Regulation,[33] which set a range of labelling requirements for quality

---

[31] Para 17.

[32] Case 8/1974, n 1 above.

[33] Council Regulation (EEC) No 355/1979 of 5 February 1979 laying down general rules for the description and presentation of wines and grape musts [1979] OJ L 54/99. Arts 12–18 of the Regulation, and in particular Art 12 thereof, sets out a series of labelling and identification requirements for quality wines produced in specified regions within the Member States.

wines which, it was stated, were 'particularly comprehensive and enable the feared confusion to be avoided'.[34] The rules on bulbous bottle use were therefore found to be a measure equivalent to a quantitative restriction on imports, deemed to be unnecessary and unjustifiable on grounds of consumer protection.

EU Member States have also used the health protection exception to the prohibition on measures equivalent to quantitative restrictions, contained in Article 36 TFEU, to justify their food packaging requirements which could potentially inhibit trade. In *Schwarz*, the Court of Justice examined whether it was permissible for Austria to have a ban in place on the sale of unwrapped chewing-gum from vending machines.[35] Normally, questions such as this would be examinable for compatibility with EU hygiene regulations, but these did not apply to machine-vended confectionery at this time.[36] They therefore needed to be tested for compliance with free movement requirements only. The Court found that the rule at issue was an impediment to trade. Importers who wished to sell their confectionery through vending machines in Austria would have to ensure that it was pre-packaged, making importation into that State more expensive and cumbersome. They might even have been required to change the type of machine that they use for this purpose as those designed for non-packaged goods could not usually be used to vend packaged goods also. However, the Court did find that the rule was justifiable on health protection grounds. The Austrian Health and Food Safety Agency demonstrated to the Court how non-pre-packaged goods sold from vending machines were often contaminated with insects. Unwashed hands were used to retrieve chewing-gum from the machines, also leading to the spread of contamination between consumers. For these reasons, the prohibition on selling unwrapped goods was deemed both adequate and, most importantly, proportionate to the aim pursued, namely the protection of health.

4.2.4 Determining 'Substantial Difference' when Considering Consumer Protection

National laws on a whole range of issues related to the manufacture and marketing of food can be assessed for compatibility with EU rules on the free movement of goods. However, it is those rules which prescribe a minimum or maximum quantity for one of the food's constituents that often leads to these rules facing Court examination, just as it originally was in *Cassis*.

---

[34] Para 29 of the judgment in Case 16/1983 *Prantl* [1984] ECR 1299.

[35] Case C-366/2004 *Georg Schwarz v Bürgermeister der Landeshauptstadt Salzburg* [2005] ECR I-10139.

[36] The EU legislation on hygiene standards in the food sector was Council Directive 1993/43/EC [1993] OJ L 175/1 at the time. The hygiene regulations, and their application in English law, are dealt with in much more detail in ch 6.

French rules on the fat content of cheese were examined by the Court of Justice in *Deserbais*.[37] Here, the national rules at issue prohibited the marketing of cheese in France, in this case a consignment of German Edam, where the fat content was below 40 per cent. The German cheese in this case had a fat content of around 34 per cent. The trader responsible for bringing the cheese onto the German market was facing criminal prosecution in France for failing to comply with this requirement. As a defence, he claimed that the French law at issue was in contravention of Article 34 TFEU, in that it was a measure equivalent to a quantitative restriction on imports. The cheese was lawfully produced and marketed in another Member State. Under the principle of mutual recognition, developed by the Court in *Cassis*, it would, therefore, have to be lawfully marketable in France as well, regardless of the French law on the matter. The Court of Justice agreed. Information on the packaging disclosing the actual fat content of the cheese would be a more proportionate response in the circumstances than would be a prohibition on the sale of the product. It did, however, also determine that in some circumstances consumers may not be adequately protected by such labelling disclosures. This could be the case where there was such a 'substantial difference' between the imported product and foods normally marketed using the same sales name that there was the probability of confusing consumers. This is potentially a key exception to the principle of mutual recognition—the test of 'substantial difference'—and it has come before the Court of Justice on a number of occasions.

Having followed the usual post-*Cassis* jurisprudence on the proportionality of labelling requirements, the Court turned its attention to those circumstances where there is a measure equivalent to a quantitative restriction on imports, but where there may also be a potential justification for the maintenance of such a measure due to the level of difference between the imported variety of a product and that with which it could be confused were the national law at issue not applied. It queried whether the principle of mutual recognition

> must be applied where a product presented under a particular name is so different, as regards its composition or production, from the products generally known by that name in the [Union] that it cannot be regarded as falling within the same category.[38]

The Court went on to find that 'no situation of that kind arises ... in this case'. It reached this conclusion by looking at the defining characteristics of the 'product generally known by that name' to test whether there was substantial difference between this and those of the lower-fat cheese at issue. In particular here the Court looked to the international standards for Edam cheese, noting that both the United Nations Codex Alimentarius Commission and the 1951 Stresa Convention on Cheese state that the minimum fat content should be 40 per cent. This was not deemed to be sufficient to illustrate a substantial difference between the products. The Court also clearly stated that it would not be bound by such international

---

[37] Case 286/1986 *Ministère Public v Gérard Deserbais* [1988] ECR 4907.
[38] Para 13.

instruments, noting that the Stresa Convention predated the existence of EU obligations on the free movement of food and should not therefore apply to trade between Member States. It could continue to place obligations on Member States, but only in relation to third countries who were not members of the EU.[39] If there was no substantial difference between the cheeses at issue, then there could be no grounds for maintaining a prohibition on the use of a food name for the imported product in the interests of consumer protection. This would be a disproportionate response in the circumstances. Labelling disclosures on fat content would suffice.

Substantial difference is really the only basis upon which the protection of consumers can be readily used by EU Member States as justification for the maintenance of national trade-impeding compositional requirements, although, again, rarely with success. Any test for substantial difference will require an identification of the key characteristics of the foodstuff normally known by the name at issue in the importing State. If the imported alternative does not possess these characteristics, or does not possess them to a similar or significant level, then there may be substantial difference, and the prohibition or restriction on the import will stand. The product at issue before the Court of Justice in *Smanor* was frozen yoghurt.[40] Here, the French authorities sought to ban the sale of the respondent's product as 'yoghurt', preferring instead that it should be marketable only as 'deep-frozen fermented milk'. The argument was that the term 'yoghurt' should only be used for fresh fermented milk products which contained live bacteria at the rate of 100 million per gram.[41]

The first issue in this case related to the fact that it was dealing with a wholly internal situation. All of the relevant prior decided cases dealt with some inter-State element. They examined national measures which placed restrictions on the sale of imported foodstuffs. Here, the measure at issue was a French ban on a French product being sold in France. The free movement of food between Member States was not really a concern here. It was therefore queried as to whether Article 34 TFEU could still apply in the circumstances. The French Government argued that it should not, as there was no restriction being placed on imports or exports. However, the wording of the *Dassonville* formula clearly stipulates that a national measure must only affect trade 'actually or potentially', meaning that the French decree on yoghurt products could apply to frozen products made and lawfully marketed in other Member States should they be imported into France at some stage in the future. There was the 'potential' for French law to impede interstate trade. Such rules could therefore be examined for compatibility with EU rules on measures equivalent to quantitative restrictions on trade, even where the facts of the case related to a wholly internal situation at that time.

---

[39] As held in Case 812/1979 *Attorney General v Burgoa* [1980] ECR 2787.

[40] Case 298/1987 *Proceedings for compulsory reconstruction against Smanor SA* [1988] ECR 4489.

[41] Art 2 of French Decree No 63-695 on the prevention of fraud with regard to fermented milk products and yoghurt (Official Journal of the French Republic of 16 July 1963, p 6512) as amended by Decree No 82-184 of 22 February 1982 (Official Journal of the French Republic of 25 February 1982, p 676).

On the issue of 'substantial difference', the Court of Justice found that consumers could be provided with adequate information on the nature of the product without placing any prohibition on the use of the name 'yoghurt' if the description 'deep-frozen' preceded it on the labelling. This would clearly show the treatment that the product had undergone in production. It was recognised, however, that the consumer may not be properly protected where the deep-frozen version of the product did not possess or retain the same characteristics as regular yoghurt. As in *Deserbais*, the Court looked at international standards to help it determine what the key characteristics of yoghurt are. Both the Codex Alimentarius standards and the regulations of other Member States indicated that the main distinguishing feature of yoghurt was the presence of live bacteria at an abundant level. Therefore, substantial difference could be shown if these levels were significantly less for the product after it had undergone a process of deep-freezing. It would be for the national court to ultimately determine whether the bacteria levels dropped to a level that meant that the product could no longer carry the term 'yoghurt' in its sales name. This level would, however, have to be so substantial as to justify the obligation to use a different name. If not, the consumer would, in the opinion of the Court of Justice, be adequately and appropriately protected where the deep-frozen variety was properly labelled.

The test of 'substantial difference' is, of course, a very subjective one. In *Deserbais* the Court ruled that a reduced fat content was insufficient to show this difference. In *Smanor*, it left this to the national court to decide on the basis of the facts before it. In both cases it was made clear that the difference would have to be at a level that rendered the product very different in some way. Minor difference is clearly not enough. The difference must be sufficient to alter or remove the defining characteristic or characteristics of the food in question. The Court of Justice has clearly articulated this point in *Foie Gras*,[42] where it stated that while

> it is legitimate to enable consumers, who attribute specific qualities to products which are manufactured from particular raw materials or which have a given content of a characteristic ingredient, to make their choice in the light of such criteria [this] objective may be attained by means, other than the reservation of certain trade descriptions to products possessing particular qualities, which would be less restrictive on the marketing of products coming from a Member State which satisfy the rules laid down by that State, such as affixing suitable labels concerning the nature and characteristics of the product for sale.

However, this does

> not exclude the possibility that Member States could require those concerned to alter the denomination of a foodstuff where a product presented under a particular denomination is so different, as regards its composition or production, from the products generally known under that denomination in the [Union] that it cannot be regarded as being in the same category.[43]

[42] Case C-184/1996 *Commission v France* [1998] ECR I-6197.
[43] ibid, para 23.

This was mostly a restatement of what was delivered in *Deserbais*, but it provides a good summary of the position on 'substantial difference'. The Court did also provide further guidance here on what can be examined to establish whether the level of difference is at the level necessary to be deemed 'substantial'. It stated, first of all, that the mere fact that a product does not wholly conform to national composition requirements is not enough to warrant a prohibition. However, it also found that national authorities are entitled to monitor the way in which suspected products are made in order to establish whether the raw materials and production methods used match up with the information that is provided on the label. This could then entitle the authorities to bring proceedings against those responsible for selling foodstuffs which are described as being identical to those which are covered by the national requirements, but which in reality 'are so different in content as to give rise to suspicion of deceit'. For this level of difference to be reached the imported foodstuff must 'depart markedly from the requirements imposed by the legislation of the State concerned'.[44] There must be evidence of this level of difference before a prohibition on imports can be justified. Mere suspicion of incomplete compliance with national compositional requirements is not enough. There must still be mutual recognition of products which are lawfully made and marketed in other Member States, unless substantial difference can be proved.

The Court in *Deserbais* provided the only ground upon which a Member State may successfully justify the existence of national compositional requirements as being necessary for the protection of consumers. The Court has restated its position from *Cassis* on many occasions—the protection of consumers is a legitimate basis for derogating from the law on the free movement of goods as set out in Article 34 TFEU. Despite this, it is rare that the Court will accept that a prohibition on the marketing of a food under a particular sales name is proportionate for this purpose. It will, on some occasions, leave this to the national court to decide, as it did in *Smanor*. However, it is clear that it is only where there is a considerable, or substantial, difference between the imported product and the foodstuff normally known by that name that it will allow the State to act to prevent confusion amongst consumers. It can only be looked at on a case-by-case basis, and it remains relatively unclear as to just what constitutes 'substantial' in the level of difference between the products concerned.

The European Commission has attempted to give some guidance in this regard in a Communication to the Member States, which was designed to provide some clarity in the aftermath of *Smanor* and *Deserbais*.[45] It stated that any test of substantial difference should be carried out on the subjective basis of consumer expectations and the objective basis of already existing rules and standards, including those of the Codex Alimentarius Commission and the other EU Member States.

---

[44] Para 25.

[45] Commission interpretative communication on the names under which food products are sold [1991] OJ C 270/2.

It should also involve some scrutiny of the ingredients and manufacturing methods used in the production of the foods that are being compared for equivalence. The Commission sets out that a substantial difference in any one of these tests may be sufficient to facilitate the Member State in its prohibition on the use of a particular generic sales name for products not meeting the requirements set. However, there is no further clarity provided on the degree of difference that there must be before it can be rendered 'substantial'.

The Court of Justice will not always look to the test of 'substantial difference' in its examinations of national measures that have an effect equivalent to a quantitative restriction on trade, even where the circumstances are almost identical to those which were scrutinised in cases such as *Deserbais*. In *Nespoli and Crippa*, for example, the Court examined whether Italian legislation which set minimum fat content for cheese was compatible with EU rules on the free movement of food.[46] It was found that these requirements, which were effectively a prohibition on those products which failed to meet the standard set, were a measure equivalent to a quantitative restriction on trade, and that they were disproportionate to the aim pursued. They were an obstacle to trade that could not be justified on consumer protection grounds. While the usual solution of using labelling to disclose actual fat content was offered by the Court, it made no assessment of whether there was a level of difference between the varieties of cheese at issue to warrant an investigation into the existence, or otherwise, of 'substantial difference' between them.

4.2.5 Protecting Human Health

It is quite common for two, or even three or more justifications to be put forward by Member States in support of their own trade-impeding measures. It is very common for both consumer protection and human health protection arguments to be made together. Other potential lines that can be taken include the promotion of a fair-trading environment, where it is claimed that facilitating those who use cheaper substitute ingredients, for example, puts the more traditional producer at a competitive disadvantage. This often arises in those circumstances where the protection of consumers has been used as a justification for a national measure that is, on the face of it, at odds with the objectives of Article 34 TFEU. They are often two sides of the same argument—the consumer is protected by an assurance that certain ingredients have been used in the production of a particular foodstuff and the producer has been consequently protected as only he will be able to use the disputed food name by meeting the compositional requirement that has been set. It has also been argued that promoting the same aims as those of the Union should be a valid justification for the application of national standards.

---

[46] Case C-196/1989 *Criminal proceedings against Enzo Nespoli and Giuseppe Crippa* [1990] ECR I-3647.

In the *Milk Substitutes* cases, for example, it was put forward by the respondent Member State that a prohibition on the marketing of substitute milk favoured the consumption of regular milk and dairy products, which was, it was pointed out, also one of the aims of the Common Agricultural Policy.[47] This has been rejected on a number of occasions on the basis that national measures cannot exist contrary to a fundamental principle of Union law, such as the free movement of goods, unless clearly justified by a reason recognised in EU law.[48] The strongest argument that can be put forward by a Member State in such circumstances is that the measure at issue is necessary to protect human health.

While Article 34 TFEU provides that quantitative restrictions on trade and all measures of equivalent effect are prohibited, Article 36 TFEU states that

> [this] shall not preclude prohibitions or restrictions on imports, exports or goods in transit justified on grounds of ... the protection of health and life of humans, animals or plants [provided that] such prohibitions or restrictions shall not, however, constitute a means of arbitrary discrimination or a disguised restriction on trade between Member States.

While the Court of Justice developed the consumer protection exception to the prohibition on measures of equivalent effect to quantitative restrictions on trade, the Treaty has always clearly provided for an exception based on the need to protect human health. A more practical distinction between these two exceptions is that a ban on the sale of a foodstuff on health grounds more readily satisfies the proportionality test than one based on consumer protection. The case law already discussed in this chapter clearly shows just how difficult it is for Member States to ever demonstrate that a prohibition based on consumer protection is the most proportionate response available in the circumstances. Labelling will, in the opinion of the Court, be less restrictive on trade but just as effective in protecting the interests of the consumer. If, however, a foodstuff includes ingredients that may pose a threat to human health, a prohibition on the sale of that product may be the only reasonable option available in the circumstances.

Both consumer protection and health protection arguments were put forward by Member States to justify their trade-impeding measures in many of the early cases on the free movement of food. In *Cassis*, for example, a weak argument was made that the maintenance of minimum alcohol level requirements for fruit liqueurs was necessary to prevent the over-exposure of consumers to cheaper, low-alcohol varieties.[49] Failure to do this, it was claimed, could lead to a greater tolerance for alcohol amongst Germans. Unsurprisingly, this was rejected by the Court, who found that many moderately alcoholic products were widely available on the German market. It also noted that many of those products with a higher

---

[47] Case 216/1984 *Commission v France* [1988] ECR 793 and Case 76/1986 *Commission v Germany* [1989] ECR 1021.

[48] The argument was similarly rejected by the Court of Justice in Case 274/1987 *Commission v Germany* [1989] ECR 229 in relation to the promotion of meat consumption.

[49] Case 120/1978, n 3 above.

alcohol content were often consumed in diluted form. A stronger health protection argument was put forward by Germany in the *Beer Purity* case.[50] While the consumer protection justification was based on reserving the name 'Bier' for those beverages which were made entirely from a limited list of ingredients, it was stated that the rules were also necessary for health protection purposes in that they banned the inclusion of additives.

The German authorities sought to minimise the quantity of additives being ingested by their populace. They considered that the long-term dangers of consuming additives were not fully known, and in particular that there was uncertainty about how health could be affected by the interaction of additives with alcohol in the body. As beer was consumed in large quantities in Germany, it would be desirable to prohibit the use of additives in production and, as was pointed out, their use was technologically unnecessary if the purity requirements were followed in the first place.

Noting its seminal decision in *Sandoz*,[51] which is discussed in more detail below, the Court accepted that uncertainty about the use of particular ingredients could be used by Member States to justify national measures designed to protect human health. This would, however, be limited to that which was absolutely necessary to protect health, in particular where the measure at issue was a prohibition. The German rules prohibited all additive use in beer production. There was no assessment, therefore, of individual additives to test for their safety. Some expert reports were submitted by Germany in support of their claim that the ingestion of additives in general could be harmful to health. However, many of the additives used in the manufacture of beer in other Member States were permitted for use in the manufacture of food in Germany. It would be difficult, therefore, to stand over a claim that the purity requirements for beer were premised on a desire to protect health.

The extent to which Member States can legitimately limit the use of additives in food production is a controversial one. In the *Beer Purity* case, the German authorities pointed out that there was no technological need for the use of additives if only the prescribed natural ingredients were used in production. The Court, however, countered this by finding that a lack of necessity does not equate to a lack of technological function. This is discussed in more detail below in the context of additive use in food production more generally, but it does demonstrate a fundamental point about the jurisprudence of the Court of Justice when it comes to the health protection justification. It is only where there is a clear and identifiable danger to human health, attached to the use of a specific ingredient or production process, that the Article 36 TFEU exception can be used by Member States to justify their related national measures. This point is also made more clearly in other cases, in particular those which deal with the nutritional value of food.

---

[50] Case 178/1984, n 21 above.
[51] Case 174/1982 *Criminal proceedings against Sandoz BV* [1983] ECR 2445.

The Court of Justice has found, in a number of cases, that national measures designed to promote or maintain the nutritional quality or value of food is not an acceptable use of the health protection exception set out in Article 36 TFEU. This was established in *Meat Purity*, where national requirements on the use of additional ingredients in meat products were assessed for compatibility with EU rules on the free movement of food.[52] German regulations prohibited the marketing of meat products which contained ingredients other than meat, subject to some exceptions. The national law on foodstuffs banned the importation of products that were not in compliance with this requirement. The German Government maintained that the contested prohibition was justified on grounds of health protection because it was necessary to ensure a sufficient intake of essential nutrients from meat, especially proteins. Two reports, produced by the German Government, actually showed that protein intake levels were, in general, more than adequate. Even where consumption was at a level below that which was recommended, in particular amongst younger sections of the population, this was found to pose no threat to health. The reports also showed that some meat ingredients could contain harmful substances, such as purine, cholesterol and saturated fatty acids and that therefore there should actually be concern about increased consumption.

What is most significant in the *Meat Purity* judgment, however, is what the Court had to say on national measures designed to maintain nutrient levels and the health benefits that could be derived therefrom. The German Government argued that vegetable proteins, present in the ingredients typically added to meat in these products, have a lower nutritional value than animal proteins. Referring to its earlier decision in the *Milk Substitutes* case,[53] the Court restated the position that

> a Member State may not invoke public health grounds in order to prohibit the importation of a product by arguing that its nutritional value is lower than another product already available on the market in question, since it is plain that the choice of foodstuffs available to consumers in the [Union] is such that the mere fact that an imported product has a lower nutritional value does not pose a real threat to human health.[54]

This is crucial to understanding the limits that are placed on Member States by EU rules on the free movement of food. This effectively prohibits the adoption of measures at national level which are designed to promote good health. National law cannot be used to ensure that the nutritional quality derived from foods is maintained or improved. The reason for this is clear. The absence of nutritional value poses no 'threat' to human health. The Court, in its case law on the use of the health protection exception set out in Article 36 TFEU, distinguishes between 'danger' and 'harm'. The former is deemed by EU law makers to be something

---

[52] Case 274/1987 *Commission v Germany* [1989] ECR 229.
[53] Case 216/1984, n 47 above.
[54] Para 10 of Case 274/1987, n 52 above.

that needs regulating, the latter is not. This is discussed more in chapter nine, but it should be noted at this stage that this position, combined with the other jurisprudence of the Court on measures equivalent to quantitative restrictions on trade, bars Member States from taking meaningful interventionist action to deal with a public health crisis like obesity. It limits the Government options to certain campaigns, promotions and enticements, rather than direct action, such as prescribing clearer labelling on food. Needless to say, the German Government's argument in the *Meat Purity* case was ultimately rejected. A national measure designed to maintain the nutritional value of food was not justifiable on the basis of being necessary to protect human health.

This issue of promoting nutritional content had previously been dealt with by the Court in the *Milk Substitutes* cases.[55] In the first of these enforcement actions, taken against France, the Commission had brought the proceedings on the basis of the contention that national rules which prohibited the same of substitute milk were contrary to Article 34 TFEU. The French Government sought to justify the ban on a number of grounds, such as the protection of consumers, and the promotion of the aims of the Common Agricultural Policy, which was discussed earlier in this chapter. It also argued that it was necessary to ban substitute milk in order to protect human health.

It was claimed that there were two reasons as to why a prohibition such as this was necessary for health protection. The first related to nutritional value. A similar argument was made to that which was put forward by the German Government in *Meat Purity*. The Court immediately rejected this on the basis that public health grounds could not be used by a Member State to justify a prohibition by arguing that a product's nutritional value is lower or its fat content higher than another similar product already available on the market in question. It also agreed with the Commission's contention that a ban could not persist where other products were available in the Member State which were also of lower nutritional value or which had similar fat content to substitute milk. This line of reasoning indicates a flawed understanding of human diet and nutrition. While it is, of course, perfectly correct to find that there are products of similar nutritional inferiority available on the market, the judgment, and the precedent that it sets, fails to take into consideration the type of product at issue, or its importance to meeting personal dietary requirements.

The foods at issue in both *Meat Purity* and the *Milk Substitutes* cases are staples of the European diet. Their consumption contributes significantly to meeting recommended daily intakes for the key nutrients, such as proteins, carbohydrates, fats, vitamins and minerals. Comparing their replacements to 'other' products available on the market fails to take this into consideration. These 'other' foods should be consumed in addition to the staples, not as a substitute for them. It is as if the Court is saying that you cannot restrict the marketing of

---

[55] Case 216/1984 *Commission v France* and Case 76/1986 *Commission v Germany*, both n 47 above.

substitute milk when you do not place similar restrictions on the sale of sweets or crisps. This is not to say that, on balance, the Court has not come to the right ultimate conclusion in the circumstances, namely that a prohibition is disproportionate to the aim pursued. The way in which it has reached this decision is questionable. It is not comparing like with like to underpin its position, or that of the Commission. The Court did not accept that any measure was necessary to protect health in the circumstances, so the fact that we happen to be dealing with a prohibition is not necessarily the crucial factor. The way in which the Court has refused to accept that there is any health protection purpose underlying the national law indicates that there is no proportionate measure that it would be deemed permissible to adopt either. It simply refuses to accept that placing restrictions on the marketing of nutritionally inferior substitutes is ever justifiable on health protection grounds.

The second argument put forward by France in the first of the *Milk Substitutes* cases was that these products could have harmful effects on certain groups of people. The Court rejected this contention on the ground that the consumption of milk itself is also potentially risky for people who suffer from certain diseases. This was backed up with a claim that there was disagreement between specialists as to the actual or potential dangers posed by the consumption of animal and vegetable fats. This, however, fails to recognise the key basis upon which national measures designed to protect health can be taken by Member States. Originally in *Sandoz*,[56] and later followed up through the development of the precautionary principle, it is precisely when there is uncertainty, or disagreement between the experts, as to the level or nature of risk involved that national measures can be adopted until the reality of those risks becomes realised. According to the Court, proper labelling of the list of ingredients and an identification of the characteristics of the milk substitutes being offered would enable those with an intolerance to these products to make their own decision on consumption. Had the Court followed its earlier decision in *Sandoz*, the Member State could have been facilitated in the adoption of interim measures to deal with any potential threat posed.

The respondent in *Sandoz* had been charged with selling unauthorised fortified foods in the Netherlands. The company was marketing sports bars and drinks with added vitamins. All of the products in question were lawfully marketed in Germany or Belgium. It had applied for authorisation of the products, as was required under Dutch law. This was rejected on the basis that the addition of these vitamins, mostly A and D, to the products in question posed a danger to public health. On querying whether the authorisation process was compatible with EU Treaty rules on the free movement of food, the Court held that it was perfectly acceptable to have such a procedure in place, provided permission was granted to market products which are both safe and necessary. The company and the

---

[56] Case 174/1982 *Criminal proceedings against Sandoz BV* [1983] ECR 2445. The Court had previously come to a similar conclusion in Case 272/1980 *Frans-Nederlandse Maatschappij voor Biologische Producten* [1981] ECR 3277.

Commission had been of the view that these products would only ever be harmful if consumed to excess. Expert reports showed that the over-consumption of vitamins over a prolonged period could have detrimental effects on health. However, the scientific research available at the time was not conclusive on the quantities that could be consumed at a safe level, nor was it clear as to what the harmful effects could be. Most significantly, for the development of EU jurisprudence on the degree to which Member States can act in such circumstances, the Court of Justice stated that

> [where] there are uncertainties at the present state of scientific research it is for the Member States, in the absence of harmonisation, to decide what degree of protection of the health and life of humans they intend to assure, having regard however for the requirements of the free movement of goods within the [Union].[57]

This principle was found by the Court to apply to substances such as vitamins which were not really harmful but which could become so if taken to excess. National rules restricting the fortification of foods, requiring, for example, that prior authorisation is granted before these products can be sold to consumers, could therefore be justified, on principle at least, under the terms of Article 36 TFEU. They could be deemed necessary for the protection of human health.

By this stage in the judgment in *Sandoz*, the Court had accepted two things. The first was that scientific uncertainty surrounding a practice in food production could warrant the adoption of national measures by Member States. Second, these measures could, in principle, be justified under the Article 36 TFEU exceptions to the general prohibition on measures equivalent to quantitative restrictions on trade. However, the Court also held that all of this is subject to the principle of proportionality. Trade can be restricted on food safety grounds, but only if this happens in a way that has the most minimal impact on trade that is available in the circumstances. These restrictions were therefore justifiable, provided that authorisations were granted wherever possible. This would make them proportionate. The Court recognised, however, that it was difficult to assess such authorisations. It would be hard, for example, to monitor consumption levels that could be deemed excessive. This would be further complicated by the fact that vitamins are also present in everyday foods. Consuming fortified foods in addition to a recommended diet could itself lead to excessive consumption, as could eating large amounts of a particular food which was also high in the same vitamins which were being used for fortification. There would therefore have to be a wide level of discretion afforded to the Member States on this issue, provided any response taken was proportionate in the circumstances. This would have to involve the granting of authorisations by national authorities to foodstuffs lawfully marketed elsewhere in the Union, in particular where the fortification was designed to meet a real need, especially a technical or nutritional one.

---

[57] ibid, para 16 of *Sandoz*.

National laws restricting the fortification of foods, such as those at issue in *Sandoz*, have been a persistent problem for producers. They have also led to the Court of Justice being called upon to adjudicate on a number of occasions, in particular where prior authorisation is required for marketing a new nutrient or product. In *Greenham and Abel*, criminal proceedings had been brought against the joint directors of a food company on two grounds, one of which was selling products fortified with the nutrient coenzyme Q10.[58] This substance was not authorised for human consumption, as was required under French law. The respondents claimed that this was contrary to EU rules on free movement, in particular as the products were lawfully marketed in other Member States and no serious risk to health had been shown. It was submitted that the mere fact that a food supplement is freely marketed in other Member States is not sufficient for its marketing to be permitted automatically in all Member States. It should have to undergo the authorisation procedure first. The Commission disagreed. It was of the view that if a nutrient could be used in fortification in one Member State, then products which were fortified with this nutrient must be granted access to the importer's market, provided that international scientific research and the nutritional habits of the populace showed that this did not pose a risk for public health. This would not necessarily require the use of a full authorisation procedure. According to the Commission, national courts could decide whether the competent authorities of the Member State concerned had properly evaluated the risks related to the nutrient in question. No information was submitted to the Court showing that coenzyme Q10 was dangerous. However, the Court did find that the use of national authorisation procedures, such as that at issue here, could be justified despite their trade-restricting impact. Several conditions would, however, have to be met.

First, any national rule requiring that prior authorisation is granted before marketing must involve a procedure that facilitates ready access for applicants to have their products included on the approved list. The procedure must be completed within a reasonable time. Any refusal to authorise must be open to appeal, including to a court of law. Second, applications for authorisation may only be refused where the substance is shown to pose a genuine risk to public health.[59] Provided they meet these conditions, Member States are entitled to have authorisation procedures in place if this is necessary to protect health due to certainty about risk. Following *Sandoz* they should also have a wide discretion in this regard where there is uncertainty about the risk type and/or level, although the *Milk Substitutes* cases might suggest otherwise. This discretion will always be subject to the principle of proportionality, and nothing can be done which is really just a disguised restriction on trade. Where alternative, less trade-restricting measures are available, which will still be effective to the level required in the circumstances,

---

[58] Case C-95/2001 *Criminal proceedings against Greenham and Abel* [2004] ECR I-1333. Coenzyme Q10 is an antioxidant needed for basic cell function. Its level in the body usually decreases with age.

[59] As first established by the Court in Case C-192/2001 *Commission v Denmark* [2003] ECR I-9693.

these must be chosen instead of a cumbersome authorisation procedure or refusal to authorise. Any such refusal must therefore be based on an assessment that establishes a definite or probable risk to human health.[60]

In *Greenham and Abel* the Court found that a decision to prohibit the marketing of a foodstuff could only, therefore, be adopted 'if the alleged risk for public health appears to be sufficiently established on the basis of the latest scientific data available at the date of the adoption of such decision'.[61] A Member State can take action based on the precautionary principle where this assessment indicates that there is still uncertainty as to the nature of the risk involved. The precautionary principle is discussed in more detail in the next chapter, in the context of food safety. However, it can be said at this stage that it permits the taking of interim measures on health protection grounds until the science is more certain about the existence and/or nature of a risk. Here, it was argued that the products at issue possessed no nutritional benefit. The Court found that 'nutritional need' was a legitimate consideration in the assessment of risk, but also that the absence of such a need was not enough to justify a total prohibition. There would have to be an identifiable risk, or at the very least 'the likelihood of real harm to public health ... should the risk materialise'. It would ultimately be for the national court to decide if evidence provided warranted use of this precautionary approach in the circumstances. Member States can, therefore, subject to these conditions, have authorisation procedures for fortified foods in place. This is an important exception to the wide-scale application of the EU Treaty prohibition on measures equivalent to quantitative restrictions on imports. It allows Member States to ban the sale of foodstuffs lawfully manufactured and marketed elsewhere in the Union, provided that this decision follows a process that is readily accessible, timely, and subject to appeal where required. Any refusal to authorise must also be based on a detailed risk assessment, which is based on the most reliable scientific data available and the most recent results of international research.

The significance of the position that developed out of *Commission v Denmark* and *Greenham and Abel* on the legitimacy of prohibitions based on valid authorisation procedures was further highlighted by the decision of the Court in *Red Bull*.[62] Multiple complaints had been made by operators based in several Member States to the European Commission. Their claims related to the difficulties they were encountering when attempting to market their fortified foods in France. The Commission brought proceedings on the basis that the applicable French law on the sale of fortified foods did not facilitate the mutual recognition of products lawfully marketed elsewhere in the Union. The French Government accepted that its national legislation was capable of hindering trade but that this was justified by its objectives of protecting public health and consumers, and that it was proportionate. All fortified foods had to be approved by the authorities before they could be sold on the French market.

---

[60] ibid, para 47.
[61] ibid, para 42.
[62] Case C-24/2000 *Commission v France* [2004] ECR I-1277.

The Court accepted that the authorisation procedure at issue was not, in principle, contrary to EU law. However, it reiterated the conditions that must be satisfied before any refusal to authorise a fortified food would be deemed compatible with EU law. As held previously, the national authorisation procedure would have to be readily accessible by operators from other Member States. It would have to be completed within a reasonable time. It would also have to be open to challenge, including before the courts. Finally the addition of the nutrient concerned would have to pose a genuine risk to human health.[63]

The Court has provided significant elaboration on how these conditions can be satisfied in its deliberations in *Red Bull*. It stated first of all that accessibility to the procedure should be assessed on the basis of its transparency and openness. This should include the provision of clear information on what the process involves, and what the applicant is required to do. Any refusal must also provide clear reasons underlying the decision, in particular to provide the applicant with potential grounds for an appeal. Decisions should be made as quickly as possible in each individual case.

In order for a national authorisation procedure to be deemed accessible it must be 'expressly provided for in a measure of general application which is binding on the national authorities'.[64] The procedure at issue in *Red Bull* was not established in national legislation. A notice was provided to operators setting out the rules on marketing fortified foodstuffs, but this was not sufficient to meet the requirements stipulated. Applications were not routinely considered in a timely manner either. The application for the authorisation of the energy drink Red Bull, for example, was not even formally acknowledged until seven months after its receipt by the assessing authorities. The decision to refuse authorisation was not communicated to the applicant for more than two years. The complaints against the French authorities about their failure to have an authorisation procedure in place that was compatible with EU law was therefore clearly well founded on the first two grounds.

On the third contention, that the refusal to authorise the marketing of Red Bull in France was not justifiable for health protection purposes, the Court found, as it had in *Sandoz*, that Member States have wide discretion in this regard where there is scientific uncertainty about the risk attached to the use of a particular substance. However, it also recognised that any exercise of this discretion must remain proportionate to the aim pursued. Whichever means they choose to achieve this should therefore be limited to that which is actually necessary to safeguard public health. Any exception to a fundamental principle of EU law, such as the free movement of goods, should thus be interpreted strictly. A prohibition, which is of course the most trade-restricting of all measures that can be adopted, would have to be based on a proper risk assessment, which clearly showed that a

---

[63] Case C-192/2001 *Commission v Denmark* [2003] ECR I-9693.
[64] Para 41 of Case 176/1984 *Commission v Greece* [1987] ECR 1193.

ban was necessary in the circumstances.[65] After dismissing the evidence offered by the French authorities in support of their action on a range of fortified foods, the Court did find that the existence of a Scientific Committee on Human Nutrition (SCHN) report, which gave an adverse opinion on the presence of certain nutrients, such as taurine and glucuronolactone, in caffeinated drinks could be sufficient to support a French ban. It also held that if the right sort of evidence showing potential risks can be produced, this switches the burden of proof from the Member State to the Commission in these enforcement actions. It stated that in such circumstances

> the Commission [would have] to state explicitly why the [Member State's] argument based on that [evidence] cannot suffice to justify the refusal to authorise the marketing of [fortified products].[66]

The Commission's contention that the refusal to authorise the energy drink Red Bull was unjustifiable, was thus rejected. The Court found that it had not shown why the SCHN report failed to substantiate the ban. The Member State was required to have a more accessible authorisation procedure in place. It was also obliged to identify clear risks to health where it refused to authorise products lawfully available elsewhere in the EU. However, it was perfectly acceptable to prohibit the marketing of fortified foods and drinks where there was sufficient scientific evidence to support this, even where the reports and opinions were not entirely conclusive on the nature or level of the risks involved in consumption.

If we consider the SCHN report presented in *Commission v France* to be the type of scientific study which can be used as a legitimate basis for refusing the authorisation of certain foods, it must also be established as to what constitutes insufficient evidence in such cases. In the same case, the French authorities sought to rely on a report issued by the Conseil supérieur d'hygiène publique de France (French Public Health Authority—CSHPF) in defence of its refusal to authorise the marketing of food supplements and dietary products containing L-tartrate and L-carnitine. Their claim was that the addition of these substances to foods provided no significant nutritional benefit. The Court of Justice first made it clear that the absence of nutritional need or benefit was not sufficient to justify a prohibition where the products were lawfully manufactured and marketed elsewhere in the EU. Products making nutritional or health claims are now subject to specific EU legislation.[67] The Court also stated here that aspects of the CSHPF report that were being relied upon were not the type or quality of evidence required by them to show that a restriction placed on the free movement of food was warranted. The report had cited 'digestive problems which affect 13 per cent of the population' without specifying their nature. It also mentioned the absence

---

[65] Case C-24/2000, n 62 above, paras 53–56.

[66] Para 72 thereof.

[67] Regulation (EC) No 1924/2006 of the European Parliament and of the Council of 20 December 2006 on nutrition and health claims made on foods [2007] OJ L 12/3. Nutrition and health claims are discussed in more detail in ch 7.

of proof supporting claims about the usefulness or benefits of adding L-tartrate and L-carnitine to supplements, but no detailed assessment of the effects which the addition of these substances could have on human health. The Court found that this was not sufficient to support what amounted to a marketing ban. It was deemed to be more of a generalised opinion than a rigorous scientific survey. Article 36 TFEU could not, therefore, be successfully used by the French authorities in these circumstances. Something more substantial was required for this— something like the SCHN report on the use of taurine and glucuronolactone, which was sufficient to allow for similar action to be taken in banning Red Bull.

Comparing the response of the Court of Justice to the French CSHPF opinion on the one hand, and the SCHN report on the other, could bring us to the conclusion that the EU institutions are favouring their own scientific investigations over those undertaken in the Member States. There are other examples of this, and these are discussed in the context of the use of the precautionary principle by the Council and the Commission in chapter five. However, the Court did also use the CSHPF opinion in support of the action on Red Bull. The difference between those aspects of the opinion which dealt with food supplements and those which set out the position on energy drinks was the Commission's own response to these. In relation to the former the Commission challenged the nature of the evidence submitted and the Court supported this. On the latter, the Commission did not adequately explain why the CSHPF opinion was insufficient to justify a prohibition on marketing energy drinks with a caffeine content higher than that which was authorised in France. It produced no evidence that called into question the French authorities' analysis of the dangers which these drinks could present to public health.[68] Coupled with the findings of the SCHN report on taurine and glucuronolactone use, this was sufficient to reverse the burden of proof requirements onto the Commission. It was then unable to stand over its claims about the illegitimate use by France of the Article 36 TFEU exception.[69]

The imposition of national compositional requirements, such as the inclusion or exclusion of certain ingredients, can potentially be justified by Member States on health protection grounds. A key feature of any such argument put forward by a State is the production of evidence that there is some threat posed to health by the inclusion or exclusion of substances in food production. As seen above, this came before the Court in cases such as *Milk Substitutes* and *Meat Purity*, but in these circumstances there was little in the supporting documentation to show

---

[68] The safety, or otherwise, of consuming energy drinks resurfaced following a 2013 report published by the French Food Safety and Environment Agency, which showed that these can have dangerous cardiovascular and psychological effects in some circumstances. For further discussion on this see E Amat and L Rihouey-Robini, 'A scientific report rekindles the controversy over energy drinks in France' (2013) 8 *European Food and Feed Law Review* 414.

[69] The fortification of foods is now legislated for by Regulation (EC) No 1925/2006 of the European Parliament and of the Council of 20 December 2006 on the addition of vitamins and minerals and of certain other substances to foods [2006] OJ L 404/26. This Regulation has since been amended by Article 50 of the newer Food Information Regulation 1169/2011 [2011] OJ L 304/18, which is discussed in much more detail in ch 7.

that there was any real safety or health concern. In *Bellamy* the respondent argued that a national law setting a maximum salt content for bread was contrary to EU rules on the free movement of goods.[70] The State, in this case Belgium, contended that this was justifiable under the terms of Article 36 TFEU, as it was necessary to keep salt consumption low in the interests of protecting human health. Here, English Shop Wholesale imported foodstuffs from Britain for sale in Belgium, including bread with a salt content of 2.88 per cent. Belgian law prescribed that the salt content of bread sold there could not exceed 2 per cent. In considering whether prohibiting the sale of the bread imported from Britain was a measure equivalent to a quantitative restriction on trade, which it obviously was, and also if this could be justified as being necessary for the protection of human health, the Court, referring to its earlier judgement in *Van der Veldt*,[71] found that it was not compatible with EU obligations. No additional or different arguments in support of the maximum salt requirement were made, beyond those which had been offered in *Van der Veldt*. The rule remained likely to hinder trade between Member States and was not seen as justifiable by the Court.

It is often presumed that the over-consumption of salt has a range of detrimental consequences for human health. In particular, there is sufficient evidence to show that it can lead to a high rate of blood pressure and also heart disease.[72] Despite this, the European Court of Justice in *Van der Veldt* refused to support a Belgian ban on salt content in bread above 2 per cent on the basis that it was a disproportionate response in the circumstances. The respondent in this case imported practically all of its bread and other bakery products from the Netherlands. Food inspections discovered that the salt content of these products were at a level between 2.11 per cent and 2.17 per cent. Charges were brought against the retailer.

The argument was made in *Van der Veldt* that the disputed Belgian rule was necessary to protect humans from the health implications of the over-consumption of salt. On rejecting this, the Court found that exceeding the maximum permitted levels by the small amounts which the imported bread did was not sufficient to pose the type of risk needed to justify a prohibition. It must be remembered that the baked products at issue only surpassed the 2 per cent salt content requirement by between 0.11 per cent and 0.17 per cent. No scientific evidence was produced to show that this was a dangerous level. The Court also found that a more proportionate response was available to the Belgian authorities in the circumstances. According to it, the prescription of suitable labelling would have provided consumers with full information on the composition of the products concerned. It was stated that '[t]he protection of public health would thus have been ensured

---

[70] Case C-123/2000 *Criminal proceedings against Christina Bellamy and English Shop Wholesale SA* [2001] ECR I-2795.

[71] Case C-17/1993 *Criminal proceedings against Van der Veldt* [1994] ECR I-3537.

[72] See, eg, P Meneton, X Jeunemaitre, H de Wardener and G Macgregor, 'Links between dietary salt intake, renal salt handling, blood pressure, and cardiovascular diseases' (2005) 85 *Physiological Reviews* 679.

without such serious restrictions on the free movement of goods'.[73] This raises two questions on the suitability of the Court's approach to this issue, not only in its reasoning in *Van der Veldt*, but also that which was later based upon this in *Bellamy*.

It is certainly arguable that labelling disclosures may not have any real impact on health protection in the circumstances. The Court stated that disclosing the amount of salt in the bread would address any concerns about excessive sodium consumption. First, this fails to account for the fact that many bread and bakery products are exempt from all labelling requirements. It has always been the case that the EU framework labelling legislation, since first developed in 1979, does not apply to highly perishable freshly baked foodstuffs. Perhaps more significantly, however, is the failure to account for the fact that mere statements in the ingredients list, or nutrient declaration, about a 2.17 per cent salt level will mean little to the average consumer. There is unlikely to be much awareness of the recommended 2 per cent maximum permitted level. Providing indirect information about exceeding this provides no meaningful information at all. A requirement to include this in the nutrient declaration would not have been permitted under EU law at the time. The provision of any of this information was not even compulsory, except for those products about which some health or nutrition claim was being made. An obligation to include this for the products concerned would surely have been deemed a measure equivalent to a quantitative restriction itself, as the exporter would not have been met with the same requirement in their own State.

The second difficulty with the decision making in these cases relates to the manner in which the Court in *Bellamy* relies so heavily on its previous judgment in *Van der Veldt*, without any consideration of a key distinction between the two sets of circumstances involved. A key part of the reasoning for rejecting the Member State's claim that the measure was necessary to protect health related to the fact that the difference between the maximum level of salt permitted under national law and the actual amounts of salt contained in the breads was not very significant. It only exceeded the 2 per cent limit by around 0.15 per cent. In *Bellamy*, however, the salt content of the products concerned exceeded the maximum permitted level by nearly five times as much as that in *Van der Veldt*. Despite this, the Court in the former dismissed the Member State's claim on the basis that 'a ruling must be given in the same terms' as that in the latter. It did not consider it any further than this. It gave no consideration to the much higher levels of salt contained in the products at issue in *Bellamy*.

Finally, EU Member States have also attempted to use the health protection exception to argue that national laws restricting the sale of alcohol are necessary in the pursuit of this aim. Swedish law prescribed that only authorised wholesalers were permitted to import alcohol from other EU Member States. This rule was

---

[73] Para 19.

tested in *Rosengren* after several Swedish residents mail-ordered the importation of cases of Spanish wine.[74] The wine was confiscated by Swedish customs authorities and criminal proceedings were brought against those who had ordered the wine. The fact that private individuals were prohibited from importing alcoholic beverages was clearly a quantitative restriction on trade. One of the grounds on which the Swedish authorities argued that their authorisation system for alcohol importation was justifiable was the need to protect young people from the harmful effects of alcohol. This was rejected. Although the system included provision for the granting of permission to applicants only if they are at least 20 years old, and therefore did prevent some younger persons from purchasing alcohol, the ban at issue in the proceedings applied to everyone, of all ages. The Court therefore held that it was an effective health protection measure, but also a disproportionate one. It would, according to both the European Commission and the Court, be less of an impediment to trade if an effective age-checking system were put in place instead.

4.2.6 National Rules on Additive Use

Other substances may be added to foods for a variety of reasons. These additives can be used, for example, to preserve, colour, thicken or enhance the flavour of a foodstuff. All must be approved at EU level before use—usually indicated in the ingredients list by the presence of an assigned 'E' number.[75] Consumers are often averse to the inclusion of additives in food. Many are natural ingredients, extracted from other foods, such as E100 Curcumin, which is taken from the root of the turmeric plant, E162 Beetroot Red, and E170 Calcium Carbonate, which is a natural chalk, or which can be extracted from eggshells. Their inclusion in production is usually therefore no more, and sometimes less, of a threat to the health or well-being of the consumer than any other ingredient used. Some additives may, however, have adverse consequences for some consumers, and certainly may not be appealing to most. E153 Carbon Black or Vegetable Carbon, for example, can be obtained from charcoal, bones, blood oils or the incomplete combustion of natural gas. It is found in some concentrated fruit juices and jams. It has been banned in food production in the USA as it is suspected to be a carcinogenic agent. Non-vegetable varieties of this additive are also banned in Australia. It is recommended that it should not be consumed by children. E110 Tartrazine Yellow is also not recommended for consumption by children. It is a

---

[74] Case C-170/2004 *Klas Rosengren and others v Riksåklagaren* [2007] ECR I-4071.

[75] Originally set out in Art 8 of Council Directive 1989/107/EEC of 21 December 1988 on the approximation of the laws of the Member States concerning food additives authorised for use in foodstuffs intended for human consumption [1989] OJ L 40/27. This is transposed into English law by, amongst other provisions, s 14(9) of the Food Labelling Regulations 1996, SI No 1499/1996. It is now also covered by Art 23 of Regulation (EC) No 1333/2008 of the European Parliament and of the Council of 16 December 2008 on food additives [2008] OJ L 354/16.

synthetic yellow dye that is often found in dilutable cordial and fizzy soft drinks, or in the shells of medicine capsules. It can cause allergic reactions, in particular amongst asthmatics and those with an intolerance to aspirin. It is also suspected of causing hyperactivity in children.[76] Its use has been banned in both Norway and Austria, but it is commonly used in the UK. While the majority of additives pose no real threat to human health, they are often used to provide a cheap substitute for more wholesome or substantial ingredients. In *Commission v Germany* the Court of Justice examined a situation where a Member State tried to restrict the use of E160f in sauces and pastries as an alternative to eggs.[77] This colouring provided the finished product with a deep yellow appearance, suggesting that there had been plenty of eggs used in production, when in fact there were possibly none. This presents two possible problems. First, the consumer is presented with a product that appears to contain certain ingredients in significant quantities, but in reality these have been substituted for additives specifically designed to mislead the purchaser. The product is presented as having a certain appearance but it is the additives, rather than the ingredients, that have given it this more appealing look, or provided it with some other organoleptic property. Second, if additives are used to replace more wholesome ingredients, the nutritional value of the food is also misrepresented in its final appearance. It may look and taste more wholesome than it actually is solely because of the use of colourings and flavour enhancers designed to present the product as having increased quantities of certain ingredients, which may actually only have been used at very low levels. In some cases additives are used to replace an ingredient altogether, even possibly when the name of this ingredient has been used in the marketing of the product, such as 'chocolate flavoured' or 'strawberry flavoured'. This is all perfectly lawful. Neither chocolate nor strawberries have to be present in either of these two examples. Additives that present the products as being made with either chocolate or strawberries can have been used instead. As is discussed in chapter seven, EU rules on food labelling allow this to happen. This legislation, coupled with EU rules on the free movement of food, prevent Member States from taking any action at national level to prevent it from happening.

The maintenance of national rules in EU Member States which prohibit the use of additives in certain foodstuffs is contrary to Article 34 TFEU. They are very difficult to justify. They almost always have to be withdrawn. The case law of the Court of Justice makes it very clear that laws which place limits on the additive use can only be applied where this is necessary for the protection of human health of consumers. As discussed above, these are both very difficult arguments to make successfully, in particular if the same additives are permitted for use either in

---

[76] See, eg, D McCann and Others, 'Food additives and hyperactive behaviour in 3-year-old and 8/9-year-old children in the community: a randomised, double-blinded, placebo-controlled trial' (2007) 370 *The Lancet* 1560. The website www.ukfoodguide.net provides an excellent assessment of, and information on, all additives approved for use in food production.

[77] Case C-51/1994 *Commission v Germany* [1995] ECR I-3599.

other foods or elsewhere in the EU. The decision in the *Beer Purity* case made it very clear that a general prohibition on additive use in these circumstances was not compatible with Article 34 TFEU obligations.[78] It could only be successfully argued that such a ban was necessary if it could be shown that there was a real risk to human health or that consumers could be misled, coupled with a demonstration that the additives in question served no technological function and could not be used in the production of other foods. These conditions still stand. However, there are some circumstances where the Court of Justice will permit the maintenance of national rules which place limitations on the use of certain additives.

Italian law which prohibited the use of chemical additives, such as nitrates, in cheese production was found to be compatible with Article 34 TFEU. These rules could be allowed if they did not involve a total ban on additive use, as was the case in *Beer Purity*, and the authorisation process met certain conditions which were designed to ensure that appropriate additive use was allowed. In *Commission v Italy* the Court found that national rules which require that an additive must be specifically authorised for use are in compliance with EU law if they are, as usual, readily accessible by applicants, if decisions on authorisation are made within a reasonable period of time, and if resulting in a rejection this must be open to a proper appeal process.[79] Also, applications could only be rejected if the additive in question did not meet any real need, in particular a technological need. The Court held that the Italian rules on additive use, in this case the addition of nitrate to cheese, were applied in the same way to both Italian producers and those from other Member States and were therefore compatible with EU provisions on free movement. Article 34 TFEU would only be breached if the national procedure unjustifiably rejected an application for the inclusion of a substance on the list of authorised additives.

The Court of Justice has also allowed the non-authorisation of additives by Member States where their use is permitted elsewhere in the EU. In *Eyssen*, for example, the Court held that a Dutch ban on the addition of nisin to cheese was justifiable on the grounds that it was necessary for the protection of human health.[80] This was decided despite the fact that this additive could be lawfully used in cheese production elsewhere in the EU. French restrictions on the use of sorbic acid in pastry products were also found to be justifiable on health protection grounds in *Bellon*.[81] This allowance was made even though the First Preservatives Directive specifically permitted the use of sorbic acid in food production.[82] It was, however, subject to the condition that a Member State must have a suitable authorisation procedure in place before introducing such a ban. The Court

---

[78] Case 178/1984, n 21 above.
[79] Case C-95/1989 *Commission v Italy* [1992] ECR I-4545.
[80] Case 53/1980 *Officier van Justitie v Kaasfabriek Eyssen BV* [1981] ECR 409.
[81] Case C-42/1990 *Criminal proceedings against Jean-Claude Bellon* [1990] ECR I-4863.
[82] Council Directive 1964/54/EEC of 5 November 1963 on the approximation of the laws of the Member States concerning the preservatives authorised for use in foodstuffs intended for human consumption [1964] OJ L 12/161. English Special Edition Series I, Chapter 1963–1964, p 99.

also held in *Muller* that allowing Member States to prohibit or restrict the use of EU-listed additives is actually necessary to ensure that the Treaty provisions on free movement, in particular those contained in Article 36 TFEU designed to protect human health, are properly observed.[83] Some limitations on Member State actions in this regard were, however, set out in the decision in *Grunert*, where it was held that they could not introduce absolute prohibitions on additives approved for use under the terms of the Preservatives Directive.[84] They could, however, prohibit the use of approved additives in some circumstances, such as limiting this to pastry products, as was the case in the later decision in *Bellon*. While Member States have traditionally enjoyed some flexibility in their application of the legal requirements on authorised additive use, it is clear that this is more limited where it can be shown that the substance in question meets a real need—either technological, physiological or economic.[85]

The issue of 'genuine or technological need' is controversial. The Court has interpreted this to mean that the possibility of using another substance,[86] or no substance at all,[87] to meet the same function as the banned additive does not mean that it does not serve a technological need. Also, an additive that significantly affects the appearance of a finished product does not necessarily serve a 'technological function' in that product, if its original function was to alter a characteristic of an ingredient.[88] Additives do not have to be listed as an ingredient on the labelling of a food product if they do not serve a technological function in the finished product.[89] The lists of additives permitted for use are now set out in Annex II to the EU Food Additives Regulation 2008,[90] the domestic application of which is provided for by the Food Additives (England) Regulations 2009.[91]

4.3 Measures Equivalent to Customs Duties on Imported Food

There are three ways in which EU rules on the free movement of goods can impact on what can be done to regulate the food sector at national level. The first, and by far the most significant, of these is that which has already been discussed at length in this chapter—the prohibition on quantitative restrictions on trade and

---

[83] Case 304/1984 *Criminal proceedings against Claude Muller* [1986] ECR 1511.
[84] Case 88/1979 *Criminal proceedings against Siegfried Grunert* [1980] ECR 1827.
[85] Case 247/1984 *Criminal proceedings against Léon Motte* [1985] ECR 1329.
[86] Case C-95/1989 n 79 above.
[87] Case 178/1984, n 21 above.
[88] Case C-144/1993 *Pfanni Werke Otto Eckart KG v Landeshauptstadt München* [1994] ECR I-4605.
[89] As stipulated by Art 20 of Reg 1169/2011, n 69 above. This is discussed in more detail in ch 7.
[90] Reg 1333/2008, n 75 above.
[91] SI No 3238/2009.

measures of equivalent effect. As has been demonstrated, the application of this provision of EU law places plenty of limitations on the Government in relation to, for example, setting compositional or packaging requirements or the operation of authorisation procedures. As will be particularly evident from the discussion in chapter nine, this has also severely curtailed Government efforts to tackle obesity through the introduction of clearer food labelling formats. The impact of this, on both human health and on the economy, is considerable.[92]

The other two ways in which EU rules on the free movement of goods can impact on what happens at national level are the prohibition on customs duties on trade between Member States, and measures of equivalent effect, and also restrictions that are placed on the taxation of foods sold in the domestic market, in particular where these appear to discriminate against imported products in some way. The former is set out in Articles 28–30 TFEU. Article 28 TFEU sets out the general position that

> [t]he Union shall comprise a customs union which shall cover all trade in goods and which shall involve a prohibition between Member States of customs duties on imports and exports and of all charges having equivalent effect, and the adoption of a common customs tariff in their relations with third countries.

Article 30 TFEU more specifically provides that

> [c]ustoms duties on imports and exports and charges having equivalent effect shall be prohibited between Member States.

The Common Customs Tariff referred to in Article 28 TFEU is important for the food sector for a number of reasons. It sets out the tariff rate for all foods, amongst other things, imported into the EU Member States from third countries. These tariffs can be set at a level that is deliberately designed to afford protection to EU producers. The rates set for garlic offer a very good example of this.[93] There can also be different rates set for different times of the year, dependent on whether the food in question is in season in the Member States at that time. So, for example, apples imported from third countries during the months of January

---

[92] Health problems associated with being overweight or obese were estimated to cost the NHS more than £5 billion per year by 2012, possibly rising to £6.4 billion by 2015 and nearly £10 billion per year by 2050. Overall costs to the economy through poor health and reduced productivity were estimated to be at £16 billion by 2007, rising to £50 billion by 2050. See P Scarborough, P Bhatnagar, K Wickramasinghe and others, 'The economic burden of ill health due to diet, physical inactivity, smoking, alcohol and obesity in the UK: an update to 2006–07 NHS costs' (2011) 330 *Journal of Public Health* 527.

[93] Commission Regulation (EU) No 1006/2011 of 27 September 2011 amending Annex I to Council Regulation (EEC) No 2658/1987 on the tariff and statistical nomenclature and on the Common Customs tariff [2011] OJ L 282/1 provides that almost all of the import duty on garlic coming into the EU from third countries is to be set at 9.6% plus €120.00 per 100 kg. There is then a complex licensing mechanism to be employed to determine just how much of the garlic imported from countries such as Argentina and China is to be taxed at this higher rate. As was pointed out in the Irish Court of Criminal Appeal, in the case of *DPP v Begley* [2013] IECCA 32, this could result in a tax rate as high as 232% on the importation of garlic from third countries. The same 2011 Regulation provides that similar foods, such as shallots and onions, are only to be taxed at the much lower rate of 9.6% across the board.

and February are met with a 6.4 per cent tariff, plus an additional tonnage charge. The same apples imported between April and June have this rate lowered to 4.8 per cent plus a tonnage charge as apples are not so in season across the EU at that time. Between August and December, prime harvesting time in Europe, the tariff rate jumps to 11.2 per cent plus tonnage charge. This is all set out in the Combined Nomenclature, which lists and defines all of the goods most commonly imported into the EU and attaches a tariff rate to each of them.[94] The Common Customs Tariff is also used to help the EU institutions to come to decisions on other free movement of goods matters. For example, nomenclature definitions have been used to help the Court to establish whether a food name has become generic, or whether it remains firmly associated with production in a particular region or country.[95] However, it is also usual for the Court to find that these definitions are not binding on them in any way, and that they may be of a persuasive authority only.[96]

Treaty provisions provide that all food and drink traded between Member States must carry an importation and/or exportation duty of 0 per cent. This is clear enough. However, the second part of the Article 30 TFEU prohibition can be more problematic. Charges imposed by Member States on imported or exported goods may be classified as 'charges of equivalent effect to a customs duty', even when they may be something else entirely. Where this is so, and the charge cannot be justified by the Member State, the Member State must cease the charge and make refunds. The real difficulty with the Article 30 TFEU prohibition is that a charge can be deemed incompatible with EU legal obligations even where domestic producers are met with a similar charge at a similar level. The charge must be imposed on all traders at the same stage and in the same manner for it to be deemed something other than of equivalent effect to a customs duty, and to therefore escape Court scrutiny.[97]

4.3.1 Unlawful Charges and Exceptions to the Rule

Any charge imposed by a Member State on a foodstuff imported from another Member State is deemed to be of equivalent effect to a customs duty if it is imposed at the point of importation or exportation. The purpose behind the imposition of the charge is irrelevant to this. It need not be protectionist in any

---

[94] Commission Regulation 1006/2011, n 93 above.

[95] Joined Cases C-289/1996, C-293/1996 and C-299/1996 *Denmark, Germany and France v Commission* [1999] ECR I-1541.

[96] In para 71 of its judgment in *Denmark, Germany and France v Commission*, n 95 above, the Court stated that 'the Community rules on export refunds and customs nomenclature relied on by the applicants reflect an approach specific to customs matters and are not in any way intended to govern industrial property rights relating to particular names or to reflect consumers' perceptions in that area, so that such rules are not relevant in determining whether a name is generic'.

[97] Case 87/1975 *Bresciani* [1976] ECR 129.

way to still be caught by the Article 30 TFEU prohibition.[98] It need not have any revenue-raising purpose either.[99] It will be prohibited by Article 30 TFEU once it has a restrictive effect on trade. There are, of course, some exceptions to this, but they are very limited in both scope and application.

The first of these possible exceptions is that the charge was not imposed due to the importation or exportation of the products, but it was actually passed on to the importer as a payment due for a service provided. In *Commission v Italy* the Member State was placing a small charge on all exported goods.[100] The idea behind the charge was that its collection could be used to gather statistics on Italian export and trade patterns. The Court found that Article 30 TFEU provided an absolute prohibition. The purpose underlying the charge imposed was not relevant to this. The existence of the charge at all was enough to subject it to Court scrutiny. The low rate of the charge was also deemed irrelevant to any defence put forward in support of its imposition. The Member State further claimed that the charge was effectively a payment for a service provided, and therefore outside the scope of Article 30 TFEU scrutiny. The Court disagreed, finding that the advantage conferred on exporters by the collection of the trade flow data was too general in nature and that it was too difficult to identify the service which individual payers of the charge were receiving. Consequently, the charge was deemed to be of equivalent effect to a customs duty, as prohibited by the State's EU Treaty obligations. It is clear, therefore, that for a Member State to successfully argue that the services exception to Article 30 TFEU applies, it must be able to show the specific benefit conferred on the importing or exporting payer of the charge.

There is a second possible exception to the application of the prohibition on charges of equivalent effect to a customs duty. This applies in those circumstances where the fee is charged to cover the costs of meeting a specific obligation imposed on the Member State by EU law. A good example of this was seen in *Bauhuis*.[101] Here, Dutch exporters were met with charges imposed by the national authorities to cover the cost of inspecting live animals. There were two charges at issue here. The first arose out of obligations placed on the Member State by the provisions of an EU directive.[102] This was not therefore based on unilateral action taken by the Member State. The Court decided that this would not be considered a charge of equivalent effect to a customs duty, provided that the amount charged was not

---

[98] Cases 2 and 3/1969 *Diamond Workers* [1969] ECR 211. In para 18 of this judgment the Court encapsulated the essence of what constitutes a charge of equivalent effect to a customs duty when it stated that '[a]ny charge, however small and whatever its designation and mode of application, which is imposed unilaterally on goods by reason of the fact that they cross a frontier constitutes a charge having equivalent effect [to a customs duty] even if it is not imposed for the benefit of the State, is not discriminatory or protective in effect'.

[99] Case 7/1968 *Commission v Italy* [1968] ECR 423.

[100] Case 24/1968 *Commission v Italy* [1969] ECR 193.

[101] Case 46/1976 *Bauhuis v Netherlands* [1977] ECR 5.

[102] Council Directive 1964/432/EEC of 26 June 1964 on animal health problems affecting intra-Community trade in bovine animals and swine [1964] OJ L 121/1977; English Special Edition Series I, Chapter 1963–1964, p 164.

more than the actual cost of carrying out the obligatory inspection. The second charge was for inspections that were not carried out pursuant to any specific provision of EU law. The Court did hold that the inspecting itself was justifiable under Article 36 TFEU as being necessary for the protection of human health, but also that the charge imposed to cover the cost of this was not justifiable as it related to the unilateral action of a Member State, placing an additional impediment in the way of the free movement of goods. The charge for the inspection carried out under national law was unlawful. The charge imposed for the execution of an obligation arising out of a specific provision of EU law was not. The Court later held that this exception could only be granted if four conditions were satisfied.[103] These are: (i) that the charge does not exceed the actual cost to the Member State; (ii) that the inspections, or other similar obligations, are obligatory across the Union; (iii) that the action that led to the cost is prescribed by Union law; and (iv) that the action promotes the free movement of goods in some way.

The third possible court-created exception to the prohibition set out in Article 30 TFEU is that the nature of the charge is such that it is really part of the national system of internal taxation, rather than any fee attached to the importation or exportation of food. Charges of equivalent effect to customs duties cannot, therefore, be 'justified' in the same way that measures of equivalent effect to quantitative restrictions can. Exceptions to the rule set out in Article 30 TFEU have been created by the Court of Justice. These determine that the status of the charge is outside the scope of Article 30 TFEU altogether, rather than providing grounds for Member States to argue that the fee imposed is necessary in some way. Customs duties and charges of equivalent effect can never really be justified. Where an additional cost is imposed by the Member State, and the Court has determined that it is not within the scope of Article 30 TFEU, it is possible that the charge may be examinable under other provisions of the Treaty, usually those on discriminatory internal taxation, now set out in Article 110 TFEU.

4.4 Discriminatory Taxation on Food and Drink

There are situations when it can be difficult to distinguish between charges imposed by Member States on importers and exporters which are to be classified as being of equivalent effect to customs duties, and those which may instead be seen as part of the internal taxation regime. While this can be a difficult distinction to make, it is also a very important one for the Member States and those who are met with the charge, as the consequences of being classified as one or the other can be very different.

---

[103] Case 18/1987 *Commission v Germany* [1988] ECR 5427.

A charge of equivalent effect is always prohibited and, once identified, must be abolished. A tax that is deemed to discriminate against products from other Member States does not have to be abolished. It just has to be modified to remove the discriminatory element. The limitations placed on the way in which Member States can tax foodstuffs once they have come onto the market in a Member State are set out in Article 110 TFEU. Paragraph 1 of this provision states that

> [n]o Member State shall impose, directly or indirectly, on the products of other Member States any internal taxation of any kind in excess of that imposed directly or indirectly on similar domestic products.

A national rate of tax must usually have three features for Article 110(1) TFEU to have any potential effect on it. First, there must be different rates of tax charged on different products. Charging a higher rate of tax on the same imported product would be blatantly discriminatory. Second, the higher rate of tax must be charged on the product that the imposing Member State does not produce at all, or does not produce at any significant level. Third, the products on which the different tax rates are being compared must be in competition with each other. They must be 'similar products'.

It should be noted at this stage that it is not just the difference in a rate of taxation that can lead the Court to conclude that it is discriminatory. It can be the manner in which the tax is imposed that can render it prejudicial to imports. In *Commission v Ireland*, the Court held that national rules which permitted national producers of alcoholic products to delay the payment of their tax were contrary to Article 110 TFEU.[104] Allowing domestic operators an additional period of up to six weeks to pay the taxes due on their products was seen by the Court to be a small, but obvious, advantage. The Irish authorities had tried to claim that the wording of Article 110 TFEU related to rates of tax only, but the Court disagreed. It is the effect of the tax that is decisive in determining whether Article 110 TFEU is applicable. The allowance made to Irish producers, which was not available to those from other Member States, was deemed to be directly discriminatory against non-nationals.

Unlike the prohibition on customs duties and measures of equivalent effect, there are circumstances where the Court accepts that seemingly discriminatory national taxes may in fact be justifiable. In *Commission v France*, for example, the higher rate of tax payable on the sale of liqueurs when compared to 'traditional natural sweet wines' was deemed justifiable, on the grounds that the lower rate for the latter was designed to support producers in areas which suffered from difficult environmental conditions.[105]

The French Government presented the argument that these wines were made in regions which were characterised by low rainfall levels and relatively poor soil quality, which limited the possibilities for growing other types of crop.

---

[104] Case 55/1979 *Commission v Ireland* [1980] ECR 481.
[105] Case 196/1985 *Commission v France* [1987] ECR 1597.

Consequently, sweet wine production was vital to the agricultural economies of these areas. The tax advantage enjoyed by the producers of these wines was, according to the French authorities, designed to offset the more severe conditions under which they were being produced and to support the continued output of high-quality produce. This scheme of preferential taxation was, crucially, also extended to imported sweet wines. No evidence was produced by the Commission to show that the application of the scheme provided more favourable conditions for French wines than for those which possessed the same characteristics but which were produced in other Member States. The Court stated that

> national provisions which cover both domestic and imported products without distinc-
> tion cannot be regarded as contrary to [EU] law merely because they might lend them-
> selves to discriminatory application, unless it is proved that they are actually applied in
> that way.[106]

The Court, just as it did in *Commission v Ireland* above, therefore made it clear that it is always the effect of the national taxation measure that is key to determining whether it is contrary to the Treaty or not. The effect must be discriminatory. Different rates of tax may be charged for similar products. Article 110 TFEU will only be breached where unjustifiable discrimination occurs.

The situation is more complicated, however, where the products that are subjected to different rates of tax are not necessarily 'similar' to each other, but they could be considered as being in at least partial competition with each other. Article 110(2) TFEU provides that

> no Member State shall impose on the products of other Member States any internal
> taxation of such a nature as to afford indirect protection to other products.

Products are seen as being 'similar' where they 'have similar characteristics and meet the same needs from the point of view of consumers'.[107] 'Other' products include those which 'without being similar ... are nevertheless in competition, even partial, indirect or potential with certain products of the importing country'.[108]

Taxing different types of spirit drinks at different rates, depending on the raw materials used in their production, was tested for compatibility with Article 110 TFEU in *Commission v France*.[109] The Member State placed a higher rate of tax on those spirits which had been made with cereals, such as whisky, when compared to those made with fruit, like brandy. Other Member States had similar provisions in place, and the Commission took issue with three of them on this.

---

[106] Para 10.
[107] Para 12 of Case 45/1975 *Rewe-Zentrale des Lebensmittel-Grosshandels GmbH v Hauptzollamt Landau/Pfalz* [1976] ECR 181.
[108] Para 6 of Case 168/1978 *Commission v France* [1980] ECR 347.
[109] ibid.

The argument was made that this was an indirect way of protecting national producers, who produced the lower-taxed varieties in significantly larger quantities. The Member States contended that Article 110 TFEU was not applicable to the circumstances as each type of spirit operated in a distinct market. According to the Commission, all spirits, regardless of the raw materials used in their manufacture, possess similar characteristics and 'in essence meet the same needs of consumers'. Spirits should therefore be considered as operating in a single general market and taxation should be calculated on the basis of a single rate for all products that is based on their alcohol content, rather than raw material type.

The Court found that three factors should be taken into consideration when determining whether all spirits were operating, at least partially, in the same market, which would be necessary for Article 110 TFEU to apply. The first was an assessment of the existence of common generic features. As all of the spirits at issue were made by distillation procedure and were characterised by their high alcohol content, the Court found that it followed that, due to their similarities, these drinks formed an identifiable and unified group of products. However, on the second consideration, the assessment of more pronounced individual characteristics, the Court did accept that there were differences between spirit types. These were related to either the raw materials used in their production, be they cereals or fruits, the manufacturing processes employed, or the flavourings added. These characteristics were distinguishable to a level which entitled some of the drinks to registered designation status.[110] The third factor in the Court's assessment was related to the use to which these drinks were usually put. It stated that despite the distinctions that could be drawn between spirit types, it was impossible to disregard the fact that there were a range of unifying characteristics between them as well.

Two conclusions could be drawn from all of this. The first was that there was clearly a group of 'similar' products operating in the market for spirits. The tax on these was covered by Article 110(1) TFEU. Second, even where a sufficient degree of similarity between spirits was difficult to determine, there were still, in the case of all such drinks, common characteristics which were 'sufficiently pronounced to accept that in all cases there is at least partial or potential competition'. Article 110(2) TFEU would thus apply in such circumstances.

The Court deemed that it was unnecessary for the purposes of this dispute to determine whether the spirits were either wholly or partly similar products because there was at least partial competition between them, meaning that Article 110 TFEU would apply in the circumstances regardless. It was also clear to the Court that the French system of charging different rates of tax depending on the raw materials used was deliberately designed to be protective of domestic spirit production. Spirits made from wine and fruit were within the most favourable tax category, whereas products that were usually imported from other Member States

---

[110] See ch 8.

were subject to the higher rates. This was deemed to be a protective charge, and the fact that there was one domestically produced drink, aniseed spirit, which was also subject to the higher rate did not, in the opinion of the Court, change this. Even the fact that the whisky's share of the market appeared to be on the increase did not alter the Court's findings in any way. The existence of at least partial competition between the types of product concerned, coupled with the fact that it was mostly imported products that were met with higher taxes, was sufficient to show the Court that the French methods of calculating charges on spirits was discriminatory, in a manner which was contrary to Article 110 TFEU.

Many of the key cases on the prohibition on discriminatory national taxes, and in particular those on the issue of goods that are in partial competition with each other, concern alcoholic drinks. The methods used to calculate the amount of tax paid by consumers when purchasing wine in the UK has also been the subject of Court scrutiny in the past.[111] The Commission was of the view that the higher rates charged on wine were deliberately designed to protect the domestic beer-producing industry. The Government argued that there was no real competition between wine and beer as consumers would not readily substitute a preference for the former to the latter because of a difference in price. It was argued that any comparison should be between beer and wines with a lower alcohol content, which also tended to be less expensive. The Court agreed, finding that 'the decisive competitive relationship between beer, a popular and widely consumed beverage, and wine must be established by reference to those wines which are the most accessible to the public at large, that is to say, generally speaking, the lightest and cheapest varieties'.[112] The Court also considered that, to a certain extent at least, the two drinks in question were capable of meeting the same needs. There was, therefore, the potential for there to be some degree of 'interchangeability' between them, meaning that consumers would be willing to change their preference for one of the product types for the other, in particular if some other factor, such as price, were taken into consideration. The existence of 'interchangeability' is crucial in determining whether Article 110 TFEU is applicable. There must be a willingness, or at least a potential willingness, amongst consumers to alter their choice should the price of one product go up or down relative to that of another. It is only where there is interchangeability that the existence of some level of competition between products can be shown. The Court considered that there was some competition between beer and low-alcohol and cheap wines. It therefore compared the way in which these products were taxed, in assessing whether there had been a breach of the Treaty. Comparisons on the level of tax were difficult to make due to the different characteristics of wine and beer. In particular, comparisons relating to the different volumes of each which would be normally drunk by a consumer were hard to quantify. Nevertheless, the Court did find that regardless of which method was used to determine the rates applied, it was clear that

---

[111] Case 170/1978 *Commission v UK* [1983] ECR 2265.
[112] Para 12.

wine was met with a much higher burden than beer. The cheaper wines, which were deemed to be those that were the most directly in competition with beer, were also subjected to this 'considerably higher tax burden'. This, according to the Court, afforded protection to domestic beer production to the detriment of wine imported from other EU Member States. It went on to state that

> the effect of the United Kingdom tax system is to stamp wine with the hallmarks of a luxury product which, in view of the tax burden which it bears, can scarcely constitute in the eyes of the consumer a genuine alternative to the typical domestically produced beverage.[113]

The levying of taxes on wine at a relatively higher rate than beer was, therefore, contrary to the UK's obligations as set out in Article 110(2) TFEU.

4.4.1 Distinguishing Between Customs Duties and Taxes

As mentioned above, there are cases where it can be difficult to determine whether the facts lend themselves to an examination of a national measure for its compliance with Article 30 TFEU prohibiting customs duties and charges of equivalent effect on the one hand, and discriminatory internal taxation on the other.

Customs duties, or any equivalent charges, are unlawful under EU law and, where found to exist, must be abolished. Internal taxation is not unlawful, and does not have to be abolished, but where it is found to discriminate against products from other Member States it may need to be modified to bring it into compliance with TFEU obligations to remove the discriminatory element.

There are, in general terms, two situations where it may be difficult to establish whether the charge at issue comes within the scope of Article 30 TFEU or Article 110 TFEU. The first is where the charge is imposed as part of a system of internal dues, applicable to all similar products at the same rate and at the same stage of production or marketing. An example of this type of charge was seen in *Denkavit*,[114] where proceedings were brought against the Danish Ministry of Agriculture by a Dutch manufacturer of animal feed over the imposition of a charge of an annual authorisation levy. It was queried whether charging importers this fee was compatible with what are now Articles 30 and 110 TFEU.

The annual authorisation levy that was at issue in *Denkavit* was also charged to national manufacturers of animal feed which contained additives. On first querying whether this levy was a charge of equivalent effect to a customs duty, the Court noted that Article 30 TFEU was not applicable in those circumstances where any fee imposed on importers

> relates to a general system of internal dues applied systematically and in accordance with the same criteria to domestic products and imported products alike, in which case it does not come within the scope of [Article 30 TFEU] but within [Article 110 TFEU instead].[115]

---

[113] Para 27.
[114] Case 29/1987 *Dansk Denkavit ApS v Danish Ministry of Agriculture* [1988] ECR 2965.

The fact that the levy was imposed on all traders in animal feed who were selling on the Danish market, and given that it was charged in the same manner on all, regardless of nationality, made this authorisation levy a part of 'a general system of internal dues' and not something equivalent to a customs duty, that was being passed on to importers only. It would have to be examined as a part of the domestic system of taxation, and tested for compatibility with Article 110 TFEU instead. On making this examination, the Court held that

> [Article 110 TFEU] is complied with where an internal tax applies in accordance with the same criteria, objectively justified by the purpose for which the tax was introduced, to domestic products and imported products so that it does not result in the imported products bearing a heavier charge than that borne by the similar domestic product.[116]

The charge was not equivalent to a customs duty just because it had to be borne by importers. It had to be paid by all, importers and domestic producers alike. It directly related to the costs incurred by the State in checking samples. It was not within the scope of Article 30 TFEU. It was not imposed in a manner that was contrary to Article 110 TFEU. While importers were met with this authorisation fee, they could not successfully claim that it should be abolished, provided it was charged to all traders at the same rate, at the same stage of marketing and for the same purpose—here to cover the cost of the analysis of samples.

The situation can be a bit more complicated where a charge is payable on a type of food that is not widely produced by the imposing Member State. Obviously, if the Member State does not produce the good, the charge is being met by importers only. However, it is also obvious that such a charge can not be automatically deemed incompatible with EU law. To do so would require that Member States could not impose any taxes or charges on foods that they do not produce themselves. The tax or charge could still be contrary to Treaty obligations, however. This would be the case if a higher rate of tax was placed on imported foods that the State did not produce, and a lower rate on those foods which it did produce and which were in at least partial competition with the imports.

Italy does not produce many bananas. However, its taxation of them was the subject of Court of Justice scrutiny in the case of *Co-frutta*.[117] The applicant imported bananas into the Benelux countries from Colombia, which it then exported to markets elsewhere in the Union. The goods were therefore subject to the requirements of 'free circulation' once they had entered any Member State. They were to be treated as if they had been produced in the EU. They were therefore entitled to the same free movement protections available after entering the Union, including the prohibition on customs duties and the elimination of discriminatory national taxes. Italian tax law established a system of 19 consumer

---

[115] Para 33.

[116] Para 35.

[117] Case 193/1985 *Cooperativa Co-Frutta Srl v Amministrazione delle finanze dello Stato* [1987] ECR 2085.

taxes, of which three were charged on goods which were classified as 'tropical products', including coffee, cocoa and bananas.

There were two key issues for the Court to determine here. First, it needed to be established whether the tax was actually a customs duty, given that in practice it really only applied to imported goods. If it were found to be a duty or a charge of equivalent effect then, as stated above, it would have to be abolished. Second, if the charge was alternatively found to be an internal tax, then the Court would have to establish whether it was discriminatory against foods imported from other EU Member States.

On the first question, the Court recognised that a charge borne by imported goods only does not necessarily mean that it is a customs duty, as prohibited by Article 30 TFEU, if it

> relates to a general system of internal dues applied systematically to categories of products in accordance with objective criteria irrespective of the origin of the products.[118]

This tax was seen to form part of 'a general system of internal dues'. The 19 categories of tax were charged on categories of products, regardless of their origin. The 'objective criterion' in this situation was the fact that the charge was imposed as the food in question, bananas, fell within a specific broader category, tropical products. The place of production of goods that were subjected to these taxes was not found by the Court to have any bearing on the rate charged, the basis of assessment or the manner in which the tax was being levied. Revenue generated by this system of taxation was used to finance State spending across all sectors. It was not being applied just because the goods at issue were imported. It was applied as part of a general system of revenue-raising for the State, and it could also be applied to imported varieties of the products at issue, where these existed. The charge on bananas constituted internal taxation and would therefore be examinable for compatibility with Article 110 TFEU instead.

For the tax at issue to be deemed discriminatory, it would have to be shown that it favoured domestic production in some way. If the small quantity of bananas produced in Italy were taxed at a lower rate than those which reached the Italian market via another Member State, discrimination would be obvious, and any difference in rates charged would have to be removed. The Court in *Co-frutta* examined this on the basis of both Article 110(1) and 110(2) TFEU. The former was not seen to apply in this case. Looking to its deliberations in *Commission v Italy*,[119] the Court reiterated that bananas were not 'similar' to those fruits which Italy did produce. Any test of similarity would have to be based on a comparison between a set of objective characteristics of the foods, such as their organoleptic properties (impact on the senses) and water content, as well as an assessment of whether they satisfy the same needs or wants of consumers.

---

[118] Para 10.

[119] Case 184/1985 *Commission v Italy* [1987] ECR I-2013. See also Case 45/1975 *Rewe-Zentrale des Lebensmittel-Grosshandels GmbH v Hauptzollamt Landau/Pfalz*, n 107 above.

Making this comparison, it was accepted that bananas differed from typical Italian-grown fruits in a number of ways. For example, it was agreed that fruits such as pears have a high water content which gives these a thirst-quenching property that bananas do not possess. Bananas were also recognised for their higher nutritional value and energy content. Article 110(1) did not therefore apply.

However, in its assessment in *Commission v Italy*, and then supported by the Court in its judgment in *Co-frutta*, the Court did find that Article 110(2) TFEU could apply in the circumstances. Bananas present consumers with an alternative to other fruits and must therefore be regarded as being in partial competition with Italian-grown varieties.[120] The tax at issue could not therefore afford any indirect protection to domestic produce if it were to be deemed compatible with EU Treaty obligations.

Three factors were crucial here. First, the higher rate of tax did not apply to most typical Italian-produced fruit. Second, the tax on the imported bananas was so high that it could amount to half of the import price. Third, the difference in tax rates was significant enough to have an influence on the market and the purchasing preferences of consumers. Article 110(2) TFEU is breached, in circumstances like these, where it protects the domestic production of 'other' products. It would have to be amended to remove, or at the very least reduce, this protective element.

4.5 Conclusion

The impact of the TFEU requirements on the free movement of goods has been most significant. The way in which these provisions have been interpreted and applied by the European Court of Justice has led to (i) a reduction in the need for harmonising EU legislation, as the principle of mutual recognition means that the compositional requirements or production standards of a Member State must be accepted by all other Member States, reducing the need for the setting of these at EU level; (ii) the scrutinising of existing national measures for compliance, many of which have been deemed contrary to Treaty obligations and thus struck from the statute book; and (iii) perhaps most significantly, the prevention of the introduction by Member States of new measures that they may feel are necessary to protect consumers, their health or that of the environment. The latter of these is most obviously presented in the Government's attempts to deal with obesity. As will be discussed in chapters seven and nine, EU rules on free movement have prevented the compulsory application of one of the most favoured methods of dealing, from a legal perspective, with this and other epidemics. The free movement of goods continues to be the most significant influence on the rules that must, and those which cannot, be applied at national level to the food sector.

---

[120] Para 12 of Case 184/1985 *Commission v Italy*, n 119 above, and para 21 of Case 193/1985 *Co-frutta*, n 117 above.

5

Food Safety

5.1 Introduction

Food should not be sold, in any form, if it is 'unsafe'.[1] It is not safe if it is 'injurious to health' or 'unfit for human consumption'.[2] The fact that the primary focus of food law is on safety is, however, problematic. Many other important considerations are often overlooked as a result of this emphasis on what is classified as 'unsafe'. There are other ways in which food can harm health, but these are not all directly related to, or covered by, the legal provisions on the marketing of safe food.

The consumption of nutritionally deficient food has a far greater impact on human health than unsafe food ever has. Many more people die as a result of consuming a poor diet than from contracting a food-borne illness.[3] Despite this, the emphasis for policy makers and legislators remains firmly fixed on those areas that are categorised as 'food safety' considerations. The definitions of 'injurious to health' and 'unfit for human consumption' form the foundation of this serious shortcoming with the law and politics that dictate what happens in the food sector. This course, directed at EU level, has a profound effect on English law and, consequently, national public health.

The General Food Law Regulation states that ascertaining whether food is 'injurious to health' is to be based upon an assessment of the probable immediate and/or short-term and/or long-term effects of that food on the health of a person consuming it, as well as on subsequent generations.[4] Account should also be taken

---

[1] Art 14(1) of Regulation (EC) No 178/2002 of the European Parliament and of the Council of 28 January 2002 laying down the general principles and requirements of food law, establishing the European Food Safety Authority and laying down procedures in matters of food safety [2002] OJ L 31/1. This legislation is more commonly referred to as 'the General Food Law Regulation'. For more on this see B van der Meulen, 'The core of food law' (2012) 7 *European Food and Feed Law Review* 117.

[2] Art 14(2).

[3] The National Institute for Health and Clinical Excellence (NICE) estimates that there are 40,000 deaths per year in England related to the consumption of unhealthy foods. See 'Prevention of cardiovascular disease', NICE public health guidance 25, June 2012; available at: www.nice.org. The Food Standards Agency estimates that there are around 590 deaths per year in the UK from food poisoning, or at least from infectious intestinal disease. See www.food.gov.uk.

[4] Art 14(4).

of any probable cumulative toxic effects and/or the particular health sensitivities of a specific category of consumers where that food is intended for them. The Regulation makes specific reference to the effect on health, whether this is immediate, short-term or long-term. It is clear, however, that this is in reality limited to the potential for food to spread disease, contaminate or toxify. Equally clearly, it does not include the potential for food to cause nutrition-related illness such as stroke, cancer, diabetes or heart disease.

Many foods are marketed, uninhibited by the law, which have a serious long-term detrimental impact on human health. They contain substances that, when consumed on an ongoing basis, can ultimately lead to premature death. As discussed in chapter seven of this book, food laws, such as those on labelling, facilitate this. Other regulations, which could control the use of these unhealthy substances in food production, are not introduced, despite overwhelming evidence of the damaging consequences of consumption. EU rules on the free movement of goods, and those existing in related secondary legislation, prevent Member States, such as the UK, from intervening. As seen in the previous chapter, the European Court of Justice has made it clear that national authorities cannot justify the maintenance of national laws on the ground that they are necessary for guaranteeing that food has any nutritional value. There can be no minimum standards for nutrition.

While the definition of a food that is 'injurious to health' has the potential to offer a framework for raising the nutritional qualities of food, it is not used in this way. Determining whether food is 'unfit for human consumption' is even less helpful in this regard. The Regulation states that assessment of whether food falls into this latter category should be based upon an examination of its intended use, any contamination, putrefaction, deterioration or decay.[5] Again, these considerations usually relate to the short-term consequences of eating rotting food. They clearly do not relate to harmful substances, such as trans-fats and fructose syrups, the long-term consumption of which can lead to the development of terminal illness. These foods are 'fit for human consumption'. Yet, their impact on overall health is usually much more damaging than the consumption of milk or cheese that has passed its use-by date.

Since the BSE crisis, many new laws governing a range of issues related to 'food safety' have been introduced onto the English statute books, either in the form of directly applicable EU regulations, or as a result of the transposition of EU directives. The key problem with this is that the regulation of food safety has developed in a way that ignores many of the most unsafe aspects of food consumption. Efforts to make foods cheaper, longer-lasting and, in some cases, more palatable, has led to the increased use of unhealthy ingredients in production.

Yet this unwelcome result remains mostly outside the scope of the controlling legislation. As a consequence, those foods that contain these substances, often to dangerously high levels, are manufactured entirely within the law. The presence of these constituents is often kept concealed from consumers due to lax labelling requirements. These foods are made and marketed in compliance with the law.

---

[5] Art 14(5).

This, according to the General Food Law Regulation, makes them, legally, 'safe'.[6] As a consequence, they must also be deemed 'safe' under English law, and specifically under the terms of the Food Safety Act 1990 and related legislation.

5.2 Food Safety Act 1990

Issued to replace the Food Act 1984, the Food Safety Act 1990 provides much of the framework for English food law, in a whole range of areas. It deals primarily, but not exclusively, with health protection and safety matters. However, it does much more than that. It defines 'food', for legal purposes.[7] It establishes who is covered by, and who has responsibility for, food law and its implementation. It puts protections in place for the consumer, with a view to ensuring that foods are not mis-sold or falsely described. It grants the Minister the power to issue codes of practice for the sector.[8] The primary focus of attention in this chapter, however, is on the key safety provisions. Other elements of the Food Safety Act 1990 are dealt with elsewhere in this book.

5.2.1 Offences under the Food Safety Act

The Food Safety Act 1990, as originally presented, must now be read alongside the General Food Regulations 2004, which are dealt with later in this chapter, and also with a few amendments made by the Food Safety Act (Amendment) Regulations 2004.[9] These instruments together cover all stages in the production and marketing of food, from farming through to consumption. The legislation applies to both commercial and non-profit-making organisations.[10] It includes all activities related to the sale, delivery, preparation, labelling, packaging, storing or transporting of food. It also extends to food given away as a prize, regardless of whether there was any sort of payment involved prior to its winning.[11]

---

[6] Art 14(7).

[7] 'Food' is now defined the same way as it is in the EU General Food Law Regulation, n 130 below. This newer definition was inserted into the Food Safety Act 1990 by reg 3(1) of the Food Safety Act 1990 (Amendment) Regulations 2004, SI No 2990/2004.

[8] Section 40. In some circumstances the Minister may be obliged to enter into consultations with others before issuing a code of practice, under the terms of Art 9 of Reg 178/2002, n 130 below. This obligation has since been introduced into the Food Safety Act by reg 4 of the Food Safety Act 1990 (Amendment) Regulations 2004, n 7 above.

[9] SI No 2004/2990.

[10] Section 1(3) of the Food Safety Act 1990.

[11] Section 2(2).

There are three main offences that can be committed under the 1990 Act. The first is 'rendering food injurious to health', as defined in the EU General Food Law Regulation. An 'injury' is caused if there is any impairment, permanent or temporary, to the health of the consumer.[12] It is the person who 'renders' the food unsafe who is responsible under the Act. This can be done by adding or abstracting an article or substance to or from the food, or by subjecting the food to a process or treatment that makes it unsafe.[13] The second main offence under the Act is selling food that does not comply with food safety requirements.[14] Non-compliance with these requirements is assessed on the basis of an analysis of whether the food in question has been rendered injurious to health, unfit for human consumption or is contaminated to an unsafe level.[15] The third type of offence that can be committed under the Act is failure to accord the consumer with sufficient protection. This can happen in one of two ways. Food cannot be sold where its nature, substance or quality is not at the type or level expected by the purchaser.[16] Similarly, food cannot be sold where it is falsely described or is misrepresented on the label.[17] An offence can still be committed under this section of the Act where an accurate statement about the composition of the food appears on the label, if other elements of the labelling are deceptive or misleading.[18]

5.2.2 Investigating Breaches of the Food Safety Act

A range of powers exist within the Food Safety Act which facilitate the inspection and analysis of products to determine whether they are being produced or sold in breach of the legislation. Authorised officers are entitled to inspect any food which is intended to be sold for human consumption.[19] An 'authorised officer' is anyone who is granted, in writing, the power to act on behalf of a designated food authority. This is not limited to 'officers' of the food authorities.[20] It includes anyone who has been given the explicit authority to act.[21] Such people are granted a range of powers to enter premises where this is necessary to facilitate their investigations into the safety of food, provided they are in possession of the required warrant.[22] The only restriction on this relates to private residences. These can only be

---

[12] Section 7(3).
[13] Section 7(1).
[14] Section 8(1).
[15] Section 8(2).
[16] Section 14(1).
[17] Section 15(1).
[18] Section 15(4).
[19] Section 9(1).
[20] Section 5(6). For a full explanation of what is meant by 'food authority', see the discussion in ch 3.
[21] Section 5(6) of the Act also states that food safety regulations may prescribe that anyone granted the authority to act in such matters must be suitably qualified for this role. These qualifications must be set out in the associated regulations.
[22] Section 32.

entered when at least 24 hours' notice of the entry has been given to the occupant. Reasonable force can be used to enter a premises in some circumstances, provided this has been previously approved by application to a justice of the peace. It is an offence to obstruct authorised officers in the carrying out of their duties, either physically or by failing to provide appropriate assistance or information.[23]

There is a range of options open to an authorised officer where he is of the opinion that food is likely to cause poisoning or disease. The first of these is the 'serving of notice'. An authorised officer can serve notice on the person in charge of food, which prevents him from using it for human consumption.[24] It is an offence to knowingly contravene the requirements of this notice. Alternatively, the food can be seized for further investigation, possibly leading to judicial inquiry.[25] However, the notice must be withdrawn where the authorised officer's inquiries indicate that there has been no breach of the food safety regulations. In either case, a decision on the safety of the food must be made within 21 days of the notice being served.[26] Where the matter does proceed to further judicial inquiry, undertaken initially by a magistrate, the person responsible for the food must be presented with the opportunity to be heard and to call witnesses before any decision on liability is made.[27] Initial liability may be limited to covering the expense involved in destroying the offending food. On the other hand, the food authority may have to compensate the owner of the food where the justice of the peace has found that there has been no breach of the legislation.[28]

Being issued with an 'improvement notice' usually indicates that there has been a more serious, or persistent, breach of the food safety legislation. This is served where the authorised officer has reasonable grounds for believing that a food business is failing to comply with the relevant safety regulations.[29] An improvement notice must contain certain information, including a statement of the grounds on which it is based, an identification of the specific matters which illustrate the failure to comply with the regulations, an outline of the measures that need to be taken in order to secure compliance and a date by which this must happen— which must allow at least 14 days for this to happen. It is an offence to fail to act on an improvement notice.[30] Improvement notices are usually issued where hygienic conditions or practices have not been employed by the food business operator.[31] They may also be issued to compel or prohibit the use of a particular process or treatment in the preparation of food, such as freezing, refrigeration, ionisation or

---

[23] Section 33.
[24] Section 9(3)(a).
[25] Section 9(3)(b).
[26] Section 9(4).
[27] Sections 9(5) and (6).
[28] Section 9(7). Disputes over the amount of compensation payable should be resolved by arbitration.
[29] Section 10(1).
[30] Section 10(2).
[31] The law related to hygienic production is discussed in more detail in ch 6.

pasteurisation. It is possible to appeal against the issue of an improvement notice, at which stage it can be either cancelled or confirmed by the court.[32]

The most serious breaches of the Food Safety Act can lead to the serving of prohibition orders or, where required, emergency or control orders. Prohibition orders can effectively be used to close a food business, often by preventing it from using its premises or equipment.[33] The order can also be issued against an individual, prohibiting him from being involved in the management of any food business.[34] The seriousness of such an order is reflected in the fact that they must be issued by a court.[35] They usually follow the conviction of a food business operator for a breach of the regulations that is likely to carry a public health risk. The order continues to have effect until the authority can be satisfied that sufficient measures have been taken to eliminate the health risk that was previously identified.[36] In some circumstances, however, the order can only be lifted by the court.[37] Emergency prohibition notices can be served by authorised officers following an application to a magistrate.[38] They are issued to food business operators where an immediate risk to health is identified. It continues to have effect until sufficient measures have been taken to address the problem.[39] Emergency control orders are only issued in the most serious of circumstances, usually where some wide-scale threat to public health is identified. They can be used to prohibit all operations that could contribute to the development or spread of this risk.[40] Both prohibition orders and emergency prohibition orders can be appealed to the Crown Court.[41]

While the issuing of notices and orders can help to immediately alleviate food safety concerns, convictions for a breach of the Act may of course follow. Certain defences are available to those against whom such an action has been brought.

Three specified defences can be made. The first is that the offence was actually committed because of the act or omission of another person.[42] A defendant who successfully employs this defence must be acquitted. The proper defendant is the person whose act or omission caused the situation to occur. The second available defence is that due diligence was exercised, provided that the accused can demonstrate that he took all reasonable precautions to avoid the commission of the offence by himself or by a person under his control.[43] Due diligence can also be demonstrated by those

---

[32] Section 39.

[33] Section 11(3).

[34] Section 11(4).

[35] Section 11(1).

[36] Section 11(6)(a).

[37] Section 11(6)(b). For example, the order has to be lifted by a court where it was originally issued following the conviction of the food business operator for a breach of the regulations.

[38] Section 12(1) and (2).

[39] Section 12(8).

[40] Section 13(1). Under section 13(3), some exemptions can be granted where the continuation of certain operations may be either necessary and/or carry a different level of risk to health.

[41] Section 38.

[42] Section 20.

[43] Section 21(1). See also: *Walker Snack Foods Ltd v Coventry City Council* [1998] 3 All ER 163. A company with a chain of shops must be able to show that it devised a proper system designed to ensure that the law was complied with. This system should include the regular organisation of checks, and the company must also be able to demonstrate that it properly selected, instructed and supervised staff. See *Tesco Supermarkets Ltd v Nattrass* [1971] 2 All ER 127.

who did not prepare or import the offending food if it can be shown that the food was made unsafe by someone else and that all reasonable safety checks were carried out.[44] Due diligence can only be used as a defence where the accused identifies, or takes all reasonable steps to identify, the other party involved, that is the one who it is claimed is responsible for making the food unsafe.[45] The third defence relates to those provisions of the Food Safety Act that deal with consumer protection.

As discussed in chapter seven, the descriptions that appear on food packaging are primarily dealt with by the Food Labelling Regulations 1996. However, there is also provision made in the Food Safety Act 1990 for aspects of this area of the law. As stated above, any person who sells food which is not of the nature or quality expected is guilty of an offence.[46] Any person who sells food that is falsely described on the label or which is likely to mislead the purchaser about the nature or quality of the food is also guilty of an offence.[47] This provision also applies to the advertising of food.[48] It may be argued as a defence in any proceedings brought under the advertising provisions that the offending advertisement was organised by and for someone else and that the accused could not have known, nor had any reason to suspect, that an offence was being committed.[49]

The sampling and analysis of food is central to any investigation into its safe use for human consumption. All food authorities must appoint qualified analysts for this purpose.[50] They must also establish suitable facilities for the necessary microbiological examinations.[51] Authorised officers are entitled to take samples of food or contact materials for examination, possibly also through an agent.[52]

---

[44] Section 21(2)–(4). It is also considered due diligence to have relied on a third party, as was the case in *Carrick District Council v Taunton Vale Meat Traders Ltd* (1994) 158 JP 347, where the respondent meat processors were cleared of selling food that did not meet the requirements of the Food Safety Act 1990 when they relied on a local authority authorised meat inspector who had deemed its product to be fit for human consumption. For further discussion on due diligence in this context see *Halsbury's Laws of England*, vol 18(2) para 465.

[45] Section 21(5).

[46] Section 14(1). However, it may not be an offence if the operator has carried out sufficient checks on his machinery to ensure that labelling accurately reflects, for example, the net quantity contained in the product. In *Bibby-Cheshire v Golden Wonder Ltd* [1972] 3 All ER 738, it was accepted by the court that machinery producing 20 million bags of crisps per week could not reasonably be expected to do so without some errors being made in the quantity included in some of these bags. An efficient system of random checking of the bags was deemed sufficient to show that there had been due diligence on the part of the producer.

[47] Section 15(1).

[48] Section 15(2).

[49] Section 22.

[50] Section 27. The reports of analysts are deemed to be vital evidence in cases brought for breaches of the Food Safety Act. The analyst or examiner therefore has to be very careful that the correct procedures are followed and the prescribed forms are used. It was found in *Newby v Sims* [1984] 1 QB 478 that a statement on the purity of rum, submitted in evidence, was too vague as it did not make specific reference to the water content percentage in the allegedly offending product. Similarly, in *Lee v Bent, Barlow and Noblett* [1901] 2 KB 290 a certificate stating that '[w]e are of opinion that the said sample contains a serious quantity of arsenic' was insufficiently precise. A statement that a sample contained 'milk, 94%; added water, 6% based on the fact that the sample contained 7.97% solids not fat, whereas genuine milk contains not less than 8.5% solids not fat' submitted in *Bridge v Howard* [1897] 1 QB 80, was held to be good due to the level of clarity and substantiating information provided.

[51] Section 28.

[52] Section 29. See also *Horder v Scott* (1880) 5 QBD 552; *Farley v Higginbotham* (1898) 42 Sol Jo 309; and *Tyler v Dairy Supply Co Ltd* (1908) 72 JP 132.

An analyst's certificate should usually be accepted and acted upon by the court, especially if there is no other evidence submitted to contradict it.[53] Further detail on the sampling and analysis of food is set out in the Food Safety (Sampling and Qualifications) (England) Regulations 2013.[54]

Immediate food safety concerns can be addressed by the issuing of notices and orders. In some circumstances, however, the act or omission of the accused can be so serious that criminal proceedings need to be taken. Any prosecution brought under the Food Safety Act 1990 must begin within three years of the commission of the offence or within one year of its discovery by the prosecutor.[55] Obstructing authorised officers in the course of their work is punishable by a significant fine (level 5 on the standard scale) or three months imprisonment, or both, on summary conviction.[56] Other offences committed under this Act can carry a fine and/ or imprisonment for up to two years, on indictment.[57]

5.3 BSE Crisis

Bovine spongiform encephalopathy (BSE) or 'mad cow disease' is a neurodegenerative disorder affecting cattle. It has a fatal effect on the brain and central nervous system. There is no treatment and no cure. There is strong evidence that BSE can be transmitted to humans as variant Creutzfeldt-Jakob disease (vCJD). Those infected can suffer hallucinations, delusions and unpleasant physical sensations, such as pain and numbness in the limbs. This can develop into poor balance, uncontrollable muscle movements and dementia. Finally, patients may have eating and swallowing difficulties and an inability to function for themselves. Again, there is no treatment or cure available. Average life expectancy following infection is around one year.

According to the Southwood Report, the first cases of BSE were detected in British cattle during the 1970s.[58] This had risen to 10,000 confirmed cases by the end of 1989. The BSE Inquiry reported that cattle had died from BSE infection as early as 1987.[59] In all probability, the disease was being spread amongst herds by

---

[53] *Harrison v Richards* (1881) 45 JP 552; *Robinson v Newman* (1917) 81 JP 187; and *Broughton v Whittaker* [1944] 2 All ER 544.

[54] SI No 264/2013.

[55] Section 34.

[56] Section 35(1). The obstruction should usually be deliberate and intentional in order to constitute an offence. See *R v Senior* [1899] 1 QB 283, CA; *Eaton v Cobb* [1950] 1 All ER 1016.

[57] Section 35(2).

[58] Report of the Working Party on Bovine Spongiform Encephalopathy (Southwood Report) (London, Department of Health/MAFF, 1989).

[59] The BSE Inquiry: The Report, The Inquiry into BSE and variant CJD in the United Kingdom (Phillips Report, 2000).

the consumption of animal feed that contained infected bone-meal. Early realisa-tions about this led to the introduction of domestic legislation on the matter in 1988.

5.3.1 Bovine Spongiform Encephalopathy Order 1988

The BSE Order 1988 was the first piece of domestic legislation passed to assist in dealing with the emergence and spread of the disease through contaminated ani-mal feed.[60] It prescribed that anyone who was in possession of a cow or carcass that was suspected of being affected with the disease was obliged to notify an appointed veterinary inspector as soon as possible.[61] It also provided veterinary inspectors with the power to prohibit the movement of suspected animals.[62] Perhaps most significantly, the Order prohibited the use of animal feed that contained material derived from a carcass—but only between July 1988 and January 1989.[63] This Order was the first in a series of inadequate responses to the growing crisis.[64]

5.3.2 EU Response to the BSE Crisis

One of the conclusions of the BSE Inquiry was that there was confusion during the period of the spread of the disease as to who had regulatory responsibility for dealing with the crisis. It was accepted, for example, that once definitive measures had been adopted by the European Commission, the national authorities ceased to be entitled to adopt any unilateral action designed to deal with the risks posed by the disease. The first Decision taken by the Commission was in 1989.[65] This obliged the UK authorities to do two things. First, it prohibited the export to other EU Member States of all live cattle born before July 1988—the date of the introduction of the animal feed ban by the BSE Order—and those born to female cattle suspected or confirmed as having the disease.[66] Second, the health certifi-cate that had to accompany all other exports, and which had been prescribed by EU Directive since 1964,[67] had now to include a statement that the BSE measures

---

[60] SI No 1039/1988.

[61] Art 4(1).

[62] Art 6.

[63] Art 7.

[64] The prohibition on using meat and bone meal in animal feed was officially recognised as being relatively ineffective in Recital 6, Preamble to Decision 1994/474, n 78 below.

[65] Commission Decision 1989/469/EEC concerning certain protection measures relating to bovine spongiform encephalopathy in the United Kingdom [1989] OJ L 225/51.

[66] ibid, Art 1.

[67] Art 3(2) and Annex F of Council Directive 1964/432/EEC of 26 June 1964 on animal health prob-lems affecting intra-Community trade in bovine animals and swine [1964] OJ 121/1977. For further discussion on EU rules on meat inspection systems see J Lawless and K Wiedemann, 'European meat inspection: continuity and change in building a (more) risk-based system of regulation' (2011) 6 *Euro-pean Food and Feed Law Review* 96.

adopted by this Decision had been complied with.[68] The Commission undertook to monitor developments in the evolving crisis.[69] However, there was no recognition of the potential dangers posed to human health at this time.[70]

The 1989 Commission Decision was amended soon after.[71] The limited ban on live cattle exports was altered, so that only those aged under six months old could be traded.[72] It was believed that these younger animals were unlikely to transmit the infection.[73] Obviously, the prohibition on the export of the offspring of infected cattle remained.[74] This Decision was supplemented in June 1990.[75] This extended the restrictions on exports of beef still attached to the bone which could not be certified as coming from holdings where there had been no cases of BSE for at least two years.[76] All nervous and lymphatic tissue had also to be removed.[77] Despite the fact that instances of BSE were now at a peak, there was no further legislative intervention until 1994. As will be discussed below, this lack of action was just one part of a whole range of negligent omissions, at both national and EU level, over the period.

By 1994 the crisis had deepened. In 1990, there were 14,181 confirmed cases of BSE in Britain, 12,611 of which were discovered in England. By 1994 this had risen to 23,943 and 20,322 respectively. The outbreak had peaked at almost 37,000 confirmed cases in Britain in 1992, and 1993 had been an almost equally bad year. Despite this, there was no significant legislative activity at EU level again until the end of July 1994.[78] This extended the restriction on the exportation of 'bone-in' beef to that which came from herds which were BSE free for at least six years.[79]

It had been presumed that the measures already taken were significant in reducing the levels of BSE incidents by 1994.[80] While the numbers of confirmed cases was in decline, these were still at very high levels—ten times what they had been

---

[68] Art 2.

[69] Art 4 of Decision 1989/469, n 65 above.

[70] The Preamble to Decision 1989/469, n 65 above, only makes reference to the disease being considered as a 'new serious contagious or infectious animal disease whose presence may constitute a danger to cattle in other Member States' (Recital 2).

[71] Commission Decision 1990/59/EEC of 7 February 1990 amending Decision 1989/469/EEC concerning certain protection measures relating to bovine spongiform encephalopathy in the United Kingdom [1990] OJ L 41/23.

[72] ibid, Art 1.

[73] Recital 4 of Preamble to Decision 1990/59, n 71 above.

[74] Art 1 of Decision 1990/59.

[75] Commission Decision 1990/261 of 8 June 1990 amending Decision 1989/469/EEC concerning certain protection measures relating to bovine spongiform encephalopathy (BSE) in the United Kingdom and Decision 1990/200/EEC concerning additional requirements for some tissues and organs with respect to bovine spongiform encephalopathy [1990] OJ L 146/29.

[76] ibid, Art 2.

[77] Art 2(2).

[78] Commission Decision 1994/474/EC of 27 July 1994 concerning certain protection measures relating to bovine spongiform encephalopathy and repealing Decisions 1989/469/EEC and 1990/200/EEC [1994] OJ L 194/96.

[79] ibid, Art 4(1).

[80] Recital 3 of Preamble to Decision 1994/474, n 78 above.

when the BSE Order was introduced in 1988. The EU Commission did undertake to keep the situation under continual review.[81] The most significant development of all in this regard came with the Spongiform Encephalopathy Advisory Committee (SEAC) Report to the Government in 1996, which concluded that there was probably a link between the consumption of beef from BSE-infected cattle and the development of vCJD in humans. This resulted in the taking of highly interventionist action by both the EU Commission and the UK authorities.

In March 1996, the Commission decided to ban the exportation of all live cattle, all beef, all products obtained from slaughtered cattle and all animal feed containing meat and bone meal, with immediate effect.[82] The Commission obliged the UK to report every two weeks on the application of all protective measures taken to control the spread of BSE.[83] The UK would, however, also be provided with the opportunity to present further proposals to the Commission on alternative control measures.[84] While there was recognition that the outright ban on all UK exports was temporary,[85] the Decision was highly controversial and thought to be unnecessary, going beyond that which was required to control the spread of the disease. This belief that the prohibition on all exports was disproportionate would ultimately face examination by the European Court of Justice in two significant cases,[86] which are discussed in more detail later on in this chapter.

While it continued to be accepted that infected meat and meat products could lead to the development of vCJD in humans, a position that was given further support by the conclusion of the Advisory Committee on Dangerous Pathogens (ACDP) in September 1997 that the BSE agent should be classified as a human pathogen, it was also acknowledged that the measures adopted by the EU and the UK were having some impact on reducing the spread of the disease. New findings also showed that the ban on exports could be lifted for some products, such as gelatin and tallow. Research suggested that the use of these, along with bovine semen, was safe.[87] However, a traceability system would have to be put in place for these products to ensure that they could be easily recalled from the market should any concerns about their use resurface.[88]

The ban on the exportation of British beef and cattle ended up lasting, in various forms, for an entire decade. The first partial resumption of the exportation of

---

[81] ibid, Recital 4.

[82] Commission Decision 1996/239/EC of 27 March 1996 on emergency measures to protect against bovine spongiform encephalopathy [1996] OJ L 78/47.

[83] ibid, Art 3.

[84] ibid, Art 4.

[85] Art 1 of Decision 1996/239, n 82 above, states that the ban is introduced '[p]ending an overall examination of the situation'.

[86] Case C-180/1996 *United Kingdom v Commission* and Case C-157/1996 *Queen v National Farmers' Union*, n 146 below.

[87] Preamble to Council Decision 1998/256/EC of 16 March 1998 concerning emergency measures to protect against bovine spongiform encephalopathy, amending Decision 1994/474/EC and repealing Decision 1996/239/EC [1998] OJ L 113/32.

[88] ibid, Art 5.

some beef products from the UK was permitted only from 1 August 1999.[89] Some EU Member States, most notably France, refused to lift the ban and were consequently threatened with legal action by the Commission, the Court of Justice later deciding that they were in breach of their obligations under the relevant Decisions.[90] The ban on exporting 'bone-in' beef (meat attached to bone) and live cattle remained in place until 2006.[91] The decision to reverse the prohibition on exports was made following a unanimous opinion of the EU Standing Committee on the Food Chain and Animal Health, supporting a Commission proposal to lift the embargo. Two conditions had to be satisfied before the EU institutions would consider this course of action. First, there had to be an incidence of less than 200 BSE cases per million adult bovine animals. The European Food Safety Authority confirmed that this was the case in May 2004. Second, there would have to be a positive report from the EU Food and Veterinary Office (FVO) indicating that there was proper enforcement of BSE controls in the UK. An inspection carried out by the FVO in June 2005 confirmed that this was the case.

5.3.3 Domestic Response to the BSE Crisis

While there were many EU Decisions and Regulations established in the effort to restrict the spread of BSE during the 1990s and beyond, there was also a plethora of domestic controls designed to deal with this crisis introduced at the same time, dating back to the BSE Order in 1988 discussed above. Further examples include the Beef (Emergency Control) Order 1996[92] and the Specified Bovine Material Order 1996,[93] both of which were published the day after the EU announced that it was banning British beef exports. This body of domestic legislation introduced a further range of significant measures restricting the conditions under which beef could be produced and sold in the UK.

The Specified Bovine Material Order was one of the most significant of the domestic measures introduced to deal with BSE. Under the Order, anything classified as 'specified bovine material', or anything containing any of this material, could not be sold by anyone.[94] This included all parts of the head (except for the

---

[89] Art 1 of Commission Decision 1999/514/EC of 23 July 1999 setting the date on which dispatch from the United Kingdom of bovine products under the date-based export scheme may commence by virtue of Art 6(5) of Council Decision 1998/256/EC [1999] OJ L 195/42. Initially, this partial resumption was to be for cattle born, reared and slaughtered in Northern Ireland only, but this was later amended to include other parts of the UK by Commission Decision 1998/692/EC of 25 November 1998 amending Decision 1998/256/EC as regards certain emergency measures to protect against bovine spongiform encephalopathy [1998] OJ L 328/28.

[90] Case C-1/2000 *Commission v France* [2001] ECR I-9989.

[91] Annex to Commission Regulation (EC) No 657/2006 of 10 April 2006 amending Regulation (EC) No 999/2001 of the European Parliament and of the Council as regards the United Kingdom and repealing Council Decision 1998/256/EC and Decisions 1998/351/EC and 1999/514/EC [2006] OJ L 116/9.

[92] SI No 961/1996.

[93] SI No 963/1996.

[94] Art 4.

tongue), spinal cord, spleen, thymus, tonsils and intestines of all cattle over six months old, or younger in some circumstances.[95] The Order also prohibited the use of meat recovered from the vertebral column by mechanical means, although it could be used for gelatine production.[96] A lot of these parts of the animal could not even be removed from the slaughterhouse, except for veterinary or scientific examination.[97] Incineration and rendering plants would face tighter controls.[98]

The Beef (Emergency Control) Order 1996 was used to introduce what is widely regarded as the most interventionist of all of the domestic legislative responses to the crisis. It prohibited the sale of all beef that came from cattle that were more than 30 months old at the time of slaughter.[99] This ban was to last until November 2005, when it was lifted by the Bovine Products (Restrictions on Placing on the Market) (England) Regulations.[100] The use of meat from cattle was now only limited to that coming from animals born before 1 August 1996,[101] provided that it was slaughtered at an approved abattoir, and in accordance with the provisions of the EU Transmissible Spongiform Encephalopathy Regulation 2001, which is discussed in more detail below. The 'over 30 month' rule was only revoked after the Food Standards Agency was satisfied that the system for testing cattle for disease was suitable and robust.

Huge volumes of domestic legislation was, and continues to be, introduced in the UK to first, deal with BSE at its most rampant and then, to minimise the possibility of its devastating impact reoccurring.[102] The primary measures that continue to apply include strict controls over slaughterhouses, animal feed and testing methods, including all of those set out in applicable EU regulations.

5.3.4 Transmissible Spongiform Encephalopathies Regulation 2001

By the time the ban on the exportation of beef from the UK was lifted in 2006, the direct cost to the sector was estimated to be in the region of £675 million. There were, of course, many other significant costs attached to the range of measures introduced to deal with the BSE crisis. According to the Report of the BSE Inquiry, domestic beef consumption declined by around 35 per cent,[103] although this rose

---

[95] Art 2(1).

[96] Art 5. The ban on the use of the vertebral column was originally introduced by the Specified Bovine Offal (Amendment) Order 1995, SI No 3246/1995.

[97] See, eg, Arts 12 and 13.

[98] Arts 17 and 18.

[99] Art 2, as amended by the Beef (Emergency Control)(Amendment) Order 1996, SI No 1043/1996.

[100] SI No 2719/2005.

[101] Art 3.

[102] For example, cattle must carry 'passports' if they are to be moved around, or into or out of, Britain under the terms of the Cattle Passports Order 1996, SI No 1686/1996.

[103] Findings of a report to the Minister of Agriculture, Fisheries and Food and the Secretary of State for Health. *The BSE Inquiry: The Report* (London, The Stationery Office, 2001).

again after the introduction of the 30-month rule. The Inquiry itself was estimated to have cost around £27 million. Beef prices fell by around 25 per cent. The
total cost of aid and compensation was thought to stand at around £5 billion, in
an industry that employed 130,000 workers. Millions of cattle were slaughtered.[104]

There were two significant reports on the way the BSE crisis was handled. The
first of these, the British BSE Inquiry, chaired by Lord Phillips, found that there
were a whole range of problems identifiable with the way in which the disease
was dealt with during the 1990s. These ranged from the practical, such as using
meat and bone meal as an ingredient of animal feed, to the legal, including both
the lack of suitable measures and the failure to apply those restrictions that were
introduced. A series of shortcomings were identified with the way in which EU
law and domestic regulation interacted on the matter. It stated, for example, that it
was generally accepted that the UK was not entitled to adopt unilateral measures
to deal with BSE as soon as the EU Commission started taking action. National
authorities were also constrained by the terms of secondary EU legislation, such as
directives on veterinary checks,[105] and zootechnical checks.[106] This, in turn, could
call into question the lawfulness of those domestic measures that were adopted,
such at the Specified Bovine Offal (Amendment) Order 1995.[107] The Inquiry concluded that this could all potentially have important consequences for the way in
which any future food crises could be responded to at national level, although the
significance of this is now probably reduced by the inclusion of safeguard clauses
in the relevant EU legislation.[108]

The second report, the European Parliament Report, identified shortcomings
with both the UK and the EU responses.[109] It noted how, despite the incidence
of BSE being at peak levels in the early 1990s, EU legislative activity to control
the spread of the disease was suspended during this period. The Council held
no debates on the matter between 1990 and 1994. Ultimately, the Parliament
found that the Council and the Commission, along with the UK authorities, had
neglected their duties.

The framework legislation that was finally introduced to deal properly with the
potential for BSE or similar diseases to create another crisis in the future, reducing

---

[104] Most of this data comes from a report by Nigel Atkinson, Head of Economics (International)
Division, Ministry of Agriculture, Fisheries and Food, entitled 'The impact of BSE on the UK economy'
(1999). The figures presented here are revised to take account of other estimates. They are for indicative
purposes only, as the estimates vary depending on the method of calculation used. The exact costs are
substantial, but uncertain.

[105] Council Directive 1989/662/EEC of 11 December 1989 concerning veterinary checks in intra-
Community trade with a view to the completion of the internal market [1989] OJ L 395/13.

[106] Council Directive 1990/425/EEC of 26 June 1990 concerning veterinary and zootechnical checks
applicable in intra-Community trade in certain live animals and products with a view to the completion of the internal market [1990] OJ L 224/29.

[107] SI No 3246/1995; see also n 96 above.

[108] Such as that set out in Reg 999/2001, n 110 below.

[109] European Parliament Report on alleged contraventions or maladministration in the implementation of Community law in relation to BSE, without prejudice to the jurisdiction of the Community
and national courts, as established by EP Decision of 17 July 1996, OJ C 239/1.

the need for ad hoc and piecemeal legislative responses, is the Transmissible Spongiform Encephalopathies (TSE) Regulation 2001.[110] This Regulation sets classifications for EU Member States and third countries or regions, according to their BSE status.[111] A State can be deemed as being either 'BSE free', 'BSE provisionally free with no reported cases', 'BSE provisionally free with at least one reported case', 'low incidence of BSE' or 'high incidence of BSE'.[112] Categories are determined after a detailed risk analysis has been conducted, as well as other factors, such as the extent to which there is an education programme for veterinary practitioners, breeders and those who transport, trade in and slaughter cattle which seeks to encourage them to report all cases of neurological manifestations in adult animals. Account is also taken of whether there is compulsory reporting and examination of cattle showing signs of BSE, continuous surveillance and monitoring systems and laboratory testing.[113] A country is 'free of BSE' if it complies with all of these conditions for at least seven years and it has had no reported cases of BSE or, where there have been reported cases, these were shown to have affected imported cattle only. A country or region has a 'high incidence of BSE' where it complies with the conditions but still has a BSE incidence rate of greater than 100 cases per million cattle over 24 months of age. There can be no trade in live cattle or beef products with States who have not had their BSE status classified by the European Commission.[114] The degree to which a State can engage in cross-border trade in meat and live animals is determined on the basis of their BSE status.[115] For example, there are no restrictions on trade with countries or regions whose status is 'BSE free', provided that imports are accompanied by an international animal health certificate attesting that the country of origin complies with the conditions set out in the Regulation. However, if the imports are coming from a State where there is a 'high incidence of BSE', then additional supporting evidence must be provided to show that the use of animal feed containing any meat or bone has been banned and that all affected cattle are killed and completely destroyed. Live animals can only be imported into any EU Member State if they were born after the date on which the animal feed ban was introduced and properly enforced. Further, such animals must have been born, raised and have remained in herds in which no case of BSE has been confirmed for at least seven years.

The TSE Regulation also introduces a monitoring system, to be systematically applied in each EU Member State.[116] Details are provided on how sampling is to

---

[110] Regulation (EC) No 999/2001 of the European Parliament and of the Council of 22 May 2001 laying down rules for the prevention, control and eradication of certain transmissible spongiform encephalopathies [2001] OJ L 147/1.

[111] Art 5(1).

[112] Annex II, Chapter C to Reg 999/2001, n 110 above.

[113] Annex II, Chapter A to Reg 999/2001, n 110 above.

[114] Art 5(1) of Reg 999/2001.

[115] Annex IX to Reg 999/2001.

[116] Art 6.

take place, to test for incidence of one of the TSE diseases—scrapie—and BSE.[117] The results of this analysis must be submitted on an annual basis by DEFRA to the European Commission. There are two categories of surveillance of TSEs that take place in the UK. The first is 'passive surveillance'. This involves the reporting of suspected cases of BSE and scrapie to the local DEFRA Animal Health Divisional Office, branches of which are located all around the country. As outlined above, TSEs are known as 'notifiable diseases', meaning that it is an offence not to report suspected cases. Farmers are compensated for animals that have to be destroyed as a result of this reporting.[118] The second type of monitoring is 'active surveillance'. This is that which is prescribed by the TSE Regulation. It is carried out on an ongoing basis by the DEFRA executive agency, the Animal Health and Veterinary Laboratories Agency (AHVLA), formed after the merger of the Veterinary Laboratories Agency with Animal Health in April 2011.

Other significant provisions set out in the TSE Regulation include the prohibition on using protein derived from mammals in ruminant feed (that for cattle and sheep),[119] the removal and destruction of specified risk material,[120] restrictions on the use of ruminant material in the production of certain products,[121] restrictions on the movement of suspected animals,[122] and details of the measures to be taken following confirmation of the presence of a TSE.[123] All of these requirements are incorporated into English law. Finally, the Regulation provides that the legislation and its implementation is to be kept under review by the European Commission, assisted by the Standing Committee on the Food Chain and Animal Health, and is therefore subject to change at any time should circumstances dictate this.[124] The Regulation came into effect on 1 July 2001.[125]

5.4 White Paper on Food Safety

The need for a radical overhaul of food safety regulation became obvious during the BSE crisis. Existing legislation was shown to be inadequate, unable to deal with outbreaks of deadly transmissible disease. Ad hoc measures, when introduced,

---

[117] Annex III, Chapter A to Reg 999/2001, n 110 above.

[118] Under the terms of the Bovine Spongiform Encephalopathy Compensation Order 1996, SI No 3184/1996.

[119] Art 7.

[120] Art 8. Specified risk material, for the purposes of Reg 999/2001, includes spinal cord, brain, eyes, intestines and spleen, amongst others, as listed in Annex V to the Regulation. Other details on the removal and destruction of these animal parts is also set out in this section of the legislation.

[121] Art 9.

[122] Art 12.

[123] Art 13.

[124] Arts 22–25. Alterations to the requirements set out in the Annexes to the Regulation are made using the comitology procedure (Art 23 in conjunction with Art 24(2)).

[125] Art 26.

had two major flaws. First, they often fell some way short of achieving their stated aim by dealing with only one element of what really needed to be a more far-reaching and holistic response. This reduced public confidence in the efficacy of the entire regulatory system. The introduction of measure after measure after measure suggests that those charged with controlling a crisis are not intervening at an appropriate level at any stage, otherwise there would be no need for a range of different responses or rules to be introduced over a protracted period of time— much the same way as the handling of the EU financial crisis from 2009 onwards failed to satisfy the markets that any of the steps taken to deal with sovereign debt would actually ever resolve the matter. Second, from a legal perspective, the failure to deal with BSE at the earliest possible stage led to the taking of questionable action by the Commission when introducing the ban on British exports in 1996.[126] This was contrary to Treaty provisions on the free movement of goods. The only support for this lay in principles that did not exist. This is discussed in more detail below, but for now it is sufficient to say that the Court of Justice, in upholding the ban, used reasoning that was based on aspects of environmental law and, given that the Treaty of Amsterdam had not come into existence, could not yet be applied to food law.

The proposals for amending EU-wide rules and systems for ensuring that food is safe were presented in the White Paper on Food Safety in January 2000.[127] A 'radical new approach' was proposed, with a view to 'enabl[ing] food safety to be organised in a more co-ordinated and integrated manner'.[128] There would be an overhaul of the existing system at five different levels to ensure that this happened.

The first, and in some ways most significant, proposal for change was the establishment of a new 'European Food Authority'.[129] This was deemed to be 'the most appropriate response to the need to guarantee a high level of food safety'. Food safety legislation would be amended to make it more coherent, 'covering all aspects of food products from farm to table'. This would involve over 80 separate alterations being made in the short term to existing legislation. The third area identified as being in need of reform was food controls. The evidence suggested that there were wide variations in the manner in which EU food law was being implemented and enforced, meaning that consumers were not receiving the same level of protection across the Union. It was therefore proposed that, in co-operation with the Member States, a new framework for the development and operation of national control systems would have to be developed. It was also envisaged that there would be an increased role for consumers in the development

---

[126] Commission Decision 1996/239, n 82 above. Some of the other reasons as to why BSE was able to spread in the way in which it did are discussed in H Pennington, *When food kills: BSE, E. coli and disaster science* (Oxford, OUP, 2003).

[127] COM (1999) 719.

[128] ibid, Executive Summary.

[129] For an insider's background into the formation of the European Food Safety Authority see D Byrne, 'The genesis of EFSA and the first 10 years of EU food law' in A Alemanno and S Gabbi (eds), *Foundations of EU Food Law and Policy* (Farnham, Ashgate, 2013).

of food safety policy. Lines of communication between the Commission and the public would have to be improved in times of crisis or concern. New labelling legislation that would bring about 'helpful and clearly presented' information would be introduced. Finally, the EU would undertake to play an active role in international bodies as 'an important element in explaining European developments in food safety'. All the other actions proposed would have to be effectively presented and explained to EU trading partners, especially considering that the Union, as a whole, is the world's largest importer/exporter of food.

5.4.1 Principles of Food Safety

Chapter 2 of the White Paper set out a series of general principles that would be applied to 'transform EU food policy into a proactive, dynamic, coherent and comprehensive instrument to ensure a high level of human health and consumer protection'.

The first of these was that this policy should be based on a comprehensive and integrated approach. This meant that controls had to be systematically applied throughout the food chain, at all stages of production and across all food sectors, regardless of where any of the production activity takes place.

The second principle set out was that responsibility for safety would have to rest firmly with all stakeholders. Those involved in manufacturing feed, farmers, manufacturers, Member State and third country competent authorities, the Commission and consumers would all have a clearly defined role in ensuring that food was safe to eat.

Third, traceability would be central to food safety policy. This would become central to ensuring that concerns could be properly addressed at the earliest opportunity, and in the most effective way, as soon as issues arise.

Transparency in decision making was declared to be another of these principles. All stakeholders would be allowed to make effective contributions to policy development. Publicising scientific opinions and inspection reports would be extended to more aspects of food safety.

The fifth principle espoused in the White Paper was to use systematic risk analysis as the foundation upon which food safety policy should be based. The best scientific information available would be used in developing new measures.

Related to this is the precautionary principle, which would now have to be applied in the taking of all risk management decisions.

Finally, the seventh general principle guiding food safety policy is that other legitimate factors relevant for the protection of consumer health and the promotion of fair practices in food trade should be taken into account. This includes consideration for the environment, animal welfare, sustainable agriculture, quality expectations and the provision of fair information on the essential characteristics of products and their method of production.

5.5 General Food Law Regulation

The White Paper on Food Safety was itself subject to the very type of stakeholder interest that the report itself saw as critical. A consultation process followed its publication. Comments and analysis were received from the European Economic and Social Committee, the European Parliament, Member States, select committees—including that of the House of Lords, as well as food and drink federations and associations. The final product of all of this was the publication of a new General Food Law Regulation in January 2002,[130] which now forms the framework for all food safety law in the EU and the Member States, including Britain.

5.5.1 Key Provisions of Regulation 178/2002

The General Food Law Regulation 'provides the basis for the assurance of a high level of protection of human health and consumers' interest in relation to food'.[131] One of the main ways in which it will achieve this is through providing 'a strong science base, efficient organisational arrangements and procedures to underpin decision-making in matters of food and feed safety'.[132]

Defining 'Food' and 'Food Law'

The Regulation defines 'food' as 'any substance or product, whether processed, partially processed or unprocessed, intended to be, or reasonably expected to be ingested by humans'.[133] This includes drink, chewing gum, and any other substance, including water, which was intentionally incorporated into food during manufacture or treatment. It does not include animal feed, which is defined elsewhere in the Regulation, live animals, plants prior to harvesting, medicinal products,[134] cosmetics,[135] narcotics,[136] or residues and contaminants. 'Food law' is defined as:

> [T]he laws, regulations and administrative provisions governing food in general, and food safety in particular, whether at [Union] or national level; it covers any stage of production, processing and distribution of food, and also of feed produced for, or fed to, food-producing animals.[137]

---

[130] Regulation (EC) No 178/2002 of the European Parliament and of the Council of 28 January 2002 laying down the general principles and requirements of food law, establishing the European Food Safety Authority and laying down procedures in matters of food safety [2002] OJ L 31/1.

[131] ibid, Art 1(1).

[132] Also Art 1(1).

[133] Art 2.

[134] As defined by Council Directives 1965/56/EEC, [1965] OJ 22, and 1992/73/EEC, [1973] OJ L 297/8.

[135] Within the meaning prescribed by Council Directive 1976/768/EEC, [1976] OJ L 262/169.

[136] As classified by the United Nations Single Convention on Narcotic Drugs 1961.

[137] Art 3(1).

Finally, 'feed' is 'any substance or product, including additives, whether processed or unprocessed, intended to be used for oral feeding to animals'.[138]

General Principles of Food Law

The Regulation sets out a number of objectives for food law. These are listed as including the protection of human life and health, the protection of consumers' interests, fair practices in food trade, the protection of animal health and welfare, and the protection of plant health and the environment.[139] In addition to this, food law is also to be designed in a way that facilitates free movement. International standards, where they exist or where their completion is imminent, should, according to the Regulation, be taken into account when food laws are being developed or adapted in any way, unless these are deemed to be inappropriate or sufficiently different from EU policy or norms.[140]

The principles of food safety, listed in the White Paper, are to be used in order to ensure that these general objectives of food law are met. This includes the use of appropriate risk analysis in the development and application of food law.[141] 'Risk analysis' is defined as 'a process consisting of three interconnected components: risk assessment, risk management and risk communication'.[142] The assessment element is to be based on available scientific evidence, considered in 'an independent, objective and transparent manner'.[143] A decision is then made on how best to deal with the nature and level of the risk identified as a result of this assessment. This is 'risk management'. The Regulation makes it clear that the opinion of the European Food Safety Authority is central to deciding on what steps to take to manage the risk.[144] A further consideration is that any measures taken should be based on the need to prevent identified risks from being fully realised. This is known as the 'precautionary principle', and it has become a central part of all food safety law, as well as other aspects of food law more generally.

Precautionary Principle

The General Food Law Regulation provides that

> [i]n specific circumstances where, following an assessment of available information, the possibility of harmful effects on health is identified but scientific uncertainty persists, provisional risk management measures necessary to ensure the high level of health

---

[138] Art 3(4).
[139] Art 5(1). For more on this see B van der Meulen, 'The function of food law: on the objectives of food law, legitimate factors and interests taken into account' (2010) 5 *European Food and Feed Law Review* 83.
[140] Art 5(3).
[141] Art 6(1).
[142] Art 3(10).
[143] Art 6(2).
[144] Art 6(3).

protection chosen in the [Union] may be adopted, pending further scientific information for a more comprehensive risk assessment.[145]

This is the formal legal presentation of the 'precautionary principle', as it applies to food law across the EU. It is a relatively simple proposition. Its application is fraught with difficulties.

Article 191 TFEU provides that 'Union policy ... shall be based on the precautionary principle and on the principles that preventive action should be taken'. This relates to environmental law only.

This is the first problem with the precautionary principle. Its application to food law has no legal basis in the Treaty. Despite this, the European Court of Justice formally extended the principle to food law on the basis of this Treaty provision. When deliberating in the BSE cases,[146] the Court stated that '[w]here there is uncertainty as to the existence or extent of risks to human health, the institutions may take protective measures without having to wait until the reality and seriousness of those risks become fully apparent'.[147] This is merely a restatement of previous decisions, such as that in *Sandoz*.[148] It is, in essence, the precautionary principle, and it had already been an accepted part of the Court's jurisprudence for some time. However, the Court then went on to formalise this as a principle of EU law derived from the Treaty. It stated that '[the purpose of Article 191 TFEU determines that Union] policy on the environment is to pursue the objective *inter alia* of protecting human health [and] that policy is to aim at a high level of protection and is to be based in particular on the principles that preventive action should be taken and that environmental protection requirements must be integrated into the definition and implementation of other [Union] policies'.[149]

Food safety and environmental protection are not connected, in law or in fact. Using teleological interpretative techniques to make a connection between Article 191 TFEU and the BSE crisis, or matters of food safety more generally, is taking this to a new, unjustifiable level. It makes no sense. This is especially so when one considers that Treaty provisions on health protection did not even exist in their current, stronger form at the time. While the Treaty of Amsterdam did amend the Treaty to include the provision that '[Union] action ... shall be directed towards improving public health, preventing human illness and diseases, and obviating sources of danger to human health',[150] this did not happen until after the judgments in the BSE cases were delivered. There was not therefore any relevant Treaty

---

[145] Art 7(1).

[146] Case C-180/1996 *United Kingdom v Commission* [1998] ECR I-2265 and Case C-157/1996 *Queen v National Farmers' Union* [1998] ECR I-2211.

[147] Para 99 of *UK v Commission* and para 63 of *Queen v NFU*, n 146 above.

[148] Case 174/1982 *Criminal proceedings against Sandoz BV* [1983] ECR 2445, where the Court stated, in para 16, that '[i]nsofar as there are uncertainties at the present state of scientific research it is for the Member States to decide what degree of protection of the health and life of humans they intend to ensure'.

[149] Para 100 of *UK v Commission* and para 64 of *Queen v NFU*, n 146 above.

[150] Former Art 152 EC. For more on this see ch 2.

provision in existence at the time that could be used in conjunction with Article 191 TFEU to formalise the application of the precautionary principle to human health protection. The real legal basis for the application of the principle to food safety matters is that which now appears in Article 7 of Regulation 178/2002. It continues to have no foundation for food law in the TFEU.[151]

The legislation remains open to serious criticism given that the real basis for the application of one of the most important principles of the entire food safety regime may be undermined because it is not found in any substantive Treaty provision. While this may seem like an academic point, it remains a significant one, despite the existence of Article 7 of the General Food Law Regulation. Use of the precautionary principle provides one of the most significant and potentially far-reaching exceptions to the free movement of goods between EU Member States. It allows the EU institutions to prohibit trade in goods where it has reason to believe that this is necessary to protect human health. However, this reason does not need to be conclusive. There just has to be a 'possibility of harmful effects on health'.

Despite the significance of this exception to a fundamental freedom enshrined in EU law, it continues to have no proper legal basis in the TFEU, unlike other grounds permitting derogation from this principle, such as that set out in Article 36 TFEU.[152] The key difference here is that Article 36 TFEU sets out when Member States, such as the UK, can justify taking action or adopting measures that are contrary to the free movement of goods. The same right for the EU institutions is not provided for anywhere in the Treaty. It has not therefore been negotiated and/or accepted by the Member States on the same basis. No unanimity was required to introduce this vitally important exception to free movement into EU law. Instead, it was codified into the law by the use of secondary legislation, relying on the Court's previous extension of the precautionary principle from environmental protection into food law, the reasoning for which was, and has remained, flawed. The EU institutions have become empowered to take precautionary action on the basis of poor legal reasoning. The consequences of this type of action are potentially devastating, as British beef farmers are only too aware.

This brings us to the second problem with the precautionary principle. Neither the legislation, nor the related case law, makes it clear as to what is considered sufficient evidence supporting the taking of precautionary action. Article 7 of the General Food Law Regulation makes reference to 'an assessment of available information'. A European Commission Communication makes reference to three conditions that must exist before there can be recourse to the precautionary principle.[153]

First, there must be an identification of potentially negative effects. Some risk, or potential risk, to human health must be identified. This alone is not,

---

[151] For further discussion on this see C MacMaoláin, 'Using the precautionary principle to protect human health' (2003) 28 *EL Rev* 723, 732.

[152] As discussed in ch 4.

[153] Communication from the Commission on the precautionary principle, COM (2000) 1.

of course, enough. The risk must be evaluated. This is the second condition. A scientific assessment of the potential adverse effects must be undertaken. There must be reliable scientific data presented which, on logical reasoning, leads to the conclusion that there is a possibility of negative impact on health. The potential severity of the risk must be evaluated, taking consideration of all relevant factors, including possible damage levels, persistency, reversibility and delayed effect. This assessment should be as comprehensive as the circumstances allow. The Communication states that it must consist of four components: hazard identification, hazard characterisation, appraisal of exposure and risk characterisation. An attempt should be made to complete these four steps before any decision to take action is taken. The third condition that must exist before the precautionary principle can be invoked is that there must be some degree of scientific uncertainty. This may arise, for example, because the evidence is incomplete or is contested. The assessment indicates that the data is insufficient, inconclusive or imprecise, making it impossible to determine the level or nature of the risk with sufficient certainty.

If the three conditions are met, and the precautionary principle is invoked, it will lead to the adoption of some sort of measure, unless, of course, it is determined that no measure is necessary. The decision to take action is a political one. Decision makers are charged with weighing up the results of the assessment process with the degree to which the level of risk identified would be acceptable to society. It is then for the Court of Justice to determine whether action taken by the EU institutions, if challenged, is valid. The Commission Communication on the precautionary principle makes it clear that the Court accepts that its role at this stage is limited to examining whether the institution involved 'committed a manifest error or misuse of power or manifestly exceeds the limits of its power of appraisal'. This should mean that measures adopted in an arbitrary fashion should not apply.[154]

This brings us to the third identifiable problem with the precautionary principle—it can be used to make arbitrary, political decisions that are unsupported by sufficiently sound scientific evidence. A clear example of this happening in practice is evident from the judgment in one of the most significant cases in this area, *Pfizer*.[155] Here, the applicant contested the validity of a 1998 Council Regulation which prohibited the use of four previously approved antibiotics in animal feed.[156] The applicant was, at the time, the only producer of one of the

---

[154] Arbitrariness in precautionary decision making should also be avoided to prevent conflict with WTO obligations. For discussion on the operation of the precautionary principle in the international legal context see N Salmon, 'A European perspective on the precautionary principle: food safety and the free trade imperative of the WTO' (2002) 27 *EL Rev* 138.

[155] Case T-13/1999 *Pfizer Animal Health SA v Council* [2002] ECR II-3305. A very similar judgment, based on similar facts, was delivered on the same day in Case T-70/1999 *Alpharma Inc v Council* [2002] ECR II-3495.

[156] Council Regulation (EC) No 2821/1998 of 17 December 1998 amending, as regards withdrawal of the authorisation of certain antibiotics, Directive 1970/524 concerning additives in feedingstuffs [1998] OJ L 351/4.

banned antibiotics, virginiamycin, in the world. They were thus able to bring an application under Article 263 TFEU to the General Court, seeking an annulment of this Regulation.

It was accepted by all parties to the case that the contested Regulation had been introduced as a precautionary measure, as neither the reality nor the seriousness of the risk had been scientifically proven. The main argument put forward by the applicant was that the risk assessment used to take this action was incomplete and erroneous. It was claimed that the Union institutions, in particular the Commission and the Council, had failed in two ways. First, they arbitrarily chose one body of evidence, supplied by Denmark, over another, which included a negative appraisal by the Scientific Committee for Animal Nutrition (SCAN) of this Danish dossier. Second, they re-interpreted the advice which suggested there was no risk posed to human health by continued use of the antibiotics. It is not within the scope of this book to evaluate whether the concerns raised about the studies which showed the need for a ban were valid. It is however, questionable as to whether the legislative institutions should take such interventionist action on the basis of a re-interpretation of conclusions which stated that the evidence used in support of the ban was both misleading and artificial. The General Court even concluded that the institutions involved were aware of the methodological limitations of these studies. Despite this, it was considered acceptable for the Commission to ignore the opinion of SCAN, on the basis that sufficient reasons were not provided supporting their view that the Danish evidence did not suggest that any real risk existed. While the legislative institutions are not bound to follow the opinions of advisory committees, such as SCAN, it does leave them vulnerable to accusations of arbitrariness in the use of the precautionary principle, which is exactly what the Communication states they should seek to avoid.[157]

Public Consultation in Devising Food Laws

One of the beliefs about the way in which the BSE crisis was mishandled, at both UK and EU levels, was that it led to reduced levels of confidence amongst consumers about the safety of food. Advice on the consumption of beef was mixed. Initial presumptions about the transferability of the disease to humans were later shown to be ill-founded. Neither science nor politics were shown to be capable of offering the type of reassurance that was sought.

Apart from the general overhaul of food safety rules and processes by the General Food Law Regulation, the legislation also seeks to regain the trust of consumers by actively involving them 'during the preparation, evaluation and revision of food law, except where the urgency of the matter does not allow it'.[158] This involves 'open and transparent public consultation, directly or through

---

[157] For more on the operations of the precautionary principle in food law see A Szajkowska, 'The impact of the definition of the precautionary principle in EU food law' (2010) 47 *CML Rev* 173.
[158] Art 9.

representative bodies'. This policy of involving stakeholders, including the general public, in the legislative process is now commonplace. Very few food law initiatives come to the statute book without some prior dialogue with, amongst others, consumer groups. This is not limited to food safety laws. It has become the norm across almost all areas of food law. For example, the initial proposal to introduce a new food labelling regulation followed a series of public consultations on a range of related matters, including nutrition labelling and origin marking, as well as a general call for suggestions on how the framework legislation could be improved.[159]

The General Food Law Regulation also provides that the public should be properly communicated with and informed about any suspected or confirmed food safety concern. It provides that

> where there are reasonable grounds to suspect that a food or feed may present a risk for human or animal health, then, depending on the nature, seriousness and extent of that risk, public authorities shall take appropriate steps to inform the general public of the nature of the risk to health, identifying to the fullest extent possible the food or feed, or type of food or feed, the risk that it may present, and the measures which are taken or about to be taken to prevent, reduce or eliminate that risk.[160]

This applies across all areas of food law. This 'risk communication' is a vital element of risk analysis, and one of the three components identified by the Regulation. The other two elements of this, risk analysis and risk management, are dealt with in more detail above.

Food Business Operator Responsibilities

The General Food Law Regulation makes food businesses more accountable for failures to comply with the legislation and to prevent crises. The 'food business operator' is defined in the Regulation as 'the natural or legal persons responsible for ensuring that the requirements of food law are met within the ... business under their control'.[161] This applies across all stages of production, including any processing and distribution.[162] There are three main responsibilities placed on food business operators. The first is to ensure that they operate according to the applicable food safety regulations. The second is to ensure that they do all within their power to withdraw unsafe foods from the market.[163] The designated competent authorities, usually the Food Standards Agency or the local authority, must be notified about the need to do this, and the measures that must be taken

---

[159] See DG SANCO, 'Labelling: competitiveness, consumer information and better regulation for the EU' Consultative Document, February 2006. Available at: ec.europa.eu/food.

[160] Art 10.

[161] Art 3(6).

[162] Art 17(1).

[163] Art 19(1). The responsibilities of food business operators and national competent authorities in this regard are also set out in the General Food Regulations 2004, SI No 3279/2004.

to achieve it, without delay.[164] Consumers must be informed about the reasons for the withdrawal of the product and they may, in some circumstances, be asked to return it to the place of purchase or to the producer or importer. This responsibility may be extended to include retailers and distributors in the process.[165] All are also under an obligation to collaborate with the designated competent authorities when action needs to be taken to avoid or reduce risks posed by a food which they have supplied.[166]

The third main responsibility of the food business operator is to ensure that they have a proper traceability system in place. This is defined as 'the ability to trace and follow a food, feed, food-producing animal or substance intended to be, or expected to be incorporated into a food or feed, through all stages of production, processing and distribution'.[167] Proper systems of traceability have become a feature of food law since the BSE crisis. The idea is that where a problem or safety concern with a particular food or ingredient is identified, all products which contain or have been associated with that food or ingredient can be readily identified and withdrawn from the market if necessary. This is the practical development of the 'farm to fork' approach advocated in the White Paper on Food Safety. Those operating in the food sector are obliged to be in a position where they can identify any other operator who has supplied them with any food or ingredient.[168] They must, therefore, ensure that they have systems in place which guarantee that this information can be made available to the competent authorities on demand. Similarly, they must also be able to readily identify other businesses that they have supplied.[169] One of the best ways of ensuring that a proper system of traceability exists is through the use of proper labelling and documentation.[170] While the General Food Law Regulation provides the framework for developing traceability systems in the sector, other legislation establishes specific procedures and obligations related to foods for which this is deemed to be of particular importance. A good example of this can be seen in the GMO regulations.[171] These are discussed in more detail in chapter ten.

5.5.2 European Food Safety Authority

One of the most heralded proposals put forward in the White Paper on Food Safety was the establishment of a 'European Food Authority'. This was claimed to

---

[164] Arts 19(1) and 19(3).
[165] Art 19(2).
[166] Art 19(4).
[167] Arts 3(15) and 18(1).
[168] Art 18(2).
[169] Art 18(3).
[170] Art 18(4).
[171] Regulation (EC) No 1830/2003 of the European Parliament and of the Council of 22 September 2003 concerning the traceability and labelling of genetically modified organisms and the traceability of food and feed products produced from genetically modified organisms and amending Directive 2001/18/EC [2003] OJ L 268/24.

be central to the priority of the Commission to take effective measures designed to ensure a high level of consumer protection. The Authority, once established, would play a key role in this, having particular responsibility for risk assessment and communication on food safety matters. However, it was decided that at that particular stage in the development of EU law, it would be unwise to assign any risk management role to the Authority, especially where this involved the need to introduce legislation. It was thought that the transfer of regulatory powers to an independent body could lead to 'an unwarranted dilution of democratic accountability'. It would also have required for amendments to be made to the EU Treaties.

Chapter III of the General Food Law Regulation deals with the tasks and functioning of the European Food Safety Authority, which was established in 2002.[172] Its primary role is to provide scientific advice and scientific and technical support for the implementation of Union law and policy in all areas that have a bearing on the safety of food.[173] It is organised and functions in a way that, it is hoped, will ensure that it is widely regarded as a trustworthy point of reference for all in food safety matters, recognised for its independence, transparency and rigour.[174] It is responsible for the collection and analysis of data that can be used to evaluate risks within the food chain,[175] and the subsequent communication of noteworthy dangers to the public, when required.

The European Food Safety Authority is assigned a series of tasks to enable it to carry out these important functions properly. These include providing the EU institutions and the Member States with the best possible scientific opinions; promoting and co-ordinating the development of uniform risk assessment methodologies; providing scientific and technical support to the Commission and, when requested, interpreting and considering risk assessment opinions; commissioning scientific studies; collecting, analysing and summarising scientific and technical data; identifying and characterising emerging food safety risks; establishing a network of organisations operating within the sector; advising in crisis management procedures; improving co-operation between the Union, applicant countries, third countries and international organisations on food safety matters; and finally, providing independent conclusions on food safety or related concerns.[176]

The organisational structure of the European Food Safety Authority consists of a management board, an executive director, an advisory forum, a scientific committee, scientific panels and staff.[177] The management board consists of 14

---

[172] Art 22(1) of Reg 178/2002, n 130 above. For an assessment of the role of EFSA as set out in the Regulation see K Kanska, 'Wolves in the clothing of sheep? The case of the European Food Safety Authority' (2004) 29 *EL Rev* 711.

[173] Art 22(2).

[174] Art 22(7).

[175] Art 22(4).

[176] Art 23.

[177] Art 24. Members of the Management Board, the Advisory Forum and the Executive Director are all obliged to act independently and in the public interest, under the terms of Art 37 of the General Food Law Regulation, n 1 above.

members, who are appointed by the Council in consultation with the European Parliament, from a list drawn up by the Commission.[178] At least four of the members of the management board must be representatives of consumer and other interest groups. The composition of the board should be structured in a way that ensures the presence of a high level of competence, a broad base of expertise and a good geographic distribution from within the EU Member States. Members of the Board serve a term of four years, renewable once. It meets at the request of the Chair or at least one-third of the members.[179] Its main role is to ensure that the rest of EFSA properly performs the tasks assigned to it by the Regulation.[180] It also sets a programme of work for the Authority, on an annual basis.[181]

The Executive Director is appointed by the Management Board, from a list of candidates proposed by the European Commission.[182] The Executive Director's responsibilities include the day-to-day administration of the Authority and overseeing the implementation of the work programmes assigned by the Management Board;[183] and the annual production of a draft report on EFSA activities which, once adopted, is then circulated to the EU Commission, Council, European Parliament and the other Member States.[184]

The Advisory Forum is made up of representatives from the designated competent authorities of the Member States, including the Food Standards Agency.[185] Its key role is to advise the Executive Director in his orchestration of EFSA.[186] It also provides a focus for the exchange of information of potential food safety risks and the pooling of information.[187] The Advisory Forum can also include representatives of the European Commission and the European Parliament in its work.[188]

The Scientific Committee and permanent Scientific Panels are more directly responsible for providing the scientific opinions issued by EFSA.[189] The Committee is composed of the Chairs of each of the Scientific Panels, as well as six independent scientific experts.[190] Eight original panels were established at the time of the formation of EFSA. These include panels on additives, plants, genetically modified organisms, animal welfare, contaminants, biological hazards and dietetic products, nutrition and allergies.[191] The remits and range of panels can be

---

[178] Art 25(1). Art 38(2) provides that EFSA Management Board meetings must be held in public.
[179] Art 25(6).
[180] Art 25(7).
[181] Art 25(8). For further discussion on the governance of EFSA see S Gabbi, 'The scientific governance of the European Food Safety Authority: *Status quo* and perspectives' in A Alemanno and S Gabbi (eds), Foundations of EU Food Law and Policy: Ten years of the European Food Safety Authority (Ashgate, 2014).
[182] Art 26(1).
[183] Art 26(2).
[184] Art 26(3).
[185] Art 27(1).
[186] Art 27(3).
[187] Art 27(4).
[188] Art 27(7).
[189] Art 28(1).
[190] Art 28(3).
[191] Art 28(4).

altered as and when required by EFSA and the European Commission, using the comitology procedure.[192] Again, there is a strong link between the work of these panels and the Commission. Representatives of the latter, for example, can be present at both panel and committee meetings, but they may not 'seek to influence discussions'.[193] Smaller working groups of both the Committee and the Panels may be formed to deal with more specific matters.[194]

As stated, one of the key functions of EFSA is issuing scientific opinions. This can happen in one of three ways.[195] The first is where this is requested by the Commission. The vast majority of opinions are initiated in this way. Second, requests can also be made by the European Parliament or a Member State. Finally, EFSA may take the initiative and decide to deliver an opinion itself. Any request made for an opinion must include contextual information explaining the issue that needs to be addressed, as well as some reasoning as to why the investigation to be undertaken is of interest to the EU.[196] The Authority can refuse to issue an opinion where it is of the view that it has already delivered a similar, previously requested one and that there are no new scientific elements which justify a re-examination.[197]

EFSA is not the only point of reference on the scientific issues surrounding food safety matters. Other opinions are delivered by other bodies. EFSA is a significant point of reference, but it is obliged to consider the views and conclusions of others and seek to deal with any divergence of opinion that may exist.[198] It does this by contacting the other body involved with a view to sharing all relevant scientific information in order to properly identify potentially contentious scientific issues.[199] Where this other body is one of the EU's own agencies, or that of a Member State, the two are obliged to co-operate with a view to either resolving the divergence or coming together to present a joint document to the Commission which clarifies the contentious points.[200] These documents must be made public.[201] EFSA can also commission others to undertake studies on its behalf.[202]

Much of the work of EFSA involves the collection and analysis of relevant scientific and technical data from studies undertaken elsewhere.[203] It then uses these studies to assist it in identifying emerging risks, which are in turn communicated

---

[192] Art 28(4) in conjunction with Art 58(2) of Reg 178/2002, n 130 above.
[193] Art 28(8).
[194] Art 28(9).
[195] Art 29(1).
[196] Art 29(2).
[197] Art 29(5).
[198] Art 30(1).
[199] Art 30(2).
[200] Art 30(3).
[201] Art 38 of the Regulation also provides that EFSA must carry out other activities with a high level of transparency. In particular, it must publicise all agendas and minutes of the Committee and Panel meetings, scientific opinions, reasons for any decisions taken and the annual report.
[202] Art 32. For more on the role of EFSA in the provision of scientific advice on risks associated with the food chain see A Smith, S Terry and D Detken, '10 years of the European Food Safety Authority' (2012) 7 *European Food and Feed Law Review* 111.
[203] Art 33.

to the European Parliament, the Commission and the Member States.[204] Central to the proper functioning of these lines of communication is the 'rapid alert system'. EFSA is a key figure in this process, being responsible for the analysis of the content of messages relayed through the system, providing the Commission and the Member States with any information that they need to make a proper risk analysis.[205] It is designated a similar role in the crisis management process.[206] The Authority can also, on its own initiative, communicate with the public on any risks that are identified.[207] It is also under an obligation to develop meaningful contact and dialogue with consumer and producer groups and representatives.[208]

Rapid Alert System

It is widely recognised that one of the best ways of dealing with a food safety crisis once it develops is to ensure that all affected parties are kept informed about the nature and extent of the problem so that they can act accordingly. The General Food Law Regulation sets up a network, designed to formally open and maintain these vital lines of communication and information. This is known as the 'Rapid Alert System'. Notification of all direct and indirect risks caused by food or feed to human health happens through this network. The main players in this are the EU Member States, the Commission and EFSA. All are required to have a designated contact point as part of the network, with the Commission having overall managerial control of the system.[209]

Members of the network must immediately notify the Commission where they have any information about a food safety risk.[210] The Commission then has responsibility for transmitting this information to the other members of the Rapid Alert System network. EFSA can intervene at this stage to provide additional scientific or technical information that can assist in the appropriate risk management decisions being taken. Member States have a clear obligation under the system. They must notify the Commission immediately about a risk, in the first place, and about any management measures that they adopt, such as a restriction on marketing or a product recall.[211] They must also provide a detailed explanation of the reasons underlying any course of action that they have taken.[212] The Commission must then notify the other members of the network about this risk management decision and the reasons for it, providing them with the opportunity to take their own action or, of course, to object to the measures adopted elsewhere where this affects their interests. Details of all further action taken by Member

---

[204] Art 34.
[205] Art 35.
[206] Art 56(2).
[207] Art 40.
[208] Art 42.
[209] Art 50(1).
[210] Art 50(2).
[211] Art 50(3)(a).
[212] Art 50(3)(c).

States must be relayed back through the network.[213] Participation in the Rapid Alert System is also open to EU applicant countries, third countries and international organisations.[214]

As with many other areas of food safety regulation and control, documents and information related to the Rapid Alert System must be made available to the public. Any information about food safety risks that is available to the network must also be available to consumers, including details of the products involved, the nature of the risk and any measures that have been, or which will be, taken.[215] This does not, however, extend to the disclosure of information that needs, for commercial reasons, to be kept secret. The only exception to this is that which must be made public to ensure that any risk posed to health is minimised or averted.

Emergencies and Crisis Management

In some circumstances, the use of the Rapid Alert System may not be sufficient to deal with the seriousness of the risk posed. These situations require the adoption of emergency measures instead.[216] The key distinguishing factor that identifies the risk as an 'emergency' is that it is thought that Member State intervention will not be sufficient to contain the risk.[217] The safety concern is deemed to be so serious that only Commission action, applicable across all EU Member States, will suffice. There are several different types of emergency measure that can be adopted, depending on the circumstances. The most obvious one is the suspension of marketing the food in question. Alternatively, 'special conditions' of use can be prescribed instead. The ban on British beef exports would be an example of the former. Bone-in beef restrictions would be an illustration of the latter. Emergency measures can apply with immediate effect. They are, however, subject to review within 10 days of their passing, at which stage they should be confirmed, amended, revoked or extended.[218] Decisions on the continuance or otherwise of the emergency measure are made using comitology procedures. They should also be made public. Finally, the Commission is obliged, under the terms of the General Food Law Regulation, to have a proper crisis management plan in place to deal with wide-scale food safety concerns.[219] This should specify the practical procedures that should be followed to manage a crisis, including the principles of transparency to be applied and a communication strategy.[220] It should also establish a 'crisis unit', responsible for collecting and evaluating all information

---

[213] Art 50(5).

[214] Art 50(6).

[215] Art 52(1) in conjunction with Art 10 of Reg 178/2002, n 130 above.

[216] Art 53(1).

[217] Art 54 of Reg 178/2002 further provides that Member States can adopt interim protective measures where the Commission fails to take an emergency decision. These national interim protective measures can be maintained until the Commission does act.

[218] Art 53(2).

[219] Art 55(1).

[220] Art 55(2).

relevant to the crisis and for identifying the options that are available to minimise the risk to human health.[221] Details of the work and the conclusions of the crisis unit must also be made publicly available.[222]

5.5.3 General Food Regulations 2004

The specifics of the domestic application across Britain of Regulation 178/2002 are set out in the General Food Regulations 2004.[223] Cross-references to the Food Safety Act 1990 are made throughout the Regulations. Essentially, these 2004 Regulations update and add to the 1990 Act, to ensure the proper implementation of the General Food Law Regulation at national level.

The 2004 Regulations set the designated competent authorities in food safety matters as the Food Standards Agency, local authorities and port authorities, depending on the circumstances at issue.[224] The powers assigned to these authorities include taking measures designed to restrict or withdraw the marketing of foods that pose a threat to health,[225] demanding information to trace the origins of a potentially harmful food,[226] and dealing with food business operators to avoid or reduce the risks posed by a food.[227]

The 2004 Regulations also set out details on the range of offences that can be committed under the terms of the EU Regulation. Any person who fails to comply with the provisions of the General Food Law Regulation is guilty of an offence,[228] punishable by a fine up to the statutory maximum, or imprisonment for up to two years, or both.[229] This includes breaches of any food safety requirements,[230] presentation requirements,[231] traceability requirements,[232] or any of the responsibilities set for food business operators.[233] Finally, the Food safety Act 1990 is amended to account for changes made by the EU General Food Law Regulation. This includes, for example, references to Regulation 178/2002 definitions, such as that which is used to identify whether 'food is injurious to health'.[234]

---

[221] Arts 56 and 57.
[222] Art 57(3).
[223] SI No 3279/2004.
[224] Reg 3(1).
[225] As set out in Art 14(8) of Reg 178/2002, n 130 above.
[226] As set out in Art 18 of Reg 178/2002, n 130 above.
[227] As set out in Art 19 of Reg 178/2002, n 130 above. The powers themselves are set out in reg 3(2) of the General Food Regulations 2004, n 163 above.
[228] Reg 4.
[229] Reg 5.
[230] Set out in Art 14(1) of Reg 178/2002, n 130 above.
[231] Art 16 of Reg 178/2002, n 130 above.
[232] Art 18 of Reg 178/2002, n 130 above.
[233] Art 19 of Reg 178/2002, n 130 above.
[234] Reg 9(a) of the General Food Regulations 2004, amending section 7(2) of the Food Safety Act 1990.

6

Chemical and Biological Safety of Food

6.1 Hormone Use in Food Production

The EU has been traditionally averse to the use of hormones in food-producing animals. These substances are often used in farming as growth-promoters, designed to create additional muscle in animals, leading to increased food production levels. Testosterone, progesterone, trenbolone acetate, melengestrol acetate and oestradiol can all be used for this purpose. While most of these substances can be used for veterinary medicinal purposes, the EU has banned their use for growth-promoting purposes since 1981.[1]

6.1.1 Hormones Directive

The original 1981 legislation, which had been transposed into English law by the Animals and Fresh Meat (Hormonal Substances) Regulations 1988,[2] was replaced by a new directive in 1996.[3] This Hormones Directive goes even further than its predecessor, and amendments to it have reduced the circumstances in which certain listed substances can even be administered to farm animals for medicinal purposes. The ban on hormone use was introduced, and later maintained, due to

---

[1] Council Directive 1981/602/EEC of 31 July 1981 concerning the prohibition of certain substances having a hormonal action and of any substances having a thyrostatic action [1981] OJ L 222/32. Art 2 of the Directive prescribed that 'Member States shall ensure that the following are prohibited: (a) the administering to a farm animal, by any means whatsoever, of substances having a thyrostatic or substances having (a), oestrogenic, androgenic or gestagenic action; (b) the placing on the market or slaughtering of farm animals to which [these] substances have been administered; (c) the placing on the market of meat [from such] farm animals; (d) processing of the meat referred to'.

[2] SI No 849/1988.

[3] Council Directive 1996/22/EC of 29 April 1996 concerning the prohibition on the use in stock-farming of certain substances having a hormonal or thyrostatic action and of beta-agonists, and repealing Directives 1981/602/EEC, 1988/146/EEC and 1988/299/EEC [1996] OJ L 125/3. The Directive has since been amended by Directive 2003/74/EC of the European Parliament and of the Council of 22 September 2003 amending Council Directive 96/22/EC concerning the prohibition on the use in stockfarming of certain substances having a hormonal or thyrostatic action and of beta-agonists [2003] OJ L 262/17.

the potential dangers that their residues could pose for human health. Under the terms of the Directive, all EU Member States are obliged to prohibit

> the placing on the market of stilbenes, stilbene derivatives, their salts and esters and thyrostatic substances for administering to animals of all species [and] the placing on the market of beta-agonists for administering to animals the flesh and products of which are intended for human consumption.[4]

Thyrostatic substances are administered to reduce or stabilise the production of thyroid hormones in animals. Beta-agonists can be used to enhance lean muscle gain and growth. The Directive also bans the importation of animals, meat or other products derived from animals which have been treated with listed substances.[5] The Hormones Directive 1996 has been transposed into English law by the Animals and Animal Products Regulations 1997.[6]

The ban on hormones use in food-producing animals is controversial as many of the substances have been approved for use in food production elsewhere, most notably by the Food and Drug Administration (FDA) in the USA. As discussed in chapter two, it has also created much disagreement at World Trade Organization level, where the Dispute Panel and the Appellate Body both found that prohibitions on importing products made from hormone-treated animals was inconsistent with the EU's WTO obligations, in particular those arising under the SPS Agreement.[7]

6.2 Pesticides

Pesticides can be used in the production of food for a variety of reasons. The term itself really covers a whole range of chemical compounds which are used to control pests that can damage crops, kill weeds and alter the growth rate of a plant. They include insecticides, herbicides, fungicides, plant growth regulators and biocides. Pesticides can only be used if they have been approved by the European Commission.

6.2.1 Pesticides Regulation

The key piece of legislation on the lawful use of pesticides in all EU Member States is the 2009 Regulation.[8] It is designed to take account of all factors which can be

---

[4] Art 2.
[5] Art 11.
[6] SI No 1729/1997.
[7] DS 26 and DS 48, *EC—Measures Concerning Meat and Meat Products (Hormones)*.
[8] Regulation (EC) No 1107/2009 of the European Parliament and of the Council of 21 October 2009 concerning the placing of plant protection products on the market and repealing Council Directives 1979/117/EEC and 1991/414/EEC [2009] OJ L 309/1.

affected by pesticide use, including the need to protect human health, animal health and the environment. The Regulation defines 'plant protection products' as being those which contain, or which consist of, active substances intended to protect plants against harmful organisms, or influence the life processes of plants including their growth (other than as a nutrient), preserving plants or destroying undesired parts of plants.[9] Additional requirements are also set for the use of pesticides in the production of ingredients for specific products, such as baby foods. The Infant Formula and Follow-on Formula (England) Regulations 2007 provide, for example, that much lower levels of permitted pesticide residues should be established for these products.[10] The Processed Cereal-based Foods and Baby Foods for Infants and Young Children (England) Regulations provide similar restrictions on residue levels for these products.[11]

The primary potential problem with pesticides is not necessarily their use but, as alluded to above, it is more that 'residues' of the substances will remain in the plants, drinking water or in the environment, possibly causing pollution or causing harm to humans and/or animals. A pesticide can only be approved for use under the terms of the Regulation if it can be shown that

> they shall not have any harmful effects on human health, including that of vulnerable groups, or animal health, taking into account cumulative or synergistic effects … or on groundwater [and] they shall not have any unacceptable effect on the environment.[12]

Not being harmful is not enough, however, to result in an approval for use. The substance must also be sufficiently effective, have no unacceptable effects on plants and it should cause no unnecessary suffering to the vertebrates it is designed to control.[13]

Applications for the approval of active substances are submitted by the producer to a rapporteur Member State, usually the State in which they are established.[14] A dossier of information related to the application is then assessed by the Member State, or a group of Member States in some circumstances,[15] before a 'draft assessment report' on this is forwarded to the European Commission and the European Food Safety Authority.[16] The draft assessment report should also include the proposed set maximum residue levels to be permitted for the substance under review.[17] The Authority is responsible for making this report public, although some elements can be kept confidential at the request of the applicant.[18]

---

[9] Art 2(1).
[10] SI No 3521/2007, reg 14.
[11] SI No 3207/2003, reg 7.
[12] Art 4(2).
[13] Art 4(3).
[14] Art 7.
[15] Arts 8 and 9.
[16] Art 11.
[17] Art 11(2).
[18] Art 12.

There is then a period allowed for the submission of written comments from interested parties and the possible organisation of a consultation with experts on the content of the report and the suitability of the product for approval. At the end of this stage of the process, the European Food Safety Authority issues an opinion, which it is then up to the Commission to accept, reject or modify. This takes place by the issuing of a new Regulation by comitology, involving the Standing Committee on the Food Chain and Animal Health.[19] The Regulation either (i) approves the active substance, subject to conditions and restrictions; (ii) does not approve the use of the active substance; or (iii) amends the conditions previously attached to the approval for use.[20] First approvals are for a maximum period of 10 years.[21] These can then be re-approved for a further 5–15 years, depending on the type of substances at issue.[22] The Commission can, of course, also review any approval granted at any time, in particular where there is new scientific and technical knowledge and/or monitoring data available.[23]

Once an 'active substance' is approved for use under the procedure outlined above, it can then be used in plant protection products, which must then also be authorised for use. A plant protection product can only be authorised where its active substances have been approved and its overall technical formulation is such that user exposure or other risks are limited as much as possible without compromising the functioning of the product.[24] Its physical and chemical properties must have been determined and deemed acceptable for the appropriate uses and storage of the product. The maximum residue levels for the product must have previously been set by Regulation 396/2005.[25] The applications for plant protection products are examined by the Member State to which it was sent.[26] Member States are obliged under the terms of the Regulation to make an 'independent, objective and transparent assessment in the light of current scientific and technical knowledge using guidance documents available at the time of application'.[27] The Member State has 12 months to make a decision on authorisation, which it then communicates to the other EU Member States.[28] This authorisation, if granted, should then be recognised in the other Member States in the same region.[29] Some substances and products can be authorised for a temporary period, even where

[19] Arts 13 and 79 of the Regulation.

[20] Art 13(2). The different types of conditions and restrictions that can be set are listed in Art 6 of the Regulation. They include, for example, changes to the level of purity of the substance that can be used, the ways in which it is applied, limiting its use to professional users and additional post-approval monitoring.

[21] Art 5.

[22] Art 14.

[23] Art 21.

[24] Art 29.

[25] Regulation (EC) No 396/2005 on maximum residue levels of pesticides in or on food and feed of plant and animal origin and amending Council Directive 1991/414/EC [2005] OJ L 70/1.

[26] Art 35.

[27] Art 36.

[28] Art 37.

[29] Art 40.

this would not normally be allowed, to deal with an emergency situation that cannot be treated in any other way.[30] Also, an approval or authorisation can be suspended at any time where there is a potential risk to human health, animal health or the environment from its continued use.[31] Approved products are also subject to additional packaging,[32] labelling,[33] and advertising controls.[34] Each EU Member State is obliged under the terms of the 2009 Regulation to designate a competent authority charged with carrying out the obligations arising under the terms of the legislation.[35] The competent authority for this purpose in the UK is the Chemicals Regulation Directorate, which is part of the Health and Safety Executive. The provisions necessary for the application of the 2009 Regulation at national level are set by the Plant Protection Products Regulations 2011, which also set the terms for monitoring compliance with, and enforcement of, the EU provisions.[36] It should also be noted at this stage that all European and national authorities, manufacturers and importers of chemicals in all sectors must operate under the terms of REACH—the EU Programme and Regulation for the Registration, Evaluation, Authorisation and Restriction of Chemicals.[37]

6.3 Materials in Contact With Foodstuffs

Materials, such as packaging and containers that are used to store products during transit or before preparation or consumption can, of course, affect the composition or properties of the food. They also have the potential to contaminate food. Regulation of these materials is thus necessary to ensure that both human health and consumers are protected.

Contact materials are legislated for through the application of a 2004 EU Regulation on the matter.[38] It covers both traditional food packaging and the more contemporary 'active food contact materials and articles'. The latter are defined in the Regulation as being those that

---

[30] Art 53.
[31] Art 69.
[32] Art 64.
[33] Art 65.
[34] Art 66.
[35] Art 75.
[36] SI No 2131/2011.
[37] Regulation (EC) No 1907/2006 of the European Parliament and of the Council of 18 December 2006 concerning the Registration, Evaluation, Authorisation and Restriction of Chemicals (REACH), establishing a European Chemicals Agency, amending Directive 1999/45/EC and repealing Council Regulation (EEC) No 793/1993 and Commission Regulation (EC) No 1488/1994 as well as Council Directive 1976/769/EEC and Commission Directives 1991/155/EEC, 1993/67/EEC, 1993/105/EC and 2000/21/EC [2007] OJ L 136/3.
[38] Regulation (EC) No 1935/2004 of the European Parliament and of the Council of 27 October 2004 on materials and articles intended to come into contact with food and repealing Directives 1980/590/EEC and 1989/109/EEC [2004] OJ L 338/4.

are intended to extend the shelf-life or to maintain or improve the condition of the packaged food [and which] are designed to deliberately incorporate components that would release or absorb substances into or from the packaged food or the environment surrounding the food.[39]

All materials and articles must be made and used in a way that neither endangers human health nor brings about an unacceptable change in the composition or organoleptic properties of the product that it is packaging.[40]

The Regulation also provides for more specific measures to be adopted for a range of contact materials, including cork, glass, ink, plastics, paper and metals.[41] As a result, legislation can be adopted that sets specific requirements for these materials on purity standards, conditions of use, migration limits (transferring components into food in unacceptable quantities), sampling and traceability. Consequently, there are specific additional legislative requirements in place for materials such as cadmium and lead,[42] cellulose film[43] and plastics,[44] amongst others. There is also a prohibition in place on the use of specified materials in plastic infant-feeding bottles.[45] Any provisions of the contact materials legislation that is liable to affect public health must involve consultation with the European Food Safety Authority.[46] This includes applications for the authorisation of new substances, where EFSA has a very significant role to play.[47]

The Contact Materials Regulation 2004 contains a range of provisions designed to best deal with situations where some risk with the substances used is identified. Traceability is required for materials and articles used at all stages in order to facilitate the recall of defective products, the provision of accurate consumer information and the attribution of responsibility where necessary.[48] As with many other areas of food law, Member States are entitled, under the terms of the Regulation, to adopt appropriate safeguard measures where they receive new information or following a reassessment of existing information that suggests a possible risk to human health.[49] This would usually involve the temporary suspension of the use of the substances identified. The usual procedures for such action apply, including

---

[39] Art 2(2).

[40] Art 3.

[41] Art 5(1).

[42] Council Directive 1984/500/EEC of 15 October 1984 on the approximation of the laws of the Member States relating to ceramic articles intended to come into contact with foodstuffs [1984] OJ L 277/12.

[43] Commission Directive 2007/42/EC of 29 June 2007 relating to materials and articles made of regenerated cellulose film intended to come into contact with foodstuffs [2007] OJ L 172/71.

[44] Commission Regulation (EU) No 10/2011 of 14 January 2011 on plastic materials and articles intended to come into contact with food [2011] OJ L 12/1.

[45] Commission Implementing Regulation (EU) 321/2011 of 1 April 2011 amending Regulation (EU) No 10/2011 as regards the restriction of use of Bisphenol A in plastic infant feeding bottles [2011] OJ L 87/1.

[46] Art 7 of Reg 1935/2004, n 38 above.

[47] Art 9 and 10 of Reg 1935/2004.

[48] Art 17.

[49] Art 18.

immediate informing of the other EU Member States and the Commission. Any final decision on the appropriateness of the measure adopted is made by the Commission.

Member States must designate national competent authorities as a contact point for authorisations and other matters arising under the 2004 Regulation. In the UK, this is designated as the Food Contact Materials and Veterinary Medicine Residues unit of the Food Standards Agency. National measures designed to give effect to the Regulations and Directives are set out in the Materials and Articles in Contact with Food (England) Regulations 2012.[50]

6.4 Ionisation

The use of ionising radiation could be considered as being either a chemical or a biological food safety issue. It usually involves the use of high-energy ionising radiation to destroy micro-organisms or bacteria in food. This can have a range of benefits, including killing off potentially harmful bacteria, preventing germination, slowing down ripening and prolonging shelf-life. Two directives on treating foods with ionising radiation were introduced by the EU in 1999.[51] These are transposed into English law by the Food Irradiation (England) Regulations 2009.[52]

The English Regulations provide that the use of ionisation is to be limited to certain types of food including fruit, vegetables, cereals, fish, poultry, herbs and spices.[53] It also limits the amount of radiation that can be used for each of these categories of foodstuff.[54] The use of these types of treatment is also limited to licence holders.[55] Irradiated food can only be imported into a State where the facility where it was treated has been specifically approved by the authorities of another EU Member State or by the EU authorities where the food is coming from a third country.[56] The Food Standards Agency is given primary responsibility for the enforcement of these provisions.[57] Failure to comply with these Regulations

---

[50] SI No 2619/2012.

[51] Directive 1999/2/EC of the European Parliament and of the Council of 22 February 1999 on the approximation of the laws of the Member States concerning foods and food ingredients treated with ionising radiation [1999] OJ L 66/16; and Directive 1999/3/EC of the European Parliament and of the Council of 22 February 1999 on the establishment of a Community list of foods and food ingredients treated with ionising radiation [1999] OJ L 66/24.

[52] SI No 1584/2009.

[53] Reg 3(2)(c).

[54] Reg 3(2)(e).

[55] Reg 4.

[56] Reg 5.

[57] Reg 9.

is a criminal offence.[58] A major review of the use of food irradiation undertaken by the European Food Safety Authority in 2011 led to a reassertion that the use of this treatment for these purposes continues to be safe.

6.5 Food Hygiene

Legislation on the hygienic production and marketing of food comes directly from three EU regulations, introduced in 2004.

The first of these is the Food Hygiene Regulation.[59] This legislation lays down the general rules on the hygiene standards that must be met for all commercially traded foods. It is clear from the Regulation that the primary responsibility for food hygiene rests with the food business operator.[60] The operator is required to ensure that all of the hygiene requirements set out in the Regulation are met at every stage of the production, processing and distribution of his foods and products.[61] This includes compliance with microbiological criteria for foodstuffs, compliance with temperature control requirements for foodstuffs, maintenance of the 'cold chain' and sampling and analysis.[62] The only exceptions to the application of these rules are for those foods produced for private domestic use, or which are supplied in small quantities directly from the producer or local retailer to the consumer.[63] 'Food hygiene' is defined in the Regulation as 'the measures and conditions necessary to control hazards and to ensure fitness for human consumption'.[64] The primary measure that must be employed to ensure that standards of hygiene are met is the use of the 'hazard analysis and critical control points' or 'HACCP' procedure.

6.5.1 Hazard Analysis Procedures

All food business operators must have a permanent hazard analysis and critical control points procedure in place.[65] This is to be based on a set of defined principles, which are to be used to identify hazards that must be prevented or reduced

---

[58] Reg 10.

[59] Regulation (EC) No. 852/2004 of the European Parliament and of the Council of 29 April 2004 on the hygiene of foodstuffs [2004] OJ L 226/3. For more on this see J Lawless, 'The complexity of flexibility in EU food hygiene regulation' (2012) 7 *European Food and Feed Law Review* 220.

[60] Art 1(1)(a).

[61] Art 3.

[62] Art 4. The targets and procedures referred to here are established and reviewed in consultation between the European Commission and the European Food Safety Authority, under the terms of Arts 4(4) and 15 of Reg 852/2004, n 59 above.

[63] Art 1(2)(c).

[64] Art 2(1)(a).

[65] Art 5(1).

to acceptable levels, identifying the critical points at which action must be taken to minimise these hazards—the 'critical control points' in the process; establishing what level of hazard is acceptable at these points; implementing effective monitoring procedures at the critical control points; establishing what corrective action can be taken when required; setting up regular procedures to verify that the system is working; and documenting and recording, commensurate with the size of the food business, in a way that verifies that the other measures are working effectively.[66]

While there is clearly a responsibility placed on food business operators to ensure that they have suitable HACCP procedures in place as a key way of maintaining the hygienic and safe production and marketing of food, they are also obliged, under the terms of the Regulation, to provide all of this information to the competent authority when required.[67] The information must be recorded and it must be up-to-date and descriptive. National and EU guides must also be developed to assist in the promotion and uniform application of HACCP principles and hygienic practices.[68] Examples of these at national level include the HACCP in Meat Plants Guide, developed by the Food Standards Agency,[69] and a range of guides tailored for different types and sizes of operators and developed by local authorities.[70]

6.5.2 General Hygiene Provisions

The Food Hygiene Regulation provides that food business operators must comply with the general hygiene provisions laid down in Annex I (primary production) and Annex II (other operators) to the Regulation.[71] Primary production provisions also apply to all transportation, including that of live animals, as well as storage and handling of primary products, provided this does not substantially alter their nature or characteristics.

Primary Production Provisions

Food business operators must, under the terms of the Regulation, ensure that their products are protected from contamination, including that which may arise from exposure to the air, soil, water, feed, fertilisers, veterinary medicines, plant protection products and biocides. There is also provision in this part of the Regulation for the adoption of measures relating to animal health and welfare and

---

[66] Art 5(2).

[67] Art 5(4).

[68] Art 7 and Annex I, Part B to the Regulation.

[69] Available at: www.food.gov.uk.

[70] Such as that produced by the London Borough of Hammersmith and Fulham, 'A guide to HACCP for caterers', available at: www.lbhf.gov.uk; and Trafford Council, 'Your guide to HACCP', available at: www.trafford.gov.uk.

[71] Arts 4(1) and (2).

plant health that have implications for human health, including programmes for the monitoring and control of zoonoses.

Other additional requirements are put in place for those food business operators who are rearing, harvesting or hunting animals or who are producing primary products of animal origin, such as milk or eggs. They are under an obligation to keep the animals, facilities, equipment and any vehicles that they use for this production clean, including those facilities that are used for the storage and handling of feed. This should include disinfecting where appropriate. Any staff used in this process must be in 'good health' and well trained on potential health risks.[72] All measures taken must be designed to keep the threat of contamination to a minimum level. This extends to taking any necessary steps designed to prevent the introduction and spread of contagious diseases transmissible to humans through food, including by taking precautionary measures when introducing new animals and reporting suspected outbreaks of disease to the relevant competent authority. Similar provisions apply for those food business operators who produce or harvest plant products or crops. Records should be kept of details related to the origin of animals kept, their feed, any veterinary medicines or plant protection products used, any incidence of health issues or disease, and any results of sampling analyses undertaken.

General Hygiene Requirements for all Food Business Operators

Annex II to the Food Hygiene Regulation sets out the main requirements for those food business operators who are not engaged in what can be classified as 'primary production'. These apply across all stages of the production, processing and distribution of food. Conditions are set for food premises, preparation areas, temporary facilities such as market stalls and mobile sales vehicles, and transportation.

Chapter I of Annex II provides that permanent food premises must be kept clean and maintained in good repair and condition. The layout, design, construction, siting and size of food premises must allow for adequate maintenance and cleaning, limit air-borne contamination and provide sufficient space for the hygienic performance of all operations. They must also be established in a way that protects against pests, contamination and the accumulation of dirt, and which prevents contact with toxic materials, the shedding of particles onto food and the formation of condensation and mould. Requirements are also set on the positioning and availability of changing facilities for staff, storage for cleaning agents, lavatories, sinks, water, drainage, lighting and ventilation. Chapter II sets similar requirements for rooms which are used, on an ongoing basis, for the

---

[72] Annex II, Chapter XII further states that '[f]ood business operators are to ensure that food handlers are supervised and instructed and/or trained in food hygiene activities commensurate with their work activity; that those responsible for the development and maintenance of the [HACCP procedure] have received adequate training in the application of the HACCP principles; and compliance with any requirements of national law concerning training programmes for persons working in certain food sectors'.

preparation, treatment and processing of food, excluding dining areas. Floor, door and wall surfaces are to be kept clean and disinfected. Ceilings and windows must be constructed in a way that prevents the accumulation of dirt, condensation and mould. Equipment and work surfaces must be maintained in good condition and be easy to clean and disinfect.[73] There must be a sufficient supply of hot and cold water and adequate provision for washing food.[74]

Chapter III of Annex II sets the requirements for those premises and rooms not covered by the other sections of this part of the Regulation. This includes all movable and/or temporary food premises, such as marquees, markets and mobile sales vehicles, as well as premises that are primarily used as a private residence but which are also regularly used for commercial food preparation. All premises covered by this section must be sited, designed and constructed in a way that facilitates cleanliness and minimises the risk of contamination, in particular by animals and pests. There must be appropriate personal hygiene facilities, such as washbasins and changing facilities, available.[75] Surfaces and work utensils must be clean. There must be an adequate supply of hot and cold water. A system must be in place for the proper storage and disposal of waste. Foods must be stored at the appropriate temperatures.

Chapter IV deals with the transportation of food. All containers used for food transportation must be kept clean and be designed in a way that facilitates cleaning and disinfection. Any receptacles or containers used for the transportation of food cannot be used for any other purpose, or for the transportation of anything other than food, where this could lead to contamination. There must be an effective cleaning of these receptacles or containers where they have previously been used to transport something other than food. Different foods should be separated during transit where necessary. Foodstuffs transported in bulk that are in liquid, granulate or powder form should be contained in suitable receptacles or tankers that are clearly marked as being 'for foodstuffs only'. There should also be proper temperature control, appropriate to the foodstuff concerned, during transportation. The rules are designed to keep the risk of contamination or deterioration of the food to the minimum level possible.

The separation and disposal of food waste is dealt with in Annex II, Chapter VI. This provides that all food waste, non-edible by-products and other refuse must

---

[73] Annex II, Chapter V provides further specific requirements on the hygienic use of equipment in the production and processing of food.

[74] Annex II, Chapter VII provides further detail on water supply and use, including more specific provision on the use of steam and ice in food preparation.

[75] Annex II, Chapter VIII further provides that '[e]very person working in a food-handling area is to maintain a high degree of personal cleanliness and is to wear suitable, clean and, where necessary, protective clothing'. It also states that '[n]o person suffering from … a disease likely to be transmitted through food or afflicted, for example, with infected wounds, skin infections, sores or diarrhoea is to be permitted to handle food or enter any food-handling area in any capacity if there is any likelihood of direct or indirect contamination'. Responsibility for the reporting of any such symptoms is, in the first instance, with the person affected, who must let the food business operator know about his illness or disease.

be removed from food preparation and storage areas as quickly as possible. This material should be deposited in closable containers, unless it can be demonstrated to the competent authorities that some other sort of disposal system is appropriate in the circumstances. Refuse stores must also be kept clean and, where possible, free from animals and pests. Waste should be destroyed or disposed of in a hygienic and environmentally friendly way. It should not itself become a direct or indirect source of contamination.

The final chapters of Annex II to the Food Hygiene Regulation set out more stipulations on the hygienic preparation, packaging and treatment of foods. Food business operators cannot accept raw materials or ingredients, other than live animals, if they are known to be, or might reasonably be expected to be, contaminated with parasites, pathogenic micro-organisms or toxic, decomposed or foreign substances to the extent that, even after the application of hygienic processes, the final product would be unfit for human consumption. All raw materials and ingredients should also be stored in conditions that prevent harmful deterioration or contamination. Food businesses that manufacture and wrap processed foods must have suitable rooms for these activities, which are large enough for the separate storage of raw and processed materials. Separate refrigeration space should also be available. Cooling, freezing and thawing should all be done in a way that poses minimal risk to health, including ensuring that material is thawed so as to minimise the growth of pathogenic micro-organisms or the formation of toxins in the foods. Finally, materials used for wrapping and packaging should not themselves be a source of contamination.

6.5.3 Specific Hygiene Rules

The second of the three hygiene regulations, all introduced in April 2004, lays down more specific hygiene rules for foods produced from animals.[76] The need for this regulation was identified as being related to the fact that incidence of microbiological and chemical hazards tends to be reported more frequently for foods of animal origin.[77] 'Products of animal origin' includes the obvious, for example eggs, dairy, meat and fish, but also foods such as honey and those produced containing blood.[78] The rules laid down in this Regulation are designed to supplement those set out in the Food Hygiene Regulation.[79] This Regulation does not apply to food production for private domestic use or to the direct supply of small quantities by producers to consumers or local retail establishments.[80]

---

[76] Regulation (EC) No 853/2004 laying down specific hygiene rules for food of animal origin [2004] OJ L 226/22.

[77] ibid, Preamble, Recital 2.

[78] Annex I to Reg 853/2004, n 76 above.

[79] Reg 852/2004, n 59 above.

[80] Art 1(3) of Reg 853/2004, n 76 above.

The Regulation does not define what is meant by 'small quantities' or 'local retail establishments' but instead leaves this up to national authorities, provided that the relevant domestic laws are drafted in a way that ensures that the objectives of the EU Regulation are achieved.[81]

The Animal Hygiene Regulation sets out more specific obligations for food business operators.[82] These include applying the required identification mark to products of animal origin. The mark can only be applied if the product has been manufactured in accordance with this Regulation and in a registered and approved establishment.[83] Food business operators who run slaughterhouses must comply with the HACCP provisions of the Food Hygiene Regulation,[84] as well as more specific requirements tailored to meet the additional needs of producing food from animals.[85] This includes a range of stipulations on animal welfare, both during transportation to, and arrival at, the abattoir. Animals brought into the slaughter hall must be slaughtered as soon as possible thereafter.[86] Parts of the animal that are to be used for human consumption must be treated in a way that minimises the risk of any contamination.[87] Those parts that are not to be used must be removed from the clean sector at the first available opportunity. Carcasses and offal must not come into contact with floors, walls or work stands. Cutting, boning, storage and later transportation must take place in an environment with a set maximum temperature. As is usual with this type of Regulation, the European Commission is assisted by the Standing Committee on the Food Chain and Animal Health,[88] and the European Food Safety Authority where necessary.[89]

The second of the more specific EU Food Hygiene Regulations, and the third part of the overall corpus of rules on the hygienic production and marketing of food, is the Organisation of Official Controls Regulation.[90] This Regulation is designed to establish a framework for EU Member States to establish and apply national rules for the implementation of the hygiene rules set out in the other regulations. Again, it only applies to products of animal origin.[91] 'Official controls' are defined in the Regulation as being 'any form of control that the competent authority performs for the verification of compliance with food law, including

---

[81] Art 1(4).

[82] Art 3 in conjunction with Annexes II and III to Reg 853/2004.

[83] Art 5. The mark itself is dealt with in more detail in Reg 854/2004, n 90 below. Establishments must have been approved and registered under the terms of Reg 852/2004, n 59 above.

[84] Art 5 of Reg 852/2004, n 59 above.

[85] Annex II to Reg 853/2004, n 76 above.

[86] Annex III to Reg 853/2004.

[87] Full detail of this is set out in Annex III to the Regulation.

[88] Art 12.

[89] Art 13.

[90] Regulation (EC) No 854/2004 of the European Parliament and of the Council of 29 April 2004 laying down specific rules for the organisation of official controls on products of animal origin intended for human consumption [2004] OJ L 226/83.

[91] Art 1(1).

animal health and animal welfare rules'.[92] As will be seen here, this Regulation links up with the other two hygiene regulations discussed above, setting out how Member States such as the UK should practically apply the requirements set out therein. For example, the other regulations provide that food establishments must be 'approved' before they can operate legitimately.

This Regulation states that where such approval is required, the competent authority must first make an on-site visit to assess the establishment.[93] It can only then approve the establishment if the food business operator can demonstrate that he has met all of the requirements of the Food Hygiene Regulation and the Animal Hygiene Regulation. In some cases, conditional approval can be granted if it appears from the on-site visit that the establishment does meet all of the infrastructure and equipment requirements. It can then only grant full approval if a demonstration is made during a second on-site visit, which must take place within three months of the first one, that all of the other requirements set by those Regulations have been met as well.[94] Member States must then keep up-to-date lists of approved establishments.[95]

The Regulation also sets out a series of general principles for official controls in respect of all products of animal origin. These include that Member States must ensure that food business operators provide all assistance necessary to enable the national competent authorities to carry out their investigative tasks effectively.[96] This means that there must be facilitation, through national law, of access to all food establishment buildings, premises and installations. There should, in the same way, be full disclosure of documentation and records that enable the authorities to properly judge any given situation of business that they are investigating. All investigations carried out under the terms of this Regulation must be related to the Food Hygiene Regulation, the Animal Hygiene Regulation and the Animal By-products Regulation.[97] These official controls should include audits of good hygiene practices and HACCP procedures in general, as well as the more specific examinations related to different types of animal-based foodstuffs.[98] The general hygiene practice audits should verify that food business operators continuously apply the proper procedures related to the design and maintenance of premises and equipment, personal hygiene, employee training, pest control, water quality, temperature control and documentation.[99] The HACCP audits should verify that food business operators are also applying the correct procedures related to this on a continuous basis.[100]

---

[92] Art 2(1)(a).
[93] Art 3(1)(a).
[94] Art 3(1)(b).
[95] Art 3(6).
[96] Art 4(1).
[97] Regulation (EC) No 1774/2002 of the European Parliament and of the Council of 3 October 2002 laying down health rules concerning animal by-products not intended for human consumption [2002] OJ L 273/1.
[98] Art 4(3).
[99] Art 4(4).
[100] Art 4(5).

The more specific official controls take account of the type of food produced by the food business operator. There are requirements set by the Regulation for fresh meat,[101] molluscs,[102] fish,[103] and milk and dairy products.[104] The national competent authority is obliged to take action where any of these audits show that there has been non-compliance with the Regulations.[105] This action should include the imposition of any necessary sanitation procedures.[106] However, it may also include marketing restrictions or prohibitions, product recalls or closure of the business.[107]

6.5.4 Food Hygiene (England) Regulations 2006

The 2006 Hygiene Regulations deal with the domestic aspects of the interpretation and implementation of the three main EU Regulations in this area, outlined above.[108] Given that much of the content of the EU rules is aimed at food intended for human consumption, the English regulations clarify that

> [a]ny food commonly used for human consumption shall, if placed on the market or offered, exposed or kept for placing on the market, be presumed, until the contrary is proved, to have been ... intended for ... human consumption.[109]

This is then extended to include that

> any food commonly used for human consumption [or substance commonly used in the manufacture of food] which is found on premises used for the preparation, storage, or placing on the market of that food, shall be presumed, until the contrary is proved, to be intended for placing on the market [... for human consumption.[110]

This can also include any article or substance which is capable of being used in the composition or preparation of food.[111]

As we have seen from the EU regulations, the national competent authority is central to the application of the hygiene rules at national level. The Food Hygiene (England) Regulations 2006 designate the Food Standards Agency as the relevant authority for England in most circumstances.[112] They play a key role in monitoring the food business operators' discharge of their wide range of responsibilities and obligations set out in the three EU regulations. There is, however, also a

---

[101] Art 5.
[102] Art 6 in conjunction with Annex II.
[103] Art 7 in conjunction with Annex III.
[104] Art 8 in conjunction with Annex IV.
[105] Art 9(1).
[106] Art 9(2)(a).
[107] Art 9(2)(b), (c) and (e).
[108] The Food Hygiene (England) Regulations 2006, SI No 14/2006.
[109] Reg 3(2).
[110] Reg 3(3).
[111] Reg 3(4).
[112] Reg 4.

substantial role for local food authorities.[113] The demarcation of these respective roles is set out in the 2006 Regulations, but it should be noted that in some circumstances this responsibility is shared. This primarily depends on the type of production or activities of the food business operator concerned.

Hygiene Enforcement Responsibilities

Regulation 5(1) of the Food Hygiene (England) Regulations 2006 provides that the Food Standards Agency or the local food authority is responsible for executing and enforcing the EU Hygiene Regulation where the food business under review is carrying out primary production and comes within the scope of application of the Food Hygiene Regulation,[114] but not the Animal Hygiene Regulation.[115] However, the Agency has sole responsibility for the enforcement of these EU regulations where the food business is a slaughterhouse or cutting plant.[116] Food Authorities regain this responsibility for the enforcement of the Hygiene Regulations where this relates to the sea transportation of food,[117] temperature control requirements,[118] the direct supply of small quantities of poultrymeat,[119] and raw milk.[120]

Failure to comply with the requirements of the Hygiene Regulations can result in the initial serving of a 'hygiene improvement notice' on the food business operator by an authorised officer.[121] This outlines to the business how it has been in breach of the regulations, indicating what must be done to remedy the matter and when this must be done by.[122] It is an offence to fail to comply with the terms of this notice.[123] More serious breaches of the regulations, which lead to a conviction, can result in the serving of a 'hygiene prohibition order'.[124] The order itself can prohibit the food business operator from using a process, treatment, premises and/or equipment.[125] In some circumstances the food business operator may even be prohibited from participating in the management of any food business.[126] The order can only be lifted where the enforcement authority is satisfied that sufficient

---

[113] As defined in section 5(1) of the Food Safety Act 1990.

[114] Reg 852/2004, n 59 above.

[115] Reg 853/2004, n 76 above.

[116] Reg 5(2).

[117] Specifically the transportation by sea of liquid oils or fats and sugar, as set out in Sch 3 to the 2006 English Regulations.

[118] As set out in Sch 4 to the 2006 Regulations, n 108 above.

[119] As set out in Sch 5 to the 2006 Regulations.

[120] As set out in Sch 6 in conjunction with reg 5(4) of the 2006 Regulations. This responsibility does not extend to raw cows' milk. The Food Standards Agency retains control over this.

[121] Reg 6(1).

[122] Under the terms of reg 6(1) a minimum notice period of 14 days must be served on the food business operator.

[123] Reg 6(2).

[124] Reg 7(1).

[125] Reg 7(2).

[126] Reg 7(4).

measures have been taken to address the health risk that was previously posed or by the direction of a court.[127] 'Hygiene emergency prohibition notices' can be approved by a Magistrates' Court, following an application by an authorised officer, where the risk to health or safety is deemed to be imminent.[128] This converts the notices into orders. The defence of due diligence can be pleaded in any proceedings for an offence under these regulations. It is up to the accused to show, in such circumstances, that he 'took all reasonable precautions and exercised all due diligence to avoid the commission of the offence by himself or by a person under his control'.[129] Appeals can be made to a Magistrates' Court against the serving of any notice.[130] The dismissals of these appeals can themselves be appealed to the Crown Court, as can any decision made by the Magistrates' Court to make a hygiene prohibition order or a hygiene emergency prohibition order.[131]

Sampling and Analysis

Authorised officers are afforded wide powers under the 2006 Hygiene Regulations to enter premises, take samples and undertake analysis to assist them in ascertaining whether there has been a breach of the legislation. An authorised officer of any enforcement authority can purchase or take any sample of food, or substance used in the preparation of food, or of any contact material, such as packaging, for further analysis.[132] He can also take articles and substances from the premises of the food business where this may be required as evidence in any proceedings brought under the Regulations.[133] Samples taken are then sent for analysis by the public analyst or a food examiner.[134] The public are also entitled to submit samples of food that they have purchased to a public analyst or examiner where there is reason to believe that it poses some sort of health risk.[135] A certificate detailing the results of the analysis is sent to the applicant and can be used as evidence in any subsequent complaint.[136]

The procurement of samples by an authorised officer is supported by those provisions of the Regulations that empower entry into food premises for this purpose. The officer has the right, at all reasonable hours, to enter any premises within his area of authority for the purpose of ascertaining whether there is or

---

[127] Reg 7(6).
[128] Reg 8.
[129] Reg 11(1).
[130] Reg 20.
[131] Reg 21.
[132] Reg 12(1) and (2).
[133] Reg 12(3).
[134] Reg 13(1).
[135] Reg 13(2).
[136] Reg 13(7) and (8). The certificate should be in the form set out in Sch 3 to the Food Safety (Sampling and Qualifications) Regulations 1990. The certificate, if it shows a breach of the Hygiene Regulations, must be acted upon by the court. See *Allan Rich Seafoods v Lincoln Magistrates' Court* [2009] EWHC 3391.

has been any contravention of the provisions of the Hygiene Regulations.[137] The only exception to this is where the premises concerned are also a private dwelling house. These can still be entered for this purpose, but only where at least 24 hours' notice has been provided. This power is provided to both local authority authorised officers and those appointed by the Food Standards Agency. A warrant can be provided, allowing for the use of reasonable force to enter a food premises where this admission has been refused or prevented by the food business operator.[138] Obstructing those who are charged with enforcing the Hygiene Regulations is an offence.[139] Once inside the premises, the officer has the right to inspect and seize records, including those held on computer.[140] Supplying false records is also an offence under the Regulations.[141] Conviction of any offence under the Hygiene Regulations can result in the imposition of a fine, or imprisonment for up to two years, or both.[142]

There are, as we know, three main EU hygiene regulations. Two of these deal specifically with meat and food produced from animals. While the general rules set out in the Food Hygiene (England) Regulations 2006 apply across the entire food sector, additional specific provision related to the monitoring of the hygienic production of food from animals is set out in further pieces of domestic legislation, such as the Official Feed and Food Controls (England) Regulations 2006[143] and the Official Controls (Animals, Feed and Food) (England) Regulations 2006,[144] as was discussed in chapter three.

---

[137] Reg 14(1).

[138] Reg 14(3).

[139] Reg 15(1).

[140] Reg 14(6) and (7).

[141] Reg 15(2).

[142] Reg 17. This is limited to a three-month prison sentence and/or a lower level fine for conviction of a breach of reg 15, which prohibits the obstruction of authorised officers or furnishing false information.

[143] SI No 15/2006.

[144] SI No 3472/2006.

7

Food Labelling and Advertising

7.1 Framework Food Labelling Legislation

Compulsory indications that must appear on the labelling of all pre-packaged foods have been standardised at EU level since the late 1970s.[1] This legislation first appeared in English law as the Food Labelling Regulations 1980.[2] Although there have been multiple amendments to the original EU directive, including a re-draft in 2000,[3] current provisions have remained almost identical to those first set out in 1979. Some new additions have been included in the list of mandatory particulars but, by and large, food labelling requirements have remained relatively unchanged for several decades. This, however, will change when the much-heralded proposals for a new EU regulation come into effect during the period 2014–2016.[4] For the purposes of this chapter, both the existing national and incoming EU regulations are discussed. The existing provisions of the Food Labelling Regulations are referred to throughout,[5] with specific reference to the EU Food Information Regulation where this will make a change to existing laws after its full implementation in 2016.[6]

---

[1] Council Directive 1979/112/EEC of 18 December 1978 on the approximation of the laws of the Member States relating to the labelling, presentation and advertising of foodstuffs for sale to the ultimate consumer [1979] OJ L 33/1.

[2] SI No 1849/1980.

[3] Directive 2000/13/EC of the European Parliament and of the Council of 20 March 2000 on the approximation of the laws of the Member States relating to the labelling, presentation and advertising of foodstuffs [2000] OJ L 109/29.

[4] Proposal for a Regulation of the European Parliament and of the Council on the provision of food information to consumers, COM (2008) 40. Now Reg 1169/2011, n 6 below.

[5] The Food Labelling Regulations 1996, SI No 1499/1996.

[6] Regulation (EU) No 1169/2011 of the European Parliament and of the Council of 25 October 2011 on the provision of food information to consumers, amending Regulations (EC) No 1924/2006 and (EC) No 1925/2006 of the European Parliament and of the Council, and repealing Commission Directive 1987/250/EEC, Council Directive 1990/496/EEC, Commission Directive 1999/10/EC, Directive 2000/13/EC of the European Parliament and of the Council, Commission Directives 2002/67/EC and 2008/5/EC and Commission Regulation (EC) No 608/2004 [2011] OJ L 304/18. For more on its implementation see, eg, L González Vaqué, 'The new European regulation on food labelling: are we ready for the "D" day on 13 December 2014?' (2013) 8 *European Food and Feed Law Review* 158.

7.1.1 Labelling Definitions

The labelling and advertising of food is regulated at domestic level by the Food Labelling Regulations 1996[7] and the Food Information Regulation 2011 from 2014–2016 onwards.[8] Labelling is defined in the English regulations as being:

> any words, particulars, trade mark, brand name, pictorial matter or symbol relating to the food and appearing on the packaging of the food or on any document, notice, label, ring or collar accompanying the food.[9]

Although the legal definition is clearly a broad one, it is not all-encompassing. The European Court of Justice has clarified that details provided on the packaging will only be classified as forming part of the labelling if its purpose is 'specifically intended to inform the consumer as to the characteristics of the product in question'.[10] A national cheese mark, essentially a serial number, designed to demonstrate to the authorities that the product had been made in compliance with certain rules, does not satisfy this 'consumer information' requirement. It is not, therefore, 'labelling' within the legal definition of the term.[11] The information imparted to the consumer should therefore be related to the nature, identity, properties, composition, quality, durability, origin or manufacturing method of the foodstuff for it to constitute 'labelling'.[12]

Other important definitions set out in the Food Labelling Regulations 1996 include that for the 'ultimate consumer' who is described as 'any person who buys other than for the purpose of resale, for … a catering establishment or for … a manufacturing business'.[13] This, however, fails to account for the fact that the purchaser and the consumer are often different people. This is an important consideration to make in the context of food labelling because the information imparted is as significant for the person who actually prepares or consumes the food as for the one who bought it, a point also clearly recognised by the European Court of Justice.[14]

---

[7] SI No 1499/1996.

[8] Reg (EU) No 1169/2011, n 6 above. For more on the protracted process of introducing this regulation, see P Dévényi, 'The new regulation on the provision of food information to consumers: is new always better?' (2011) 6 *European Food and Feed Law Review* 210.

[9] Reg 2(1). This definition is the same as that which was set out in Art 1(3) of the framework food labelling directive, Directive 2000/13, n 3 above. It is similarly defined as such in Art 2(2)(j) of the Food Information Regulation 1169/2011.

[10] Case C-285/1992 *Criminal proceedings against Coöperatieve Zuivelindustrie "Twee Provinciën" WA* [1993] ECR I-6045.

[11] Paras 16–18 of the judgment.

[12] Art 7(1)(a) of the Food Information Regulation 1169/2011, n 6 above, and para 30 of Case 298/1987, *Proceedings for compulsory reconstruction against Smanor SA* [1988] ECR 4489.

[13] Reg 2(1).

[14] Paras 24 and 25 of Case C-85/1994, *Groupement des Producteurs, Importateurs et Agents Généraux d'Eaux Minérales Etrangères, VZW (Piageme) and others v Peeters NV* [1995] ECR I-2955; and para 24 of Case C-385/1996, *Criminal proceedings against Hermann Josef Goerres* [1998] ECR I-4431. This more pragmatic definition of 'consumer' is not, however, properly clarified in Art 2 of the General Food Law Regulation, Regulation 178/2002 [2002] OJ L 31/1, where the 'final consumer' is deemed to be the 'ultimate consumer of a foodstuff who will not use the food as part of any food business operation or activity'. It is not properly defined in the Food Information Regulation either.

The Food Labelling Regulations 1996 consistently make reference to the 'purchaser', and not the 'consumer'. This is something that will be addressed by the introduction of the Food Information Regulation, which specifically refers to 'consumers' throughout, making only two references to 'purchasers'. In particular, Article 7(1) of the EU Food Information Regulation provides that '[f]ood information shall be accurate, clear and easy to understand for the consumer'.

The compulsory indications that must appear on all food labels, apart from those which are specifically excluded from the provisions of the Regulations, such as natural mineral water,[15] or those which have their own labelling requirements set out in other legislation,[16] are as established by the Food Information Regulation. These include the name of the food, a list of ingredients, the appropriate durability indication, any special storage conditions or conditions of use, the name or business name and an address or registered office of either or both of the manufacturer or packer or a seller established within the EU, particulars of the place of origin or provenance of the food if failure to provide this might mislead a purchaser as to the true origin of the food and, finally, instructions for use where necessary.[17] One of the most obvious changes to be made by the introduction of the EU Food Information Regulation is that nutrient declarations will be included in this list of compulsory indications from December 2016.[18] This is discussed in more detail in chapter nine.

'Food' is not defined, nor is there any reference to any such definition, in the Food Labelling Regulations. It is, of course, defined elsewhere.[19]

7.1.2 Labelling Format

All of the labelling particulars must appear either on the packaging, on a label attached to the packaging or on a label that is clearly visible through the packaging.[20] There are, of course, some exceptions to this where labelling is not required or where the packaging does not facilitate the use of standard labels. These instances are identified where appropriate throughout this chapter. For example, the removable foil cap or lid on a bottle of milk can be used to display the required information to the purchaser.[21]

All particulars must be provided in a manner that is easy to understand. It must be clearly legible and indelible. It must also be clearly visible to the consumer.[22]

---

[15] Reg 3(4).

[16] Eg honey, which is dealt with by the Honey Regulations 1976, SI 1832/1976; chocolate, which is regulated by the Cocoa and Chocolate Products (England) Regulations 2003, SI 1659/2003; and coffee, which is covered by the Coffee and Coffee Products Regulations 1978, SI 1420/1978, as amended by the Coffee and Coffee Products (Amendment) Regulations 1987, SI 1986/1987.

[17] Reg 5.

[18] Art 54 in conjunction with Art 9(1)(l) of Reg 1169/2011, n 6 above.

[19] Eg the Food Safety Act 1990 and EU Regulation 178/2002 [2002] OJ L 31/1.

[20] Reg 35.

[21] Reg 37.

[22] Reg 38(1).

It cannot be hidden or obscured in any way.[23] This does not preclude providing information, when required, at catering establishments, which may use temporary media such as chalk and blackboards.[24]

The main information provided by the labelling requirements must all appear in the same field of vision. This includes the name of the food, the indication of durability, the alcohol content where required, any cautionary words indicating the use of raw milk, warnings about unsuitability for use as baby food,[25] the net quantity[26] and, from 2016, the nutritional information.

7.1.3 Food Names

Food names that appear on labelling should be as prescribed by law,[27] such as a 'recipe' law,[28] or some other form of set compositional or quality-based requirements.[29] These are known as 'legal names'. A detailed list of specific food names is also set out in Schedule 1 to the Food Labelling Regulations 1996, including those for different varieties of fish, as well as for melons and potatoes, which must always be sold with an indication of their variety. If no name is prescribed for a food by a specific law, the name that is customarily used where the food is sold should be on the label.[30] This is known as a 'customary name'. Where neither a legal nor a customary name exists, a 'descriptive name' should be used. This is a name that is 'sufficiently precise to inform a purchaser of the true nature of the food and to enable the food to be distinguished from products with which it could be confused'.[31] Trademarks, brand names or 'fancy names' should not be substituted for the name of a food.[32] The latter are not defined in either the English or the EU legislation. Indications of physical condition or treatment, such as dried, frozen, concentrated or smoked, should be provided alongside the name of the food where necessary.[33]

---

[23] Reg 38(2).

[24] Reg 38(3).

[25] As set out in reg 32.

[26] Reg 39. Quantity declarations are also dealt with by the Weights and Measures Act 1985.

[27] Reg 6(1).

[28] Eg those set for honey, chocolate and coffee, as set out in n 16 above.

[29] Such as that set for 'butter' by Council Regulation (EC) No 2991/94 of 5 December 1994 laying down standards for spreadable fats [1994] OJ L 316/2, or that set for 'sugar' by the Specified Sugar Products (England) Regulations 2003, SI No 1563/2003.

[30] Reg 7.

[31] Reg 8. In *Birds Eye Walls Ltd v Shropshire County Council* (1994) 158 JP 961, it was held that describing a product as a 'prize burger' lacked the precision necessary in a food name to enable it to distinguish the product from others with which it could be confused. This was considered to be so because the same producer sold another product named the '100% burger' for the same price, even though the latter contained 100% meat, while the former contained nearly 15% vegetable protein.

[32] Reg 10.

[33] Reg 11.

7.1.4 Ingredients

The list of ingredients which must be included on all food products, subject to some exceptions,[34] must be headed or preceded by an appropriate heading which consists of or includes the word 'ingredients'.[35] The ingredients should usually be listed in descending order of weight used in the preparation of the product.[36] The main exception to this ordering of ingredients occurs when water is used, as its position in the list is calculated on the basis of the quantity of it present in the finished product, rather than on the quantity used in preparation.[37] Water does not have to be listed as an ingredient at all where it is used to reconstitute an ingredient or it is not consumed as part of the product or if it does not exceed 5 per cent of the finished foodstuff.[38] Ingredients themselves are defined as being:

> any substance, including any additive and any constituent of a compound ingredient, which is used in the preparation of a food and which is still present in the finished product, even if in altered form.[39]

Compound ingredients, mentioned above, are 'composed of two or more [ingredients]'.[40] In some circumstances, the names of all of the ingredients of a compound ingredient are to be listed, usually in a way that makes it clear that they are the ingredients of the compound ingredient.[41] A compound ingredient is often just listed by its generic name. This is so because under the terms of the Regulations, the full list of components of the compound ingredient need not be provided where it constitutes less than 25 per cent of the finished product.[42] The only exception to this is where additives are used. These must be listed beside the name of the compound ingredient.[43] Foods that consist of, or which contain, mixed fruit, nuts, vegetables, spices or herbs and no single fruit or nut, etc predominates the mixture by weight, then these ingredients may be listed as a group, with details about the components of the mixture and a statement that they are contained 'in variable proportion'.[44]

---

[34] The exceptions are set out in reg 18, and are discussed in more detail later in this section.

[35] Reg 12.

[36] Reg 13. Ingredients used in concentrated or dehydrated form and later reconstituted during preparation of the food should be placed in the list of ingredients according to the pre-concentration or pre-dehydration condition, reg 13(3). Also, where a food is sold in concentrated or dehydrated form and is usually reconstituted by the addition of water, its ingredients may be listed in descending order of their weight post-reconstitution, reg 13(4). When this is the case, the list of ingredients should be preceded by the heading 'ingredients of the reconstituted product' or similar.

[37] Reg 13(2).

[38] Reg 16(1).

[39] Reg 2(1).

[40] Reg 2(1).

[41] Reg 15(1) and 15(2).

[42] Reg 15(4).

[43] Reg 15(4)(b).

[44] Reg 13(5).

Ingredients should usually be listed using the name that would be used if the ingredient were being sold as a food.[45] Flavourings should be clearly identified in the list of ingredients.[46] The word 'natural', or similar, should only be used for ingredients when derived from material of animal or plant origin, which is either raw or which has only been subjected to processes normally used in food production.[47] Additives should be identified by their type,[48] as set out in Schedule 4 to the Regulations. Those listed include acidity regulators, anti-caking agents, colours, emulsifiers, flavour enhancers, gelling agents, humectants, preservatives, raising agents, stabilisers, sweeteners and thickeners. If an additive serves more than one of these functions then it should be listed by its principal purpose and its name or 'E' number.[49]

Ingredients Listing Exceptions

All of the above requirements on the listing of ingredients are subject to two important exceptions. First, some ingredients do not need to be named. Second, some foodstuffs do not need to bear a list of ingredients at all.

The most significant exclusion from the ingredients listing requirement is the additive that is contained in an ingredient and serves 'no technological function' in the finished product.[50] This means that any additive used in the production of an ingredient does not have to be listed on the label, once it does not affect the nature of the finished product. This is a complicated matter, perhaps best explained by reference to the European Court of Justice's assessment of what constitutes an additive in an ingredient that serves no technological function in the finished product.

In its decision in *Pfanni Werke*,[51] the Court of Justice discussed the fact that EU law provides that additives serving no technological function are not considered to be ingredients.[52] This provision was transposed into German law in a similar manner to the English transposition of the same provision by the Food Labelling Regulations 1996. A German manufacturer of dehydrated potato products had

---

[45] Reg 14(1). There must be an appropriate declaration when any ingredients have been irradiated, Reg 14(2). This latter provision reflects the requirements of Art 6(3) of the Framework Food Labelling Directive, Directive 2000/13, n 3 above. This requirement is now also contained in Annex VI to Reg 1169/2011, n 6 above.

[46] Reg 14(5).

[47] Reg 14(6), 14(7) and 14(8).

[48] Reg 14(9).

[49] The lists of permitted 'E' numbers that can be used to identify additives as ingredients, or 'serial numbers' as they are called in the Food Labelling Regulations 1996, are set out in the Flavourings in Food Regulations 1992, SI No 1971/1992; the Food Additives Labelling Regulations 1992, SI No 1978/1992; the Sweeteners in Food Regulations 1995, SI No 3123/1995; the Colours in Food Regulations 1995, SI No 3124/1995; the Miscellaneous Food Additives Regulations 1995, SI No 3187/1995; and the Bread and Flour Regulations 1998, SI No 141/1998. Additives, and some of the issues surrounding the use of 'E' numbers as an identification method, were discussed in more detail in ch 4.

[50] Reg 17(b).

[51] Case C-144/1993 *Pfanni Werke Otto Eckart KG v Landeshauptstadt München* [1994] ECR I-4605.

[52] As now set out in Art 20(b)(i) of Reg 1169/2011, n 6 above.

added diphosphate (E450a) to one of its products, potato purée flakes, to prevent discoloration during the manufacturing process. Local authorities warned the manufacturer that failing to list this additive as an ingredient was contrary to labelling laws and could lead to the imposition of a fine. The company subsequently brought an action against the authorities, claiming that the additive in question did not play any role in the finished product and did not, therefore, have to be listed. It was, they claimed, added to potato pulp to prevent it from changing colour and that the production of this pulp was only one stage in the manufacture of 'potato purée flakes'. After the dehydration of that pulp the colour of the potato flakes could not change. Initial domestic judgment went against the applicant, the local court considering that the inclusion of an additive that ultimately altered the appearance of a product had to be included in the list of ingredients. On second appeal, on a point of law, to the Federal Administrative Court, the case was referred to the Court of Justice to establish whether an additive such as this, used to prevent the discoloration of an ingredient, continues to serve a technological function in the finished product. The Court accepted that the purpose of the labelling legislation was to inform consumers by, inter alia, requiring producers to list ingredients. However, derogations from this provision, such as that on the technological function of additives, exist to ensure that information provided to consumers is effective. Requiring the publication of an exhaustive list of ingredients used would, according to the Court, deprive the legislation of its substance.

In this particular case, the fact that discoloration was no longer possible in the finished product meant that the presence of diphosphate E450a was no longer necessary in the finished product. Accordingly, this additive 'no longer serves a technological function in the finished product so that, if the consumer is not to be misled, it should not be included in the list of ingredients'.[53] Diphosphate E450a did not, therefore, have to be listed as an ingredient used in the manufacture of potato purée flakes.

This 'no technological function' exemption from the list of ingredients as interpreted by the Court of Justice in *Pfanni Werke* raises a number of concerns. First, the Court accepted that the purpose of the original Framework Food Labelling Directive, as transposed into English law by the Food Labelling Regulations 1996, was to 'inform and protect the consumer'.[54] The Directive further stated that 'labelling ... must not be such as could mislead the purchaser ... as to the characteristics of the foodstuff and, in particular, as to its ... composition'.[55] The Court goes on to accept that the additive is present in the finished product. However, having served its irreversible function, it does not have to be listed as

---

[53] Para 18.

[54] Para 15 of *Pfanni Werke*, n 51 above. Recital 6 of the Preamble to Directive 2000/13, n 3 above, also stated that '[t]he prime consideration for any rules on the labelling of foodstuffs should be the need to inform and protect the consumer'.

[55] Art 2(1)(a) of Directive 2000/13, n 3 above. Now contained in Art 7(1) of Reg 1169/2011, n 6 above.

an ingredient. This misleads the consumer about the composition of the product. If an additive is contained in a foodstuff, the fact that the function that it serves is irreversible should not mean that it does not have to be listed as an ingredient. Should several additives contained in the finished product serve no ongoing 'technological function', the list of ingredients may deceptively portray the product as containing relatively few additives. This appears entirely at odds with the declared purpose of informing the consumer.

Second, the Court does present one good argument for removing the need to list all additives—the 'de-cluttering' of the ingredients list to make the information provided more effective. However, if we work on the basis that consumers tend to see additives as a group of constituents to be avoided, or at worst to be taken in minimal quantities, then an ingredients list that reveals less than the total quantity of additives present could be considered simple, but very misleading. Effectively, product A could contain fewer additives than product B, but it must be labelled in a way that makes it appear as if it contains more of them, depending on whether the additives present in product A serve a reversible or an irreversible function in the finished foodstuff.

Other ingredients that do not need to be listed on the label include additives used solely as a processing aid,[56] and substances other than water which are used as a solvent or carrier for an additive and which are used in an amount that is no more than that which is absolutely necessary for that purpose.[57]

The second key exception to the ingredients listing requirement is that some foods do not need to bear a list of ingredients at all. This includes fresh fruit and vegetables that have not been peeled or cut; carbonated water that contains no other ingredients; fermentation vinegar produced from a single basic product; cheese, butter, fermented milk and fermented cream where no ingredients other than lactic products, enzymes, micro-organism cultures or, in the case of cheese, salt essential to manufacture have been added; single ingredient foods; and drinks with an alcoholic strength above 1.2 per cent by volume.[58] If a substance is added to any food contained in this list, a full list of ingredients is not required. A statement of 'added ingredients' can appear on the label instead.[59]

Quantitative Ingredient Declarations

When a food is marketed by 'special emphasis' on the inclusion of a specific ingredient, the actual percentage quantity of this ingredient that is used in the

---

[56] Reg 17(c).
[57] Reg 17(d).
[58] Reg 18(1).
[59] Reg 18(2).

production of this foodstuff must be stated on the label.[60] This is known as the 'quantitative ingredient declaration' or 'QUID'.[61]

By 'any reference' the Regulations are referring to any words, symbols or pictures that suggest to the consumer that the product contains a particular ingredient.[62] Where this happens, the producer is required to make a declaration of the quantity of that ingredient, or ingredients, contained in the product. This should be listed as a percentage, appearing next to the name of the food or next to the name of the ingredient as it appears in the list.[63] Therefore, for example, if a label makes reference to the inclusion of strawberries in a cereal bar, either by stating this in words or by some sort of pictorial reference, like a photograph of a strawberry, then the overall quantity of strawberries contained in that bar must be listed beside the name of that ingredient in the ingredients list, or in the description of the product. References to the use of an ingredient which is only used in a small quantity as a flavouring does not constitute 'special emphasis' and is not, therefore, subject to the quantitative ingredient declaration requirements.[64]

The requirements on quantitative ingredient declarations set out in the Food Labelling Regulations 1996 are much less stringent than those originally set out in the Framework Food Labelling Directive.[65] The Directive stated that QUID was to be employed whenever the ingredient concerned appeared in the name of the product or was usually associated with that name by consumers, where there is 'emphasis'—as opposed to 'special emphasis'—on the inclusion of the ingredient or the ingredient characterises the foodstuff and distinguishes it from products with which it might be confused.[66] 'Special emphasis' is not defined anywhere in the 1996 Regulations. The EU Food Information Regulation continues to refer to the presence of the ingredient(s) being 'emphasised'.[67] The wording of the English regulations indicates, however, that some use of pictures or wording that suggests the inclusion of certain ingredients may be allowed without any quantitative ingredient declaration being made. This addition of the word 'special' in the English regulations will have to be altered or removed after Regulation 1169/2011 comes into effect, given that it makes no reference to anything other than mere 'emphasis', and it will be directly applicable in national law.

---

[60] Reg 19(1).

[61] Quantitative ingredient declaration requirements were not included in the original Framework Food Labelling Directive, Directive 1979/112, n 1 above. They were, however, inserted into Art 7 of the first framework directive by Directive 97/4/EC [1997] OJ L 43/21. They remained one of the only significant amendments to the framework legislation when the second framework food labelling directive, Directive 2000/13, n 3 above, was introduced several years later.

[62] Art 7(2)(b) of Directive 2000/13, n 3 above, refers to 'words, pictures or graphics'.

[63] Regs 19(1) and 19(3).

[64] Reg 19(5).

[65] Art 7(2) of Directive 2000/13, n 3 above.

[66] Art 7(2) of Directive 2000/13, n 3 above.

[67] Art 22 of Reg 1169/2011, n 6 above.

7.1.5 Date of Durability

Under the terms of the 1996 Regulations, a 'best before' date should appear on the label to indicate to the purchaser/consumer 'the date up to and including which the food can reasonably be expected to retain its specific properties if properly stored'.[68] This should be expressed in terms of a day, month and year, in that order.[69] There are some exceptions to this. These are based on the degree to which the product is perishable. For example, foods that are expected to 'go off' within three months of manufacture need not have a year stated as part of the best before date on the label.[70] Foods that last more than three months, but less than 18 months, do not need to have a date included, just month and year details, provided that the words 'best before' that must precede the date are replaced with the words 'best before end'.[71] Foods that remain edible and retain their specific properties for more than 18 months are only required to carry details about the end of the year by which they should be beyond their prime.[72] The words 'best before' or 'best before end' do not need to appear directly beside the date, provided that reference is made to the place on the packaging where the date and/or the recommended storage conditions do appear.[73]

Under the terms of the EU legislation, foods which are highly perishable, and are therefore likely to constitute a danger to health if consumed after expiry, should replace the 'best before' date with the 'use by' date instead.[74] The UK Regulations make provision for the use of the latter, but, rather unhelpfully, do not indicate the circumstances in which this should be used. They merely state: '[w]here a "use by" date is required in respect of a food',[75] without actually stating when this may be required to happen.[76] The 'use by' date should be set according to the date up to and including which the food, if properly stored, is recommended for use.[77] Suitable storage conditions must also be listed.[78] It should be expressed as a day and month, or a day, month and year.[79] As with the 'best before' date, the 'use by' date may also be printed separately from the words 'use by', provided that this

---

[68] Reg 20(1).

[69] Reg 20(2).

[70] Reg 20(2)(a).

[71] Regs 20(2)(b) and 20(1).

[72] Reg 20(2)(c).

[73] Reg 20(3).

[74] Art 10 of Directive 2000/13, n 3 above and, from December 2014 onwards, Art 24 in conjunction with Annex X to Reg 1169/2011, n 6 above.

[75] Reg 21(1).

[76] While a food is no longer 'highly perishable' after it has been frozen, the 'use by' date continues to apply. Sale of the previously frozen food after this date continues to be an offence under the terms of the Food Labelling Regulations 1996. See: *Torfaen Borough Council v Douglas Willis Limited* [2012] EWHC 296.

[77] Reg 21(1)(a).

[78] Reg 21(1)(b).

[79] Reg 21(2).

is followed by a reference to the place where the date and storage conditions do appear, such as 'for use by date see lid'.[80] There is an obvious practical reason for allowing this. It means that the producer does not need to alter the label on the main form of all of his packaging, just on one element of it, such as the lid. This is likely to be more convenient and more cost-effective.

Some foods do not have to be marketed with any details about the durability date stated on the label. Untreated fresh fruit and vegetables, wine or any drink with an alcohol content above 10 per cent, bread and pastry products normally consumed within 24 hours, vinegar, salt and chewing gum, amongst others, are all exempt from this requirement.[81]

7.1.6 Indications of Origin

There are two main types of origin marking on food labels. Both are controversial. The first, which is examined in more detail here, relates simply to the place of production. Statements on the label, such as 'English chicken' or 'EU honey' are both examples of this first type of origin indication. They are contentious because they are often deceptive. 'English chicken' may not actually be produced in England. Shortcomings in the law as it stands facilitate the deception of consumers who may have a preference for locally or nationally produced food in some circumstances. However, this has now been addressed to a significant degree by the introduction of new meat origin labelling requirements by the Food Information Regulation. This is discussed further below.

The second type of origin indication on food, the geographical indication, is assessed in much more detail in the next chapter. All that needs to be said here, therefore, is that this type of labelling disclosure relates to foods that have been registered for protection throughout the EU, and potentially beyond, because they have satisfied the decision-making authorities that they possess special characteristics that distinguish them from other similar products. Registered geographical food names can only be used by those producers who are covered by the terms of the registration. This is usually a group of producers who all obtain their ingredients and operate within a clearly defined geographical area, possibly manufacturing their wares using traditional or alternative methods of production.

The first type of origin marking, which is within the scope of this chapter, and which is directly legislated for in the Food Information Regulation, is the statement about where a foodstuff has been produced, such as 'Made in …' or 'Product of …'. This can often be the most misleading piece of information to appear on food labels, either by giving the false impression that a product has been made in

---

[80] Reg 21(3).
[81] Reg 22.

a place, and/or with ingredients from that place, or by the total absence from the label of any meaningful information about the place of provenance at all.[82]

The Food Information Regulation provides that indication of the country of origin or place of provenance shall only be mandatory[83]

> where failure to indicate this might mislead the consumer as to the true country of origin or place of provenance of the food, in particular if the information accompanying the food or the label as a whole would otherwise imply that the food has a different country of origin or place of provenance [and] for meat falling within the Combined Nomenclature codes listed in Annex XI.[84]

These meats referred to in the latter part of this extract include that from pigs, poultry, sheep and goats. To be clear about this, origin labelling is therefore only mandatory, under the terms of the Regulation, where the product is either a particular type of meat or where the labelling and/or packaging would be misleading otherwise. Since the BSE crisis, beef has already had its own specific labelling requirements.[85]

7.1.7 Labelling Exemptions

According to the Regulations, and the application of the law, food labels can often omit as much significant information as they impart. In some circumstances, foods sold to consumers do not have to disclose anything on the label at all. This can lead to difficulties, especially when many of those foods that are exempt from the labelling requirements are often high in fat, sugar and/or salt content. Competent authorities may wish to reduce the consumption of these in the interests of improving health. However, the law may prevent them from ensuring that this inclusion is disclosed to consumers. A properly informed choice cannot therefore be made in the circumstances.

Pastries, breads and cakes that are sold in transparent packaging or which are not packaged at all, but are instead intended to be sold as single items, do not have to comply with the standard labelling requirements.[86] In other words, cakes, buns, breads, doughnuts, etc that are sold in bakeries or other outlets and which are not

---

[82] It has been held that the sale of American made 'Greek' yoghurt in England and Wales 'plainly involves a material misrepresentation', and was therefore passing off. A permanent injunction against the sale of this product as such was thus granted by the court in *FAGE UK Ltd v Chobani UK Ltd* [2013] EWHC 630.

[83] Art 33(5) of Reg 1169/2011, n 6 above.

[84] ibid, Art 26(2).

[85] Reg (EC) 1760/2000 of the European Parliament and of the Council establishing a system for the identification and registration of bovine animals and regarding the labelling of beef and beef products and repealing Council Regulation 820/1997 [2000] OJ L 204/1 (in conjunction with Commission Regulation (EC) 1825/2000 laying down detailed rules for the application of Regulation 1760/2000 as regards the labelling of beef and beef products [2000] OJ L 216/8, as amended by Commission Regulation (EC) 275/2007 [2007] OJ L76/12).

[86] Reg 23. The standard labelling requirements are set out in Reg 5.

packaged, usually because they are meant for near-immediate consumption, do not have to carry the compulsory indications required for other, less perishable and properly packaged products. Foods that consequently escape the labelling requirements will, of course, have no list of ingredients on the packaging. They must, however, still indicate the inclusion of additives in the preparation of the product where this would usually have to appear on the label—where a technological function is still served.[87] Alternatively, this information can be relayed to the purchaser through the use of a display, placed in a prominent position near the product's point of sale.[88] Irradiated ingredients must, however, be included on the labelling of all foodstuffs, regardless of whether the exemption usually applies.[89]

All of the labelling requirements set out in the 1996 Regulations do not apply to any pre-packaged food that is contained in an indelibly marked glass bottle intended for reuse that has no label, ring or collar, or the largest surface of whose packaging has an area of less than 10 cm².[90] Only the food name must be listed and, in some circumstances, the best before or use by date.[91]

Perhaps the most significant type of food that is exempted from the requirements of the Food Labelling Regulations is that which is sold in catering establishments. Food sold in cafés, bars and restaurants does not have to be labelled with any of the otherwise compulsory indications.[92]

7.1.8 Additional Labelling Requirements

While some foods do not have to carry a label containing any of the compulsory indications, others have to display details in addition to those set out as standard. There are some additional obligations for food sold from vending machines.[93] Alcoholic drinks must include an indication on the label of the strength by volume where this is more than 1.2 per cent.[94] The use of raw milk must be clearly disclosed by use of a statement such as 'this milk has not been heat-treated and may therefore contain organisms harmful to health'.[95] Milk substitutes, consisting of skimmed milk and non-milk fat, which are not designed for use as an infant formula or follow-on formula, must carry a clear statement that the product is unfit for use as food for babies.[96] Foods that have their durability extended by

[87] Reg 24(1).
[88] Reg 24(2).
[89] Reg 25.
[90] Reg 26(1).
[91] Reg 26(1).
[92] Reg 27(1). Irradiated foods must, of course, be labelled to indicate that they have been subject to this treatment (Reg 27(3) and (4)).
[93] Reg 29.
[94] Reg 30. For the purposes of the Regulation, the alcoholic strength of any drink is to be determined at 20 °C.
[95] Reg 31.
[96] Reg 32. Baby and infant foods are dealt with in more detail later in this chapter.

the use of packaging gas must be labelled with the indication that they have been 'packaged in a protective atmosphere'.[97] Foods containing sweeteners must also clearly indicate this. Simple statements, such as 'with sweeteners', 'with sugars and sweeteners' or 'contains a source of phenylalanine' may be used.[98]

Selling food that is not marked or labelled in accordance with the provisions of the 1996 Regulations, or which has passed its 'use by' date, is an offence, and those convicted are liable to a fine.[99] Enforcement of the labelling requirements is the responsibility of designated food authorities, usually local authorities.[100]

7.2 Nutrition Labelling and Claims

Requirements relating to the disclosure of the nutritional value of foods did not exist until the introduction of an EU directive on the matter in 1990.[101] These have since been incorporated into the Food Labelling Regulations 1996. Nutrition and health claims made on foods were not the subject of specific regulation until 2006.[102] Prior to this, they were only subject to the general, and less certain, requirement that they should not be misleading in any way. Nutrition labelling remains voluntary, unless a nutrition or health claim is made. However, as already alluded to earlier in this chapter, this will change during 2016 when the presentation of nutrient declarations becomes compulsory for the labelling of all pre-packaged foodstuffs, subject to some limited exceptions.

In order to properly understand the nutrition labelling and claims provisions set out in the 1996 Regulations, one needs to look at both Part III of the legislation and Schedules 6, 7 and 8 to it. Some claims are prohibited.[103] These include any claims that the food has tonic properties,[104] or that the food can prevent, treat or cure a disease.[105] 'Tonic' is not defined in the Regulations. Presumably it refers to

---

[97] Reg 33. The use of packaging gases is permitted by Council Directive 1989/107/EEC of 21 December 1988 on the approximation of the laws of the Member States concerning food additives authorised for use in foodstuffs intended for human consumption [1989] OJ L 40/27.

[98] Reg 34. The use of sweeteners is authorised more generally by the Sweeteners in Food Regulations 1995, SI No 3123/1995, as amended by the Sweeteners in Food (Amendment) Regulations 1996, SI No 1477/1996.

[99] Reg 44(1).

[100] Reg 45.

[101] Council Directive 1990/496/EEC of 24 September 1990 on nutrition labelling for foodstuffs [1990] OJ L 276/40.

[102] Regulation (EC) No 1924/2006 of the European Parliament and of the Council of 20 December 2006 on nutrition and health claims made on foods [2007] OJ L 12/3. The original publication of the Nutrition and Health Claims Regulation contained errors and was therefore republished in January 2007 as a corrigendum.

[103] Reg 40(1).

[104] This does not include use of the word 'tonic' in the description 'Indian tonic water' (Schedule 6, Part I).

[105] Schedule 6, Part I.

claims made that consumption of the food can make you feel invigorated, or at least physically or psychologically better.

7.2.1 Restricted Claims

Any claim that a food has particular nutritional properties must be capable of substantiation.[106] The aspects of the composition or manufacturing process that provide the food with these properties must be clearly labelled. The food must also carry nutrition labelling information. This is a key point about nutrition labelling. As stated, until 2016, the information only has to be displayed on the label where some sort of claim about the nutritional value or health benefit is made.[107] However, it should also be noted that where nutrition labelling is not prescribed, but it is used, then it has to be presented as if it were prescribed nutrition labelling.[108] The format for presenting this information relating to the nutritional values of the food is set out in Schedule 7 to the Regulations. Standard nutrition labelling must provide details on the energy level (calories), protein, carbohydrate (including the portion of this which is sugars), fat (including the portion which is saturated), and possibly also the amount of fibre, sodium and, where necessary, vitamins and minerals.[109]

Claims can also only be made where set requirements on the level of reduction/increase in the absence/presence are met. These are also set out in Schedule 6 to the Regulations. If a claim is made that a food has a 'low energy' value, it cannot contain more than 40 calories per 100 grams or millilitres. For claims that a product is a 'source of protein', the quantity of the food that can reasonably be expected to be consumed in one day must contribute at least 12 grams of protein. A claim that a food is a 'source of vitamins' can only be legitimately made when at least one half of the recommended daily intake of vitamin or vitamins specified is contained in the quantity of the food that it could be reasonably expected would be consumed within a single day. A reference to a vitamin in the name of a food does not in itself constitute a nutrition claim if the food consists solely of vitamins or minerals, such as in the form of a tablet or capsule supplement.[110] Similarly, a reference to a substance in a list of ingredients or in any nutrition labelling does not of itself constitute a claim.[111]

Nothing in the Regulations or the Schedule prevents the dissemination of information or recommendations that are intended exclusively for persons who are qualified as medical or dental practitioners, or those who have qualifications

---

[106] Reg 40(2) and Schedule 6, Part II.
[107] This is clearly set out in Art 2(2) of Directive 1990/496, n 101 above, and Art 7 of Reg 1924/2006, n 102 above.
[108] Reg 41(4).
[109] Schedule 7, Parts I and II.
[110] Schedule 6, Part II.
[111] Reg 41(2).

in nutrition, dietetics or pharmacy.[112] The other labelling requirements for products that carry claims do not have to be adhered to where the food is not pre-packaged and is sold to the ultimate consumer at a catering establishment, or if the claim itself has been made and contained within a generic advertising campaign.[113]

All misleading descriptions are prohibited by the Regulations.[114] This includes descriptions that a food may be 'dietary' or 'dietetic'.[115] These words can only be used when the food that they describe is suitable for a particular nutritional use for people who, because of their physiological condition, obtain special benefit by limiting their consumption of certain substances. The description 'low calorie' cannot be used for any non-alcoholic drink unless it contains less than 10 calories per 100 millilitres. The name 'tonic wine' can not be used for any drink unless there is also a statement, in immediate proximity to the description, that this does not imply any health-giving or medicinal properties.

7.2.2 Nutrition and Health Claims

One of the more significant legislative developments in relation to food labelling has been the introduction of regulations controlling the use of nutrition and health claims. It was recognised that an increasing number of foods for sale across the EU bore some sort of statement indicating that the product possessed properties that may be beneficial to health.[116] Many of these claims were unsubstantiated. Many more were false, or at least highly misleading. Consumers required protection from unscrupulous producers who were using concerns over the link between diet and health to create new or additional markets for their products. Some of these products had no or negligible additional health benefits.

Apart from the need to protect consumers, who may be deceived into purchasing, and possibly paying a premium for products that carried nutrition or health claims, there was also a threat posed to the free movement of goods across the EU as Member States applied their own, often differing, laws to counter misleading claim making. This could have a direct impact on the functioning of the internal market. It would also distort competition. A combination of these factors led to the belief that harmonised EU rules were thus required to regulate the use of claims.[117]

---

[112] Reg 41(1).

[113] Reg 41(3).

[114] This is not limited to nutrition and health claims, but extends to all statements or words used to describe a food that may be deemed misleading. A list of these is set out in Schedule 8 to the Regulations.

[115] Schedule 8, Part I.

[116] Recital 1 of Preamble to the Nutrition and Health Claims Regulation, n 102 above.

[117] Recital 2 of Preamble to the Nutrition and Health Claims Regulation, n 102 above.

Defining 'Claims'

The Nutrition and Health Claims Regulation covers a broad range of statements or suggestions made on food labelling. 'Claims' are defined in the Regulation as

> any message or representation, which is not mandatory under [EU] or national legislation, including pictorial, graphic or symbolic representation, in any form, which states, suggests or implies that a food has particular characteristics.[118]

A 'nutrition claim' is that which

> states, suggests or implies that a food has particular beneficial nutritional properties due to [the energy (calorific value) it provides; provides at a reduced or increased rate; or does not provide; and/or the nutrients or other substances it contains; contains in reduced or increased proportions; or does not contain].[119]

Essentially, a nutrition claim is made where there is any suggestion on the label that the food contained inside has an altered calorie or nutrient content. 'Health claims', on the other hand, are those which suggest that there is a relationship between a food and good health.[120] Nutrition and health claims may only be used if they comply with the terms of the Regulation.[121] They may never be false, ambiguous or misleading; give rise to doubts about the safety and/or the nutritional adequacy of other foods; encourage or condone excess consumption of a food; suggest or imply that a balanced or varied diet cannot provide appropriate quantities of nutrients in general; or refer to changes in bodily functions which could cause fear amongst consumers.[122]

Nutrient Profiles

The Nutrition and Health Claims Regulation works on the basis that the Commission, using comitology, establishes a set of 'nutrient profiles' with which foods must comply before a claim can be made.[123] These profiles are calculated after consideration of the quantities of nutrients and other substances, such as fats and sugars, that are contained in the food. Nutrient profiles are to be based on scientific knowledge about the relationship between diet and health. They are to be set following consultation with the European Food Safety Authority, food business operators and consumer groups. They can, of course, be updated on the basis of scientific developments. Again, comitology is used to make any necessary amendments.

Nutrition claims that make reference to reduced levels of fat, trans-fat, sugar or salt are allowed without reference to a profile for the nutrient concerned.[124]

---

[118] Art 2(2)(1).
[119] Art 2(2)(4).
[120] Art 2(2)(5).
[121] Art 3.
[122] Art 3.
[123] Art 4(1).
[124] Art 4(2)(a).

Controversially, nutrition claims can also be made where a single nutrient, such as fat or sodium, exceeds that permitted by the profile, provided that a statement to this effect appears beside the claim.[125] This means, for example, that a food that is high in fat may still carry a nutrition claim if it is also high in some beneficial nutrient, such as vitamin C. This is controversial because it means that foods that are bad for you can carry nutrition claims, which suggest that they are actually good for you.[126] Any drink that has an alcohol content above 1.2 per cent can never carry a health claim.[127] They may, however, carry nutrition claims, such as 'low alcohol', 'reduced alcohol' or 'reduced calories'. The Commission is free to add to the list of foods upon which restrictions on the use of claims may be placed. The regulatory procedure set out in the Comitology Decision is to be used to do this.[128]

Conditions for the Use of Claims

The use of nutrition and health claims is only permitted if certain conditions are fulfilled. First, the presence or absence of a nutrient about which a claim is made must have been shown to have some beneficial nutritional or physiological effect. This must be supported by generally accepted scientific evidence.[129]

Second, the nutrient concerned must also be contained in the finished product in a quantity that is sufficient to provide the defined benefit to the consumer. This level is determined by that set in EU legislation, where it exists. Otherwise, scientific evidence must show that the amount of the nutrient contained in the food will have a positive effect on human health.[130] Of course, claims can also be made about the absence of a particular nutrient, such as fat or energy, and the benefits that this may have for consumers. Similar evidence must also be provided to support these claims, showing that the level by which this nutrient has been reduced is beneficial.[131]

The third condition is that nutrients that are the subject of a claim must be present in the food in a form that can be properly used by the body.[132] It must

---

[125] Art 4(2)(b).

[126] For other criticisms of the way in which the Nutrition and Health Claims Regulation has come to work, see A Bast *et al*, 'Scientism, legalism and precaution: contending with regulating nutrition and health claims in Europe' (2013) 8 *European Food and Feed Law Review* 401; P Coppens, 'Regulation (EU) No 432/2012 establishing a list of permitted health claims' (2012) 7 *European Food and Feed Law Review* 162; and B Haber and A Meisterernst, 'Proposals for a revision of Regulation (EC) 1924/2006' (2011) 6 *European Food and Feed Law Review*.

[127] Art 4(3).

[128] Art 4(5). The regulatory procedure is set out in Art 5 of Council Decision 1999/468/EC [1999] OJ L 184/23.

[129] Art 5(1)(a). For further discussion on the types of health claims that can be made, see B Klaus, 'Restriction of use for health claims in regard to water: interpretation in conformity with the EU law' (2012) 7 *European Food and Feed Law Review* 251.

[130] Art 5(1)(b)(i).

[131] Art 5(1)(b)(ii).

[132] Art 5(1)(c).

be capable of being absorbed and transformed in a manner that benefits health. Another requirement relates to the fact that the quantity of the product that can reasonably be expected to be consumed must provide sufficient amounts of the nutrient about which the claim is made.[133] These first four conditions are set for the valid use of all claims. Additional requirements are also established for health claims specifically. These include prescribed statements that must appear on the labelling.[134] For example, there must be a statement indicating the importance of a varied and balanced diet. The quantity of the food that must be consumed for a benefit to be derived should be indicated. Where required, there should also be disclosures about the dangers of excessive consumption of the food in question. Some types of health claim can never be made.[135] Producers are prohibited from making a statement to the effect that health could be affected by not consuming the food. References to amounts of weight loss are not permitted.

Finally, the use of nutrition and health claims is only permitted if the 'average consumer', as defined in EU law, can be expected to understand the beneficial effects as expressed in the claim.[136] The 'average consumer' is categorised as being 'reasonably well informed and reasonably observant and circumspect'.[137] Nutrition and health claims must always relate to the food as it is to be consumed, according to the manufacturer's instructions.[138]

Scientific Substantiation and Authorisation

All nutrition and health claims must be based, in one way or another, on generally accepted scientific evidence.[139] Any 'food business operator' who makes a claim about their products must be able to justify this use.[140] It is up to the competent authorities in each EU Member State to require that these operators produce all of the necessary data to support any claims that they make and to ensure that they comply with their other obligations set out in the Regulation.[141] The competent authority responsible for this in England is the Food Standards Agency,[142] in association with the local authorities.[143] Just who is responsible for ensuring that the terms

---

[133] Art 5(1)(d).

[134] Art 10.

[135] Art 12.

[136] Art 5(2).

[137] As most recently set out by the Court of Justice in para 22 of its judgment in Case C-421/2013 *Apple Inc v Deutsches Patent- und Markenamt*, 10 July 2014, not yet reported. Also set out previously in, amongst many others, para 41 of the judgment in Cases C-53–55/2001 *Linde and others* [2003] ECR I-3161. For further discussion on the classification of 'consumers' in food law see M Zboralska, 'Trap of stereotypes: the EU model of a consumer' (2011) 6 *European Food and Feed Law Review* 283.

[138] Art 5(3).

[139] Art 6(1).

[140] Art 6(2).

[141] Art 6(3).

[142] Regulation 3(a) of the Nutrition and Health Claims (England) Regulations 2007, SI No 2080/2007.

[143] ibid, reg 3(b).

of the Regulation have been complied with depends on which aspect of the legislation is at issue. This will be discussed in more detail below, but as a general rule we can say that the FSA deal with authorisation issues, while the local and port authorities are responsible for ensuring that there is proper substantiation for claims made.

The conditions that must be met before a claim can be made depend on the type of claim that is being made. Nutrition claims can be made if they are one of those listed in the Annex to the Regulation and if they comply with all of the other terms of the legislation as well.[144]

Examples of this type of nutrition claim include 'low fat' which, under the terms set out in the Annex, can only be used where the product contains no more than 3 g of fat per 100 g for solids, or 1.5 g of fat per 100 ml for liquids (with the exception of semi-skimmed milk, which can contain up to 1.8 g of fat per 100 ml). A product can only claim to be 'fat-free' where it contains no more than 0.5 g of fat per 100 g or 100 ml. Most significantly, claims that a product is 'X per cent fat-free' are now, quite rightly, prohibited. Foods that were relatively high in fat content could previously carry such a claim—they could have a fat level of 10 per cent, yet could be marketed as being '90 per cent fat-free'! Other examples of permitted nutrition claims set out in the Annex to the Regulation include 'high fibre', which can only appear where the product contains at least 6 g of fibre per 100 g.

A food can be described as a 'source of fibre', however, if it contains only 3 g of fibre per 100 g. The list set out in the Annex can be amended under the comitology procedure, usually after consultation with EFSA.[145] The Commission can also call upon interested parties, such as food business operators and consumer groups, to assist it in establishing perceptions about nutrition claims and evaluating the degree to which they are readily understood.

Health claims, which must be based on generally accepted scientific evidence and which must also be easily understood by the average consumer,[146] may only be made if authorised. This can happen in two ways. First, under the terms of the Regulation, Member States were free to provide the Commission with lists of health claims and accompanying scientific substantiation by 2008.[147] Once received, and following consultation with EFSA and use of the comitology procedure, these lists would be combined to form a 'Community list' of permitted claims and any conditions of use.[148] Changes can, of course, be made to this list, again using comitology and following consultation with EFSA, either on the initiative of the Commission or following a request by a Member State.[149] However,

[144] Art 8(1) of Reg 1924/2006, n 102 above.
[145] Art 8(2) of the Regulation.
[146] Art 13(1).
[147] Art 13(2).
[148] Art 13(3).
[149] Art 13(4). Under the terms of Art 18 of Reg 178/2002, n 14 above, a food business operator who wishes to have a health claim included on the approved list can make an application for this through their national competent authority. The request is then made by the Member State where the competent authority deems it appropriate to do so. EFSA assesses the application. The Commission then decides whether to include the claim on the list, usually on the basis of the EFSA opinion.

health claims that make reference to a reduction in the risk of contracting a disease, or which refer to the health or development of children, may not avail of the list scheme.[150] This type of claim is strictly subject to the second way in which these can be authorised—the formal procedure set out in the Regulation.

Formal Authorisation Procedure for Health Claims

All health claims that are not on the pre-approved list must first be authorised for use following a Commission decision, usually based on an EFSA opinion. Applications for any such authorisation must initially be made to the national competent authority of a Member State, which is the Food Standards Agency in the UK. The FSA, or other relevant authority, must then inform EFSA about this application.[151] EFSA is then obliged to relay this information to all other Member States, the Commission and the public.[152] Applications should contain information relating to the applicant, the beneficial nature of the health claim, copies of all relevant studies and proposed wording for the claim.[153] Both the Commission and EFSA are obliged, under the terms of the Regulation, to provide technical assistance to food business operators, and in particular small and medium-sized enterprises, in preparing applications for authorisation.[154]

It must be remembered that EFSA does not authorise the use of health claims, it only provides an opinion prior to formal authorisation by the Commission in consultation with the Standing Committee on the Food Chain and Animal Health.[155] This opinion must be provided within a time limit of five months from the date of receipt of a valid application.[156] This can be extended by up to two months where the provision of additional information is requested by EFSA from the applicant. EFSA must verify that the health claim is properly substantiated by scientific evidence and that the wording of the proposed claim is in compliance with the criteria laid down in the Regulation.[157] Once made, the opinion of EFSA is then forwarded to the Commission, the Member States and the applicant.[158] This should be accompanied by a report describing the assessment that was made of the application and the reasons and information upon which it was based. The opinion must also be made public.[159] The applicant or the public may make comments on the opinion to the Commission within 30 days of its publication.[160]

---

[150] Arts 13 and 14.
[151] Art 15(2)(a).
[152] Art 15(2)(b).
[153] Art 15(3).
[154] Art 15(5).
[155] For more on this relationship between EFSA and the Commission in the context of health claims, see M Hagenmeyer and A Hahn, 'EFSA's secret health claims' (2013) 8 *European Food and Feed Law Review* 10.
[156] Art 16(1).
[157] Art 16(3).
[158] Art 16(5).
[159] Art 16(6). This must happen with all such EFSA opinions in accordance with the terms of Art 38(1) of Reg 178/2002, n 14 above.
[160] Art 16(6).

As stated above, the actual decision on whether or not to authorise the use of the health claim rests with the Commission, although it usually follows the opinion presented by EFSA.[161] The Commission has two months from the date of the EFSA opinion to provide the Standing Committee with a draft decision.[162] It must also provide an explanation of its decision where this differs from that of EFSA.[163] A final decision on the application must then be adopted using the comitology regulatory procedure.[164] The Commission must then immediately inform the applicant of the decision taken.[165] It must also be published in the Official Journal. Once approved, a health claim can be used by any food business operator,[166] subject to data protection provisions.[167] All approved health claims can, of course, be modified, suspended or revoked at any time following an EFSA opinion and Commission decision.[168] Records of all approved and authorised nutrition and health claims, and the conditions attached to their use, are detailed on a community register.[169] These are listed online (nutrition claims, authorised health claims and rejected health claims),[170] in the annex to Regulation 1924/2006 (nutrition claims), and in individual regulations, such as Regulation 665/2011 (health claims).[171]

Most EU food legislation introduced after the publication of the White Paper on Food Safety in 2000 carries safeguard measures. The Nutrition and Health Claims Regulation is no different in this regard. It permits Member States to suspend the use of any claim where it has grounds for considering that it does not comply with the terms of the Regulation, or that it has been validated with insufficient supporting scientific evidence.[172] Of course, it must inform the other Member States and the Commission about any such action and the reasons for it. As with other aspects of this Regulation, an EFSA opinion is sought before a Commission decision is made on the appropriateness of the action taken by the Member State.[173]

---

[161] For a more detailed analysis of this, see A Alemanno, 'The European Food Safety Authority before European Courts: some reflections on the judicial review of EFSA scientific opinions and administrative acts' (2008) 5 *European Food and Feed Law Review* 320.

[162] Art 17(1).

[163] Art 17(1).

[164] Arts 17(3) and 25(2) of Reg 178/2002, n 14 above. The regulatory procedure is set out in Art 5 of Decision 1999/468/EC [1999] OJ L 184/23.

[165] Art 17(4).

[166] Art 17(5).

[167] As set out in Art 21 of Reg 178/2002, n 14 above.

[168] Art 19.

[169] As established by Art 20 of Reg 1924/2006, n 102 above.

[170] Available at: http://ec.europa.eu/food/food/labellingnutrition/claims/community_register/index_en.htm.

[171] Commission Regulation (EU) No 665/2011 of 11 July 2011 on the authorisation and refusal of authorisation of certain health claims made on foods and referring to the reduction of disease risk [2011] OJ L 182/5 . This Regulation authorised the use of health claims related to the beneficial effects of chewing sugar-free gum. Annex I to the Regulation permits use of the claim that 'sugar-free chewing gum helps neutralise plaque acids'.

[172] Art 24(1) of Reg 1924/2006.

[173] Art 24(2).

However, the Commission may also initiate this procedure on its own initiative when it so chooses.[174] The Member State is entitled to maintain the suspension until any decision has been made and notified by the Commission.[175]

Nutrition and Health Claims (England) Regulations 2007

It was emphasised in chapter two that EU directives must be formally transposed into English law, but EU regulations do not require this. They automatically become part of English law once published and from the date that they enter into force.[176] They are thus directly applicable in the Member States. However, some form of domestic legislation is often required to provide further detail on those aspects of the application of the Regulation that are particular to the individual Member State concerned. The Nutrition and Health Claims (England) Regulations 2007 provide such details here.[177]

These 2007 Regulations weave and contextualise the EU Nutrition and Health Claims Regulation into English law. They link the EU Regulation to various provisions of the Food Safety Act 1990.[178] They establish the Food Standards Agency and relevant authorities as the designated national competent authorities.[179] Penalties are set.[180] Offences are outlined.[181] Finally, the Food Labelling Regulations 1996 are amended as necessary to give effect to the EU Regulation.[182]

7.3 Labelling Codes of Conduct and Practice

There are a series of codes of practice and conduct that directly impact upon the application of food labelling laws in England. The codes of practice deal with the practical application of existing laws setting, for example, clear instruction on which authorities are responsible for taking action in different areas. The codes of conduct set non-binding parameters within which various operators in the food sector should act. These provide guidelines for producers and retailers about the ways in which they should go about producing and marketing their wares. They are often created in the hope that they will lead to a modification in behaviour that reduces or eliminates the need to introduce binding legislation. They may

---

[174] Art 24(2).
[175] Art 24(3).
[176] Art 29 of the Nutrition and Health Claims Regulation provides that it is to enter into force from 1 July 2007, approximately six months after its publication in December 2006.
[177] SI No 2080/2007.
[178] Reg 6.
[179] Regs 3 and 4.
[180] Reg 5.
[181] Regs 5 and 7.
[182] Reg 8.

also exist because EU law prevents domestic legislators from introducing new laws that create some direct or indirect impediment to the free movement of food.

7.3.1 Food Law Code of Practice (England) 2008

One of the complications with the domestic application of food law is ascertaining who is responsible for its enforcement. EU rules make reference to 'competent authorities', but these are to be determined by each individual Member State. It has been noted already that in England for labelling matters this is usually either the Food Standards Agency or the local authority, depending on the circumstances. However, a further uncertainty can arise in those parts of England where there are two tiers of local government, and both have responsibility for food regulation. This is addressed by the Food Law Code of Practice (England), issued in June 2008. This horizontal code, applying to many aspects of food control, divides responsibility between County and District Councils. County Council Food Authorities must investigate and take enforcement action in cases that involve the advertising, presentation and labelling of food, except for those that relate to aspects of the Hygiene Regulation,[183] which is enforced by the District Council, and those provisions of the Food Labelling Regulations relating to 'use by' and 'best before' dates, which are to be enforced jointly by both the District and County Councils.

The Food Law Code of Practice also establishes that various 'interventions' can be made by food authorities in England to ensure that there is proper compliance by food business operators. 'Interventions' include, but are not restricted to, 'official controls', which are defined as

> any form of control that the competent authority or [Union] performs for the verification or compliance with food and feed law, animal health and animal welfare rules.[184]

They include inspections, monitoring, surveillance, verification, audit and sampling.[185] These interventions are to be applied in a risk-based manner, meaning that more intensive regulation is directed at those food businesses which present the greatest possible risk to public health. These interventions are an important part of ensuring that food meets the requirements of the labelling rules, in particular to prevent confusing or misleading consumers, to ensure compliance with compositional requirements, and to verify the absence of non-permitted excessive levels of additives and contaminants.

---

[183] Regulation (EC) No 853/2004 of the European Parliament and of the Council of 29 April 2004 laying down specific hygiene rules for food of animal origin [2004] OJ L 226/22.

[184] Art 2(1) of Regulation (EC) No 882/2004 of the European Parliament and of the Council of 29 April 2004 on official controls performed to ensure the verification of compliance with feed and food law, animal health and animal welfare rules [2004] OJ L 191/1.

[185] ibid, Art 10(1).

7.3.2 Code of Practice for the Labelling of Pork

The Pig Meat Supply Chain Task Force has introduced a voluntary code of conduct for the labelling of pork and pork products in 2010. Other meats, such as beef and poultry, are required under EU law to provide specific labelling information.[186] Pork was not subject to similar requirements until the introduction of the Food Information Regulation, and even then these provisions apply to origin labelling only.[187] The Pig Task Force was thus established in 2009 by DEFRA and chaired by the Secretary of State. Establishing a labelling code of conduct was seen to be integral to supporting the British pig meat industry by satisfying the recognised consumer preferences for pork that it is clearly labelled, in particular by indicating the origin of the product and aspects of the method of production and agricultural practices employed. Code signatories should be fully compliant with the provisions set out below, subject to some very limited exceptions, by 2011.

As discussed above, the Food Labelling Regulations 1996 set a general principle that the specific place of origin of food only needs to put on the label if a failure to do so could mislead consumers. This is arguably one of the more controversial aspects of the Regulations and related EU legislation. The lack of a definitive obligation to include origin details on labels means that unless specific legislation is introduced, as has been the case for beef and poultry, there will be widespread confusion and deception, both deliberate and consequential. For example, the existing provisions permit products produced elsewhere to be labelled in a way that suggests that they are actually English or British where some substantial change to the ingredients took place here.[188] A pig could be reared, slaughtered and processed in Spain, but using the pork from it for a sandwich or ready meal in England means that it can be labelled as being produced in England. This Code of Practice seeks to address this anomaly with consumer expectations, albeit in a voluntary, non-binding way.

For retail labelling, the Code calls for a commitment to place country of origin details clearly on the front of pre-packaged pork products. Where the product is not pre-packaged, these details should be displayed in close proximity to its point of sale, for example the meat counter in a butcher's shop. If the label suggests a

---

[186] The requirements for beef are set out in Regulation (EC) No 1760/2000 of the European Parliament and of the Council of 17 July 2000 establishing a system for the identification and registration of bovine animals and regarding the labelling of beef and beef products and repealing Council Regulation (EC) No 820/1997 [2000] OJ L 204/1 and Commission Regulation (EC) No 1825/2000 of 25 August 2000 laying down detailed rules for the application of Regulation 1760/2000 [2000] OJ L 216/8. The requirements for poultry are set out in Commission Regulation (EC) No 543/2008 of 16 June 2008 laying down detailed rules for the application of Regulation (EC) No 1234/2007 as regards the marketing standards for poultrymeat [2008] OJ L 157/46. The Poultry Marketing Regulation is discussed in more detail in ch 10.

[187] Art 26(2) of Reg 1169/2011, n 6 above.

[188] For more on the ways in which food law can be used to deal with fraud and deception, see M Gallagher and I Thomas, 'Food fraud: the deliberate adulteration and misdescription of foodstuffs' (2010) 5 *European Food and Feed Law Review* 347.

single country of origin, such as 'English pork', then the pig should have been born, reared and slaughtered there. Where any of these stages takes place in more than one country, there should be additional information provided on the label to indicate this. This can be either a statement that includes all of the countries where any part of the production process took place or merely a disclosure about where the pigs were born or reared.

One of the main ambiguities surrounding the use of origin indications, the statement that a product was 'Produced in the UK' or 'Packed in the UK', is also addressed by the Code of Practice. These types of disclosure should not be used in isolation. The country or countries of origin should also be listed alongside the statement about UK involvement in the process. So, for example, the label could state that the product was 'Produced in the UK using pork from country A' or that it was 'Made in the UK using country B and country C pork'. Many popular products, like sausages and pork pies, are often made from meat that has been imported from more than one country. Where this is the case then, according to the Code, all countries of origin should be listed. Alternatively, a statement that the pork is of 'EU origin' can be made where all of the meat used originated in Member States. The use of national terms and symbols used on labelling, such as the appearance of a Union Jack or Cross of Saint George, should be limited to those products which are made in the UK or England from domestically produced meat. Other ingredients can, of course, be of non-national origin.

Any product that is marketed using a UK geographical name, whether that name is legally protected or not, must be made, under the terms of the Code, using UK pork. However, pork from elsewhere can be used if a declaration to this effect appears alongside the name on the label. So, for example, the protected geographical indication 'Lincolnshire sausages' would be named simply as that where English pork is used, or as 'Lincolnshire sausages made from EU pork' where this was in fact the case. The Code also requires that the use of any imagery that suggests that the product is from the UK must be made with UK pork or, as for the use of geographical names, state clearly on the label that the pork is, in fact, from elsewhere. Where a specific breed name, such as 'Berkshire boar' is used without qualification then the pig must be the offspring of a pedigree boar and sow of the same breed. Cross-breed names can also be used on the labelling where at least one of the mating pigs was pedigree.

Finally, the Code of Practice for the Labelling of Pork and Pork Products sets standards for the use of terms relating to methods of production employed. The term 'free range' can only be used when the pigs involved are born outside in fields where they remain until they are sent for processing. They must be provided with food, water and shelter and be free to roam within defined boundaries. Very generous space allowances should be made available, subject to soil conditions and rotation practices. The breeding sows must also be kept outside in fields for their productive life. 'Outdoor bred' pork should only come from pigs who are also born outside in fields, where they are kept until weaning. Any pork or pork products labelled as 'outdoor bred' must also contain a statement describing how the pigs were farmed. This information should appear in the same field of vision as the initial statement. 'Outdoor reared' pigs are again born outside in fields, where they should remain for approximately half of their lives. Subsequent farming practice details should also be listed on the label, in a similar way. Use of the term 'outdoor' on its own should only appear where the pigs have been kept outside in fields until they are sent for processing. Minimum space allowances should be generous, but need not be as much as for 'free range' pigs. These allowances are defined and established on the basis of the individual weights of the pigs. In all cases pigs may be housed indoors for a limited period due to veterinary treatment or in emergencies, such as the outbreak of disease.

7.3.3 Advertising Standards

The Control of Misleading Advertisements Regulations 1988 sets the legal boundaries within which goods, amongst other things, can be represented to potential buyers.[189] An advertisement is deemed to be misleading if it 'deceives or is likely to deceive the persons to whom it is addressed or whom it reaches'.[190]

Ofcom (the Office of Communications), whose role was established by the Communications Act 2003, is the independent regulator which sets the standards for television advertising. It has transferred the responsibility for the Television Advertising Standards Code to the Advertising Standards Authority. Under this co-regulatory scheme Ofcom retains ultimate responsibility for all television advertising, and the Communications Act 2003 permits it to set standards which prohibit certain types of advertisement. It is also obliged, under the terms of the Television Without Frontiers Directive,[191] to take positive action to protect children from the harmful effects of advertising.[192] This is, of course, subject to the requirement established in EU law that any restriction on the freedom to provide services must be both necessary and proportionate.[193]

Advertising, therefore, can be controlled in two ways—either it is unlawful because it is misleading, or it is prohibited by an Ofcom/Advertising Standards Authority code. One such code is that on television advertising of food and drink products to children, published in 2007.

---

[189] SI No 915/1988.

[190] Reg 2(2).

[191] Council Directive 1989/552/EEC of 3 October 1989 on the coordination of certain provisions laid down by law, regulation or administrative action in Member States concerning the pursuit of television broadcasting activities [1989] OJ L 298/23.

[192] ibid, Art 16.

[193] As held in cases such as Case 33/1974 *Van Binsbergen v Bestuur Van de Bedrijfsvereniging voor de Metaalnijverheid* [1974] ECR 1299; Case C-180/1989 *Commission v Italy* [1991] ECR I-709; and Case C-198/1989 *Commission v Greece* [1991] ECR I-727.

Advertising of Food and Drink to Children

Obesity is a growing problem. Research suggests that many cases of adult obesity are determined by habits developed during childhood.[194] While this epidemic is dealt with in more detail in chapter nine, the fact that both the Department of Health and the Food Standards Agency have identified television advertising as an area where action should be considered to restrict the promotion of foods with a high fat, salt and/or sugar content to children, is more appropriately considered here.

The development of Ofcom's Statement on Television Advertising of Food and Drink Products to Children initially arose out of a political decision taken by the then Secretary of State for Culture, Media and Sport, requesting the development of proposals designed to strengthen existing relevant rules. In response, Ofcom conducted research into the role that advertising on television plays in influencing children's consumption of unhealthy foods. This study suggested that advertising had a modest direct effect on children's food choices but perhaps a larger, if unquantifiable, indirect effect on their preferences, consumption and behaviour. Ultimately, it was concluded that there was a case for the introduction of proportionate and targeted action in terms of rules for broadcast advertising to assist in addressing the issue of childhood health and obesity. It was also noted by Ofcom that a whole range of factors, including societal, environmental and cultural all play a role in food choices and related rising obesity rates—albeit in a way that was deemed to be 'not yet well understood'. It was therefore decided that in these circumstances a total ban on food advertising aimed at children would be neither proportionate nor, if an isolated action, effective.

Following a further consultation process, Ofcom has produced a set of regulatory objectives designed to curb the influence of advertising unhealthy foods to children, rather than any prohibition. These include reducing the exposure of children under 16 to advertisements for high fat, sugar and salt products, revising advertising content standards so as to reduce children's 'emotional engagement' with certain products and to reduce the risk that they and their parents may misinterpret product claims. The objectives also seek to avoid disproportionately impacting on the revenue of broadcasters by reduced levels of advertising, in particular during adult viewing times. It was ultimately decided, therefore, that a package of measures reflecting these objectives should be introduced to restrict the scheduling of television advertising of food and drink products to children. Any such restrictions would be limited to food and drink products that were assessed as being unhealthy due to their high fat, sugar and/or salt content, as defined by the Food Standard Agency's nutrient profiling scheme. Advertisements for these products cannot now be shown in or around programmes made specifically for

---

[194] See, eg, T Parsons, C Power, S Logan and C Summerbell, 'Childhood predictors of adult obesity: a systematic review' (1999) *International Journal of Obesity* 23; and W Dietz 'Health consequences of obesity in youth: childhood predictors of adult disease' (1998) 101 *Pediatrics* 518.

children. Nor should there be any programme sponsorship by these products. This therefore also means that there can be no advertising of these products on television channels dedicated to showing programmes for children. This has been the case since 2009.

Ofcom also decided that revised content rules should also be introduced, limiting the way in which the targeted products could be advertised, regardless of when they were being shown on television. This includes a prohibition after 2007 on the use of licensed characters, celebrities, promotional offers and health claims for those products which are aimed at pre-school or primary school children. Action has been brought by the Advertising Standards Authority on a number of occasions since the introduction of the Ofcom Code. Various advertisements have had to be removed from television screens because they were deemed to be misleading and/or irresponsible. These actions have made it clear that food and drink that is high in sugar or calorific content cannot be advertised as being nutritious, low-energy or a substitute for good dietary practice.

Advertising Alcohol

Ofcom has also introduced a code regulating the advertising of alcoholic products, with particular emphasis on the advertising of alcohol to young people. Under the general rules set out in the Code, no advertisements for any types of product can suggest that alcohol can contribute to a person's popularity or confidence, or that refusing alcohol is a sign of weakness. Nor should any advertising imply that the success of a social occasion is dependent on the presence or consumption of alcohol. There should be no link portrayed between alcohol and toughness or aggression. Suggesting enhanced attractiveness or sexual activity is also prohibited. Advertisements must not suggest that drinking alcohol can help a person to overcome their problems or that this will have any therapeutic effect or improved physical performance. The acceptability of immoderate levels of drinking or drink-driving should never be portrayed.

Additional rules for advertisements of alcoholic products are also set out in the Code. These include designing the advertisement in a way that could create strong appeal for the product amongst people under the age of 18. Nobody under the age of 25, subject to some minor exceptions, can play a significant role in advertisements for alcoholic drinks, nor should anyone appearing in these be behaving in a juvenile way. Drinks that are very low in alcoholic content (below 1.2 per cent) need not comply with all of the requirements set out in the code. These revised rules came into effect in 2005.

The introduction of the revised rules on the advertising of alcohol appear to have at least assisted in making some changes to the consumption patterns of young people. Research conducted by Ofcom in 2007 suggested that the proportion of 11–13 year olds who have never drunk alcohol increased from 31 per cent in 2005 to 46 per cent by 2007. 'Alcopops' also declined in popularity, particularly amongst children aged 14 or over, although consumption of cider was seen to increase. Figures for the proportion of 11–17 year olds who stated that they regularly drink to get drunk remained relatively unchanged between 2005 and 2007. However, the evidence suggests that the age at which young people start consuming alcohol appears to be rising.

7.4 Quality and Composition Labelling

Food laws, since the very earliest times, have prescribed what can and can not be used as ingredients in the manufacturing of certain products.[195] Even some of the initial EU laws specified the minimum compositional requirements for some foods. These are known as 'recipe laws', and their application in English law is discussed in more detail below. Setting harmonised EU-wide minimum standards for food has, however, become much less commonplace since the famous decision of the Court of Justice in *Cassis*.[196] Despite this, some important compositional and quality standards remain.

7.4.1 Honey (England) Regulations 2003

During the 1970s, the EEC, as it then was, introduced a series of directives setting compositional requirements for a list of specified foodstuffs. These directives were designed to harmonise standards across all of the Member States for each of the products concerned in order to facilitate the free movement of these foods and, to a lesser extent, to ensure that consumers were protected by setting absolute minimum standards. This list of foods included chocolate,[197] coffee,[198] jams,[199] fruit juices[200] and honey.[201] All of these original directives have since been updated and transposed into English law.

---

[195] See ch 1.

[196] Case 120/1978 *Rewe-Zentral AG v Bundesmonopolverwaltung für Branntwein* [1979] ECR 649, as discussed in ch 4.

[197] Council Directive 1973/241/EEC of 23 July 1973 on the approximation of the laws of the Member States relating to cocoa and chocolate products intended for human consumption [1973] OJ L 228/23.

[198] Council Directive 1977/436/EEC of 27 June 1977 on the approximation of the laws of the Member States relating to coffee extracts and chicory extracts [1977] OJ L 172/20.

[199] Council Directive 1979/693/EEC of 24 July 1979 on the approximation of the laws of the Member States relating to fruit jams, jellies and marmalades and chestnut pureé [1979] OJ L 205/5.

[200] Council Directive 1975/726/EEC of 17 November 1975 on the approximation of the laws of the Member States concerning fruit juices and certain similar products [1975] OJ L 311/40.

[201] Council Directive 1974/409/EEC of 22 July 1974 on the harmonisation of the laws of the Member States relating to honey [1974] OJ L 221/10.

The Honey (England) Regulations 2003 set domestic compositional requirements,[202] giving effect to harmonised EU law in this area.[203] 'Honey' is defined as

> the natural sweet substance produced by … bees from the nectar of plants or excretions of plant-sucking insects on the living parts of plants which the bees collect, transform by combining with specific substances of their own, deposit, dehydrate, store and leave in honeycombs to ripen and mature.[204]

Under the terms of these Regulations use of the name 'honey' is limited to those who comply with the compositional and labelling requirements set out. These include providing labelling particulars that accurately describe the product and give details of its origin.[205] The fact that much of the honey that is sold to consumers is blended is also reflected in the origin labelling requirements.[206] These provide that 'the country or countries of origin where the honey has been harvested' must be listed. However, where the honey originated in more than one EU Member State or third country, this can be replaced with a statement that it is a blend of EC, or non-EC, or a combination of EC and non-EC, honeys. Several different types of honey are defined in the 2003 Regulations.[207] These include 'comb honey', 'blossom honey', 'baker's honey' and 'filtered honey'. The sale of 'baker's honey', which 'may have a foreign taste or odour, have begun to ferment or have fermented, or have been overheated', must be accompanied by a labelling disclosure that it is 'intended for cooking only',[208] and it must be listed in the ingredients of a finished product as such.[209] Fines can be imposed on those who contravene the labelling provisions of these regulations.[210] Local authorities are responsible for their enforcement.[211]

7.4.2 Cocoa and Chocolate Products (England) Regulations 2003

Just what can be called 'chocolate', and its other forms such as 'milk' and 'dark', has been the subject of much debate since EU legislators first introduced a directive on the matter in 1973.[212] The problem first arose because the UK, along with Ireland and Denmark, were about to become members of the European Economic

---

[202] SI No 2243/2003. These Regulations replace the Honey Regulations 1976, SI No 1832/1976.
[203] As now set out in Council Directive 2001/110/EC of 20 December 2001 relating to honey [2002] OJ L 10/47.
[204] Reg 2(1).
[205] Reg 4(1).
[206] Reg 4(1)(c).
[207] Schedule 1 thereto.
[208] Reg 4(1)(b).
[209] Reg 4(3).
[210] Reg 7(1).
[211] Reg 7(2).
[212] Directive 1973/241, n 197 above.

Community. Chocolate produced in all these new Member States tended to be made with a higher milk content and lower cocoa content than that traditionally produced in existing Member States, such as Belgium and France. British and Irish chocolate was also often made with vegetable fats instead of cocoa butter, which was used elsewhere. These other States insisted that the British and Irish variety of 'milk chocolate', for example, should instead be called 'milk chocolate with high milk content'. Britain and Ireland disagreed, and were granted an exemption.[213] Thirty years of debate and proposed compromise ensued.

The controversy over the high milk, low cocoa and vegetable fat content of British chocolate was finally resolved with the introduction of a new EU directive in 2000.[214] This allowed for the derogation provided for the UK and Ireland in the 1973 directive to be maintained. However, the name 'milk chocolate with high milk content' was to be replaced with the name 'family milk chocolate', when this product (20 per cent dry cocoa, 20 per cent dry milk) was sold elsewhere in the EU. It could still be labelled as 'milk chocolate' when sold in the UK or Ireland.[215] The use of vegetable fats other than cocoa butter would also be permitted, subject to a maximum of 5 per cent of the finished product.[216]

The EU Chocolate Directive 2000 is transposed into English law by the Cocoa and Chocolate Products (England) Regulations 2003.[217] These regulations define 'chocolate' as

[t]he product obtained from cocoa products and sugars which ... contain not less than 35 per cent total dry cocoa solids, including not less than 18 per cent cocoa butter and not less than 14 per cent of dry non-fat cocoa solids.[218]

Schedule 1 of the Regulations also defines 'milk chocolate' as

[t]he product obtained from cocoa products, sugars and milk or milk products which ... contains not less than 25% total dry cocoa solids ... 14% dry milk solids ... 2.5% dry non-fat cocoa solids, 3.5% milk fat [and] 25% total fat.

'Family milk chocolate' has the exact same compositional requirements as 'milk chocolate' except for the fact that the total cocoa solids quantity can be reduced to 20 per cent, the milk solids increased to 20 per cent, and the milk fat increased to 5 per cent. The Schedule to the Regulations clarifies that the names 'milk chocolate' and 'family milk chocolate' are interchangeable in England once the

---

[213] Art 3(1) of Directive 1973/241, n 197 above.

[214] Directive 2000/36/EC of the European Parliament and of the Council of 23 June 2000 relating to cocoa and chocolate products intended for human consumption [2000] OJ L 197/19. For discussion on more recent updates in the case law in this area, see F Capelli and B Klaus, 'Chocolate can also be made from pure cocoa but one should be careful how to communicate this on the label' (2011) 6 *European Food and Feed Law Review* 88.

[215] Annex I to Directive 2000/36, n 214 above.

[216] ibid, Art 2.

[217] SI No 1659/2003. These Regulations replace the Cocoa and Chocolate Products Regulations 1976, SI No 541/1976.

[218] Schedule 1 to the 2003 Regulations.

minimum compositional requirements for family milk chocolate (the 20/20 formula) are met.

While vegetable fats other than cocoa butter may be used in chocolate products, this is limited to those which are specifically listed in Schedule 2 to the Regulations. Vegetable fats permitted for use are therefore restricted to oils from palm, shea, mango kernel, illipe, sal and kokum gurgi, only up to 5 per cent of the finished product.[219] Coconut oil can be used in the manufacture of ice cream and other similar frozen products. Chocolate can only be marketed as such if it complies with these Regulations.[220] Failure to comply with this can lead to the imposition of a fine on summary conviction.[221] Again, local authorities are charged with enforcing these Regulations.[222]

7.4.3 Coffee Extracts and Chicory Extracts (England) Regulations 2000

The Coffee Regulations are really only designed to deal with compositional and labelling requirements for extracts, such as instant coffee.[223] Only water can be used to extract the product from roasted coffee beans.[224] 'Instant coffee' as defined in the Schedule to the Regulations must contain 'coffee-based dry matter [which] is not less than 95% [and] no substances other than those derived from the extraction of coffee'. As with the other compositional regulations, coffee extract products must be labelled and described in accordance with the provisions of these rules,[225] and failure to do so can lead to conviction and a fine.[226] Finally, the ways in which the decaffeination of coffee is permitted are set out in the Extraction Solvents in Food Regulations 1993,[227] as amended in 2011.[228] Schedule 2 to the Regulations provides that the substances methyl acetate, ethylmethylketone and dichloromethane can all be used in the decaffeination of coffee, subject to set maximum residue limits of 20 mg per kg, or just 2 mg per kg in the case of dichloromethane.

---

[219] Reg 3 in conjunction with Schedule 2.

[220] Regs 5 and 6.

[221] Reg 8(1).

[222] Reg 8(2).

[223] SI No 3323/2000. Transposes Directive 1999/4/EC of the European Parliament and of the Council of 22 February 1999 relating to coffee extracts and chicory extracts [1999] OJ L 66/26 into English law.

[224] Reg 2.

[225] Regs 4 and 5.

[226] Reg 7.

[227] SI No 1658/1993.

[228] The Extraction Solvents in Food (Amendment) (England) Regulations 2011, SI No 1738/2011. This amendment did not really affect coffee decaffeination. Current EU legislation on extraction solvents is set out in Directive 2009/32/EC of the European Parliament and of the Council of 23 April 2009 on the approximation of the laws of the Member States on extraction solvents used in the production of foodstuffs and food ingredients [2009] OJ L 141/3 , which replaced Directive 1988/344/EEC [1988] OJ L 157/28.

7.4.4 Fruit Juices and Fruit Nectars (England) Regulations 2003

Giving effect to a 2001 EU directive,[229] the 2003 Regulations define 'fruit juice' as

> [t]he fermentable but unfermented product obtained from fruit which is sound and
> ripe, fresh or preserved by chilling, of one or more kinds mixed together, having the
> characteristic colour, flavour and taste typical of the juice of the fruit from which it
> comes.[230]

Juice used must come from the endocarp, or inner part, of the fruit. Where fruit
juice is 'concentrated', at least 50 per cent of the water content must have been
removed. However, 'fruit juice from concentrate' is

> [t]he product obtained by replacing, in concentrated fruit juice, water extracted from
> that juice during concentration, and by restoring the flavours and, if appropriate, pulp
> and cells lost from the juice but recovered during the process of producing the fruit juice
> in question or fruit juice of the same kind.

Vitamins, minerals and, in some cases, sugar may be added to fruit juice.[231]

7.4.5 Jam and Similar Products (England) Regulations 2003

The third type of foodstuff covered by the original 'recipe laws' is jams, jellies and
marmalades. The last to be introduced before the Court of Justice decision in
Cassis, the 1979 directive related to these products follows a similar format to that
used for honey and chocolate.[232] This was transposed into English law in 1981,[233]
and later replaced by these new regulations in 2003.[234]
  'Jam' is defined as

> [a] mixture, brought to a suitable gelled consistency, of sugars, the pulp or purée or
> both of one or more kinds of fruit and water, such that the quantity of fruit … used
> for every 1000 grams of the finished product is not less than 250 grams in the case of
> redcurrants, blackcurrants … 150 grams in the case of ginger [or] 350 grams in the case
> of any other fruit.[235]

To be called 'extra jam' the minimum compositional requirements are set at
450 grams for most fruits, such as strawberries and raspberries. 'Marmalade' must

---

[229] Council Directive 2001/112/EC of 20 December 2001 relating to fruit juices and certain similar
products intended for human consumption [2002] OJ L 10/58, as amended by Directive 2009/106
[2009] OJ L 212/42.
  [230] Schedule to the Fruit Juices and Fruit Nectars (England) Regulations 2003, SI No 1564/2003,
as amended by the Fruit Juices and Fruit Nectars (England) (Amendment) Regulations 2011, SI No
1135/2011.
  [231] Schedule 3 to the 2003 Regulations, n 230 above.
  [232] Directive 1979/693, n 199 above.
  [233] The Jam and Similar Products Regulations 1981, SI No 1063/1981.
  [234] The Jam and Similar Products (England) Regulations 2003, SI No 3120/2003.
  [235] Schedule 1 to the 2003 Regulations, n 230 above.

contain a minimum of 200 grams of citrus fruit per 1,000 grams of finished product. Minimum compositional standards are also set for curds, mincemeat, chestnut purée and jelly. Only those products that are produced in accordance with the requirements set out in Schedule 1 to the Regulations can be labelled using any of the names specified.[236] Schedule 2 sets out those additional ingredients that can be added to the foods covered by the Regulations.

7.4.6 Compositional Requirements in the Food Labelling Regulations 1996

In addition to all the specific labelling requirements set out in the 1996 Regulations,[237] there are also minimum compositional conditions established for specified types of cheese which, if not satisfied, mean that the sales name in question cannot be used in the circumstances. These names, many of them famous and protected at EU level,[238] are not to appear on labelling, for example, where the amount of water content in the cheese does not exceed a set amount.[239] For Blue Stilton this is set at 42 per cent. For others, such as Cheshire and Double Gloucester, this is slightly higher at 44 per cent. Cheddar can contain a maximum of 39 per cent water.[240] The amount of milk fat in any cheese cannot fall below 48 per cent.[241] Similar requirements are also set for cream.[242] For example, 'clotted cream' must contain at least 55 per cent milk fat, while 'double cream' should have at least 48 per cent fat content.[243] Finally, 'wine' can only be used in the labelling or advertising for a food or drink when it meets the definition set out in EU regulations on the matter.[244] 'Wine' is defined as

> [t]he product obtained exclusively from the total or partial alcoholic fermentation of fresh grapes, whether or not crushed, or of grape must.[245]

The word 'wine' can, however, be used in a composite name, such as 'non-alcoholic wine' or 'wine gums', unless this is likely to cause confusion.[246]

---

[236] Regs 4 and 5.
[237] The Food Labelling Regulations 1996, n 5 above.
[238] See ch 8.
[239] Reg 42(2)(a).
[240] Schedule 8, Part II to the 1996 Regulations, n 5 above.
[241] Reg 42(2)(b).
[242] Reg 42(3).
[243] Schedule 8, Part III to the 1996 Regulations, n 5 above.
[244] Council Regulation (EEC) No 822/1987 of 16 March 1987 on the common organisation of the market in wine [1987] OJ L 84/1.
[245] ibid, Annex I.
[246] Reg 43 of the 1996 Regulations, n 5 above.

7.4.7 Baby and Infant Foods

Processed baby and infant foods are subject to a range of additional legislative requirements beyond the framework labelling and compositional requirements. The specific hygiene and contaminant provisions relating to these products are dealt with in chapter six of this book. 'Baby foods' are defined in English law as

> foods for particular nutritional use fulfilling the particular requirements of infants and young children in good health and intended for use by infants while they are being weaned, and by young children as a supplement to their diet or for their progressive adaptation to ordinary food, but excludes processed cereal-based foods.[247]

'Processed cereal-based foods' are similar to 'baby foods' as defined above, but more specifically, they include cereals which have to be reconstituted with milk or other liquids, pasta which is to be used after cooking and rusks and biscuits which can be used directly or mixed with liquids.[248] 'Infants' are children under 12 months of age, while 'young children' includes those between one and three years old.[249] The English Regulations transpose EU Directive 1996/5,[250] as amended.[251] The Regulations do not apply to baby food which is a milk intended for young children.[252] These are instead covered by the Infant Formula and Follow-on Formula (England) Regulations 2007.[253]

Under the provisions of the Processed Cereal-based Foods and Baby Foods for Infants and Young Children (England) Regulations 2003, no ingredients can be used in the manufacture of the covered products unless they have been shown by generally accepted scientific data to be suitable for the particular nutritional needs of infants and young children.[254] They should also only contain permitted ingredients up to a level that presents no danger to infant health.[255] Vitamins and minerals, for example, must be kept at a quantity which does not present any possible health concern which could be caused by overconsumption. It is only those

---

[247] Regulation 2(1) of the Processed Cereal-based Foods and Baby Foods for Infants and Young Children (England) Regulations 2003, SI No 3207/2003. These 2003 Regulations revoke the previous Processed Cereal-based Foods and Baby Foods for Infants and Young Children Regulations 1997, SI No 2042/1997, as amended.

[248] Regulation 2(1) in conjunction with Schedule 1, Part I of the Processed Cereal-based Foods and Baby Foods for Infants and Young Children (England) Regulations 2003, n 247 above.

[249] Regulation 2(1) of the 2003 Regulations, n 247 above.

[250] Commission Directive 1996/5/EC of 16 February 1996 on processed cereal-based foods and baby foods for infants and young children, [1996] OJ L 49/17.

[251] Directive 1996/5 was amended several times. The last of these amendments was by the introduction of Directive 2003/13/EC [2003] OJ L 41/33. Directive 1996/5 was later replaced by Commission Directive 2006/125/EC of 5 December 2006 on processed cereal-based foods and baby foods for infants and young children [2006] OJ L 339/16. This is recognised in English law by reg 6(2) of the Food for Particular Nutritional Uses (Miscellaneous Amendments) (England) Regulations 2007, SI No 2591/2007.

[252] Reg 3 of the 2003 Regulations, n 247 above.

[253] SI No 3521/2007.

[254] Reg 5(1) thereof.

[255] Reg 5(2).

vitamins, minerals and other nutrients that are specifically listed in Schedule 4 to the Regulations which can be added to infant and baby foods.[256] Schedule 5 sets out the maximum permitted amounts.

The 2003 Regulations also set out a set of labelling requirements for processed cereal-based foods and baby foods beyond the specifications of the Food Labelling Regulations 1996. This includes a requirement to provide a statement as to the appropriate age from which the food may be used, with regard being had to the texture, composition and other properties of the product.[257] This age can never be younger than four months. There should also be information on the presence or absence of gluten if the age specified on the label is less than six months.[258] The usual requirements of ingredient listing, energy values, protein, carbohydrates and fat also apply.[259] However, it should be noted that this was made compulsory under the 2003 Regulations for infant foods, and not optional or limited to those products making some sort of health or nutrition claim, as has been the case for other foods prior to the introduction of the Food Information Regulation. Fines can be imposed for those found guilty of an offence under the Regulations.[260] Food produced for export to a country where similar requirements on the production and marketing of infant food do not apply are not subject to the 2003 Regulations.[261]

The Infant Formula and Follow-on Formula (England) Regulations 2007 transpose Directive 2006/141 into English law.[262] The Regulations set out a general prohibition on the marketing of infant or follow-on formula unless certain conditions are met first.[263] It is prohibited, for example, to market a product as being capable of satisfying the nutritional requirements of infants during the first months of life unless that product is infant formula.[264] Any infant formula which is designed to provide all nutritional needs on its own can only be marketed if this has been adequately demonstrated by appropriate studies and expert guidance.[265] As is the case in the Baby Foods Regulations, infant and follow-on formula cannot contain any substance, including nutrients, in a quantity that could endanger the health of infants and young children.[266] Infant formula can only contain ingredients that have been scientifically demonstrated to be suitable for the particular nutritional uses of infants from birth. This suitability has to be demonstrated

---

[256] Reg 6(1).

[257] Reg 8(1)(a).

[258] Reg 8(1)(b).

[259] Reg 8(1)(c) and (d).

[260] Reg 10. As is the case for many breaches of English food law, this is set at a maximum on summary conviction of level 5 on the standard scale.

[261] Reg 11.

[262] Commission Directive 2006/141/EC of 22 December 2006 on infant formulae and amending Directive 1999/21/EC [2006] OJ L 401/1.

[263] Reg 3.

[264] Reg 4.

[265] Reg 8.

[266] Reg 5.

through the systematic review of available data on the expected benefits and safety considerations.[267]

Similar provisions apply for follow-on formula designed for children over six months old.[268] Infant formula and follow-on formula can never require anything other than the addition of water in their preparation.[269] The proteins in infant formula can be derived from cows' milk, goats' milk,[270] or soya—either alone or in a mixture with animal proteins.[271] Food business operators cannot market a new infant formula without giving prior notice of this to the Food Standards Agency.[272] A model of the labelling to be used for the product should be forwarded with this notification to the FSA.

There are a range of additional labelling requirements set out in the Regulations for infant and follow-on formula, again beyond those stipulated in the Food Labelling Regulations. The product must be called 'infant milk' where it is manufactured entirely from cows' milk proteins.[273] Otherwise, it should be called 'infant formula'. The same provisions apply for the products 'follow-on formula' and 'follow-on milk'.[274] All infant formula must carry a set of mandatory labelling disclosures, including a statement that the product is suitable for use by infants from birth when they are not breast fed; the energy values and other relevant nutritional information; and instructions for preparation and storage.[275]

The product must also carry a statement, preceded by the words 'important notice', which indicates the superiority of breast feeding. It should never carry a statement that the product is 'humanised', 'maternalised' or 'adapted'.[276] It should also never include a picture of an infant or 'any other picture or text which may idealise the use of the product'.[277]

Follow-on formula should carry statements on the labelling which make it clear that the product is only suitable for infants over six months of age; that it forms part of a diversified diet; that is should not be used as a substitute for breast milk during the first six months of life; and that any decision to begin complementary feeding before six months of age should only be made on the advice of qualified professionals.[278]

The usual nutritional declarations must also be made. Similar restrictions on the use of terms such as 'humanised' apply to follow-on formula as well. So do

---

[267] Reg 6.

[268] Reg 7.

[269] Reg 10.

[270] Included after amendment to the 2007 Regulations by the Infant Formula and Follow-on Formula (England) (Amendment) Regulations 2013, SI No 3242/2013.

[271] As set out in Annex II to Directive 2006/141, n 262 above.

[272] Reg 13.

[273] Reg 15.

[274] Reg 16.

[275] Reg 17(1).

[276] Reg 17(2).

[277] Reg 17(3).

[278] Reg 18(1).

prohibitions on the appearance of anything on the label which could discourage breast feeding.[279] Finally, in relation to the labelling of these products, both infant formula and follow-on formula should both be presented in a way that enables consumers to make a clear distinction between the products so as to avoid any risk of confusion between them.[280]

The Infant Formula and Follow-on Formula (England) Regulations 2007 also set out a series of restrictions on the advertising and marketing of these products. Infant formula cannot be advertised except in a scientific publication, or one for the purposes of trade prior to the retail stage, and is in a publication that is not aimed at the general public. There is an exception to this. An advertisement may be published if it carries a range of statements about the superiority of breast feeding or refrains from making statements that would do anything to discourage breast feeding in any way.[281] Advertisements for infant formula can only contain information that is scientifically verifiable and factual, and they must not imply that bottle-feeding is equivalent or superior to breast feeding.[282] There are fewer restrictions placed on the advertising of follow-on formula in the Regulations. Advertisements for these products should also refrain from discouraging breast feeding or suggesting that the product is 'humanised' or similar.[283] They should also be presented in a way that clearly distinguishes the product from infant formula.

The marketing of these products is also quite restricted in ways other than those which are placed on advertising by the Regulations. It is an offence, for example, to present infant formula in a special display designed to promote retail sales of the product.[284] Free samples of infant formula cannot be given away, nor can coupons providing a discount on these products be distributed to consumers. They can never be the subject of special offers or loss-leaders in shops. All informational or educational material, written or audio-visual, that deals with the feeding of infants must include details on 'the benefits and superiority of breast-feeding', as well as indicating that the introduction of partial bottle-feeding could have negative effects on breast-feeding.[285] The Regulations even go so far as to oblige that information given out in this way on infant formula must also give details on 'the social and financial implications of its use'.[286] No pictures which 'idealise' the use of infant formula can be included in informational or educational material.[287] Finally, neither infant formula, nor follow-on formula,

---

[279] Reg 18(2).
[280] Reg 19.
[281] Reg 21(1).
[282] Regs 21(2) and 21(3).
[283] Reg 22.
[284] Reg 23(1).
[285] Reg 24(1).
[286] Reg 24(2).
[287] Reg 24(3).

can be exported to third countries from the UK unless they have satisfied the key provisions of the Regulations and the relevant Codex Alimentarius Standards.[288]

The requirements set out above on baby and infant foods are all subject to changes that will be made when an EU regulation on this, and other, matters comes into effect in July 2016.[289] The Regulation is designed to amalgamate existing provisions in a range of areas, including infant foods, foods for particular medical uses and weight-control products. More specifically, it also starts to address the need to regulate the emerging market in milk-based drinks which are promoted as being particularly suitable for young people. However, it is only a commitment to the commissioning of a Commission report on these products, which should be presented to the European Parliament and to the Council, after consultation with EFSA, by July 2015.[290] A legislative proposal on the matter may be introduced at that stage. The Regulation does not depart significantly from already existing provisions on baby and infant food. The labelling requirements for these products continue to require that nothing is conveyed which might discourage breast feeding.[291] Other stipulations, such as the prohibition on the use of pictures of infants in relation to formula, continue along the same lines as those set out in the Infant Formula and Follow-on Formula (England) Regulations 2007.

---

[288] These are Codex Standard 72/1981 for Infant Formula and Codex Standard 156/1987 for Follow-up Formula.

[289] Regulation (EU) No 609/2013 of the European Parliament and of the Council of 12 June 2013 on food intended for infants and young children, food for special medical purposes, and total diet replacement for weight control and repealing Council Directive 92/52/EEC, Commission Directives 96/8/EC, 1999/21/EC, 2006/125/EC and 2006/141/EC, Directive 2009/39/EC of the European Parliament and of the Council and Commission Regulations (EC) No 41/2009 and (EC) No 953/2009 [2013] OJ L 181/35.

[290] ibid, Art 12.

[291] ibid, Art 10(1).

8

Protected Food Names

8.1 Geographical Indications

A European Commission study, published in March 2013, found that foods produced in the EU that are protected from production or imitation by producers other than those who have registered their products are worth around £45 billion annually.[1] These protected foodstuffs account for 15 per cent of the EU's total food and drink exports. The same study found that sales of protected geographical foodstuffs were calculated to be worth almost £5 billion across the UK by 2010.

The system devised at EU level for protecting these 'geographical indications' and 'designations of origin' was first established in 1992.[2] When the Court of Justice developed the principle of mutual recognition in February 1979,[3] declaring that a product 'lawfully produced and marketed in one of the Member States' should be marketable in all of the Member States,[4] it essentially created an inter-State market without restrictions as to compositional requirements or methods of manufacture. A producer in one Member State could make cheese, call it whatever he liked, include a place in the name with which his product had no connection, and sell it using that name in any Member State. Exmoor Blue cheese could be made in another EU Member State and then trade off the good name of the Devon and Somerset version. Provided the producer could call the cheese 'Exmoor Blue' in the country where it was originally marketed, he could call it that in England as well—even where the two versions of the product differed significantly from each other in composition, texture and taste. Producers of the original version would have to share, and risk, their goodwill. Consumers could be deceived into purchasing a product, believing that it was, in fact, something else. The introduction of a register for geographical food names, such as Exmoor Blue cheese, sought to remedy this.

---

[1] AND-International report for the European Commission, 'Value of production of agricultural products and foodstuffs, wines, aromatised wines and spirits protected by a geographical indication'; available at ec.europa.eu/agriculture/external-studies.

[2] Council Regulation (EEC) No 2081/1992 of 14 July 1992 on the protection of geographical indications and designations of origin for agricultural products and foodstuffs [1992] OJ L 208/1.

[3] Case 120/1978 *Rewe-Zentral AG v Bundesmonopolverwaltung für Branntwein* (Cassis) [1979] ECR 649.

[4] Para 14.

In 2005 the World Trade Organization found that elements of the EU system for registering and protecting geographical food names were contrary to the Agreement on Trade Related Aspects of Intellectual Property Rights (TRIPs).[5] As was discussed in chapter two, it was decided that the equivalence and reciprocity conditions for access to the system established by Regulation 2081/1992 violated the national treatment obligations set out in TRIPs and the General Agreement on Tariffs and Trade (GATT).[6] As a result of this, a new Regulation on the protection of geographical food names had to be introduced by the EU, to replace the original offending legislation. This 2006 Regulation addressed the concerns that had been raised at WTO level.[7] Otherwise the system remains substantially the same as that originally developed in 1992. The key provisions of the 2006 Regulation have themselves since been incorporated into a new Food Quality Regulation.[8] The law remains relatively unchanged by this newer Regulation, most of which came into effect at the end of 2012. The 2006 regulations have been repealed.

8.1.1 Geographical Food Names Regulation

The preamble to the Food Quality Regulation 2012 states that '[c]itizens and consumers in the Union increasingly demand quality as well as traditional products'.[9] This then 'generates a demand for agricultural products or foodstuffs with identifiable specific characteristics, in particular those linked to their geographical origin'.[10] With the introduction of the compulsory indication of the protected status of registered foodstuffs, it is now easier for discerning consumers to make choices that can be based on a consistent level of quality.[11] The presence of the related symbol on labelling informs the consumer, in a clear way, that the product has been manufactured to set minimum standards, and in a specific place.

---

[5] DS 174, 290, *European Communities—Protection of Trademarks and Geographical Indications for Agricultural Products and Foodstuffs.*

[6] Art 3.1 TRIPs and Art III:4 GATT.

[7] Council Regulation (EC) No 510/2006 of 20 March 2006 on the protection of geographical indications and designations of origin for agricultural products and foodstuffs [2006] OJ L 93/12.

[8] Regulation (EU) No 1151/2012 of the European Parliament and of the Council of 21 November 2012 on quality schemes for agricultural products and foodstuffs [2012] OJ L 343/1. For a more detailed analysis of this Regulation see M Gragnani, 'The EU Regulation 1151/2012 on quality schemes for agricultural products and foodstuffs' (2013) 8 *European Food and Feed Law Review* 376.

[9] Recital 2 of the Preamble to Reg 1151/2012, n 8 above.

[10] ibid.

[11] Art 8 of Reg 510/2006 provided that the symbol and/or indication of protected status should appear on the labelling of registered foodstuffs. This was not, under the terms of Art 20 of the Regulation, a compulsory indication until 1 May 2009. The symbols that had to be used were set out in the Annex to Commission Regulation (EC) No 628/2008 of 2 July 2008 amending Regulation (EC) No 1898/2006 laying down detailed rules of implementation of Council Regulation (EC) No 510/2006 on the protection of geographical indications and designations of origin for agricultural products and foodstuffs [2008] OJ L 173/3. Art 12 of Reg 1151/2012 now provides for the establishment of a new symbol, designed to publicise PDOs and PGIs. However, this provision of the 2012 Regulation does not take full effect until 2016.

Products must first be registered for protection under the terms of the Regulation before this symbol, or other indication, can be used.

Categories of Protected Geographical Food Name

The 2012 Food Quality Regulation sets out two types of protected geographical food name. These are the designation of origin and the geographical indication. The former is defined as being:

> [A] name which identifies a product originating in a specific place, region or, in exceptional cases, a country, whose quality or characteristics are essentially or exclusively due to a particular geographical environment with its inherent natural and human factors, and the production steps of which all take place in the defined geographical area.[12]

These 'steps' were identified in the previous regulations as being 'the production, processing and preparation'.[13] The second category, the geographical indication, is mostly the same as the designation of origin except for the fact that only the production and/or processing and/or preparation must take place in the defined geographical area, described in the 2012 Regulation as being 'at least one of the production steps'.[14] English foods that have been registered as protected designations of origin (PDO) include Yorkshire forced rhubarb, which was registered in March 2010, Staffordshire cheese, which was registered in September 2007, Cornish clotted cream, which was registered in October 1998, and Stilton, which was registered in June 1996. Cornish pasties (2011), Cumberland sausages (2011), Melton Mowbray pork pies (2009), Welsh beef (2002) and Exmoor Blue cheese (1999) have, amongst others, all been registered as protected geographical indications (PGIs). Non-geographical names, such as feta, can also be registered as designations of origin or geographical indications where there is a clear link between the traditional place of production and the characteristics of the foodstuff. This was stated explicitly in the original geographical food names regulations,[15] but is indicated in the 2012 Regulation by an alteration of the definitions of PDO and PGI to being 'a name which identifies a product', rather than limiting this to the name of a region or place.[16]

Generic Names

While the geographical food names regulation goes some way to promoting and protecting minimum quality standards for foodstuffs, and the property rights of those who produce them, the majority of products can never be registered as a PDO or a PGI. Any name that has become 'generic' cannot be registered or

---

[12] Art 5(1) of Reg 1151/2012, n 8 above.
[13] Art 2(1) of Reg 510/2006, n 7 above.
[14] Art 5(2) of Reg 1151/2012, n 8 above.
[15] Eg Art 2(2) of Reg 510/2006, n 7 above.
[16] Art 5(1) and (2) of Reg 1151/2012, n 8 above.

protected.[17] As a result, some of the most well known geographical food names are excluded from the scope of the Regulation. Cheddar, for example, can never be registered. Although originally produced in Somerset, its reputation well established by the twelfth century, use of the name 'cheddar' to describe many varieties of cheese, produced in many different places, means that the name, although geographical, is also generic. Its use has become so commonplace that it cannot now be registered for protection. However, if the application for registration is made more specific, and tailored to a defined geographical area, protection is possible. 'Cheddar' cannot be registered, but 'West Country Farmhouse Cheddar' can.[18]

This previous example helps to illustrate some of the complications that exist in determining which names are generic. This is a constant source of deliberation—most famously debated in relation to the status of feta cheese. Cheddar is clearly a generic name. It is the most widely eaten cheese in the world. It is produced in the UK, Ireland, USA, Canada, New Zealand, Australia and elsewhere. The Regulation provides that generic names are those which are 'the names of products which, although relating to the place, region or country where the product was originally produced or marketed, have become the common name of a product in the Union'.[19] A range of factors must be taken into account when determining whether a name satisfies this definition and has consequently become generic for the purposes of the Regulation. The situation in the Member States and in areas of consumption must be considered, as must any relevant national or Union laws.[20] This is a flexible and objective test, requiring the examination of evidence to support a claim that the name has not, in fact, become generic and is therefore potentially eligible for protection as a PDO or a PGI. The Court of Justice has stated that

> [t]he way in which the name of a product becomes generic is the result of an objective process, at the end of which that name, although referring to the geographical place where the product in question was originally manufactured or marketed, has become the common name of that product.[21]

Tests of this nature are often problematic and open to accusations of arbitrary decision making. Flexible objectivity can sometimes lead to more subjective decision making. Never was this more evident than in relation to the long-running saga which centred on attempts to have Greek feta cheese registered as a protected designation of origin.

---

[17] ibid, Art 6(1).

[18] West Country Farmhouse Cheddar cheese was registered as a protected designation of origin under the terms of Commission Regulation (EC) No 1107/1996 of 12 June 1996 on the registration of geographical indications and designations of origin under the procedure laid down in Art 17 of Council Regulation (EEC) No 2081/1992 [1996] OJ L 148/1.

[19] Art 3(6) of Reg 1151/2012, n 8 above.

[20] Art 41(2) of Reg 1151/2012.

[21] Case C-466/2007 *Alberto Severi v Regione Emilia-Romagna* [2009] ECR I-8041, para 50.

Assessing Names

As noted above, certain considerations must be taken into account when deciding whether a geographical food name is generic. These are broad assessment criteria related to the name, its history, consumer preference for the food, the existence of relevant laws and their application and public perception. Essentially, the criteria set out in the Regulation, that there must be an examination of the situation in the Member States and of the relevant national or Community rules, facilitates the presentation of a vast variety of supporting evidence for any claim that a name is either generic, or non-generic and therefore potentially suitable for registration and protection.

The case law of the Court of Justice, and the legislation that has developed out of it, presents significant elaboration on what is meant by the ambiguous assessment criterion of 'the situation in the Member States'. In June 1996, the Greek cheese 'feta' was registered as a protected designation of origin, along with around 19 varieties of Greek cheese, and many different foodstuffs from the other EU Member States.[22] However, three Member States, Denmark, Germany and France, took exception to this, claiming that the name 'feta' was generic and should not, therefore, have been registered. They thus sought to have the decision to register feta as a PDO annulled.[23]

In *Denmark, Germany and France v Commission*,[24] it was noted that prior to making the decision to register feta as a PDO there was acceptance that 'extreme caution' would be required when determining whether the name had become generic. 'Convincing evidence' would need to be presented to support whichever decision was made.

A 'Eurobarometer' study was therefore commissioned, to gauge public perceptions about the name 'feta', and in particular to ascertain, as far as possible, whether it had become the common name for a product, detached from its original geographical connotation.[25] This study found that on average around one in five EU citizens had heard of feta, rising to almost everybody in Greece and Denmark. Of those who had heard of the name, the majority associated it with cheese, and the majority of those associated this cheese with Greece. Three-quarters of those surveyed who were familiar with the name 'feta' saw it as having a geographical connotation. More interviewees considered 'feta' to be a common

---

[22] Commission Regulation (EC) No 1107/1996 of 12 June 1996 on the registration of geographical designations and designations of origin under the procedure laid down in Art 17 of Council Regulation (EEC) No 2081/1992, OJ L 148/1.

[23] This application for the annulment of that part of Reg 1107/1996 which listed feta as a PDO was brought under Art 263 TFEU (formerly Art 230 EC, but which was Art 173 EC at the time of this case). For further discussion on the relevance of Art 263 TFEU to English food law see ch 2.

[24] Joined cases C-289/1996, C-293/1996 and C-299/1996 *Kingdom of Denmark, Federal Republic of Germany and French Republic v Commission of the European Communities* [1999] ECR I-1541.

[25] This Eurobarometer survey was based on interviews with 12,800 nationals of the then 12 Member States. It was published on 24 October 1994.

name than one which related exclusively to a particular place of origin.[26] While the range of questions posed in the study appear confusing and mostly superfluous to the aim of ascertaining consumer perceptions about feta, the results of the survey were clear. Most of those questioned had never heard of feta. Of those who were familiar with it, many considered it to be a common name. Just over half of Greeks considered it to be a geographical name. Despite this, the Commission concluded that 'feta' had not become generic. Even the Scientific Committee for Designations of Origin and Geographical Indications could only determine by the slimmest of majorities, four votes to three, that 'feta' met the conditions for registration as a protected name, although they were convinced that it was not a generic name.[27] Denmark, Germany and France contested these conclusions.

It is important to dwell on these feta cases for a while as they exemplify so much about the system of protection for registered geographical food names. They make it clear that a name need not be 'geographical' to be accepted onto the register. They illustrate the range and type of data that must be presented where there is contention over eligibility for registration. They also clearly show us how that data is then interpreted, arguably arbitrarily, in the decision-making process. The Commission was effectively accused of this arbitrariness by both the applicant Member States and the Court of Justice in *Denmark, Germany and France v Commission*. When deciding that 'feta' was not generic, the Commission had not given proper consideration to 'the situation in other Member States', as it was obliged to under the terms of the Regulation. The name had been used for a considerable time in other Member States, not just in Greece. A product called 'feta' had been lawfully produced and marketed in those States. None of this potentially persuasive evidence was taken into account by the Commission when deciding that 'feta' was not a generic name. The registration of feta as a PDO was thus annulled by the Court.[28]

The Court of Justice did not decide in *Denmark, Germany and France v Commission* that the name 'feta' was generic. All they had decided was that the Commission had erred in its decision-making process by not taking the existing situation in other Member States into consideration. It could be argued, of course, that the Commission also erred in interpreting the results of the Eurobarometer study, so central to its finding that the name should be eligible for registration as

---

[26] These findings were presented in para 37 of the judgment in *Denmark, Germany and France v Commission*, n 24 above.

[27] This Committee was established by Commission Decision 1993/53/EEC of 21 December 1992 setting up a scientific committee for designations of origin, geographical indications and certificates of specific character [1993] OJ L 13/16. In particular the Committee was not unanimously convinced that 'feta' met the terms of Art 2(3) of Reg 2081/1992, that it was a '[c]ertain traditional geographical or non-geographical [name] designating an agricultural product or a foodstuff originating in a region or a specific place, which fulfils the conditions [for a designation of origin]'.

[28] 'Feta' was removed from the PDO register by Art 1 of Commission Regulation (EC) No 1070/1999 amending the Annex to Regulation (EC) No 1107/1996 on the registration of geographical indications and designations of origin under the procedure laid down in Art 17 of Council Regulation (EEC) No 2081/1992 [1999] OJ L 130/18.

a PDO, in the way that it did. But the Court did not make any declaration on this aspect of the Commission's assessment. The possibility therefore existed for the Commission to go through the process again. It could collate data on the existing situation in other Member States and use this, along with its existing interpretations of the Eurobarometer and the Scientific Committee findings, to support its registration of 'feta' as a PDO. This is exactly what the Commission then did.

A new Regulation was introduced in 2002 to reinstate 'feta' onto the PDO register.[29] The Commission organised another poll in 1999, this one more directly related to the 'situation' regarding feta cheese in all of the Member States. The data gathered from the EU Member States at the time suggested that specific rules governing the production and marketing of feta cheese had existed in three places: Greece, since 1935; Denmark, since 1963; and the Netherlands, between 1981 and 1998. Feta cheese had been produced, at varying levels, in at least 13 of the then 15 Member States. Feta production was described as 'substantial' in four of these States: Greece (since ancient times), Denmark (since the 1930s), France (since 1931) and Germany (since 1972). Much of this cheese was exported around the world. Greek feta tended to be produced using ewe's and goat's milk. The Danish, French and German varieties were usually made with ewe's milk (especially in France) or cow's milk. The poll also showed that when Greece had joined the EU in 1981, it had accounted for around 92 per cent of feta consumption amongst all of the Member States. Consumption had increased in the other States since then, to a level where Greece now only accounted for 73 per cent of the total rate. Crucially, however, the replies to the questionnaire sent by the Member States to the Commission showed that many of the cheeses that were marketed as 'feta' tended to make some sort of reference to Greece on the label. Text, symbols or pictures suggesting a link between the product and Greek territory, culture or tradition were used to market the product—regardless of where the cheese had been produced. Practically all feta produced anywhere in the EU was being marketed in this way. Dictionary definitions of 'feta' usually specified a Greek cheese made from ewe's and goat's milk, but there was some recognition that production was now more widespread than this. The Scientific Committee unanimously concluded that 'feta' was not a generic name. It gave several reasons for this: the concentration of both production and consumption in Greece; the usual difference in the type of milk used (cow's) and the method of manufacture (ultrafiltration) in other Member States; the evocation of the Greek origin of the product amongst consumers; and the absence of specific legislation setting compositional requirements in most Member States other than Greece (Denmark being the only exception at the time).

It must be remembered that the Commission is not obliged to follow the Scientific Committee's opinion. It may, however, be of persuasive authority. Taking account of this, and an 'exhaustive overall analysis of the legal, historical,

---

[29] Commission Regulation (EC) No 1829/2002 of 14 October 2002 amending the Annex to Regulation (EC) No 1107/1996 with regard to the name 'feta' [2002] OJ L 277/10.

cultural, political, social, economic, scientific and technical information',[30] the Commission concluded that 'feta' is not a generic name. It is, instead, a traditional non-geographical name, eligible for protection under what is now Article 5 of Regulation 1151/2012.[31] The name 'feta' would now therefore be included in the register of protected designations of origin and geographical indications.[32]

The assessment by EU institutions and Member States of whether the name 'feta' is generic was described earlier as being something of a saga. This is because despite everything that has been outlined already—the regulations, the court cases, the surveying—the decision to register feta for protection came before the Court of Justice again in *Germany and Denmark v Commission*.[33]

The Court now looked at what at had been done, and discovered, by the Commission since deliberations about the generic nature of the name 'feta' had last come before it. Looking at the preamble to the reinstatement of feta on the PDO register,[34] the Court noted that information provided by the Member States indicated that products called 'feta' tend to make some explicit or implicit reference to Greece on the labelling.[35] The link between feta and Greece was being deliberately suggested on almost all of the cheese of that type being produced in other countries as part of a sales strategy aimed to capitalise on the reputation of the original Greek product.[36] This, combined with all of the data gathered by the 1999 Commission poll, suggested to the Court that 'feta' was not a generic name. This time the Court was satisfied that the Commission had taken all relevant factors taken into consideration in their assessment—the existing situation in the Member State in which the name originates and in arrears of consumption; the existing situation in other Member States; and the relevant national or Union laws—as was required by Article 3(1) of Regulation 510/2006. The action brought by Germany and Denmark was consequently dismissed.

It is clear from the wording of Article 3(1) of the Regulation, and the related case law, such as the feta cases discussed above, that a full assessment of all the listed factors is essential in determining whether a name is generic. This was further clarified by the Court in *Commission v Germany*,[37] where it stated that

> [w]hen assessing the generic character of a name, the Court has held that it is necessary, under Article 3(1) of [the Regulation,] to take into account the places of production of the product concerned both inside and outside the Member State which obtained

---

[30] Recital 33 of the Preamble to Reg 1829/2002, n 29 above.

[31] Formerly Art 2(3) of Reg 2081/1992, n 2 above.

[32] Art 1(1) of Reg 1829/2002, n 29 above.

[33] Joined cases C-465/2002 and C-466/2002 *Germany and Denmark v Commission* [2005] ECR I-9115.

[34] Reg 1829/2002, n 29 above.

[35] Preamble to Reg 1829/2002, n 29 above, recital 20.

[36] Similarly, the Court found in para 55 of Case C-132/2005 *Commission v Germany*, n 37 below, that 'Parmesan' cheese sold in Germany tended to be marketed with labels that referred to Italian culture and landscapes, and from this it could be inferred that German consumers perceived Parmesan as an Italian product, even if it had actually been produced elsewhere.

[37] Case C-132/2005 *Commission v Germany* [2008] ECR I-957.

the registration of the name at issue, the consumption of that product and how it is perceived by consumers inside and outside that Member State, the existence of national legislation specifically relating to that product, and the way in which the name has been used in [Union] law.[38]

Essentially, the Court was summarising the range of factors taken into consideration in *Germany and Denmark v Commission*. It has also been found that a food name should not be presumed to be generic until declared otherwise.[39] To do so would jeopardise the application, as generic names cannot be registered. It would also be contrary to the objectives pursued by the Regulation, namely the protection of both consumers and producers.[40]

Applications for Legal Protection

Geographical food names must be registered with the European Commission before they can be legally protected in all Member States, and potentially throughout the World Trade Organization as well. Applications for protection commence with the completion of a product specification.[41] This should provide the Commission with details about the foodstuff for which protection is sought, including the name of the product; a description of the product, including information about the raw materials used in production and the key characteristics of the food, such as its physical, chemical, microbiological and organoleptic qualities (texture, taste, smell, appearance); a definition of the geographical area where the food is traditionally produced; evidence that the product originates in that defined geographical area; a description of the method of production; and packaging details.[42] All of this information may not be required for all applications. For example, the foodstuff under consideration may not traditionally have any specific type of packaging, making the provision of details on this superfluous to this application. Finally, information must be furnished which demonstrates that there is a link between the characteristics of the foodstuff and its traditional place of production.[43] The product specification can be amended, even after protected status has been finalised.[44]

Only groups are entitled to apply for registration under the terms of the Regulation.[45] A 'group', for the purposes of the Regulation, is an association of producers or processors working with the same agricultural product or foodstuff. A natural or legal person may be treated as a group in some circumstances.[46] This can be the case where the person concerned is the only producer in the defined

---

[38] Para 53.
[39] Case C-446/2007 *Alberto Severi v Regione Emilia-Romagna* [2009] ECR I-8041.
[40] Para 53.
[41] Art 7 of Reg 1151/2012.
[42] Art 7(1)(a)–(e) of Reg 1151/2012.
[43] ibid, Art 7(1)(f).
[44] Art 53.
[45] Art 49.
[46] Art 49(1).

geographical area who is willing to submit an application and the defined geographical area in question possesses characteristics which differ appreciably from those of neighbouring areas or the characteristics of the product for which registration is sought differ from those produced in neighbouring areas.[47] Applications may also be lodged by several groups joined together seeking the registration of a trans-border geographical name.[48] The application must include the specification details, outlined above, as well as the name and address of the applicant group or groups, and a single document that sets out details on the main points of the specification and the link between the product and its area of production—basically a clear and summarised version of all relevant information.[49]

Where an application relates to a product made or processed within a single Member State, the dossier of evidence supporting the request for registration should be addressed to that Member State. The application must then be scrutinised by the relevant authority within the State to check that it is justified and meets the conditions necessary for registration as a protected geographical food name. In England, applications are evaluated by DEFRA.[50] There is also an obligation placed on the relevant authority to establish a national objection procedure. This involves publishing details of applications made, providing a reasonable period of time for potential objectors to lodge a claim that the application should not proceed.[51] Any natural or legal person who has a legitimate interest in the application, and who is established within the State, may lodge an objection to an application. DEFRA must consider the admissibility of any objections lodged, taking into account whether the foodstuff for which an application has been made is in compliance with the terms of the Regulation, in particular whether it is the type of name that is eligible for protection, whether it is a generic name or whether registration would jeopardise an existing trade mark.[52]

A final decision is then to be taken by DEFRA on the eligibility of the application. If this is favourable, the application is forwarded to the European Commission, alongside further publication of the details of the application, giving potential objectors one more opportunity to try to stall the process. Once all outstanding issues have been resolved, the Commission then considers the application lodged by DEFRA. Objections from other Member States and/or third countries are dealt with at a later stage in the process. Member States may grant transitional protection, extending to the host State only, while the application is considered.[53] This interim status must cease as soon as the Commission has made its decision on eligibility for protection.

---

[47] Art 49(1)(a) and (b). Both criteria must be satisfied.
[48] Art 49(1).
[49] Art 8(1).
[50] Under Art 36 of Reg 1151/2012 Member States are responsible for designating their own competent authorities.
[51] Art 49(3).
[52] Art 10.
[53] Art 9.

It is the European Commission that makes the ultimate decision on whether or not to include a foodstuff on the protected designations of origin or protected geographical indications register. DEFRA sends the details of applications that it has pre-assessed on to the Commission for EU approval. Only the summarised version, not the full version, of the product specification has to be included in this submission, along with details of the name and address of the applicant group and details of its own publication and declaration that it considers that the foodstuff in question is eligible for protection.[54] The Commission then has a maximum of six months in which to consider the application.[55] A list of applications received should be published on a monthly basis, as well as including details of applications that are being considered for registration in the Official Journal of the European Union.[56] The application is then subject to Commission scrutiny.

Objections to Protection

Objections to the registration of geographical food names may be made by any Member State or third country within six months after publication of the details, mentioned above, in the Official Journal.[57] In order to do so, the Member State or third country must lodge a document of objection with the Commission. This right to object is also extended to natural or legal persons who have a legitimate interest in the application that has been made, whether resident in an EU Member State or a third country.[58] This does not extend to residents of the Member State from which the application has been made, as they have already had the opportunity to object when the application was initially under the consideration of the relevant national authority, such as DEFRA, as outlined above.

The objection by others from within the EU is made through the relevant body in their own Member State. Attempts to block the registration by interested parties from third countries are made by way of application to the Commission, either directly by themselves or through their national authority. All statements of objection, regardless of where they come from, have to be made within the set three-month time period.[59] Objections are only admissible where they can demonstrate that the product for which registration is sought does not fall within the definitions of designation of origin or geographical indication, or that its registration would jeopardise an existing trade mark, or that the name is generic or potentially misleading to consumers. Admissible objections are then considered, with a view to agreement being reached between all of the interested parties on how to proceed, or if that fails to produce a result the Commission will make a decision on

---

[54] Art 8(2).

[55] Art 50(1). It was allowed 12 months for this under Art 6(1) of Reg 510/2006, n 7 above.

[56] Art 50(2).

[57] Art 51(1)(1).

[58] Art 51(1)(2).

[59] Art 10. Again, this time frame has been reduced by Reg 1151/2012. It was set at six months under the terms of Art 7(3) of Reg 510/2006.

the basis of the evidence presented to it.[60] If no admissible objections are received, the name is registered for protection.[61] Protected names can be cancelled at a later date, should circumstances change in a way that warrants this course of action.[62]

Effects of Protection

Once registered, the protected name can be used by any operator who markets a product that conforms to the standards set out in the specification.[63] Obviously, this will only extend to those who produce or process within the specified region. Member States may not use national law to alter the nature or the terms of the protected designation of origin after registration.[64] A statement that the product is a protected designation of origin or designation of origin must appear on the labelling, and since May 2009 the standard EU PDO or PGI symbol, as appropriate, must also be included.[65]

Registered food names are accorded a high level of legal protection under the scheme.[66] Primarily, they are protected against any use of the name by operators who are not covered by the terms of the product specification,[67] or any other practice that is liable to mislead the consumer about the true origin of the product.[68] They are specifically protected from any 'misuse, imitation or evocation', even where the actual origin of the product has been indicated on the label.[69] Prohibiting 'evocation' of registered food names means that the producers of another similar product cannot use a similar name to that of its protected counterpart. This is so even where the other, similar name has been in use for some time and predates the registration of the protected geographical indication or designation of origin.

In *Gorgonzola*,[70] for example, it was held that the name 'Cambozola' was an evocation, even though it was itself protected by an existing registered trade

---

[60] Art 52(3).

[61] Art 52(2).

[62] Art 54.

[63] Art 12(1).

[64] Joined Cases C-129/1997 and C-130/1997 *Chiciak, Chiciak and Fol* [1998] ECR I-3315.

[65] As originally established by Art 8(2) in conjunction with Art 20 of Regulation 510/2006. The approved symbols are, until 2016, set out in Annex V to Regulation 1898/2006 [2006] OJ L 369/1.

[66] While the level of protection accorded to registered names is generally high, it is exhaustive in nature, and does not extend to geographical indications for which no application for registration has been made. This was seen most clearly in case C-478/2007 *Budĕjovicky Budvar v Rudolf Ammersin GmbH* [2009] ECR I-7721, where use of the name 'Bud' was not prohibited by the protected status of three Czech beers which included this designation within the PGIs Budĕjovické pivo, Čéskobudĕjovické pivo and Budĕjovicky mĕstansky var. This was the case despite the fact that the designation 'Bud' had previously been protected under a bilateral agreement between Austria and Czechoslovakia. An application for the protection of the designation 'Bud' would have to be successfully made before restrictions could be placed on others' use of that name for marketing their beer.

[67] Art 13(1)(a).

[68] Art 13(1)(d).

[69] Art 13(1)(b).

[70] Case C-87/1997, *Consorzio per la tutela del formaggio Gorgonzola v Käserei Champignon Hofmeisted GmbH & Co KG and Eduard Bracharz GmbH* [1999] ECR I-1301.

mark. The soft blue Italian cheese, Gorgonzola, had been registered as a protected designation of origin since 1996.[71] The German soft blue cheese, Cambozola, had been protected by a trade mark there since January 1983. The consortium for the protection of Gorgonzola applied to the Commercial Court in Vienna seeking an order prohibiting the marketing of Cambozola in Austria using that name, contending that the designation of origin status was compromised due to the similarity between the two names. While leaving the ultimate decision on continued use of the trade mark name to the national court, the European Court of Justice did decide that there was evocation of a protected name due to the fact that similar names were being used to describe similar products. This created the possibility of creating confusion amongst consumers. During its deliberations, the Court described 'evocation' as covering those situations

> where the term used to designate a product incorporates part of a protected designation, so that when the consumer is confronted with the name of the product, the image triggered in his mind is that of the product whose designation is protected.[72]

Since the products at issue here were both soft blue cheeses which were similar in appearance, it would be reasonable, according to the Court, to conclude that the protected name 'Gorgonzola' was being evoked where the other name, 'Cambozola', ends in the same two syllables and contains the same number of syllables, resulting in a 'phonetic and visual similarity between the two'.[73] While the Court of Justice was clearly of the opinion that the circumstances at issue here gave rise to probable evocation, the Geographical Food Names Regulation does allow certain trade marks to continue in their application, even where they run contrary to the terms of a protected designation of origin or protected geographical indication. Article 14(2) states that

> a trademark the use of which corresponds to one of the situations referred to in Article 13 [such as evocation] which has been applied for, registered or established by use ... in good faith within the territory of the [Union] before either the date of protection of the designation of origin or geographical indication in the country of origin or before 1 January 1996, may continue to be used ... provided that no grounds for its invalidity or revocation exist.

In other words, where a trade mark was registered in good faith in a Member State prior to protection being accorded under the Regulation 510/2006 scheme, then use of the trade mark should continue, unless there is some other good reason for preventing this. In *Gorgonzola*, it was noted that 'Cambozola' was registered as a trade mark before Gorgonzola was accorded PDO status. It would have been 'in good faith' had it been done 'in compliance with the rules of law in force at the time'.[74] Assessment of this is left to the national court.[75]

---

[71] Annex to Reg 1107/1996, n 22 above.
[72] Case C-87/1997 *Gorgonzola*, n 70 above, para 25.
[73] Para 27.
[74] Case C-87/1997 *Gorgonzola*, n 70 above, para 34.
[75] Para 36.

In *Commission v Germany*,[76] where an action was brought against the Member State for failing to prevent the abuse of a protected designation of origin, it was held that there was a phonetic and visual similarity between the names 'Parmesan' and the registered 'Parmigiano-Reggiano'. Both products are hard cheeses, usually grated or intended to be grated. Both are of similar appearance. This, according to the Court, made it irrelevant that one was not a direct linguistic translation of the other. The similarities were deemed to be such that consumers could think of Parmigiano-Reggiano when confronted with Parmesan. The latter was thus found to be an evocation of the former.[77]

Where a food name has been classified as a protected designation of origin or protected geographical indication, other products cannot be marketed as being similar to them. This means that the use of terms such as 'style', 'type' or 'imitation' cannot be used in conjunction with the protected name by producers not covered by the registration specification.[78] Registered food names are also protected from

> any other false or misleading indication as to the provenance, origin, nature, or essential qualities of the product, on the … packaging, advertising material or documents relating to the product concerned, and the packing of a product in a container liable to convey a false impression as to its origin.[79]

It must be remembered that the use of a PDO or a PGI is conditional upon full compliance with the terms of the specification. This can mean that all or specific aspects of the production process must take place in the region covered by the registration, even where this has little impact on the nature of the protected product itself. Slicing, grating and/or packaging may all have to happen in the same place before a registered name can be lawfully used in the marketing of a foodstuff. In *Bellon*, for example, it was held that all stages of production, including the grating and packaging of Grana Padano cheese, could be included as conditions for the use of a protected designation of origin.[80] Limiting the use of this PDO to cheese that had been grated and packaged in the region covered by the specification was deemed a measure equivalent to a quantitative restriction on exports, as prohibited by Article 35 TFEU. However, this could be justified on the basis that the quality and authenticity of the product as presented to consumers could be compromised if these stages of production took place outside the region covered by the registration. The Court also stated that no alternative, less restrictive measures could be used to achieve this aim of guaranteeing quality—recognised as being one of the key aims of the geographical food names regulation, and of the framework of the Common Agricultural Policy more generally.[81] A condition like this, insisting that grating and packaging must take place in the region of production,

---

[76] Case C-132/2005 *Commission v Germany*, n 37 above.
[77] Para 49.
[78] Art 13(1)(b).
[79] Art 13(1)(c).
[80] Case C-469/2000 *Ravil SARL v Bellon Import SARL and Biraghi SpA* [2003] ECR I-5053.
[81] Para 48.

can, however, only be relied upon against other food business operators if it has been brought to their knowledge by adequate publicity in EU legislation, such as making specific reference to it in the relevant regulation.[82] It can be relied upon, but only against those who could reasonably have been expected to know about it.

The Court of Justice came to similar conclusions on the condition that Parma ham could only be sold as such if it had been sliced in the region of production. This matter first came before the English courts when the respondent company, Asda, had been selling packets of pre-sliced Parma ham in its supermarkets.[83] There was no dispute over whether the ham was genuine 'Prosciutto di Parma', which was registered as a protected designation of origin.[84] However, the fact that the product was sliced and packaged in England did give rise to a dispute—the producers' association claiming that the ham in question was not lawfully marketable due to the fact that the product specification stipulated that all stages of production must take place in the registered region. The House of Lords, on appeal from the Parma ham producers, referred the matter to the European Court of Justice, asking whether the PDO regulations, combined with the registered product specification, created a valid EU right, directly enforceable in the court of a Member State.[85]

Under the terms of Italian national law, Parma ham must be marked with a distinguishing five-pointed coronet (corona ducale).[86] Article 6 of this law provides that the mark must be applied and kept on the ham, indelibly stamped if necessary. It also states that the packaging operations have to take place in the typical production area, in order to ensure that the mark is only affixed to genuine products. Other related Italian legislation prescribes that the slicing and packaging of Parma ham must take place at plants in the typical production area, which have been approved by the producers' association, and in the presence of representatives of the association.[87] Having taken all of this into consideration, the European Court of Justice confirmed that the Geographical Food Names Regulation could be used to create a condition that operations, such as the slicing and packaging of a designation of origin, must take place in the region of production, where this is set out in the specification used to register the product.[88] It also held that the enforcement of this condition was a measure equivalent to a quantitative restriction on exports. It continued to point out, however, that this could be justified on the basis that the resulting restriction on trade and commercial operations was necessary to ensure preservation of the reputation of Parma ham. Despite all

---

[82] In this case, Reg 1107/1996, n 22 above.

[83] *Consorzio del Prosciutto di Parma v Asda Stores Ltd and Hygrade Foods Ltd* [1999] ETMR 319, CA.

[84] Registered by Reg 1107/1996, n 22 above.

[85] Pre-ECJ determination opinion in the House of Lords was that the respondents were infringing a valid EU right, directly enforceable in the English courts. See n 83 above.

[86] Law No 26 on protection of the designation of origin Prosciutto di Parma of 13 February 1990, GURI No 42 of 20 February 1990, p 3.

[87] Arts 25 and 26 of Decree No 253 implementing Law No 26, GURI No 173 of 26 July 1993, p 4.

[88] Case C-108/2001 *Consorzio del Prosciutto di Parma and Salumificio S Rita SpA v Asda Stores Ltd and Hygrade Foods Ltd* [2003] ECR I-5121.

of this, however, it was ultimately held that the producers could not rely on the slicing and packaging elements of the registered product specification. The specificity of the conditions attached to this had not been properly publicised. Similar to its decision in *Bellon*, the Court had found that all the terms of a registered specification are enforceable, provided that they are necessary, proportionate and brought to the attention of other operators. Setting out all the conditions attached to the use of a PDO in the relevant EU legislation is deemed to be sufficient for the satisfaction of the latter.

The existence of a protected food name cannot be used by national authorities to restrict the activities of operators who produce unregistered similar foods in the region covered by the product specification on the basis that such limitations are necessary to preserve the status of the protected name.[89] Complete protection is not always immediate on registration.[90] Existing producers of the protected product, who are not covered by the product specification, may be permitted to continue to use the name for a period of time after registration.[91] Finally, protected food names cannot, subject to one exception, ever become legally 'generic'.[92] The only circumstances in which a protected food name can later become generic is if the Regulation which entered the PDO or PGI onto the register is annulled by the Court of Justice under the Article 263 TFEU procedure, as discussed in chapter two.

8.2 Traditional Specialities

Foods that owe their qualities or characteristics to their raw materials or composition, but which are not 'geographical' within the terms of Regulation 1151/2012, may still be accorded protection under EU law if they satisfy the conditions for registration as a 'traditional speciality guaranteed' or 'TSG'.[93] The system for

---

[89] Case C-161/2009 *Kakavestos-Fragkopoulos kai v Korinthias* [2011] ECR I-915.

[90] Art 15(1) of Reg 1151/2012, n 8 above, provides that 'the Commission may adopt implementing acts granting a transitional period of up to five years to enable products originating in a Member State or a third country the designation of which consists of or contains a name that contravenes Art 13(1) to continue to use the designation under which it was marketed [where] such products have been legally marketed with that name in the territory concerned for at least five years preceding the [registration]'.

[91] For example, several producers were permitted to continue their production and marketing of Melton Mowbray pork pies for five years after the registration of that name as a protected geographical indication, despite operating outside the terms of the product specification. Art 1 of Commission Regulation (EC) No 566/2009 of 29 June 2009 entering a name in the register of protected designations of origin and protected geographical indications [2009] OJ L 168/20.

[92] Art 13(2).

[93] The 'traditional speciality guaranteed' was previously known as the 'certificate of specific character', but this changed with the introduction of the new TSG Regulation in 2006, Regulation 509/2006 of 20 March 2006 on agricultural products and foodstuffs as traditional specialities guaranteed [2006] OJ L 93/1.

registering TSGs was also originally developed in 1992,[94] updated and amended in 2006,[95] and again in 2012.[96] It is stated that the creation of TSGs was necessary as '[t]he promotion of traditional products with specific characteristics could be of considerable benefit to the rural economy … by improving the income of farmers and by retaining the rural population in these areas'.[97] Two UK products have been registered as a TSG. These are 'Traditional Farmfresh Turkey', which was granted TSG status in 2000, and 'Traditionally Farmed Gloucestershire Old Spots Pork', registered in 2010. Traditional specialities from other EU Member States that have been entered into the TSG Register include 'Pizza Napoletana' (Italy, 2010), Mozzarella (Italy, 1998), 'Faro' beer (Belgium, 1997) and 'Jamón Serrano' (Spain, 1999). Very few TSGs have been registered across the EU. It is very much an under-used system for registering traditional food names as compared to the PDO/PGI procedure.[98] It is also, however, a potentially very valuable process for producers.

'Traditional speciality guaranteed' was very simply defined in the 2006 Regulation as 'a traditional agricultural product or foodstuff recognised by the [EU] for its specific character through its registration under this Regulation'.[99] 'Specific character' was deemed to be 'the characteristic or set of characteristics which distinguishes an agricultural product or a foodstuff clearly from other similar products or foodstuffs of the same category'.[100] A product was deemed to be 'traditional' when it has been in existence for at least 25 years.[101] This has now been extended to 30 years.[102] The characteristics of a foodstuff that can be considered in determining whether the product is eligible for registration as a TSG include the physical, chemical, microbiological or organoleptic features, or the method or conditions of production.[103] Presentation is not in itself an examinable characteristic. One of the key differences between the TSG system and that for PDOs and PGIs is that the use of a registered TSG may not necessarily become the exclusive preserve of those who apply for the name to be registered, or for those who meet the conditions set out in the product specification, which must

---

[94] Council Regulation (EEC) No 2082/1992 of 14 July 1992 on certificates of specific character for agricultural products and foodstuffs [1992] OJ L 208/9.

[95] Reg 509/2006, n 93 above.

[96] Reg 1151/2012, n 8 above.

[97] Recital 2 of the Preamble to Reg 509/2006, n 93 above. Recital 34 of the Preamble to Reg 1151/2012 states that '[t]he specific objective of the scheme for traditional specialities guaranteed is to help the producers of traditional products to communicate to consumers the value-adding attributes of their product'.

[98] This was also formally recognised in Recital 34 of the Preamble to Reg 1151/2012, where it was stated that 'as only a few names have been registered, the current scheme for traditional specialities guaranteed has failed to realise its potential [and it] should therefore be improved, clarified and sharpened in order to make the scheme more understandable, operational and attractive to potential applicants'.

[99] Art 2(1)(c) of Reg 509/2006, n 93 above.

[100] ibid, Art 2(1)(a).

[101] ibid, Art 2(1)(b).

[102] Art 3(3) of Reg 1151/2012, n 8 above.

[103] Art 2(2).

be submitted as part of the application for registration. As a result, there have to date been two TSG registers: one for those names the use of which is reserved for certain producers, and one for those TSGs which can be used by other producers as well.[104]

An agricultural product or foodstuff must be produced using traditional raw materials or be characterised by a traditional composition or production method before it is eligible for registration as a traditional speciality guaranteed.[105] A name could be either 'specific in itself', as would be the case for Neapolitan pizza, or it could clearly identify the specific character of the foodstuff—such as a reference to being 'traditionally farmed'.[106] Under the terms of the 2012 Food Quality Regulation, names are now eligible for registration as a traditional speciality guaranteed where they describe a specific product or foodstuff that

> results from a mode of production, processing or composition corresponding to traditional practice for that product or foodstuff; or is produced from raw materials or ingredients that are those traditionally used.[107]

A name cannot be registered if it is merely referring to claims of a general nature used for a set of products.[108] Names already registered under the 1992 and 2006 Regulations can continue to use their TSG status. They are to be automatically entered into the new register, as established by Article 22 of Regulation 1151/2012.[109]

The TSG name cannot be used unless the product carrying it complies with the terms of the 'specification'.[110] The product specification itself should include details of the name by which it is proposed to be registered, a description of the foodstuff and its characteristics, a description of the ingredients and production method, the aspects of the product that give it a distinguishing character and evidence to support the claim that the product is 'traditional'.[111] Individuals cannot apply for the registration of a TSG. This must be done by a 'group',[112] defined in the Regulation as 'any association, irrespective of its legal form, mainly composed of producers or processors working with the same product'.[113] Several groups from different Member States or third countries may submit a joint application.[114] Applications for the registration of a TSG can only be made by those who actually produce the product or foodstuff in question.[115] This removes

---

[104] Art 3.
[105] Art 4(1).
[106] Art 4(2). Now contained in Art 18(2) of Reg 1151/2012, n 8 above.
[107] Art 18.
[108] Art 18(4).
[109] Art 25(1).
[110] Art 19(1).
[111] Art 19(1)(a)–(d).
[112] Art 49(1). As is the case for PDO and PGI applicants, a single natural or legal person may be treated as a 'group' in some circumstances.
[113] Art 3(2).
[114] Art 49(1).
[115] ibid.

the possibility of opportunistic applications being made by those with no existing interest in the traditional product. Applications should include information about the group applying and the details in the product specification.[116]

Applications should be initially lodged with relevant authorities in the Member State where the group is based. They, in turn, scrutinise the application to ensure that registration may be possible under the terms of the Regulation, and to check that the information and supporting documentation meets the requirements set out therein.[117] Applications for TSG registration can, of course, be objected to by others. It is up to the Member States to ensure that a proper national objection procedure is established and facilitated.[118] This should include ensuring that there is adequate publicising of any applications made, along with the provision of reasonable periods within which those with a legitimate interest can lodge their objections. The Member State authorities then forward the application to the Commission for consideration.[119] The Commission is then charged with publicising applications,[120] providing others with a legitimate interest with the opportunity to raise an objection to the registration of a TSG.[121]

Objections must be made within three months of the details of the application being publicised in the Official Journal. They must demonstrate that the name should not be eligible for registration as a TSG, within the terms of the Regulation. If no such objection or demonstration is made, the name is registered. Where a legitimate concern is raised, the Commission tries to facilitate consultations between the parties concerned, in the hope of reaching an acceptable agreement between them.[122]

The Commission makes the final decision on registration where no such agreement can be reached between the parties. Any registered name can have its TSG status cancelled by use of the comitology procedure if the Commission considers that it should not continue to be protected under the terms of the Regulation.[123] The Commission is assisted by the Agricultural Product Quality Policy Committee.[124]

8.2.1 Benefits of Traditional Speciality Guaranteed Status

A name that is successfully registered as a TSG can be used by any operator who markets a product that conforms to the terms of the specification.[125] Those

---

[116] Art 20(1).
[117] Art 49(2).
[118] Art 49(3).
[119] Art 49(4).
[120] Art 50(2).
[121] Art 51(1).
[122] Art 51(3).
[123] Art 54.
[124] Art 57(1). For TSGs it used to be assisted by the Standing Committee on Traditional Specialities Guaranteed.
[125] Art 23(1).

products that meet the standards set out in the specification also benefit from being able to display the TSG symbol on the labelling.[126] This is similar to the symbol used in the marketing of PDOs and PGIs. The whole system for using the TSG has thus been opened up by the introduction of Regulation 1151/2012. Any producer, including those from third countries, is able to use a registered name, provided that their product complies with the requirements of the specification. Their use remains reserved for those who meet the standards set, but the system does now provide a good opportunity for both the producers of 'traditional' products and consumers, who know that the foods they purchase, if carrying the TSG symbol, have been made according to prescribed conditions related to distinctive qualities or characteristics.

Member States are obliged, under the terms of the Regulation, to ensure that legal protection is put in place against any misuse or misleading use of the traditional speciality guaranteed term or symbol on food labelling.[127] They must also take steps to prevent the imitation of registered names by others who are not covered by the product specification, or anything else related to the misuse of registered TSGs that may cause confusion amongst consumers.[128]

8.2.2 Control of Traditional Speciality Guaranteed Use

As is the case for designations of origin and geographical indications, DEFRA is the designated national competent authority for dealing with traditional speciality applications. However, under the terms of the Regulation, responsibility for verifying compliance with registered product specifications can be passed to a product specification body.[129] These bodies, if used, must first be accredited in accordance with the 'General Requirements for Bodies Operating Product Certification Systems'.[130]

It is stipulated in these requirements that inspection bodies must act independently and with impartiality when carrying out their checks. So, for example, when the Gloucestershire Old Spots Pig Breeders' Club sought to have their product registered for its specific character, the private body, the Product Authentication Inspectorate Limited, was appointed as the Authority charged with verifying compliance with the product specification. This same body is also responsible for checking the authenticity of the protected designations of origin Stilton cheese and West Country Farmhouse Cheddar, as well as the protected geographical indication Melton Mowbray pork pies.[131]

---

[126] Art 23(2) and (3).
[127] Art 24(1).
[128] Art 24(2).
[129] Art 37(1).
[130] European standard EN 45011, ISBN: 0580294153.
[131] Art 37 of Reg 1151/2012, n 8 above, also provides that product certification bodies can be used to verify compliance with the product specifications for protected designations of origin and protected geographical indications.

8.2.3 Optional Quality Terms

Finally, Regulation 1151/2012 also establishes a new type of food name, the 'optional quality term'. This is described as being a 'second tier of quality systems, based on quality terms which add value, which can be communicated on the internal market and which are to be applied voluntarily'.[132] They are descriptive terms used for products that are related to farming methods or processing techniques. An optional quality term must relate to a distinguishing characteristic, such as a method of production, it must add value when compared to its non-use for similar products, and it should have a European dimension.[133] This suggests that names previously registered as a TSG, such as 'Traditional Farmfresh Turkey', should now be considered as a quality term rather than a speciality guarantee.

Regulation 1151/2012 specifically identifies two quality terms. The first of these is the 'mountain product'. This term can only be used to describe foods where both the raw materials and any animal feed used come from mountain areas.[134] Any processing should also take place in the mountains.[135] 'Mountain areas' are themselves defined by Article 18 of Regulation 1257/1999.[136] The second quality term recognised by Regulation 1151/2012 is the term 'product of island farming'.[137] Again, the raw materials used in production should come from islands, and use of the term should really be limited to those foods which are substantially affected by being produced in such places. The Commission is charged with introducing more detailed rules in this area.[138] Member States should ensure that these terms are used appropriately.[139]

8.3 Wine and Spirits Protection

The EU Member States combined form the world's largest producer, exporter and consumer of wine. A common market organisation (CMO) for wine, which was reformed in 1999,[140] and again in 2008,[141] is used to support this important part

---

[132] Recital 44 of the Preamble to Reg 1151/2012, n 8 above.

[133] Art 29(1).

[134] Art 31(1)(a).

[135] Art 31(1)(b).

[136] Council Regulation (EC) No 1257/1999 of 17 May 1999 on support for rural development from the European Agricultural Guidance and Guarantee Fund (EAGGF) and amending and repealing certain Regulations [1999] OJ L 160/80.

[137] Art 32.

[138] Art 33.

[139] Art 34.

[140] Council Regulation (EC) No 1493/1999 of 17 May 1999 on the common organisation of the market in wine [1999] OJ L 179/1.

[141] Council Regulation (EC) No 479/2008 of 29 April 2008 on the common organisation of the market in wine, amending Regulation (EC) No 1493/1999, 1782/2003, 1290/2005, 3/2008 and repealing Regulations (EEC) No 2392/1986 and 1493/1999 [2008] OJ L 148/1.

of the agricultural and manufacturing sectors. The idea behind having a CMO for wine is that it can be used to make EU producers more competitive in the global market. To achieve this, simpler, clearer and more effective rules governing the sector should be introduced and applied. This should result in the lifting of existing restrictions on the planting of new vines across all EU Member States by 2015.

8.3.1 Common Organisation of the Market in Wine

As was stated above, a system of registering and protecting the geographical status of wines was originally excluded from the scope of both the 1992 and 2006 food names regulations.[142] This continues to be the case with Regulation 1151/2012.[143] However, a variation on the PDO/PGI registration scheme did exist for wines since 1970, predating UK accession to the Treaty of Rome.[144] It was revised and updated in 1979.[145] Under this system, 'quality wines produced in specified regions' could be protected on the basis of satisfying a range of production factors and product characteristics. Determining whether a wine or a sparkling wine could be considered to be of a certain 'quality' would follow an assessment of the production area, vine varieties used, cultivation methods, wine-making methods, yields and analysis of organoleptic characteristics.[146] Member States could also set additional conditions of production and characteristic requirements.[147] Essentially, assessment of eligibility for protection under the terms of the Regulation was left to the Member States themselves. This resulted in nearly 3,000 wines being listed as a 'quality wine produced in specified region' prior to the establishment of the more structured PDO/PGI registration system for wines in 2008.[148] This includes, amongst others, any wine or sparkling wine with an 'Appellation d'origine contrôlée', 'Appellation contrôlée', 'Champagne' designation or 'Vin délimité de

---

[142] Reg 2081/1992, n 2 above, and Reg 510/2006, n 7 above, respectively.

[143] Art 2(2) of Reg 1151/2012, n 8 above, states that it does not apply to spirits, aromatised wines or grapevine products.

[144] Council Regulation (EEC) No 817/1970 of 28 April 1970 laying down special provisions relating to quality wines produced in specified regions [1970] OJ L 99/20. No English language version of this Regulation exists. Earlier attempts had been made to organise the EEC wine market with the introduction of Regulation 24/1962, Règlement No 24 portant établissement gradual d'une organisation commune du marché viti-vinicole [1962] OJ 989/62. Art 4 of this Regulation presents the first attempt to introduce an EU-wide quality control system for wines.

[145] Council Regulation (EEC) No 338/1979 of 5 February 1979 laying down special provisions relating to quality wines produced in specific regions [1979] OJ L 54/48.

[146] Art 2(1) of Reg 338/1979.

[147] Art 2(2) of Reg 338/1979.

[148] The Preamble to Reg 479/2008, n 141 above recognised that up to that stage, the system identifying quality wines through the use of protected designations of origin and geographical indications was 'not fully developed in this respect'. A new regime was thus required to 'allow for a transparent and more elaborate framework underpinning the claim to quality by the products concerned'. This would, according to Preamble Recital 27, 'be established ... in line with the approach followed under the [Union's] horizontal quality policy applicable to foodstuffs other than wine and spirits in Council Regulation (EC) No 510/2006'.

qualité supérieure' made in France or those awarded a 'Denominazione di origine controllata' in Italy.[149]

A new wine regulation, creating a registration system for wine similar to that which exists for food, was published in 2008.[150] This Regulation defines a 'designation of origin' for wines as

> the name of a region, a specific place or, in exceptional cases, a country used to describe a product that complies with the following requirements: (i) its quality and characteristics are essentially or exclusively due to a particular geographical environment with its inherent natural and human factors; (ii) the grapes from which it is produced come exclusively from this geographical area; and (iii) its production takes place in this geographical area.[151]

A 'geographical indication' differs from this in that only 85 per cent of the grapes used for production must come from the defined geographical area.[152] Generic names cannot be protected.[153] Issues that are considered when assessing whether a name is generic includes an examination of the existing situation in EU Member States, in particular in areas where the food is most commonly consumed. An assessment is also made of whether there are any existing relevant national or EU legal provisions which could offer some guidance on whether the name has traditionally been reserved for foods produced in defined areas. It should also be established as to whether or not these rules have been properly applied and adhered to by national authorities in the past.

Geographical names that are liable to mislead consumers because, for example, they are similar to a well-known existing trade mark, cannot be registered either.[154] Similarly, names can not be registered as trade marks where they are similar to protected geographical names.[155]

The 'technical file' is the key component of the application for the registration of a wine as a designation of origin or geographical indication. It should include details about the name to be protected, the applicant's details and a detailed, as well as summarised, product specification.[156] The 'product specification' lists information related to the name of the wine, a description of the wine—including an evaluation of its organoleptic properties, the production method, the geographical area of production, yields, grape varieties and compliance verification authority details.[157] Applicants are usually the representative of a group of producers of the wine but may, in exceptional cases, be a single producer.[158] Initial

---

[149] Art 16 of Reg 338/1979.
[150] Reg 479/2008, n 141 above.
[151] Art 34(1)(a).
[152] Art 34(1)(b).
[153] Art 43(1).
[154] Art 43(2).
[155] Art 44(1).
[156] Art 35(1).
[157] Art 35(2).
[158] Art 37.

applications are made to the designated national authorities.[159] DEFRA, which is the designated competent authority for the UK, then examines the application to assess whether it is in compliance with the terms of the Regulation. If it is, the application is published, providing those with a legitimate interest with the opportunity to object to registration.[160] If no justifiable objections are received, the application is forwarded to the Commission for their scrutiny.[161] Further objections can be received by the Commission,[162] following publication of the details of the application in the Official Journal of the European Union.[163] A decision on registration, using the comitology procedure, is then made.[164] Registered product specifications can be amended at a later date.[165] Protected status can be cancelled by the Commission where necessary.[166]

Once registered, the protected designation of origin or protected geographical indication can be used by any operator who complies with the terms of the product specification.[167] Registered wines are protected against direct or indirect commercial use of the name by comparable products that are not in compliance with the specification where this exploits the reputation of the PDO or PGI.[168] They are also protected against any misuse, imitation or evocation, even where the true origin of the product is indicated.[169] Finally, the usual protections against 'any other false or misleading indication' apply, as does that which prevents the registered name from becoming 'generic'.[170] Member States are obliged to prevent the unlawful use of protected wine names.[171] While Member States are responsible for designating their competent authorities for controlling the PDO/PGI system for wines,[172] verifying compliance with the terms of a registered name can also be designated to a private 'control body'.[173] The costs of verification are borne by the producers.[174]

---

[159] Art 38(2).

[160] Art 38(3).

[161] Art 38(5).

[162] Art 40.

[163] Art 39(3).

[164] Art 41 in conjunction with Art 113(2). A public electronic register of all protected designations of origin and geographical indications for wine is maintained by the Commission (Art 46).

[165] Art 49.

[166] Art 50.

[167] Art 45(1).

[168] Art 45(2)(a).

[169] Art 45(2)(b). For discussion on what is meant by 'evocation' see also C MacMaoláin, 'Reforming European Community Food Law: Putting quality back on the agenda' (2003) 58 *Food and Drug Law Journal* 549.

[170] Arts 45(2)(c) and 45(3).

[171] Art 45(4).

[172] Art 47.

[173] Art 48. 'Control bodies' that can operate as product certifiers are defined in Art 2 of Reg 882/2004 as 'an independent third party to which the competent authority has delegated certain control tasks', [2004] OJ L 165/1.

[174] Further details on how the whole process works are set out in Commission Regulation (EC) No 607/2009 of 14 July 2009 laying down certain detailed rules for the implementation of Council Regulation (EC) No 479/2008 as regards protected designations of origin and geographical indications, traditional terms, labelling and presentation of certain wine sector products [2009] OJ L 193/60.

Wine Regulations 2011

The Wine Regulations 2011 set out all of the domestic components of the relevant EU regulations, including those related to protected designations of origin and geographical indications. They recognise the effect of Regulation 479/2008 in English law.[175] Schedule 1 to the Regulations sets out the names, geographical areas and applicable requirements for protected geographical indications. It sets two areas for which geographical indications for wine can be used— 'English Regional' for England and 'Welsh Regional' for Wales. Eligibility for using these PGIs is subject to compliance with a set of minimum standards set out in the Schedule. For example, the alcohol content must be at least 8.5 per cent. Maximum levels are also set for acidity and the presence of sulphur dioxide, copper and iron. The wine must be sterile, with no indication of yeasts or bacteria likely to cause spoilage. The wine must be capable of retaining its properties when chilled. Different standards are set for English and Welsh Regional sparkling wines. For both sparkling and non-sparkling, however, permitted production quantities are in proportion to vineyard size—the wines must come from a batch for which the maximum yield for each hectare of land cultivated with vines for producing the wine was 100 hectolitres. The carbon dioxide present in the sparkling wine must come exclusively from fermentation. Actual alcohol content must be at least 9.5 per cent.

Schedule 2 to the Regulations sets similar, if higher-level, requirements for protected designations of origin. Wine can be either 'English' or 'Welsh' if produced according to the terms of the EU Regulations and if meeting the minimum or maximum standards included in the domestic 2011 Regulations. For non-sparkling 'English' or 'Welsh' wine the maximum yield for each hectare is 80 hectolitres. This level remains at 100 hectolitres per hectare for the PDOs 'English' and 'Welsh' sparkling wines. Also, for English non-sparkling wine, the vines must be grown at or below 220 metres above sea level. No similar requirement exists for sparkling varieties. Finally, minimum alcohol content levels are also set for both wine types, as are maximum permitted amounts of acidity, sulphur dioxide, copper and iron. Both wines must be capable of retaining their characteristics when chilled.

The system for registering wines according to their regional qualities or production characteristics has, historically, been very different from that which exists for foodstuffs. There are nearly three times as many wines registered for protected status in the EU as there are registered foods. The use of PDOs and PGIs for wines is not nearly as reliable as it has become for foodstuffs. This is primarily because 'traditional terms' used to classify wines in Member States entitle the user to claim that the product is a PDO or a PGI, despite the fact that the product

---

[175] Regs 2 and 6. Reg 479/2008 is, of course, directly applicable in English law. The domestic Wine Regulations 2011 deal with those aspects of the EU regulations that can only be dealt with domestically, such as the designation of competent authorities and national procedural matters, SI No 2936/2011.

has not undergone the same rigorous assessment of quality as that prescribed for food under the terms of Regulation 510/2006. There has been no meaningful Commission involvement in the process and there have been fewer opportunities for objections to the registration to be raised. There is also confusion over the fact that 'traditional terms' can not become generic,[176] even though they are general in nature, for example the 'Appellation d'origine contrôlée', and have been used to describe thousands of products. There is the possibility that the comitology procedure can be used to restructure this system for wines so that only those producers who make applications to the Commission through their own State authorities will be eligible for protection in the future. This would greatly assist English wine producers. It would probably mean that fewer producers in other EU Member States would be able to make legally verifiable claims about the quality of their product, leaving English producers of quality sparkling and non-sparkling wines facing less competition in this field.

8.3.2 Spirits Protection

Permitted definitions, descriptions, presentation formats and labelling content for spirit drinks are also set by EU regulations.[177] 'Spirit drinks' are defined as alcoholic beverages

> intended for human consumption; possessing particular organoleptic qualities; having a minimum alcoholic content strength of 15% vol.; having been produced either directly by [distillation, maceration or similar processing] or by the mixture of a spirit drink with one or more other spirit drinks and/or ethyl alcohol of agricultural origin or distillates of agricultural origin, and/or other alcoholic beverages, and/or drinks.[178]

Spirit drinks are further categorised in Annex II to the Regulations. This provides more detailed definitions for drinks such as rum, whisky, brandy, vodka and gin. Most are required to have a minimum alcohol content of 37.5 per cent. 'London gin' is defined as being

> obtained exclusively from ethyl alcohol of agricultural origin ... whose flavour is intro-duced exclusively through the re-distillation in traditional stills of ethyl alcohol in the presence of all the natural plant materials used ... which does not contain added sweet-ening exceeding 0.1 gram of sugars per litre of the final product nor colorants, which does not contain any other added ingredients other than water. The minimum alcoholic strength by volume of London gin shall be 37.5%. The term London gin may be supple-mented by the term 'dry'.

---

[176] Art 55(2) of Reg 479/2008, n 141 above.
[177] Regulation (EC) No 110/2008 of the European Parliament and of the Council of 15 January 2008 on the definition, description, presentation, labelling and protection of geographical indications of spirit drinks and repealing Council Regulation (EEC) No 1576/1989 [2008] OJ L 39/16.
[178] Art 2(1).

The sales names of spirit drinks can, subject to satisfaction of set conditions, be protected as geographical indications. EU regulations define geographical indications for spirits as

> an indication which identifies a spirit drink as originating in the territory of a country, or a region or locality in that territory, where a given quality, reputation or other characteristic of that spirit drink is essentially attributable to its geographical origin.[179]

Spirits registered with a geographical indication are listed in Annex III to the Regulations. These include Cognac (France), Grappa (Italy), Kirsch d'Alsace (France), Swedish Vodka, Poitín (Ireland), Scotch Whisky, and Plymouth Gin. 'London gin' is a notable absentee from this list. Its inclusion in the Annex II definitions categorises it as a generic name. Under the terms of the Regulation, generic names, or those which have come into common usage, cannot be registered as geographical indications.[180]

Applications for the registration of spirit drinks are made by the Member State of origin to the Commission.[181] Again, the technical file forms the key component of any application. This should include details about the type of spirit drink for which registration is sought, the geographical indication and area of production, a description of the drink and its defining characteristics, production methods, relevant national laws and applicant details.[182] The Commission then has 12 months to consider the application.[183] If it considers that the name is eligible for protection, it publishes the technical file in the Official Journal of the European Union, allowing six months for possible objections to registration to be raised by others.[184] Finally, if the Commission decides to proceed with the registration of the geographical indication, it should use the comitology regulatory procedure with scrutiny in making this decision. This decision is also to be publicised through its announcement in the Official Journal.[185] It is then up to the Member States and their designated authorities to ensure that the specifications set out in the technical file are complied with.[186]

Once registered, geographical indications for spirit drinks are protected against any direct or indirect commercial use by those not covered by the registration; any misuse, imitation or evocation, even where the real origin of the product is indicated; any other false or misleading indication; or any other practice liable to mislead the consumer as to the true origin of the product.[187]

---

[179] Art 15(1).
[180] Art 15(3).
[181] Art 17(1) and (2).
[182] Art 17(4).
[183] Art 17(5).
[184] Art 17(6) and (7).
[185] Art 17(8).
[186] Art 22(1) in conjunction with Art 24(1). The technical file can be altered, using the same procedure as that used for the initial application for registration (Art 21 of Reg 110/2008, n 177 above).
[187] Art 16.

Other products that have been registered as trade marks that contain or consist of a registered geographical indication must be invalidated, or refused for registration in the first place, if their use is likely to impinge upon the protection accorded to the PGI under the terms of the Regulation.[188] Some limited exceptional circumstances that may facilitate continued use of the trade mark are set out in the Regulation.[189] Registered geographical indications for spirits can, of course, be cancelled by the Commission where it is of the opinion that the specifications set out in the technical file can no longer be ensured.[190] Again, any decision made in this regard must follow use of the correct comitology procedure, involving the Committee for Spirit Drinks.[191] The same procedure is also to be used for any amendments to the Annexes to the Regulation, such as those involving an alteration to the legal definitions of the spirit drink categories or the listing or de-listing of geographical indications.[192]

---

[188] Art 23(1).

[189] Art 23(2). These limited exceptions include those circumstances where the trade mark was registered in good faith in an EU Member State prior to either the date of protection of the geographical indication in the country of origin or before 1 January 1996.

[190] Art 18.

[191] As established by Art 25 of Reg 110/2008, n 177 above.

[192] Art 26.

9

Nutrition, Obesity and Health

9.1 Introduction

It has been illustrated in earlier chapters in this book that there has been a significant legislative and political emphasis on food safety matters since the BSE crisis of the 1990s, leading to the neglect of other concerns, in particular those related to the nutritional value and quality of food. While new directly applicable regulations have been introduced on quality[1] and on food labelling,[2] it is here argued that these will contribute little, certainly in the short to medium term, to dealing with the biggest of all food concerns—poor nutrition. Studies referred to previously have highlighted the figures which illustrate this point.[3] Over 80 times as many people are estimated to die from coronary heart disease resulting from poor diet in England alone as die from food poisoning across the UK, on an annual basis. At national level, government policy can be directed towards trying to improve the health of the nation. However, legally, there is little that can be done at national level to change this. As is discussed throughout this chapter, and as has already been alluded to in this book, EU rules on the free movement of food prevent Member State governments from introducing legally binding national measures that have been identified as offering one of the best ways of reducing obesity and rates of overweightness in society. As is also discussed here, harmonising EU food labelling requirements have not adequately addressed this—despite clear recognition at institutional level that there is a problem, and that labelling can be used to help to resolve it.

[1] Regulation (EU) No 1151/2012 of the European Parliament and of the Council of 21 November 2012 on quality schemes for agricultural products and foodstuffs [2012] OJ L 343/1.

[2] Regulation (EU) No 1169/2011 of the European Parliament and of the Council of 25 October 2011 on the provision of food information to consumers, amending Regulations (EC) No 1924/2006 and (EC) No 1925/2006 of the European Parliament and of the Council, and repealing Commission Directive 1987/250/EEC, Council Directive 1990/496/EEC, Commission Directive 1999/10/EC, Directive 2000/13/EC of the European Parliament and of the Council, Commission Directives 2002/67/EC and 2008/5/EC and Commission Regulation (EC) No 608/2004 [2011] OJ L 304/18.

[3] As noted in ch 5, the National Institute for Health and Clinical Excellence (NICE) estimates that there are 40,000 deaths per year in England related to the consumption of low-quality foods. See 'Prevention of cardiovascular disease', NICE public health guidance, 25 June 2012; available at: www.nice.org. The Food Standards Agency estimates that there are around 590 deaths per year in the UK from food poisoning. See www.food.gov.uk. See also S Mayor, 'Regulation has not reduced food poisoning in Britain' (1997) 315 *British Medical Journal* 1111.

The EU Commission has produced a White Paper outlining a strategy on nutrition and obesity.[4] Understanding the stance that the EU may adopt on these matters is crucial to determining just what can be done at national level. Where legislative intervention is concerned, it is only where the EU acts that similar rules or regulations can be introduced into English law. It is recognised that colour coding, or at least clearer, more user-friendly, nutrient declarations may be one of the best ways of ensuring that consumers are informed about the composition and potential detrimental effects of the food they consume.[5] However, as is also noted, it is only where there is specific standardisation at EU level that any rules on the use of these 'traffic-light' or other systems can be enforced domestically. To date, EU law does not provide for the use by Member States of binding labelling templates that have been shown to improve consumer understanding and decision making. This is a significant shortcoming in the law. Member States cannot act to take the appropriate measures unless EU law permits this. EU legislators have not acted to either introduce, or facilitate, these alternative labelling systems, which could go some way to addressing concerns about the relationship between diet and health, when considered as part of a package of measures that need to be employed.[6]

9.2 Nutrition Labelling Requirements

No significant legal changes were made to nutrition labelling requirements between the introduction of the first directive on this matter in 1990[7] and the enactment of a new regulation in 2011.[8] Originally, all nutrition labelling was optional,[9] except for those products where a nutrition claim appeared on the label.[10] Most of the time that nutrition labelling was used, there was only an obligation to provide information on the energy value, protein level, carbohydrate and fat.[11] A different set of particulars, known as 'group two particulars', would

---

[4] Commission White Paper on a strategy for Europe on nutrition, overweight and obesity related health issues, COM (2007) 279. This is discussed in more detail below. However, for much more detailed analysis of this see chapter 2 of A Garde, *EU Law and Obesity Prevention* (Alphen aan den Rijn, Kluwer Law International, 2010).

[5] By, eg, I Borgmeier and J Westenhoefer, 'Impact of different food label formats on healthiness evaluation and food choice of consumers: a randomised-controlled study' (2009) 9 *BMC Public Health* 184.

[6] Art 35 of Reg 1169/2011, n 2 above, does allow for the use of additional labelling types if certain conditions are met. However, their use can not be made compulsory by Member States and therefore they remain subject to the same problems as already exist for the enforcement of such schemes, as identified later in this chapter.

[7] Council Directive 1990/496/EEC of 24 September 1990 on nutrition labelling for foodstuffs [1990] OJ L 276/40. Transposed into English law by the Food Labelling Regulations, most recently those of 1996, SI No 1499/1996.

[8] Reg 1169/2011 on the provision of food information to consumers, n 2 above.

[9] Art 2(1) of Dir 1990/496, n 7 above.

[10] ibid, Art 2(2).

[11] Art 4(1).

only have to appear if a nutrition claim was made specifically about the sugar, saturated fat, fibre or sodium level in a foodstuff. In this case additional information on all of these nutrients would also have to be provided.[12] The 2011 Food Information Regulation changed all of this.

The Preamble to the Food Information Regulation noted that the nutrition labelling legislation was in need of updating.[13] It also stated that the Commission White Paper on a Strategy for Europe on Nutrition, Overweight and Obesity related health issues had highlighted that nutrition labelling was an important method of informing consumers about the composition of foods and of helping them to make informed choices.[14] A Commission Communication, entitled 'EU Consumer Policy strategy 2007–2013—Empowering consumers, enhancing their welfare, effectively protecting them' had underlined how facilitating informed choice was essential to creating effective competition in the market and protecting consumer welfare.[15] Crucially, there was recognition that

> [k]nowledge of the basic principles of nutrition and appropriate nutrition information on foods would contribute significantly towards enabling the consumer to make ... an informed choice.[16]

The ultimate result was the repeal of the Nutrition Labelling Directive and the creation of a new set of provisions, setting revised requirements for the presentation of this information, and increasing its ubiquity and prominence on virtually all prepackaged foods, including, for the first time, those which are not subject to any nutrition or health claim.

As outlined in chapter seven, the Food Information Regulation provides that the inclusion of details on the nutritional characteristics of products should be mandatory on all labelling in order to enable consumers to make informed choices from 2016 onwards.[17] Section 3 of the Regulation presents us with the detail on what this compulsory requirement entails. It states that the mandatory nutrition declaration should include details on the energy value (usually calories), the fat content and quantity of this which is in saturated form, carbohydrate level, as well as that for sugars, protein and salt.[18] This minimum level of mandatory detail can also be supplemented with information on monounsaturated fats, polyunsaturated fats, polyols, starch, fibre and vitamins and minerals which are present in significant amounts.[19]

---

[12] ibid.

[13] Recital 7 of the Preamble to Reg 1169/2011, n 2 above.

[14] ibid, recital 10.

[15] Communication from the Commission to the Council, the European Parliament and the European Economic and Social Committee; EU Consumer Policy strategy 2007–2013; Empowering consumers, enhancing their welfare, effectively protecting them, COM (2007) 99.

[16] Recital 10 of the Preamble to Reg 1169/2011, n 2 above.

[17] Art 4(1)(c) of Reg 1169/2011, n 2 above. Specific provision is then made for this inclusion by Art 9(1)(l) of the Regulation.

[18] Art 30(1) of Reg 1169/2011, n 2 above.

[19] The quantity which constitutes a 'significant amount' is set out in Part A of Annex XIII to the Regulation. This usually means that there must be at least 15% of the daily reference intake (based on set nutrient reference values) supplied by 100 g or 100 ml of a food or 7.5% per 100 ml of a drink.

9.2.1 Use of Portion Sizes

The Food Information Regulation states that nutrient values should be expressed per 100 g or 100 ml as required,[20] or as a percentage of the recommended intake for vitamins and minerals,[21] but also that

> the energy value and the amounts of nutrients [present] may be expressed per portion and/or per consumption unit, easily recognisable by the consumer, provided that the portion or the unit used is quantified on the label and that the number of portions or units contained in the package is stated.[22]

The use of nutrition labelling on a per portion basis can only be done if it is in addition to the expression per 100 g or per 100 ml. The use of portion sizes as a basis for the presentation of information on nutrient values is often problematic, made more difficult by the fact that the Regulation does not go as far as the Food Standards Agency Guidelines on the use of signpost labelling in this regard. Most specifically, the Regulation makes no reference to the fact that self-determined 'portion' sizes must at least be reasonable. It only states that that where the portion size is used as a method for expressing this important information, the total number of portions contained in the package must also be provided on the label. This does little to protect the consumer who seeks out the non-high-fat food. It also facilitates deception. It allows the portrayal of a product as having a much lower fat content than it does. By reducing the portion size on which the information is based to half the quantity that we could reasonably expect to be consumed, the fat, salt, sugar and calorie levels are also halved, to a level that is based on an unrealistic and dishonest assessment of what the reasonable consumer actually consumes. There is, however, the potential for the Food Information Regulation to make a significant change in this area if Article 33(5) thereof is properly applied. It provides that

> [i]n order to ensure the uniform implementation of the expression of the nutrition declaration per portion or per unit of consumption and to provide for a uniform basis of comparison for the consumer, the Commission shall, taking into account actual consumption behaviour of consumers as well as dietary recommendations, adopt, by means of implementing acts, rules on the expression per portion or per consumption unit for specific categories of foods.

The revised comitology examination procedure is to be used to introduce any measure designed to set these uniform portion sizes.[23] Doubts remain, however,

---

[20] Art 32(1) and (2).
[21] Art 32(3) and (4).
[22] Art 33(1).
[23] Art 33(5) in conjunction with Art 48(2) of Reg 1169/2011, n 2 above. The revised comitology examination procedure is set out in Art 5 of Regulation (EU) No 182/2011 of the European parliament and of the Council of 16 February 2011 laying down the rules and general principles concerning mechanisms for control by Member States of the Commission's exercise of implementing powers [2011] OJ L 55/13. The entire revised comitology procedure is discussed in more detail in ch 2.

about the ability of the use of this provision to satisfy concerns about the exploitation by producers of the 'per portion' allowance. First, the Commission's general acceptance that it cannot introduce specific legislative requirements for each individual food type, as exemplified by its decision to cease introducing recipe laws relatively early in the development of EU food law, suggests that it would be equally reluctant, and/or unable, to provide similar provision here. Second, Article 33(5) of the Food Information Regulation explicitly states that dietary recommendations will be taken into account in determining portion sizes. This essentially means that the higher the quantity of fats, sugars and salt contained in the foodstuff, the lower the 'recommended' portion size may be. This could then continue to facilitate the setting of the unrealistic 'two squares' of chocolate or 'one-sixth of a bag of crisps' portion. While this could assist in creating consistency across portion sizes, it would not tally with the consumption behaviour of the average peckish consumer.

9.2.2 Mandatory Nutrition Declarations

The mandatory nutrition declaration, to be applicable from 2016 onwards,[24] must be presented 'in the principal field of vision',[25] and in a set minimum font size.[26] Negligible amounts of a nutrient need not be listed, other than as being 'negligible amounts'.[27]

The first key change made to the presentation of nutrition declarations on foodstuffs is, of course, this alteration from optional requirement to compulsory one in most circumstances, and insistence that the information is laid out in a set format or formats in a prominent position on the label. Many, if not most, producers were already providing this information, whether they were obliged to or not.[28] So, it is arguable, this will make little difference to the use of labelling as a mechanism for informing consumers in a way that facilitates informed decision making in a manner that improves diet. The Food Information Regulation does, however, also recognise the potential value of using additional forms of presentation of the same information in a manner that improves the imparting of this to,

---

[24] Art 55 of Reg 1169/2011, n 2 above.

[25] ibid, Art 34(3)(a).

[26] Art 34(3)(b) thereof. Minimum font sizes are set out in Art 13(2) of the Regulation, which stipulates that 'the mandatory particulars ... shall be printed on the package or on the label in such a way as to ensure clear legibility, in characters using a font size where the x-height ... is equal to or greater than 1.2 mm'. It was originally proposed that this minimum should be set at 3 mm, but this was later deemed excessive following extensive lobbying and appeals.

[27] Art 34(5).

[28] See S Bonsmann et al, 'Penetration of nutrition information on food labels across the EU-27 plus Turkey' (2010) 64 *Journal of Clinical Nutrition* 1379, which finds that, on average, 85% of products presented nutrition labelling or related information, rising to as high as 97% in Member States such as Ireland.

and the understanding of it amongst, consumers. Article 35(1) of the Regulation provides:

> In addition to the forms of expression [and presentation] referred to in [this legislation, information on] the energy value and the amount of nutrients ... may be given by other forms of expression and/or presented using graphical forms or symbols in addition to words or numbers provided that the following requirements are met: (a) they are based on sound and scientifically valid consumer research and do not mislead the consumer ...; (b) their development is the result of consultation with a wide range of stakeholder groups; (c) they aim to facilitate consumer understanding of the contribution or importance of the food to the energy and nutrient content of a diet; (d) they are supported by scientifically valid evidence of understanding of such forms of expression or presentation by the average consumer; (e) ... they are based either on the harmonised reference intakes [or] on generally accepted scientific advice on intakes for energy or nutrients; (f) they are objective and non-discriminatory; and (g) their application does not create obstacles to the free movement of goods.

In other words, signpost or 'traffic-light' labelling may be used, but only alongside the tabular form prescribed by the Food Information Regulation and provided that it can be shown that the method chosen for presenting in this additional way is both genuine and readily understood by consumers.

Member States can recommend the use of a form of presentation for this additional nutrition labelling but, as is clear from the wording of the Regulation, they remain unable to prescribe a set format or template for this.[29] This fact is further highlighted by the inclusion of the requirement that no such scheme can 'create obstacles to the free movement of goods' which, of course, a compulsory labelling format would do. They must also provide the EU Commission with the details on any such scheme which is introduced—primarily to ensure that it does not breach any of these, or other, free movement of goods rules.[30] A new labelling scheme announced by the Government in late 2012 cannot therefore be any less voluntary than its predecessor, introduced by the Food Standards Agency in 2006. The new template can be recommended to the food sector, but it need not necessarily be followed. The Government is also obliged, under the terms of the Food Information Regulation, to monitor the use of any additional labelling scheme introduced.[31] It may, however, also require that food business operators from other EU Member States notify the national authorities of any signpost or similar labelling that they wish to use. An assessment can then be made as to whether the requirements set out in the Regulation on the use of such schemes have been met.

---

[29] Art 35(2).
[30] Such as that set out in Art 34 TFEU, as discussed in detail in ch 4.
[31] Art 35(3).

The EU Commission provides a focal point for the collection and exchange of information on the use of these alternative labelling systems. Article 35(4) provides that it

> shall facilitate and organise the exchange of information between member States, itself and stakeholders on matters relating to the use of any additional forms of expression or presentation of the nutrition declaration.

While it has been made clear here, and throughout this book, that the implementation of labelling, or similar, schemes such as these are outside the control of the individual Member State authorities, the Food Information Regulation does at least provide the possibility for the setting of a harmonised form of alternative presentation in the future. Article 35(5) provides that

> [b]y 13 December 2017, in light of the experience gained, the Commission shall submit a report to the European Parliament and the Council on the use of additional forms of expression and presentation, on their effect on the internal market and on the advisability of further harmonisation of those forms of expression and presentation. For this purpose, Member States shall provide the Commission with relevant information concerning the use of such additional forms of expression or presentation on the market in their territory. The Commission may accompany this report with proposals to modify the relevant Union provisions.

This means that there is an undertaking to evaluate (i) the success of alternative labelling mechanisms; and (ii) the ubiquitousness of such schemes across the EU and, on the basis of this evaluation, to consider the introduction of a harmonised EU standard for signpost or traffic-light labels. This could, potentially, become the standard way in which nutritional information is presented, perhaps even supplanting the traditional tabular form. Only then could the Food Standards Agency prescribe that a set template is used for all alternative labelling on all foodstuffs to which this would apply.

9.3 EU Nutrition Policy and Obesity

In December 2010 DG SANCO produced the implementation progress report on the 'Strategy for Europe on nutrition, overweight and obesity related health issues'.[32] The data presented highlighted the prevalence of weight-related health issues across the EU. In seven countries that carried out measurements on adults, between 53.5 and 68.5 per cent of men, and 47.2 and 61.8 per cent of women were deemed to be overweight. Those who were 'obese' ranged from 14.2 to 26 per cent of men and from 13.3 to 30 per cent of women. The figures for men for each of the Member States for which there was comparable data, bar one—Finland, showed that those affected by the epidemic continued to rise. The graphs presented also indicated that there was a rise in the rate of overweight adult males in the UK

---

[32] Note 4 above.

during the period under review (2004–2008). Similar figures were reported for women, although increases and existing weight rates tended to be at a lower level than for men. The Health Behaviour in School-aged Children (HBSC) survey conducted in 2005–2006 indicated that up to 30 per cent of boys and 25 per cent of girls were overweight on the basis of a body mass index (BMI) assessment. The World Health Organization (WHO) European Childhood Obesity Surveillance Initiative (COSI), the first round of which took place in 2007–2008, found that, on average, 24 per cent of children aged between six and nine years were overweight or obese.

The data available all suggests that there are serious and ongoing concerns about weight and obesity issues across the EU. Yet little was done at EU level in the years that followed the publication of the White Paper on Obesity. The same position was maintained in the implementation progress report of late 2011 as had been put forward in the White Paper of 2007, and the Green Paper two years before that. Despite rising obesity rates, and the serious consequences for human health that this entailed, existing, and widely criticised, nutrition labelling and nutrition and health claims requirements would, it was claimed, be sufficient to deal with the detrimental contribution that food was making to the spread of this epidemic. As already noted, the revamped Regulation on the Provision of Food Information to Consumers does now, however, at least pave the way for more meaningful legislative intervention at a later stage. This itself is, however, not certain and subject to a range of factors developing in the years following the introduction of this Regulation.

The White Paper on nutrition and obesity sets out a starting point for any integrated EU approach to assist in reducing incidence of ill health arising out of poor diet. The Paper noted that levels of overweight and obese children and adults have risen dramatically in recent decades. It was also noted that there were repeated calls from the Council for the Commission to develop action plans in the fields of both nutrition and physical activity levels to deal with this.[33] The publication of a previous Green Paper on promoting healthy diets had already led to the finding that there was a broad consensus on the need for the Union to contribute in a meaningful way to tackling this epidemic by engaging with relevant stakeholders at national, regional and local levels.[34] Respondents to the content of the Green Paper highlighted the need for a meaningful and coherent EU-wide approach to tackling obesity.

Provisions of the EU Treaties on health policy have consistently envisaged that measures designed to promote physical wellbeing should be complementary to national policies in this area. Article 168 TFEU now provides that

[a] high level of human health protection shall be ensured in the definition and implementation of all Union policies and activities. Union action, which shall complement national policies, shall be directed towards improving public health, preventing physical

---

[33] Council Conclusions of 2 December 2002 on Obesity [2002] OJ C 11/3.
[34] Commission Green Paper on promoting healthy diets and physical activity: a dimension for the prevention of overweight, obesity and chronic diseases, COM (2005) 637.

and mental illness and diseases, and obviating sources of danger to physical and mental health. Such action shall cover the fight against the major health scourges, by promoting research into their causes, their transmission and their prevention, as well as health information and education, and monitoring, early warning of and combating serious cross-border threats to health.

While the latter part of Article 168(1) TFEU makes reference more specifically to contamination and disease, efforts made by both the Union and by Member States are clearly covered by those references in the remainder of the provision to physical health. As will be discussed in more detail later in this chapter, and as has already been alluded to in chapter four, a significant obstacle exists within EU law itself which prevents the co-operative and complementary nature of action referred to in tackling health-related issues from being realised. This is, of course, the existence of Article 34 TFEU, prohibiting Member States such as the UK from adopting or applying any national measures that inhibit trade and which cannot be justified. Member States can take action designed to protect human health; Article 168 TFEU even supports this, but they may only do so within the parameters set elsewhere in the Treaty, namely where the action taken does limit, in any way, the sale or marketing of food from other States, even where these may have a detrimental effect on health. This essentially means that it is only the EU institutions which are in a position to introduce enforceable legislation designed to combat obesity and nutrition-related illness. It cannot actually be a complementary process of the type envisaged in Article 168 TFEU.

The White Paper identified four strands to the Union-wide approach to tackling obesity. The first was that actions should aim to address the root causes of health-related risks, extending to those associated with both poor diet and limited physical activity. The over-consumption of food, or the excessive consumption of the wrong food, is, of course, only one of the factors that can lead to obesity. Second, the actions identified in the White Paper should apply horizontally across government policy areas and at different levels of government, local and national, using a range of instruments including legislation, networking, public-private approaches and to engage the private sector and civil society. Third, action will need to be taken by private actors, such as the food industry, and civil society, including local actors such as schools and community organisations.

Finally, there would have to be close monitoring of the impact that measures adopted and approaches taken were having on diet and physical activity levels, with a view to assessing that which would need to be refined in any way or even changed fundamentally. There would have to be broad stakeholder involvement, ranging from industry and researchers to civil society, community groups and the media, to make any proposals ultimately effective. This, it was hoped, would lead to better informed consumers who would be capable of making the right choices if given 'access to clear, consistent and evidence-based information when deciding which foods to buy' following exposure to 'the wider information environment [as] shaped by cultural factors, such as advertising and other media'.

Following on from this, the White Paper identified three ways in which already existing EU-developed laws could be used to help tackle nutrition-related illness and disease. The first was through the development of the nutrition labelling requirements. This, it was noted, could be used to support consumers in their efforts to make decisions that would benefit their health. At the time of the White Paper, it was suggested that this could possibly lead to mandatory nutrition labelling for all foods. As noted, the new Regulation on the Provision of Food Information to Consumers has now introduced provision for this.[35] From 2016 this information must appear, and it must be 'front of pack', that is in a clear position on the front of the food packaging. While 'signpost' nutrition labelling has not been made compulsory, there is scope in the Regulation for this to be made the subject of EU-wide legislation at a later stage.[36] The merits or otherwise of compelling producers and/or retailers to use this system on their labels is discussed in more detail below.

The second way in which existing laws could assist in combating obesity was envisaged as being through exerting proper controls over the use of nutrition and health claims. As discussed above, these types of statement only became the subject of specific Union regulation in 2006.[37] This was seen in the White Paper as presenting the opportunity of ensuring that claims made on foods about their nutritional values and/or health-promoting properties would be based on reliable scientific evidence only, ensuring that consumers would not be misled by inaccurate or confusing claims.

Finally, it was stated in the White Paper that some form of tailored regulation of the advertising and marketing of food would have to be introduced to control the ways in which these could be used to influence consumers into acting in a manner that may be detrimental to their health. It was stated that there was strong evidence that advertising aimed at children could be particularly influential in this regard. As a result, the Commission had initiated an Advertising Round Table to explore whether self-regulatory approaches could be used to develop best practice models for industry.

This resulted in the production of a report, setting out this model and determining whether it could present an effective method for controlling advertising aimed at children.[38] The Report found that there was a broad consensus that self-regulation in the advertising sector would only be able to work properly if there was a clear legislative framework which facilitated this. Self-regulation within the

---

[35] Art 9(1)(l) of Regulation (EU) No 1169/2011 of the European Parliament and of the Council of 25 October 2011 on the provision of food information to consumers [2011] OJ L 304/18. For further discussion see ch 7.

[36] Art 35(5) of Reg 1169/2011, n 2 above. This review is to take place by December 2017. For further discussion see ch 7.

[37] Regulation (EC) No 1924/2006 of the European Parliament and of the Council of 20 December 2006 on nutrition and health claims made on foods [2007] OJ L 12/3 .

[38] DG SANCO Report on Self-Regulation in the EU Advertising Sector, July 2006, available at: ec.europa.eu/dgs/health_consumer/self_regulation/docs/report_advertising_en.pdf.

sector would be delivered, primarily, through the adoption and application of codes rather than legally binding rules. However, it was noted that in order for this mechanism to be effective, there would have to be meaningful contribution from stakeholders to the development of these codes, including consumer groups, parent associations and academics. As will be discussed below, the relevant code in the UK in this regard is that which was produced by the British Committee of Advertising Practice in 2010. The European Commission made it clear in the White Paper on Obesity that it was to keep the existing voluntary approach. This was due to the fact that this method possessed the potential 'to act quickly and effectively to tackle rising overweight and obesity rates', subject to a reassessment of this position in 2010. This ultimately resulted in the publication of a progress report on the White Paper strategy in December of that year.

The 2010 DG SANCO implementation progress report also referred to the fact that the EU has introduced the Audiovisual Media Services Directive, which obliges the Member States and the Commission to encourage media service providers to establish codes of conduct on commercials aimed at children that are advertising unhealthy foods.[39] The Directive encourages self-regulation of the advertising sector in a manner that contributes to the promotion of healthy lifestyles among children. There is a reporting system established in the Directive which facilitates the monitoring of the application of these aims within the Member States.[40]

The White Paper itself also recognised that responses to nutrition-related ill health could not be limited to legislative or self-regulatory measures alone. It stated that the Commission, in conjunction with the Member States and relevant stakeholders, would undertake to develop and support scientific information and education campaigns to raise awareness of the health problems that are now associated with poor diet.

It also undertook to promote the consumption of healthier food options through its own campaigns and within the framework established by the Common Agricultural Policy. It proposed allowing surplus fruit and vegetable production to be distributed to children through schools and increasing financial support provided by the Commission for healthy eating projects aimed at young consumers. It was also noted that the Commission would initiate a study to examine the potential for more food reformulation, designed to reduce the levels of

---

[39] Art 9(2) of Directive 2010/13/EU of the European Parliament and of the Council of 10 March 2010 on the coordination of certain provisions laid down by law, regulation or administrative action in Member States concerning the provision of audiovisual media services [2010] OJ L 95/1. For an assessment of the EU's role in using the Directive to prevent children from being targeted by the alcohol and food industries see O Bartlett and A Garde, 'Time to seize the (red) bull by the horns: the European Union's failure to protect children from alcohol and unhealthy food marketing' (2013) 38 *European Law Review* 498 and chapter 5 of A Garde, *EU Law and Obesity Prevention*, n 4 above.

[40] The 2013 report recognised the 'efforts made by the advertising industry and members of the EU pledge to respond to the [Directive's] call for codes of conduct for commercial communications, accompanying or included in children's programmes, of foods and beverages high in fat, sugar and salt'. Report No 2132/2012 on the Implementation of the Audiovisual Media Services Directive, 28/02/2013.

fat, saturated and trans-fats, salt and sugar in manufactured products. This study could then be used to gauge the extent to which self-regulation was working in relation to this aspect of improving the nutritional value of food.

There were other ways envisaged in the White Paper that the EU, in co-operation with the Member States, could assist in reducing rates of obesity. These included encouraging physical activity through sport, outdoor activities and active commuting. Targeting vulnerable groups, such as children and those in low socio-economic groups, was also prioritised. Developing the evidence base to support policy and decision making designed to combat obesity and using EFSA advice in relation to nutrition and health claims were also set as key ways in which the EU institutions could have a role to play.[41] There would also have to be an improvement in, and harmonisation of, national systems for monitoring data on food consumption levels, overweight and obesity rates. This would, it was suggested, have to happen at three levels.

First, there would have to be monitoring at the macro level to ensure the consistent gathering of comparable data on progress indicators. This should happen with reference to European Community Health Indicators (ECHI), assessing weight, diet and physical activity levels across the Union.

Second, there would need to be a systematic identification of action already undertaken in the Member States and an evaluation of its impact and effectiveness.

Third, there should be an assessment of individual projects and programmes, or micro monitoring. Support for all of this would be available through the Commission-developed European Health Interview Survey (EHIS), which became operational in 2007 and is managed by Eurostat. This system of data collection takes place in five-year cycles and gathers information on participants' BMI, smoking behaviour, alcohol consumption and perceptions of personal health. DG SANCO also launched the European Health Examination Survey in 2010. All the information produced by these systems is then collated to inform policy making and action taking on obesity prevention.

While much of what happens to combat nutrition-related illness must take place at EU level, there is recognition that Member State action is essential to addressing overweight and obesity issues. The White Paper clearly states that EU activity in this area is designed to support and complement that of the Member States. Diet, and the extent to which it affects health, varies from State to State, meaning that the type of action to be taken is often best determined at local level.

Despite this recognition, however, one outstanding, and very significant, legal problem remains. Member States cannot take legislative action designed to minimise the ill-effects of poor diet. To do so would be contrary to EU Treaty rules on the free movement of food. Any measures adopted would be deemed equivalent

---

[41] For a detailed examination of EFSA's role in nutrition policy formulation see M Friant-Perrot and A Garde, 'From BSE to obesity: EFSA's growing role in the EU's nutrition policy' in A Alemanno and S Gabbi (eds), *Foundations of EU Food Law and Policy* (Farnham, Ashgate, 2013).

to a quantitative restriction on trade which, as discussed in chapter four, we know to be prohibited by Article 34 TFEU, with little chance of justification available under Article 36 TFEU.

We can conclude from this that while EU policy documents support policy decision making at Member State level, EU law prevents this national policy meta-morphosing into national law, where this would inhibit, directly or indirectly, actually or potentially, interstate trade.[42] We must therefore trust that existing EU food labelling legislation is sufficient to deal with diet-related contributors to the prevalence of overweight people in society.

There is recognition at EU level that one of the best ways that this can be achieved is through the adoption of more meaningful and comprehensible forms of nutrition labelling, along the lines of that first proposed in the 2004 Government White Paper on Public Health, and developed by the Food Standards Agency in 2006. This is discussed below. Despite this, the Food Information Regulation does not provide for compulsory alternative labelling schemes. Article 34 TFEU prevents Member States from properly implementing their own policies aimed at addressing this.

9.4 National Nutrition Policy

Concerned at the ineffectiveness of the nutrition labelling requirements set out in the Nutrition Labelling Directive 1990 and the Food Labelling Regulations 1996,[43] the development of 'a clear straightforward coding system ... in common use ... that busy people can understand at a glance' was one of the central proposals put forward by the Government in its Public Health White Paper, published in November 2004.[44] It further stated that

> [f]ood is a prime example of an area where there needs to be clear and consistent information to help people make healthy choices. A lot of information is provided on packaged and processed foods. Many people understand the importance of thinking about how much salt, fat and sugar they eat. But lists expressed in terms that few of us can understand are not enough. What we need to know is where a particular food fits in a healthy balanced diet so that we can make informed choices.

The Government undertook, therefore, to 'press vigorously for progress during the UK presidency of the EU in 2005 to simplify nutrition labelling and make it

---

[42] For a more in-depth discussion on the importance of defining the relationship between 'local' and 'European' ideals and notions of 'risk' see D Chalmers, 'Food for thought: reconciling European risks and traditional ways of life' (2003) 66 *MLR* 532.

[43] SI No 1499/1996.

[44] White Paper on Public Health, *Choosing health: making health choices easier*, Department of Health, London, 2004.

mandatory on packaged foods'.[45] The latter part of this would require a revision of the EU Nutrition Labelling Directive which, as we know from the discussion above, only set compulsory nutrition labelling requirements for those foods which carried a nutrition or health claim on the packaging.

Making this change would prove relatively straightforward given that most foodstuffs carry this information anyway, regardless of whether a claim has been made or not.[46] It has, of course, now been made mandatory to provide nutrition information for all products through the introduction of the Food Information Regulation.[47] The former part, the simplification of nutrition information, would be more difficult to achieve. This would require agreement amongst EU Member States that the system for presenting this information required a significant over-haul. It would essentially mean the introduction of an EU-wide scheme for the presentation of nutrition information in the 'signpost' or 'traffic-light' format.

This particular amendment is not contained in the Food Information Regulation. In the meantime, national authorities must continue to rely on the use of voluntary codes and the support of producers and retailers to make any such scheme workable. Initial attempts to achieve this in 2006 failed. New propos-als in this regard were thus put forward in late 2012 in the hope of developing a scheme that would result in increased adherence rates during 2013. These would, however, like their predecessor, remain entirely unenforceable by law, despite their recognised value in dealing with the problems of poor diet, overweightness, obesity and related illness and disease, such as type 2 diabetes, heart disease and cancer.

9.4.1 Signpost Labelling

It has long been contended that traditional tabular forms of nutrition labelling are difficult for most consumers to comprehend.[48] We must therefore present this important information in a format that is easier to understand. This is even more imperative where the consumer must evaluate the data on nutrition values in addition to all of the other details presented, including that on durability dates, ingredients, allergens, price, value, content and so on. It must therefore appear in

---

[45] ibid.

[46] S Bonsmann et al, n 28 above.

[47] Art 9(1)(l) of Reg No 1169/2011, n 2 above.

[48] For further discussion on consumers' ability to understand these labels see, eg, G Cowburn and L Stockley, 'Consumer understanding and use of nutrition labelling: a systematic review' (2005) 8 *Public Health Nutrition* 21; and A Shine, S O'Reilly and K O'Sullivan, 'Consumer attitudes to nutrition labelling' (1997) 99 *British Food Journal* 283. It has also been suggested that understanding of nutri-tion information seems to be more widespread than use, suggesting that there is a lack of motivation amongst consumers as well as a failure, in many cases, to understand. It is hoped that 'signpost' labels, discussed in this chapter, could address the apparent apathy issue by clearly highlighting foods of poor nutritional benefit. See K Grunert et al, 'Use and understanding of nutrition information on food labels in six European countries' (2010) 18 *Journal of Public Health* 261.

a way that imparts the relevant particulars in a manner which facilitates consumer decision making in a quick, yet informed, way. The use of a well-considered 'signpost' or 'traffic-light' labelling scheme is, it is contended, the best way of achieving this dual aim. However, the system is not without its flaws. Crucially, existing alternative nutrition labelling schemes have two main shortcomings – and both relate to the fact that the template developed by the Food Standards Agency is not enforceable by law. The first is that retailers and producers can modify the FSA template provided to suit their own needs and marketing priorities. The second relates to the fact that the portion sizes upon which the colour-coded information provided is usually based can be doctored to present the product as having less detrimental nutritional values than that which is in fact the case. This former makes the scheme unworkable and confusing. The latter facilitates the deception of the consumer. This is, of course, problematic in a system initially designed to create clarity, consistency and certainty. Ongoing and flagrant abuse of the system leads to the directly opposite result.

The idea behind signpost nutrition labelling is that it presents the relevant information in an easily understandable format. The colours used in traffic lights are also used for the key nutrients. The label expresses the quantity of the nutrient, such as fat level, present in the product. A green background to this information indicates that a safe or relatively healthy amount of fat is present in a portion of the food in question. The use of an amber background for this suggests that the quantity contained in the product is at a higher level. The use of a red background signifies that there is a high level of fat or other nutrient in the food. Similar information is usually provided for saturated fats, sugar and salt. Determining which colour should be used is made by reference to the definitions set out in the EU Nutrition and Health Claims Regulation.[49] The Annex to this Regulation provides that a food can be classified as 'low-fat' where it contains a maximum of 3 g of fat per 100 g of solids, or 1.5 g of fat per 100 ml of liquids. Similar categorisation is provided for 'low-saturated fat', 'low sugar' and 'low salt', the latter description being retained for those foods that contain a maximum of 0.12 g of salt per 100 g or per 100 ml. The Regulation does not, however, set any range for medium or high levels of fats, salt, sugar or saturated fats. The Food Standards Agency has therefore determined that the amber (medium level) and red (high) classifications for these should be based on the recommendations of the UK Scientific Advisory Committee on Nutrition (SACN) and the Committee on Medical Aspects of Food and Nutrition Policy (COMA). These scales base 'high' levels for fat, saturated fat, sugar and salt on the calculation of 25 per cent of the recommended daily intake level per 100 g, or 30 per cent (40 per cent for salt) per portion. The nutritional information provided should be based, according to the FSA, on the product 'as sold', with the exception of dried foods, where it should be expressed 'as reconstituted'.[50]

[49] Regulation (EC) No 1924/2006 of the European Parliament and of the Council of 20 December 2006 on nutrition and health claims made on foods [2007] OJ L 12/3.

[50] Food Standards Agency, 'Front-of-pack traffic light signpost labelling technical guidance', Issue 2, November 2007. Available at: www.food.gov.uk.

The first of the shortcomings with the FSA-developed signpost labelling scheme identified above is that producers and retailers can modify the template provided. This is as a direct result of the fact that EU law prohibits the national authorities from introducing any labelling requirement other than that directly introduced by the EU. As has been discussed in some detail in chapter four, this relates to the fact that EU rules on the free movement of goods, in particular the prohibition on the implementation of national measures that are of equivalent effect to quantitative restrictions on trade, prevent the adoption of any national law that restricts the flow of products between Member States. Labelling laws are clearly within the scope of this provision, set out in Article 34 TFEU. As a consequence of this lack of legal effect, UK producers and retailers adopted their own versions of the FSA-backed scheme, soon after its introduction. This resulted, according to previous estimates, in the establishment of 14 different signpost label types by as early as July 2006 – less than four months after the initial establishment of the scheme.[51] None of these were identical to the FSA template, and no two were the same as each other. A scheme designed to create clarity was adding to the confusion. No-one was obliged to adhere to the template, so no-one did. This would continue to be the case unless a compulsory scheme were to be introduced by EU legislation.

The second difficulty that the use of colour-coded signpost food labelling has encountered relates to the actual information that is presented. The Food Standards Agency Guidance provides that

> [i]nformation given in the signpost on the levels of nutrients present in a portion of a product should not be misleading and be based on realistic portion sizes [and where] possible, generally accepted portion sizes should be used.[52]

Again, given the absence of any legal backing for the UK traffic-light labelling scheme, this request, which is all it can be, is often ignored. Large packets of crisps have misleadingly represented the portion as being only one-sixth of the bag and some chocolate has proudly flaunted seemingly good news to the consumer about the profile of the product based on a 'portion' that transpires to be a meagre two squares of the bar (or in one example identified, a portion of one square of a bar of chocolate)! Again, these practices can continue legitimately and lawfully until the EU decides to take action in this area by establishing its own scheme or setting harmonised provisions on those systems used in the Member States.

It has been officially recognised that the scheme introduced in 2006 has not worked. This culminated in the announcement of a new, single system for nutri-

---

[51] C MacMaoláin, *EU Food Law: Protecting consumers and health in a common market* (Oxford, Hart Publishing, 2007) 235.
[52] Food Standards Agency, 'Front-of-pack traffic light signpost labelling technical guidance', n 50 above, p 8.

tion labelling in October 2012.[53] The Department of Health stated that this would involve the use of front-of-pack information that would clearly display how much fat, saturated fat, salt, sugar and calories are contained in food products. The scheme is to involve the use of colour coding, guideline daily amounts contained (expressed as a percentage of the GDA), and high/medium/low text. It was noted that retailers were already using variants of a hybrid system (the FSA template) but were displaying this information 'with different visuals, colour and content making it hard for consumers to compare food'. The new model would be developed following collaboration between Government, industry and other partners to agree on the detail. The importance of the development of such a labelling type, which was announced following a three-month UK-wide consultation on the matter, was underlined by the Department, which stated that

> [h]aving a clear and consistent labelling system across all retailers will allow consumers to make quick, informed decisions about the food they eat and may also help consumers to make healthier choices that address some of the serious health consequences of poor diet, including obesity, cardiovascular disease, cancer and diabetes.

Three problems remain. First, determining the portion sizes on which the labelling declarations are based remains at the discretion of the retailers. Previous calls to make these 'realistic' were not adhered to.

Second, there is no mention of the application of this 'new' scheme to producers, only to retailers. Of the 14 different signpost labelling methods identified in July 2006, five were developed by food manufacturers.

Third, the scheme must again remain entirely voluntary until the EU acts to introduce specific provisions that would facilitate making national, or EU, food labelling requirements enforceable by law. The State must therefore look elsewhere for solutions that can be adopted and implemented at national level to address this serious public health issue.

9.4.2 National Health Strategy

It has been made clear in this chapter that regardless of any proposals introduced to use food labelling as a mechanism to tackle obesity, these will always have to remain voluntary unless and until the EU introduces a harmonised standard or allowance for this. A Government White Paper, published in November 2010, has therefore presented alternative methods that can be used to combat food-related health concerns. This document, entitled 'Healthy Lives, Healthy People: Our strategy for public health in England' sees the facilitation of better food choices as an essential component of the more general aim of improving the longevity

---

[53] For further discussion on the legal implications of introducing such a scheme see also M Holle, E Togni and A Vettorel, 'The compatibility of national interpretative nutrition labelling schemes with European and international law' (2014) 9 *European Food and Feed Law Review* 148.

and well-being of the population.[54] Given the lack of legislative control over its content and format, labelling is, unsurprisingly, not mentioned anywhere in the White Paper, except when dealing with tobacco consumption and smoking. Alternative, practical and EU-permitted, interventionist measures related to food are addressed in the document. It states that '[r]esearch has shown that social networks exert a powerful influence on individual behaviour, affecting our weight, smoking habits and happiness'.[55] In addition to this, it further asserts that

> [t]he quality of the environment around us also affects any community [as] pollution, air quality, noise, the availability of green and open spaces, transport, housing, access to good-quality food and social isolation all influence the health and wellbeing of the local population.

Action points set out in the White Paper that are designed to assist in enhancing the quality of food available and the environment in which it is produced and in which people live include the promotion of community ownership of green spaces and access to land, so that people can grow their own food. It is also stipulated that there must be more collaborative work with business and the voluntary sector through the Public Health Responsibility Deal, which was discussed in chapter three, including the establishment of networks on food, alcohol and physical activity. This would be extended to specifically target changes that were deemed necessary to reduce salt intake, provide better information to consumers about food and the promotion of more socially responsible retailing and consumption of alcohol.

Other initiatives proposed in the White Paper include providing support for families to assist them in making informed choices about their diet and physical activity levels, while also maintaining the Department of Education standards for school food. There would also be consideration of the DEFRA Fruit and Vegetable Task Force recommendation that food containing fruit or vegetables along with other types of food should be added to the '5-a-day' licensing scheme.

9.4.3 Department for Environment, Food and Rural Affairs Task Force

A nutrition task force was established in October 2009, charged with increasing the consumption and production of domestic fruit and vegetables in England. This body was to come into existence for one year, after which a report would be published, outlining proposals designed to improve the competitiveness of

---

[54] Department of Health, 'Healthy lives, healthy people: our strategy for public health in England', The Stationery Office, 30 November 2010, ISBN: 9780101798525.

[55] The research referred to here includes J Hall and T Valente, 'Adolescent smoking networks: The effects of influence and selection on future smoking' (2007) 32 *Journal of Addictive Behaviour* 3054; H Achat and others, 'Social networks, stress and health-related quality of life' (1998) 7 *Quality of Life*

English farmers and to support the ability of low-income families to increase the quantity of fruit and vegetables in their diet. The task force has since published two documents: a report in August 2010, and an action plan to deliver on the recommendations made in this report, in October of the same year.

The Task Force was made up of representatives of the Guild of Food Writers, the Department of Health, the School Food Trust, the National Farmers' Union, the British Dietetic Association, retailers, and the Food Standards Agency. The Report highlighted that poor nutrition was estimated to cost the National Health Service in the region of £6–7 billion annually by 2002, suggesting that this had probably risen to £8 billion by 2009.[56] Added to this was the estimation that an overall increase in the consumption of fresh produce to five portions per day could help avoid up to 42,000 premature deaths per year. It was also noted, however, that despite widespread recognition of the '5-a-day' message, overall fruit and vegetable consumption levels were actually falling. Where there was any increase, this had tended to be in relation to fruit juices, and not vegetables. Demand for domestically produced fruit had remained relatively stable but, alarmingly, sales of British-grown vegetables had reduced by 23 per cent. Import levels had risen 51 per cent over the same period,[57] and national self-sufficiency in indigenous fruit and vegetables continued to fall. The importance of increased fruit and vegetable consumption clearly relates not only to health protection, and the associated cost benefits to the NHS, but also to the economy as a whole, highlighted by the fact that agri-food is the largest manufacturing sector in the UK, contributing over £80 billion to the economy annually and employing over 3.6 million people.[58]

The Task Force Report has identified a number of ways in which the increased consumption of fruit and vegetables can be encouraged. The first of these is to try to influence or change consumer behaviour. The Report indicated that this can be achieved in two broad ways. The first is through the use of government advertising and information campaigns. The second is by ensuring the reliable availability of good value and quality foods that the consumer can prepare or consume easily. Domestic growers would have to be able to compete with imports on this basis. It was suggested that behaviour change campaigns that simply tell people what they should do are usually ineffective or insufficient in achieving the desired aims. Other methods have to be used to complement the original information provided. These include the reinforcement of positive decision making on an ongoing and at point-of-sale basis; providing opportunities for consumer experimentation with new foods, in particular by the use of devices which suggest healthier

---

Research 735; and N Christakis and J Fowler, *Connected: the surprising power of our social networks and how they shape our lives* (New York, Little, Brown, 2009).

[56] Data taken from M Rayner and P Scarborough, 'The burden of food related ill-health in the UK' (2005) 59 *Journal of Epidemiology and Community Health* 1054.

[57] According to DEFRA and HM Revenue and Customs figures on the Adjusted National Food Survey Data 1974–2000 and the Economic and Social Data Service Expenditure and Food Surveys, available at www.esds.ac.uk.

alternatives; preparation and/or cooking instruction; normalising behaviour by demonstrating that others have already changed or maintained the preferred position; and regulating through what is termed 'supportive choice architecture', which stipulates that certain foods have to be available to consumers, for example obliging schools to provide that fruit and vegetables form an integral part of school lunches and dinners.

The second recommendation made by the Task Force to assist in increasing overall fruit and vegetable consumption levels is that there should be marketing programmes run on a collaborative basis with industry, designed to promote British fruit and vegetables when they are in season and ensuring that they are provided with adequate shelf space in retail outlets. There should also be more promotion of frozen fruits and vegetables as alternatives, in particular because of the ability of the freezing process to ensure that vital nutrient levels are maintained in the food. Freezing also helps to minimise waste and ensures that there is an availability of domestic produce all year round. It was also recommended that the Healthy Start voucher scheme, run by the Department of Health and the National Health Service, should therefore be extended to frozen produce. This has now happened, providing these products, as well as milk and infant formula, for qualifying pregnant women and children under four years of age. The '5-a-day' licensing scheme has now also been extended to include composite foods which contain at least one portion of fruit or vegetables that count towards reaching this target for individuals. Frozen fruit and vegetables are also included in this, as are dried fruits, juices and smoothies.

Value added tax (VAT) rates should, according to the Task Force Report, also be changed to ensure that fruit juices and smoothies are subject to the same lower rates of tax as biscuits and cakes, which can be subject to as little as 0 per cent VAT. The former are deemed to be fruits and vegetables for '5-a-day' licensing purposes but it was ruled in 2010 that they are also 'luxury products', and are therefore liable to the then standard VAT rate of 17.5 per cent.[59] Schedule 8 to the Value Added Tax Act 1994 stipulates that the sale of food should not be liable to VAT, with some exceptions set out. These include, for example, ice cream, frozen yoghurt, confectionery (but not including cakes or biscuits other than those with a chocolate coating) and, most significantly here, beverages. The question in *Innocent* was whether a smoothie was a 'beverage' for VAT purposes, and whether this evaluation should take aspects of social policy into consideration. The 0 per cent VAT

---

[58] Council of Food Policy Advisors, *Food: a recipe for a healthy, sustainable and successful future. Second report of the Council of Food Policy Advisors* (London, DEFRA, 2010).
[59] *Innocent Limited v The Commissioners for Her Majesty's Revenue and Customs* [2010] UKFTT 516.

rate for food has not been deemed incompatible with EU law.[60] It is potentially justifiable on the basis that it is used to pursue a legitimate social objective.

However, no such social policy, other than keeping food prices as low as possible, was ever referred to, much less elucidated. It had previously been held by Warren J in *Kalron Foods* that the VAT Act failed to establish a consistent consumer support policy.[61] If the exemption from VAT was designed to assist consumers in ensuring that they had sufficient means to purchase food, then it was questionable as to why cakes and many biscuits could benefit from this 0 per cent rate when fruit juice and bottled water were taxed at the standard rate. The argument in *Innocent* was that smoothies have significant nutritional value and should therefore be exempt from VAT on the basis that their consumption contributes to the achievement of the necessary 'social policy'. In *Kalron* it was held, and upheld on appeal,[62] that liquidised fruits and/or vegetables must be considered as 'beverages' for taxation purposes. In *Innocent* the same conclusion was reached about fruit smoothies. The Tribunal actually used the fact that other 'healthy' drinks, such as fruit juice and bottled water, were taxed at the standard rate as an explanation as to why it was consistent to subject smoothies to the same level of VAT.

No state can legitimately claim that it wishes to encourage its population to eat healthily if it imposes a significantly higher tax on fruit smoothies and blended fruit than on biscuits and cakes.[63] It is meaningless to introduce a series of unenforceable templates for signpost nutrition labelling while simultaneously making healthy alternative consumption choices more expensive through a discriminatory taxation regime. Repeatedly, studies show that one of the primary considerations in purchasing determinations is price.[64] Yet little has been done to make fruit and vegetables, in what might be considered by many as their most palatable form, more affordable. What is most alarming about the decisions in both *Innocent* and

---

[60] Case 416/1985, *Commission v UK* [1988] ECR 3127. The 0% VAT rate has not necessarily been deemed compatible with EU law either. The European Court of Justice merely found that the Commission had failed to establish that the UK was not in compliance with its obligations under what were the applicable provisions of EU law at the time, in particular those set out in Directive 1977/388/EEC [1977] OJ L 145/1.

[61] *Kalron Foods Ltd v The Commissioners for Her Majesty's Revenue and Customs* [2007] STC 1100.

[62] [2007] EWCH 695.

[63] Cakes are always 0% VAT-rated, whereas biscuits are standard VAT-rated if wholly or partly covered in chocolate. This distinction between different types of biscuits is complicated by the absence of any definition of either cakes or biscuits. This complication was most famously addressed in the case of 'Jaffa cake' biscuits, which were originally 0% VAT-rated by Customs and Excise as they were considered to be 'cakes', but which were later re-classified as 'biscuits partly covered in chocolate'. United Biscuits challenged this, arguing that they were in fact cakes. Their appeal was successful, the Tribunal finding that although 'Jaffa cakes' had the characteristics of both cakes and biscuits, they possessed enough characteristics of 'cake' to be considered as such for VAT purposes. *United Biscuits* (LON/91/0160).

[64] See, eg: T Andreyeva, M Long and K Brownell, 'The impact of food prices on consumption: a systematic review of research on the price elasticity of demand for food' (2010) 100 *American Journal of Public Health* 216; and S French, 'Pricing effects on food choices' (2003) 133 *Journal of Nutrition* 8415. The latter study showed how reducing the price of lower-fat foods led to significant increases in the sale of these products. Price reductions also led to a fourfold increase in the sale of fresh fruit, and a doubling of sales of fresh vegetables.

Kalron is that the Tribunal and the High Court respectively found that fruit and vegetables were significantly different in their pre- and post-liquidised forms. The appellants in *Kalron* argued that their products, a blend of liquidised fruits and/ or vegetables, were a soft form of food, as distinct from a beverage. Beverages were subject to the higher rate of VAT. The applicants in *Innocent* claimed that fruit smoothies are essentially the same as a fruit salad, and should therefore be treated the same for taxation purposes. In both cases the Tribunal and the Court disagreed. In the former, Warren J stated in the High Court that '[t]he blending transforms a solid, albeit soft, food into a liquid which can be drunk'. The process could, therefore, change the VAT treatment of the ingredients. In the latter it was found that

> fruit smoothies are not merely drinkable liquids, they are drinks [and] as drinks, fruit smoothies are unusual (but not unique) in that they are quite thick and do require digestion: we do not think this is sufficient to mean that they are not a beverage if they are drunk as other beverages would be drunk.

The Tribunal also chose to overlook the fact that the majority of consumers saw smoothies as being more of a snack than a drink. This was deemed inconsequential on the grounds that they were

> wary of putting too much weight on market research which gives different answers to similar questions from one survey to another and where answers depend so much on how the question was asked and what alternatives were given.

The taxation of fruit smoothies would not be reconsidered in the light of either overall nutrition policy or, perhaps more questionably, by virtue of the fact that they retain many of the key characteristics of, and are produced entirely from, food—albeit in liquidised form. The Fruit and Vegetables Task Force Report suggested that reducing the VAT to 0 per cent on these healthier options could lead to an increase in overall nutritional benefits derived from diet to the extent that it could save the NHS nearly 1 per cent of its overall budget. It could, in effect, be a cost-saving measure.

Most of the debate thus far has tended to focus on the introduction of so-called 'fat taxes', which would lead to an increase in the price of some foods and sugary drinks. This is often put forward as a potential panacea to the obesity problem. It did not work in Denmark, and was withdrawn soon after its introduction. More sensibly, it has also been suggested that the use of fiscal measures to discourage the consumption of nutritionally inferior foods can only work as one of a range of related measures, operating as part of an overall strategy, based on a mix of policy tools.[65] This could include the reduction of taxes on

---

[65] A Alemanno and I Carreño, 'Fat taxes in Europe: a legal and policy analysis under EU and WTO law' (2013) 8 *European Food and Feed Law Review* 97.

healthier foods. It could also involve the use of a well-constructed alternative labelling scheme, which makes it clear to the consumer that the food is not just 'high' or 'low' in a particular substance. Instead, it must clearly indicate the impact that the long-term consumption of the food or drink in question will have. Simply displaying fat or sugar levels is not suitable. The consumption of many types of fats is essential for good health. Similarly, sugar content arising from fruits is completely different from that present in a product due to processing.

9.5 International Policy and Recommendations

While it is recognised that most individual States or interstate organisations, such as the EU, have their own policies on nutrition and food safety, the WHO has drafted an action plan designed to assist the European region in its efforts to tackle disease associated with, in particular, obesity.[66] This plan was endorsed by the WHO Regional Committee for Europe, which called on its own Member States to develop related food and nutrition policies.

The WHO Action Plan set out four main aims. These were stated as reducing the prevalence of diet-related non-communicable disease; reversing the obesity trend in children and adolescents; reducing the prevalence of micronutrient deficiencies; and reducing the incidence of food-borne diseases. The first three of these relate directly to nutrition, both deficiency and excess. The third relates to the absence of recommended minimum quantities of certain vitamins and minerals, such as vitamin A and iron, from diets. These three nutrition-related aims would be tackled by reductions in saturated fatty acid, trans-fat, salt and sugar consumption, coupled with an increase in the quantities of fruit and vegetables eaten. Specific actions designed to achieve these aims were listed as including the promotion of school nutrition policies, such as the establishment of fruit and vegetable distribution schemes; improving the availability and affordability of fruit and vegetables; promoting the reformulation of mainstream food products in order to reduce the quantities of fats, salts and sugars used in the manufacture of food; promoting appropriate micronutrient fortification of staple food items, in particular where micronutrient deficiencies have become a public health problem; improving the nutritional quality of the food supply in public institutions, such as health services, schools and workplaces; exploring the use of economic tools,

[66] WHO, *2nd European Action Plan for Food and Nutrition Policy 2007–2012* (Copenhagen, WHO, 2008).

such as taxes and subsidies to influence the affordability of food and drinks in line with dietary guidelines; and establishing targeted programmes for the protection of vulnerable and low socioeconomic groups.

More specifically, the WHO Action Plan sets guidelines for the provision of comprehensive information and education to consumers. It states that '[a] sound communication and information strategy ... is essential for supporting the adoption of healthy lifestyles'. Specific action to assist in delivering on this was stated to include the development of dietary guidelines, aimed at both the general population and at vulnerable groups; conducting public campaigns aimed at informing consumers about food and nutrition; ensuring the employment of appropriate marketing practices for all food products in line with internationally agreed recommendations; and the promotion of adequate and suitable labelling for food products, designed to improve consumers' understanding of product characteristics and supporting healthy choices. This labelling recommendation also stipulated that regulations and guidelines should be developed that reflect best practice, such as 'front-of-pack signposting'. Whichever method is used, the Action Plan recommends that it should establish 'an efficient method for assessing the nutrient quality of food products'.

10

Ethical and Environmental
Aspects of Food Law

10.1 Introduction

It has been demonstrated throughout this book that the preponderance of English food law now comes directly from EU legislative initiative and interpretation through the case law of the European Court of Justice and European Commission policy documentation. As the High Court has put it so clearly in its examination of certain provisions of the Food Labelling Regulations 1996, '[a]s with so many current regulations concerning consumer protection, the origin of these Regulations is to be found in European Directives'.[1] These laws do not always reflect the different priorities of consumers and industry in their provisions and application. A whole range of other considerations may need to be taken account of in the drafting of new EU legal requirements. This is a difficult thing to achieve when the general moral, ethical or environmental preferences themselves differ from Member State to Member State. Issues such as animal welfare, climate change and the preservation of local ecosystems may need to be taken into account in the creation of rules which are primarily designed to promote free movement and maintain some sort of minimum quality standards. The rules are created on a European basis, but they may be at odds with more specific national or local priorities. Some of these issues are examined in more detail in this chapter.

10.2 Food Law and Climate Change

Climate change is likely to have a very significant impact on global and national food production. The Intergovernmental Panel on Climate Change (IPCC) has reported that carbon dioxide emissions need to drop to half of 1990 levels by the year 2050 to have even a 50 per cent chance of avoiding a 2 degree

---

[1] *Torfaen County Borough Council v Douglas Willis Limited* [2012] EWHC 296.

rise in temperatures.[2] This could lead to increased shortages of food. Higher temperatures lead to lower global production yields. It was reported in *Science* in 2003 that corn and soya levels could drop by 17 per cent for every degree rise in temperature.[3] This, and other estimates, suggests that billions of lives could be put at risk from lower food production levels arising out of rises in global temperatures. Agriculture is a big part of the problem. While food production levels need to increase to feed the world's ever-rising population, the growing and production of food accounts for around 20 per cent of all greenhouse gas emissions.[4] This would suggest that the way in which food is made, transported, marketed and consumed needs to change if we are to see higher population levels fed by a sector that needs to reduce its own impact on climate change. Food law has a key role to play in this.

In 2009 a report was published in *The Lancet* which suggested that a clear message needs to be made about the strong links between climate change and human health.[5] There are two parts to this. The first is that climate change is likely to have a significant impact on the ability to produce food. This could lead to starvation, malnutrition, disease and death. The second is that traditional messages about the need to change individual behaviour in a way that reduces the human factors, such as carbon emissions, in climate change are not having the desired effect. It would be preferable, therefore, to change these so that the message becomes a demonstration of how leading a low-carbon-emitting lifestyle is good for the individual's health. It can lead to lower rates of heart disease, obesity and diabetes. There would also be lower levels of pollution, making for cleaner air and better lung health.

Food law and policy can be used to address some of the issues raised here. These range from adopting regulations that support and promote environmentally friendly farming practices to the development of labelling schemes which indicate where the product has been made in an environmentally friendly manner. The former has been addressed, to some degree, by the Regulations on organic foods. This is discussed in more detail below. The latter suggestion is more problematic. Individual retailers have developed their own labelling disclosures, designed to provide the consumer with information on the impact of certain products on the

---

[2] IPCC Fourth Assessment Report, 2007. Available at: www.ipcc.ch. Further contributions have since been made to the Fifth Assessment Report, such as that on 'Climate Change 2014: Impacts, Adaptation and Vulnerability', also available at www.ipcc.ch.

[3] D Lobell and G Asner, 'Climate and management contributions in US agricultural yields' (2003) 299 *Science* 1032.

[4] This figure varies depending on how it is calculated and on what is taken into consideration. Agriculture alone has been estimated to account for 20% of emissions in C Cole et al, 'Global estimates of potential mitigation of greenhouse gas emissions by agriculture' (1997) 49 *Nutrient Cycling in Agroecosystems* 221. However, it has also been estimated to be at the lower level of 10–12% in the IPCC Report. It was noted by S Friel et al, 'Public health benefits of strategies to reduce greenhouse-gas emissions: food and agriculture' (2009) 374 *The Lancet* 2016, that these figures could rise by half by 2030, caused in particular by increased demand for meat.

[5] A Costello and others, 'Managing the health effects of climate change' (2009) 373 *The Lancet* 1693.

environment. These have, however, tended to be limited to details on 'food miles', showing whether the product has travelled a long distance to the supermarket shelf. These types of label can be both misleading and meaningless. It has been highlighted, for example, that the transportation of food makes up a very small part of the sector's carbon emissions. A whole range of factors would therefore have to be taken into account in setting any meaningful and verifiable labelling scheme that could be used to provide more useful disclosures to concerned consumers. Some foodstuffs that have travelled relatively short distances to shops are amongst the highest of carbon emitters in their production.

A DEFRA report has clearly indicated that using 'food miles' alone is not a valid indicator of sustainable development of environmental friendliness.[6] This report stated that food accounted for 30 per cent of all goods transported on UK roads. Food now travels further than was the case a few decades previously. The total mileage that food was travelling was up by 50 per cent since 1978, but the quantity was only up by 23 per cent. Air transportation of food rose 140 per cent between 1992 and 2002, accounting for just 1 per cent of the total mileage, but 11 per cent of the carbon emissions.

Air transportation of food creates 177 times the carbon output of shipping it. This all also leads to associated economic and social costs. It was estimated in the DEFRA report that the transportation of food on British roads costs the economy £9 billion per annum through added traffic congestion. The pollution costs stand at around £2 billion. All of this related to a sector where agriculture adds around £6.4 billion to the UK economy.

It is clear from this data that while the air transportation of food is a contributor to the carbon output of the food sector, it is only a small part of this. Despite this, existing carbon labelling schemes, adopted by supermarkets in particular, have tended to base their indications on the miles flown by imported food only. The reality of impact on climate change is much more complex than this.

Calculating the total carbon emissions of the production, transportation and marketing of food must be based on a range of factors. Seemingly environmentally friendly foodstuffs can sometimes be the worst offenders in this regard. 'Local' products can be grown on the farm and then transported to the packer, then on to the distribution centre, then back to the shop near where it was produced in the first place. Refrigeration of both local and organic foods can result in significant carbon output. Foods grown 'out of season' can have all sorts of damaging consequences for the environment.

It has been reported, for example, that it is less harmful in this regard to bring a consignment of tomatoes by road from Spain than it is to produce and sell them 'locally' in the UK, where the former has been produced using natural heat and sunlight while the latter has involved artificial versions of these in greenhouses. It can be better for the environment to ship lamb 11,000 miles from New Zealand

---

[6] DEFRA, 'The validity of food miles as an indicator of sustainable development: Final report' (2005); Report Number: ED50254.

for sale in the UK than to have it produced and sold in the UK. This is due to the decreased use of fertilisers and increased recourse to renewable energy sources in New Zealand production. The type of food and/or method of production can also have an effect on its environmental impact. Organic food, for example, tends to be made using less energy and lower quantities of fertilisers and chemicals.

Meat has a much higher water usage in production than most fruits and vegetables. It can take 2,400 litres of water to make a hamburger. It takes around 13 litres of water to produce a tomato. Cows emit large quantities of methane gas. In fact, the mere existence of food-producing livestock produces more carbon dioxide and greenhouse gases than all of food transportation combined. The production of red meats tends to lead to around one and a half times the emissions of the same quantities of chicken. Overall, the figures clearly show that most of the greenhouse gases from the food sector arise from the production, rather than the transportation, stage. The former has been calculated to account for 83 per cent of the sector's emissions in the US.[7] The same study noted that delivery from the producer to the retailer was responsible for only 4 per cent of the sector's carbon output there.

It has been made clear that the transportation mode and distance travelled, refrigeration, time of year, production methods and food type all contribute to the carbon output of food, yet labelling schemes operating in the UK that are designed to indicate the carbon emissions attached to foods have tended to focus on 'food miles' only. The law could be used to address this by the creation of a new labelling format that would provide the consumer with a more holistic assessment of the relationship between the product and its potential to impact on climate change and pollution.

There is no publicly regulated food labelling indication which clearly indicates the overall environmental impact of food. If food purchasing and consumption habits do not change, we will possibly see further shortages in the availability of food which are, at least partially and probably significantly, caused by any failure to bring about this required alteration.

Experiences in other areas of food law could be used for guidance in the development of such a labelling indication. Disclosures such as this should be backed up by legislation and made compulsory, rather than being introduced by a voluntary scheme. For example, it has been claimed that it is only with the introduction of compulsory indication requirements for protected geographical food names that these products could become better known to, and more readily identifiable by, consumers.[8] The use of an environmental impact labelling indication should also be introduced by way of harmonising and effective EU legislation.

---

[7] C Weber and H Matthews, 'Food-miles and the relative climate impacts of food choices in the United States' (2008) 42 *Environmental Science and Technology* 3508.

[8] Recital 28 of Preamble to Regulation (EU) No 1151/2012 of the European Parliament and of the Council of 21 November 2012 on quality schemes for agricultural products and foodstuffs [2012] OJ L 343/1.

It is clear that rules on the free movement of goods would prevent the UK from introducing its own unilateral and enforceable scheme. Applying this to domestic producers only could also put them at a competitive disadvantage, especially where products carried a negative indication. The adoption of voluntary and complementary nationally applied schemes, such as that operated by Carbon Trust UK, while very useful in some ways, are not therefore desirable or appropriate in the long term. Fair-trade labels, which have also operated without legal support, are often self-awarded and open to abuse by those using them. With no minimum criteria for certification, traders can set their own standards which may be little better, or possibly worse, than their non-fair-trade counterparts. It can also lead to the same indication being made, but being based on an entirely different set of criteria. Any labelling indication designed to indicate environmental impact must also be clear and user-friendly. The way in which nutritional information has been presented since the introduction of the Nutrition Labelling Directive in 1990 has highlighted how such disclosures can often lack usefulness, or possibly mislead, if the template is not set in a manner which offers the details in an accessible and understandable format.[9]

Most importantly, as has been made clear above, any carbon labelling scheme for food must be based on the full range of appropriate criteria rather than the more blinkered approach of indicating (air) miles travelled only. This is one factor, but consideration should also be given to the transportation method, the production emissions, the food type, water usage and storage conditions. These can have a far more significant bearing on the environmental impact than the criterion on which these assessments, where they do exist, have traditionally been based.

10.3 Organic Food

Organic food sales in the UK were worth around £1.23 billion annually by 2013. They have been higher than this in the past, peaking at £2.1 billion in 2008, but they did rise again during 2012–2013 after several years of successive falls in sales coincided with a recession in the economy. These figures, taken from the Soil Association's Organic Market Report 2013, also show that the dairy sector continues to be the strongest-performing category, as sales of organic milk, which accounts for the highest overall sales value of any organic product (£143 million), grew by 2.2 per cent. In the rest of the grocery sector, tea and yoghurts showed strong growth at 19 per cent and 9 per cent respectively, while 57 per cent of all baby food sold in the

---

[9] See, eg, G Cowburn and L Stockley, 'Consumer understanding and use of nutrition labelling: a systematic review' (2005) 8 *Public Health Nutrition* 21; and A Shine, S O'Reilly and K O'Sullivan, 'Consumer attitudes to nutrition labelling' (1997) 99 *British Food Journal* 283.

UK was organic by 2013. The online organic sales sector was also growing, roughly in line with increased sales of goods through the internet in the economy as a whole. Organic catering also accounted for around £16 million of sales by 2013.

Sales of organic food in the UK are at significantly lower levels than in other EU Member States of a comparable size. There are approximately twice as many organic products sold in France, and four times as many in Germany. The reasons as to why consumers buy, and are usually willing to pay a premium price for, organic food differ. Most think that organic food is healthier. This is often disputed.[10] Around one-third find that organic food tastes better than its conventional counterparts. Nearly half of consumers surveyed buy organic for environmental reasons. Just under one-third take animal welfare considerations into account when buying organic food.[11]

The figures for organic farming and food production for the UK are not very encouraging for that sector. Sales levels have fallen back pretty sharply during recessionary times, suggesting a lack of priority amongst many consumers for environmental and welfare considerations. Less than 4 per cent of agricultural land in England was designated for organic farming by 2012, and this figure was falling at that time. This compares to an average of 5.4 per cent of agricultural land being used for organic production across the EU. All of this is to be set against the context of the horse-meat scandal of 2013,[12] which had initially led to increased sales in organic foodstuffs.

The Soil Association has been particularly critical of the lack of Government backing for organic produce, citing the fact that European sales of these products had increased by around a quarter since the start of the global economic downturn in 2008—a trend which was reversed in the UK. It has called for the development of a new national organic action plan, similar to that developed by the Scottish Government. Similar action plans have been published in the past, such as that which was produced in 2002 with the stated aim of identifying what was required to ensure stable and strategic growth for the organic sector in England.[13] This would create a package of providing environmentally based producer support, firm targets for public sector procurement of organic produce and more investment in promoting organic products. The law on organic production is set out in EU regulations from 2007 and 2008, which are given full effect in English law by the Organic Products Regulations 2009.[14]

---

[10] See M Jensen, H Jørgensen and C Lauridsen, 'Comparison between conventional and organic agriculture in terms of nutritional quality of food—a critical review' (2013) 8 *Perspectives in Agriculture, Veterinary Science, Nutrition and Natural Resources* 1.

[11] Data all taken from the Soil Association's Organic Market Report 2013, available at: www.soilassociation.org/marketreport.

[12] In early 2013, the Food Safety Authority of Ireland tested 27 frozen beefburgers and 37% of these contained equine DNA. It emerged that equine DNA was present widely in foods in other countries, including the UK. Approximately 16 countries in total appear to have been affected by the scandal.

[13] DEFRA, 'Action plan to develop organic food and farming in England', July 2002, available at: archive.defra.gov.uk.

[14] SI No 842/2009.

10.3.1 European Union Regulation of Organic Produce

The first framework EU Regulation on the production and marketing of organic foodstuffs was introduced in 1991.[15] It subsequently became one of the most amended pieces of EU food legislation, with changes having to be made on 41 occasions by 2006. The provisions originally contained in the Regulation had become very piecemeal. This was one of the reasons underlying the need to introduce a new Organic Food Regulation in 2007.[16] The European Commission had previously launched an Action Plan for Organic Food and Farming in 2004, and this document had also called for changes to be made, in particular by simplifying the general principles contained in the Regulation and making it more transparent, improving farming standards, increasing consumer awareness, and even allowing the provision of State aids for the sector.[17] It also specifically called for clarity in relation to the labelling of foods as 'organic', even where they contained genetically modified organisms. The original 1991 Regulation did not prohibit the use of genetic modification in the production of organic food, a surprising allowance which was later certified by the Court of Justice.[18] Regulation 834/2007, the new Organic Food Regulation, came into effect in 2009.

Organic Foods Regulation 834/2007

The objectives for organic production are set out in Article 3 of Regulation 834/2007. It provides that the key objective is to establish a sustainable management system for agriculture that is natural, contributes to a high level of biological diversity, involves the responsible use of natural resources, and operates on the basis of high standards of animal welfare. The 'principles' of organic production include the use of living organisms and mechanical agricultural methods, the practice of land-related crop cultivation and livestock production and excluding the use of GMOs.[19] All of this should be based on risk assessment and the use of

---

[15] Council Regulation (EEC) No 2092/1991 of 24 June 1991 on organic production of agricultural products and indications referring thereto on agricultural products and foodstuffs [1991] OJ L 198.

[16] Council Regulation (EC) No 834/2007 of 28 June 2007 on organic production and labelling of organic products and repealing Regulation (EEC) No 2092/1991 [2007] OJ L 189/1. Recital 4 of the Preamble to this Regulation states that '[i]n its conclusions of 18 October 2004, the Council called on the Commission to review the [Union] legal framework in this field with a view to ensure simplification and overall coherence and in particular to establish principles encouraging harmonisation of standards and, where possible, to reduce the level of detail'.

[17] Communication from the Commission to the Council and the European Parliament on a European Action Plan for Organic Food and Farming, COM (2004) 415.

[18] Case C-156/1993 *European Parliament v Commission* [1995] ECR I-2019. The use of genetic modification in the production of organic food was not prohibited until amendments to Art 5(3) of Reg 2092/1991 were made by the introduction of Council Regulation (EC) No 1804/1999 of 19 July 1999 supplementing Regulation (EEC) No 2092/1991 on organic production of agricultural products and indications referring thereto on agricultural products and foodstuffs to include livestock production [1999] OJ L 222/1. Despite this, some confusion about the use of genetic modification techniques in the production of organic food remained.

[19] Art 4(a).

the precautionary principle when appropriate. Additional and specific principles are also to be applied to the production of processed organic food. The Regulation states that these foods should be made from organic ingredients except where they are not available in organic form, the use of additives and processing aids should be kept to a minimum and processes and substances should not be used where they could mislead consumers about the nature of the final product.[20]

The Regulation makes the prohibition on the use of GMOs much more explicit than that which had originally appeared in Regulation 1804/1999.[21] Article 9 of Regulation 834/2007 provides that

> GMOs and products produced from or by GMOs shall not be used as food, feed, processing aids, plant protection products, fertilisers, soil conditioners, seeds, vegetative propagating material, micro-organisms and animals in organic production.

This is an important provision. It underlines the fact that the only way that consumers and/or retailers can completely avoid the use of genetic modification is to choose the organic option. As is discussed below, meat or animal products from animals that have been fed a GM diet do not have to carry any indication of the fact that the animals in question have been fed a diet including genetically modified foods. The only exception to this is that which is contained in Article 9(1) of the Organic Foods Regulation, which explicitly prohibits the use of GM animal feed in organic production. The Regulation then further states that

> [o]perators may assume that no GMOs or products produced from GMOs have been used in the manufacture of purchased food and feed products when the latter are not labelled, or accompanied by a document, pursuant to [the GMOs regulations].[22]

Operators using non-organic products in the production of organic foods can also oblige their ingredient suppliers to confirm that the products supplied have not been produced from or by GMOs.[23] This is all a very marked departure from that which was permitted under the original regulations in the 1990s, where genetically modified micro-organisms were specifically listed as being amongst those non-organic ingredients that could be lawfully used in the manufacture of organic products. The use of ionising radiation for the treatment of organic food, feed or the ingredients of organic produce is also explicitly prohibited.[24]

For food to be lawfully labelled as 'organic', the entire agricultural holding which produces it should usually be managed in compliance with the requirements applicable to organic production.[25] There are some circumstances where this does not have to be the case, but this is only allowed when the holding is split into clearly separated units. There are additional rules for plant production,

---

[20] Art 6(a)–(c).
[21] Note 18 above.
[22] Art 9(2). The GMOs Regulations are discussed in more detail below.
[23] Art 9(3).
[24] Art 10.
[25] Art 11.

and standards for animal production. The former includes obligations to use tillage and cultivation practices that maintain or increase soil organic matter and enhance soil biodiversity, for example. It also includes the use of multi-annual crop rotation, a ban on mineral nitrogen fertilisers and a preference for the use of natural pest, weed and disease control measures.[26] A restricted list of non-organic fertilisers, soil conditioners, plant protection products, feed materials and feed additives that can be authorised for use in organic production is drafted by the Commission, using comitology.[27] However, authorisation is only to be granted where this is necessary for ensuring sustained production. This may be the case if their use is deemed essential for the control of a harmful organism or a particular disease and alternative treatments are not available.

It is certainly arguable that the very highest of welfare standards for animals are those contained in the Organic Foods Regulation. The legislation also includes a range of requirements designed to maintain the organic purity of food-producing animals. Organic livestock, for example, must be born and raised on organic holdings.[28] Some non-organically raised animals may be brought onto a holding for breeding purposes under set conditions. However, these must go through a 'conversion period' before they, or their products, can be deemed 'organic'. The same rules apply to those animals which may have been kept on a farm before the conversion to organic production began, provided all of the other requirements of the Regulation have been properly applied during this period.

Welfare of Organic Food-producing Animals

The Organic Foods Regulation sets out a range of production rules, designed to ensure that animals are raised in the most natural manner possible. One of the main outcomes of this is that welfare standards tend to be higher in the production of organic animal-derived foods than their more intensive or conventional counterparts. In particular, the Regulation stipulates that, for livestock,

> husbandry practices, including stocking densities, and housing conditions shall ensure that the developmental, physiological and ethological needs of animals are met.

This is roughly similar to the general welfare requirements applicable to all food-producing animals, which are discussed in more detail later in this chapter. However, the Regulation then further provides that

> the livestock shall have permanent access to open air areas, preferably pasture, whenever weather conditions and the state of the ground allow this unless restrictions and obligations related to the protection of human and animal health are imposed on the basis of [Union] legislation.[29]

---

[26] Art 12.
[27] Art 16.
[28] Art 14.
[29] Art 14.3(b).

This is the crucial welfare requirement for animals used to make organic produce. They have full access to the outdoors, unless there is some very good reason as to why this cannot be the case. Tethering and isolation are prohibited for organic livestock, again unless there is some significant justification for this, such as for safety, welfare or veterinary reasons.[30] The duration of the transportation of livestock is also to be minimised. As will be seen below, this is not necessarily the case for non-organic animals.

The Organic Foods Regulation also sets clear environmental protection provisions attached to the rearing of livestock. It stipulates that the quantity of livestock should usually be relatively limited in order to minimise the potential for overgrazing, erosion and pollution. Controversial breeding methods are prohibited. While artificial insemination is allowed, cloning and embryo transfer are not.[31] There are strict requirements on feed. It must be organic. It should be locally produced, where possible. There should be permanent access to pasture or roughage. Growth promoters should never be used.[32] Significantly, the Organic Foods Regulation has loosened the rules on the use of veterinary medicines. Previously, there was an emphasis on the use of alternative veterinary treatments, which arguably reduced the overall welfare standards attached to organic production. Now the Regulation states that

> disease shall be treated immediately to avoid suffering to the animal; chemically synthesised allopathic veterinary medicinal products including antibiotics may be used where necessary and under strict conditions, when the use of phytotherapeutic, homeopathic and other products is inappropriate.[33]

It could, of course, be argued that the use of these latter remedies must generally be considered inappropriate in the absence of scientific evidence to the contrary about their efficacy. Immunisation is permitted. So are treatments related to the protection of human and animal health introduced by EU laws. Adapted, but similar, rules apply to organic aquaculture.[34]

Labelling Organic Foods

The Organic Foods Regulation provides that any labelling or advertising which refers to organic production methods, including the use of terms such as 'bio' or 'eco', can only legitimately appear where a product and all of its ingredients have been produced according to the standards set out in the legislation.[35] Having said that, there may be reference to organic production for processed foods which are made from mostly organic ingredients. However, for this to be permitted, at least

---

[30] Art 14.
[31] Art 14.1(c).
[32] Art 14.1(d).
[33] Art 14.1(e).
[34] Art 15.
[35] Art 23.1.

95 per cent of the agricultural ingredients used have to be organic.[36] All of the organic ingredients used in the manufacture of such products must be clearly indicated in the ingredients list. The total percentage of organic ingredients should also be clearly labelled. The Regulation further prohibits the appearance of any terms, including those used in registered trademarks, or any practices used in labelling or advertising which are liable to mislead consumers into believing that the product is organic.[37] Unlike previous versions, the 2007 Regulation also makes it very clear that references to organic ingredients or production can never be used for foods that contain or have been produced from genetically modified organisms.[38]

One of the key changes made by the 2007 Organic Foods Regulation to the labelling requirements is that from now on all such foods must also carry the stipulated EU logo.[39] This has been compulsory since July 2010.[40] National and private logos may also be used, such as that introduced by the Soil Association.[41] Member States are also obliged under the terms of the Regulation to designate competent authorities responsible for overseeing the application of the Regulation.[42] This, along with the other necessary national implementations, has been done in England through the introduction of the Organic Products Regulations 2009.

10.3.2 Organic Products Regulations 2009

Whilst most of the focus so far in this chapter on the legal requirements related to the production and marketing of organic food has been on EU Regulation 834/2007, two other regulations contribute to the overall regulatory package here. These are Commission Regulation 889/2008,[43] which sets out more detailed rules for the implementation of the Organic Foods Regulation 834/2007, and Commission Regulation 1235/2008,[44] which provides detail on the arrangements for the sale and marketing of organic products imported from third countries. The latter two regulations are the product of the recourse to the comitology procedure referred to throughout the Organic Foods Regulation. The organic

---

[36] Art 23.4.

[37] Art 23.2.

[38] Art 23.3.

[39] Art 24.

[40] Art 97, in conjunction with Art 58, of Commission Regulation (EC) No 889/2008 of 5 September 2008 laying down detailed rules for the implementation of Council Regulation (EC) No 834/2007 on organic production and labelling of organic products with regard to organic production, labelling and control [2008] OJ L 250/1.

[41] Art 25.

[42] Art 27.

[43] Note 40 above.

[44] Commission Regulation (EC) No 1235/2008 of 8 December 2008 laying down detailed rules for implementation of Council Regulation (EC) No 834/2007 as regards the arrangements for imports of organic products from third countries [2008] OJ L 334/25.

produce of third countries can only be imported into EU Member States like the UK if produced in compliance with the terms of the 2007 Regulation or verifiably equivalent standards.[45] Port authorities must be notified at local level about the importation of consignments of organic produce from third countries.[46] This, and all other detail on the implementation and application of the EU regulatory package under national law, is provided by the Organic Products Regulations 2009.[47]

Control bodies have a very important role to play in the regulation of the organic sector. After designation, these bodies are responsible for notifying DEFRA, the local authority, and the port authority where required, about any perceived irregularities or infringements that they identify.[48] Authorised officers can then take samples for analysis to ascertain whether any offence has been committed.[49] Anyone charged under the Regulations can argue that he took all reasonable precautions and exercised due diligence in his operations,[50] or that the fault really lay in the act or omission of another person.[51] Local authorities, or port health authorities in the case of imports from third countries, are responsible for enforcing the Regulations.[52] Their authorised officers have the power to enter premises,[53] inspect documents, seize records and check computers in carrying out this assigned task.[54] Any resulting prosecutions must be commenced within one year of the commission of the offence or six months of its discovery by the prosecutor, whichever is the earlier.[55]

10.4 Genetic Modification

It is arguable that the three most significant events which have impacted upon EU food law, and consequently English food law, are the BSE crisis, the horse-meat controversy (although the full effect of this cannot really be measured until several years after news of the debacle first broke in 2013) and the use of genetically modified organisms (GMOs). What gave rise, in particular, to debate over the inclusion of GMOs in the food chain was the initial poor regulation of this sector.

---

[45] Arts 32 and 33 of Reg 834/2007, n 16 above.
[46] Reg 6 of the Organic Products Regulations 2009, n 14 above.
[47] Note 14 above.
[48] Reg 16.
[49] Reg 17.
[50] Reg 21.
[51] Reg 20.
[52] Reg 22.
[53] Reg 23.
[54] Reg 24.
[55] Reg 29.

Although EU directives were introduced as early as 1990,[56] they failed to properly account for the types of concern that consumers might have over the use of genetic modification techniques in food production. There were no proper labelling requirements indicating where foods had been made with or from a GMO.

10.4.1 Issues with Early Genetically Modified Organisms Legislation

There are really two areas where the use of GMOs has given rise to controversy and created cause for concern. The first relates to environmental law, and any in-depth examination of this is really beyond the scope of this book. However, it should be noted that the growing of genetically modified crops in the UK has raised a number of environmental issues, in particular the potential for there to be cross-contamination between these and their conventional counterparts. This can affect both the farmer, who either wishes to produce entirely GMO-free crops, and the consumer, whose choice can become restricted where the complete absence of GM ingredients cannot be guaranteed. There is also the possibility that the growing of conventional crops could be impaired if contaminated by cross-pollination with genetically modified ones. Given the existence of wind, insects and birds, it is very difficult to control cross-contamination between farms. It has been pointed out that issues surrounding the 'co-existence' between genetically modified and conventional crops are now limited to economic ones, the most obvious of which would be the potential for the non-GM grower to have a marketing advantage amongst many consumers. This is due to the fact that other environmental and/or health issues should have now been adequately addressed by the authorisation processes that must be completed before any GMO is released into the environment or onto the consumer market.[57]

The second controversial aspect to the use of genetic modification in food production relates to the fact that this practice has often been concealed from the consumer. The issue really came to broader public attention when it was reported in the late 1990s that feeding laboratory rats a diet containing genetically modified potatoes could have toxic effects on their intestines.[58] From a consumer protection perspective, this served to highlight that the original GMO directives did not create adequate labelling requirements for genetically modified food.[59] Avoiding these products would therefore prove difficult for those consumers who

---

[56] Council Directive 1990/219/EEC of 23 April 1990 on the contained use of genetically modified micro-organisms [1990] OJ L 117/1 and Council Directive 1990/220 of 23 April 1990 on the deliberate release into the environment of genetically modified organisms [1990] OJ L 117/15.

[57] See M Lee, EU Environmental Law: Challenges, Change and Decision-Making' (Oxford, Hart, 2005), esp 255–259.

[58] S Ewen and A Pusztai, 'Effect of diets containing genetically modified potatoes expressing Galanthus nivalis lectin on rat small intestine' (1999) 354 *The Lancet* 1353.

[59] Council Directives 1990/219 and 1990/220, n 56 above.

wished to make such a choice. The Novel Foods Regulation had been introduced in 1997,[60] and this had created some additional and clearer labelling requirements for those foods which were different from their conventional counterparts. Novel foods were defined in this Regulation as being those 'which have not hitherto been used for human consumption to a significant degree'.[61] They specifically included 'foods and food ingredients containing or consisting of genetically modified organisms' and those 'produced from, but not containing, genetically modified organisms'.[62] The Regulation provided that

> the following additional specific labelling requirements shall apply to foodstuffs in order to ensure that the final consumer is informed of any characteristic or food property ... which renders a novel food or food ingredient no longer equivalent to an existing food or food ingredient [and it] shall be deemed to be no longer equivalent ... if scientific assessment ... can demonstrate that the characteristics assessed are different in comparison with a conventional food or food ingredient, having regard to the accepted limits of natural variations for such characteristics.[63]

Where a food or food ingredient was accordingly deemed to be 'novel', it would have to carry labelling disclosures which clearly indicated this. This was consequently the first meaningful labelling condition set for genetically modified foods. The Regulation specifically provided that novel foods must have

> labelling [which indicates] the characteristics or properties modified, together with the method by which that characteristic or property was obtained [including] the presence of an organism genetically modified by techniques of genetic modification, the non-exhaustive list of which is laid down in [the original Deliberate Release Directive, 1990/220].[64]

Some other additional requirements for genetically modified organisms were also set in the Novel Foods Regulation, such as those related to the granting of consent for deliberate release and the supply of technical dossiers.[65] However, these related to the treatment of the GMO before it would be placed on the market and did not affect the labelling requirements as such, other than to the extent that the food could not be sold to consumers in the first place without meeting these requirements as well. Similarly, some further environmental considerations were also addressed in the Regulation.[66]

While the Novel Foods Regulation did set out additional labelling requirements for some genetically modified foods, and included a safeguard clause which

---

[60] Regulation (EC) No 258/1997 of the European Parliament and of the Council of 27 January 1997 concerning novel foods and novel food ingredients [1997] OJ L 43/1.

[61] Art 1(2).

[62] Art 1(2)(a) and (b). These provisions were later deleted from the Novel Foods Regulation by Art 38 of Reg 1829/2003.

[63] Art 8.1.

[64] Art 8(1)(a) and (d).

[65] Art 9(1).

[66] Such as that set out in Art 9(2), which dealt with the evaluation of GMO release authorisation applications and the environmental safety requirements set out therein.

facilitated the suspension by Member States of trade in GMOs where they had sufficient grounds for believing that its continued use could endanger human health or the environment,[67] it did not provide regulators with a sufficiently stable legal basis for dealing with the controversies which broke in the late 1990s. It was not just the negative results of studies measuring the impact of GMO consumption on the intestines of lab rats that gave cause for concern, it was also the fact that the regulatory framework which had developed up to that point contained too many loopholes and shortcomings to ensure that all such foods should be clearly labelled to this effect. There was potential danger to human health from the consumption of foods made from or containing a GMO, but the presence of these substances would not necessarily have to be disclosed to the consumer.

Shortcomings with the GMO legislation became apparent when a regulation was introduced in 1997 to close a loophole that had allowed genetically modified soya and maize to avoid being subject to some labelling requirements.[68] Some EU Member States had taken their own action to counter this deficiency in the law, including setting labelling requirements for these products. The Commission took action in the form of this Regulation, relying on the principle that unilateral Member State action would have implications for the EU rules on the free movement of goods, consumer protection and fair competition. Despite this, another regulation had to be introduced in 1998, as the first attempt to close the loophole identified had failed to set full and adequate labelling requirements for genetically modified soya and maize.[69] This new regulation provided that

> where the food consists of more than one ingredient, the words 'produced from genetically modified soya' or 'produced from genetically modified maize', as appropriate, shall appear in the list of ingredients provided for by [the framework food labelling directive] in parentheses immediately after the name of the ingredient concerned [or] these words may appear in a prominently displayed footnote to the list of ingredients by means of an asterisk to the ingredient concerned.[70]

While this is quite explicit about the need to indicate the presence of a genetically modified ingredient or ingredients, the provision is unsatisfactory. The disclosure did not need to be any more prominent on the label than an inclusion in the ingredients list, or a footnote to this. It was only where the product was not required under the terms of the Framework Food Labelling Directive to provide any list of ingredients at all that that words 'produced from genetically modified soya' or 'produced from genetically modified maize' had to be printed clearly on

---

[67] Art 14.

[68] Commission Regulation (EC) No 1813/1997 of 19 September 1997 concerning the compulsory indication on the labelling of certain foodstuffs produced from genetically modified organisms of particulars other than those provided for in Directive 1979/112/EEC [1997] OJ L 257/7.

[69] Council Regulation (EC) No 1139/1998 of 26 May 1998 concerning the compulsory indication on the labelling of certain foodstuffs produced from genetically modified organisms of particulars other than those provided for in Directive 1979/112/EEC [1998] OJ L 159/4. This Regulation was later repealed by Art 37 of Reg 1829/2003, n 98 below.

[70] Art 2(3).

the labelling.[71] The original Framework Food Labelling Directive, which was in effect at the time of the introduction of this 1998 Regulation, provided that a list of ingredients was not required for fresh fruit and vegetables, carbonated water, vinegar, cheese, butter, fermented milk products or single-ingredient products.[72] Therefore, it was only this limited list of foodstuffs which had to carry the clearest indication that genetic modification had been used in production. For all other products, a note in the ingredients list would suffice.

It was not just weaknesses in the legislation that caused initial issues with the regulation of genetically modified organisms in the production of food. The Court of Justice specifically supported the inclusion in the regulatory framework of genetically modified substances as being amongst those ingredients that could be used in the production of organic food.[73] When the European Parliament sought the annulment of a Commission Regulation,[74] on the grounds that the Commission had exceeded its powers by permitting the use of genetically modified micro-organisms in organic production, the Court held that this inclusion was not contrary to the principles and obligations set out in the original Organic Production Regulation.[75]

It had noted that the legislation did permit the use of non-organic ingredients and substances in organic products, albeit within set limits. The Commission argued, and the Court accepted, that the legislative institutions had not sought a prohibition on the use of genetic modification in organic farming. Genetically modified organisms and micro-organisms had not therefore been excluded from the lists of permitted substances of non-organic agricultural origin that could be used in organic food. The law was later changed, in 1999, to reflect the inappropriateness of allowing the inclusion of genetically modified substances in organic food.[76] The Preamble to this amending regulation stated that '[g]enetically modified organisms and products derived therefrom are not compatible with the organic production method' and therefore they 'should not be used in products labelled as from organic production'.[77]

The use of genetic modification in food production received widespread negative publicity following a television programme broadcast in the UK that echoed

---

[71] Art 2(3)(b).

[72] Art 6 of Council Directive 1979/112 of 18 December 1978 on the approximation of the laws of the Member States relating to the labelling, presentation and advertising of foodstuffs to the ultimate consumer [1979] OJ L 33/1.

[73] Case C-156/1993 *European Parliament v Commission* [1995] ECR I-2019.

[74] Commission Regulation (EEC) No 207/1993 of 29 January 1993 defining the content of Annex VI to Regulation (EEC) No 2092/1991 on organic production of agricultural products and indications referring thereto on agricultural products and foodstuffs and laying down detailed rules for implementing the provisions of Art 5(4) thereto [1993] OJ L 25/5.

[75] Reg 2092/1991, n 15 above.

[76] Council Regulation (EC) No 1804/1999 of 19 July 1999 supplementing Regulation (EEC) No 2092/1991 on organic production of agricultural products and indications referring thereto on agricultural products and foodstuffs to include livestock production [1999] OJ L 222/1.

[77] Recital 10 of the Preamble to Reg 1804/1999, n 18 above.

the claims that were made in a research letter to the *Lancet*, published in 1999.[78] It was stated that the research had identified that diets containing genetically modified potatoes had negative effects on the gastrointestinal tracts of rats. Much media and public attention ensued. There was such a backlash against the use of genetic modification across the UK and the majority of EU Member States that an unofficial moratorium on the approval of new GMO uses was introduced. This, coupled with further action taken by individual States, ultimately led to the US, Canada and Argentina bringing complaints to the Dispute Settlement Body of the World Trade Organization.[79] There it was decided that the EU had applied a general de facto moratorium on the approval of biotech products between June 1999 and August 2003, something which the EU had previously denied.

The Dispute Panel further found that by applying this moratorium, the EU had taken action that was inconsistent with obligations set out in the Agreement on the Application of Sanitary and Phytosanitary Measures (SPS, discussed in chapter two), in particular Article 8 thereof which provides that WTO Members must observe the terms of the Agreement on the operation of approval procedures. More specifically, the actions of individual EU Member States, which had limited and restricted the use of GMOs, was found to be contrary to Articles 2.2 and 5.1 of the SPS Agreement as the safeguard measures adopted were not based on appropriate risk assessments. The Panel Reports were adopted in November 2006.

The first decade or so of GMO regulation in the EU was a troubled one. The absence of proper labelling requirements, shortcomings with aspects of the legislation, consumer unrest, scientific uncertainty, the taking of action by individual Member States that was contrary to EU legislative requirements, and the actions of the EU that were inconsistent with its WTO obligations all combined to lead to a clear recognition that new measures were required.

An overhaul of most of the existing legislative framework thus commenced with the introduction of a new GMO directive in 2001 and two new regulations—on genetically modified food and on traceability and labelling, in 2003. The Novel Foods Regulation of 1997 has mostly ceased to apply to aspects of genetic modification but, as will be discussed in more detail below, this Regulation is now also subject to review.[80]

---

[78] S Ewen and A Pusztai, 'Effect of diets containing genetically modified potatoes expressing Galanthus nivalis lectin on rat small intestine' (1999) 354 *The Lancet* 1353.

[79] DS 291, 292 and 293, *Measures Affecting the Approval and Marketing of Biotech Products.*

[80] Commission Proposal for a Regulation of the European Parliament and of the Council on Novel Foods, COM (2013) 894. As will also be discussed further below, this is not the first time that proposals have been brought forward on changes to the Novel Foods Regulation, a previous Commission document having been published in late 2007 (COM (2007) 872). However, progress on its introduction stalled during the legislative process, primarily due to disagreement on animal cloning. For more on the regulation of animal cloning in the UK see 'L Petetin, 'The revival of modern agricultural biotechnology by the UK Government: what role for animal cloning?' (2012) 7 *European Food and Feed Law Review* 296.

10.4.2 Defining Genetically Modified Organisms

The legal definition provided in the legislation for genetically modified organisms is that they are

> [any] organism, with the exception of human beings, in which the genetic material has been altered in a way that does not occur naturally by mating and/or natural recombination.[81]

Examples of genetically modified foods include golden rice. To produce this, three genes are inserted into the seed, two of which are taken from daffodils. The other is bacterial. These insertions increases the beta-carotene levels in the rice, which turns into vitamin A in the body. The hope is that the consumption of this rice can help to fight levels of blindness arising out of nutrient deficiency in developing countries. Another example of a GM food would be sweetcorn (Bt-corn) that has been modified to produce its own poison (Bacillus thuringiensis), which can then kill insects. This would reduce the need for insecticide use. However, it could also result in the killing of other insects, such as butterflies, who have a vital role to play in the ecosystem. It would appear that there are both advantages and disadvantages to genetically modifying foods. Regardless of this, it is crucial that the sector is regulated in a manner that can ensure, as far as possible, public confidence in the use of genetic modification techniques in food production. As outlined above, early regulation failed to do this. The revised legislative package should be better equipped to deal with the controversial elements of GMO should the need arise. The first part of this package is the EU Deliberate Release Directive. This has been transposed into English law by the 2002 Regulations.

10.4.3 Genetically Modified Organisms (Deliberate Release) Regulations 2002

The GMO Regulations 2002 make a number of amendments to the Environmental Protection Act 1990.[82] This includes the insertion of the definition of a GMO,[83] as taken from the EU Deliberate Release Directive. It also sets out that there are some circumstances where the use of prescribed techniques that alter genes or genetic material may fall outside the scope of the legislation.[84] These techniques are not

---

[81] Art 2(2) of Directive 2001/18 on the deliberate release of genetically modified organisms [2001] OJ L 106/1. Transposed into English law by the Genetically Modified Organisms (Deliberate Release) Regulations 2002, SI No 2443/2002.

[82] In particular, s 106.

[83] Reg 3(4). The GMO Regulations 2002, n 81 above, more specifically provide that s 106(4)(a) of the Environmental Protection Act 1990 should now state that '[g]enes or other genetic material in an organism are "artificially modified" ... if they are altered otherwise than by a process which occurs naturally in mating or natural recombination'.

[84] By the insertion of a new s 106(4)(b) into the Environmental Protection Act 1990.

deemed to be 'artificial modification'. They include in vitro fertilisation, natural processes such as conjugation, transduction and transformation and polyploidy induction, used to make most wheat for bread.[85]

Applications to market those substances which have been produced by the forms of genetic modification that are covered by the Environmental Protection Act 1990 are made under section 111. As would be expected, these applications must include the data and results from any previous release of the organisms.[86] They should also include environmental risk assessments, conditions for marketing such as those of handling and use, post-release monitoring plans and labelling and packaging proposals.[87] All applications are made to the Secretary of State for the Environment, Food and Rural Affairs.

DEFRA must comply with the EU procedures set out in the Deliberate Release Directive after the application has been made. These include forwarding a summary version of the application to the European Commission and the competent authorities in all other Member States.[88] The application is then examined for compliance with the requirements set out in the Environmental Protection Act and in the GMO Regulations. DEFRA then has 90 days either to accept or reject the application for authorisation to deliberately release the GMO.[89] Details of this assessment should then be sent on to the European Commission. Consent for deliberate release can only be granted by DEFRA where no legitimate objection to this has been raised by either the European Commission or by another EU Member State.[90] Applications must also be made to DEFRA for the renewal of any previously approved authorisation for deliberate release of a GMO,[91] as initial permission can only be granted for a maximum of 10 years.[92] Any consent, or renewal, must also specify to the recipient details about the period of validity of this consent, marketing conditions including any specific conditions of use, post-approval monitoring plans and labelling requirements.[93] Each approved GMO must also be assigned a unique identifier, designed to facilitate this monitoring and traceability.[94]

There are, of course, safeguard clauses contained within both the EU Deliberate Release Directive and the domestic GMO Regulations 2002. Regulation 31 provides that the safeguard procedures are triggered when the relevant competent authority receives any new information about the risk, or potential risk, attached to the continued use of an approved GMO. When this happens, there is an obligation to provide the Commission with an assessment report which indicates

---

[85] Reg 5(2) of the GMO Regulations 2002, n 81 above.
[86] ibid, reg 16(2)(b).
[87] Reg 16(2)(c)–(i).
[88] In the format established by Art 13(2)(h) of the Deliberate Release Directive, n 81 above.
[89] Reg 23 of the GMO Regulations 2002.
[90] Reg 24.
[91] Reg 25.
[92] Reg 24(5).
[93] Reg 28(b)–(f).
[94] Reg 28(a).

whether the consent to release the GMO, or any of the conditions attached to the original authorisation, needs to be revoked or modified in any way. When the concern relates to a human health protection issue, this assessment report should not be forwarded to the Commission without the agreement of the Health and Safety Executive. The competent authorities of the other EU Member States, which must also have been informed about any new information about the safety or otherwise of the continued use of a GMO, can raise an objection to any of the proposals put forward by DEFRA in the assessment report. The EU Commission then ultimately determines whether a consent to market a GMO should be revoked or modified.[95] A prohibition notice may be served, following a joint decision of DEFRA and the Food Standards Agency, where a severe risk has been identified after an examination of new or additional information, or a reassessment of existing studies on the GMO concerned.[96] This form of action is, however, also subject to the scrutiny of the EU Commission, which makes any ultimate decision on the validity or otherwise of any prohibition notice made at national level.[97]

10.4.4 European Union Genetically Modified Organisms Regulations

The regulatory regime for genetically modified foods was mostly completed by the introduction of two EU regulations in 2003. Taken together, the Deliberate Release Directive—as transposed into domestic law by the GMO Regulations 2002, the EU Regulation on Genetically Modified Food and Feed,[98] and the GMO Traceability and Labelling Regulation,[99] the latter two both being directly applicable in national law, form the framework for GMO regulation in the UK. Additional implementing measures for both the GM Food and Feed Regulation and the GM Traceability and Labelling Regulation are provided for at national level by the Genetically Modified Food (England) Regulations 2004,[100] the Genetically Modified Animal Feed (England) Regulations 2004,[101]

---

[95] Reg 31(6).

[96] Reg 32.

[97] Reg 32(4).

[98] Reg (EC) No 1829/2003 of the European Parliament and of the Council of 22 September 2003 on genetically modified food and feed [2003] OJ L 268/1.

[99] Reg (EC) No 1830/2003 of the European Parliament and of the Council of 22 September 2003 concerning the traceability and labelling of genetically modified organisms and the traceability of food and feed products produced from genetically modified organisms and amending Directive 2001/18/EC [2003] OJ L 268/24. For further discussion on the introduction of, and implications of, this regulation see L Andersen, 'The EU rules on labelling of genetically modified foods: mission accomplished?' (2010) 5 *European Food and Feed Law Review* 136; and C MacMaoláin, 'The new genetically modified food labelling requirements: finally a lasting solution?' (2003) 28 *European Law Review* 865.

[100] SI No 2335/2004.

[101] SI No 2334/2004.

and the Genetically Modified Organisms (Traceability and Labelling) (England) Regulations 2004 respectively.[102]

Genetically Modified Food and Feed

The EU GM Food and Feed Regulation sets out that the key aim of the legislative framework provided must be to ensure, as far as possible, that genetic modification does not have adverse effects on human health, animals or the environment.[103] It must also be designed to ensure that consumers are not misled about the composition of foodstuffs, or the techniques used in their production. Article 4 of the Regulation also provides that genetically modified foods cannot

> differ from the food which it is intended to replace to such an extent that its normal consumption would be nutritionally disadvantageous for the consumer.

The primary way of satisfying these aims is the establishment of a rigorous authorisation procedure for all GMOs.[104] Under the terms of the Regulation, applications for authorisation are first sent to the competent authority in a Member State.[105] Regulation 3 of the GM Food (England) Regulations 2004 provides that the competent authority for this purpose is the Food Standards Agency. It is then the FSA's responsibility to send the application for authorisation on to the European Food Safety Authority, without delay.[106]

All applications for GM food use have to include a range of details on the producer, the product and its use. This includes the name and address of the applicant; the name of the food, including the transformation event used; information needed to comply with the terms of the Cartagena Protocol on Biosafety;[107] detailed descriptions of methods used in production; copies of studies, including independent and peer-reviewed studies where these exist, which demonstrate that the food is safe; data which demonstrate that the food is not significantly different from its conventional counterpart; proposed labelling details; samples of the food; and plans for post-release monitoring.[108] Full technical dossiers, in accordance with the requirements set out in the Deliberate Release Directive, should also be provided for foods containing or consisting of GMOs.[109]

After the application for authorisation has been made to the Food Standards Agency, it then turns to the European Food Safety Authority to make its assessment

---

[102] SI No 2412/2004.
[103] Art 4(1).
[104] Art 4(2).
[105] Art 5.
[106] Art 5(2)(a)(ii) of the EU GM Food and Feed Regulation, n 98 above.
[107] The Cartagena Protocol on Biosafety, adopted in January 2000, is an international agreement, signed up to by 167 states, which is designed to ensure the safe handling, transport and use of modified organisms. It entered into force in September 2003. It contains 40 articles and 3 annexes on a range of issues related to the minimisation of risks related to GMOs. Text of the Protocol is available at: bch. cbd.int/protocol/text.
[108] Art 5(3).
[109] Art 5(5).

on use of the GMO.[110] Normally, EFSA should issue an opinion on the application within six months. It can ask the applicant for additional information to help it in forming its opinion. The General Food Law Regulation also obliges EFSA to make any opinion on the use of a GMO public.[111] The public can then, in turn, make comments to the Commission on the EFSA opinion. The EFSA opinion is not binding on the Commission. EFSA delivers an opinion only. The Commission makes the decision on authorisation.[112] The GM Food and Feed Regulation just prescribes that any decision taken in respect of the application will take 'into account the opinion of the Authority'.[113] The Commission makes its decision following consultation with its own Standing Committee on the Food Chain and Animal Health. This Committee, as discussed in chapter two, was also established by the General Food Law Regulation. The Commission must explain to the Committee the reasons underlying any differences that there might be between its decision and the preceding EFSA opinion. Comitology is then employed to arrive at a final decision on authorisation.[114] All of this should happen within time limits stipulated in the Regulation.

Authorisations can be modified, suspended or revoked. EFSA is specifically entitled to issue an opinion on whether one of these three courses of action should be taken. It can do this either on its own initiative, or at the request of a Member State or the Commission.[115] Once arrived at, the EFSA opinion should then be transmitted to the Commission, the authorisation holder and the Member States. The opinion should also be made public, subject to the deletion of any information that has been identified as confidential. The public has the right to comment on the EFSA opinion to the Commission. It is up to the Commission then to examine the EFSA position and comments from the public before deciding whether the authorisation should be modified, suspended or revoked. Applications for the renewal of previously granted authorisations should be made directly to the Commission at least one year before the expiry of the original granting of consent.[116] Renewals can be for a maximum of 10 years also.

---

[110] Art 6. This has been described as being '[o]ne of the most controversial areas of EFSA's activities' in S Poli, 'Scientific Advice in the GMO area' in A Alemanno and S Gabbi (eds), *Foundations of EU Food Law and Policy* (Farnham, Ashgate, 2013).

[111] Art 38(1) of Regulation (EC) No 178/2002 of the European Parliament and of the Council of 28 January 2002 laying down the general principles and requirements of food law, establishing the European Food Safety Authority and laying down procedures in matters of food safety [2002] OJ L 31/1.

[112] Art 7.

[113] Art 7(1) thereof.

[114] As set out in Arts 7(3) and 35(2) of the GM Food and Feed Regulation 2003, n 98 above, in conjunction with Council Decision 1999/468/EC, as amended by Council Decision 2006/512/EC, [2006] OJ L 200/11. This procedure has since been altered by the introduction of Regulation (EU) No 182/2011 of the European Parliament and of the Council of 16 February 2011 laying down the rules and general principles concerning mechanisms for control by Member States of the Commission's exercise of implementing powers [2011] OJ L 55/13. The revised comitology procedures are discussed in more detail in ch 2.

[115] Art 10 of Reg 1829/2003, n 98 above.

[116] Art 11.

Labelling requirements for foods containing or consisting of GMOs are set out in each of the four pieces of EU legislation referred to above, which taken together form the regulatory framework for genetically modified products. As noted above, there are stipulations on labelling contained in both the Deliberate Release Directive and the Novel Foods Regulation. The GM Food and Feed Regulation also provides that

> [w]ithout prejudice to the other requirements of [Union] law concerning the labelling of foodstuffs, foods falling within the scope of this [legislation] shall be subject to the following specific labelling requirements: (a) where the food consists of more than one ingredient, the words 'genetically modified' or 'produced from genetically modified (name of the ingredient)' shall appear in the list of ingredients provided for in [the framework food labelling directive] in parentheses immediately following the ingredient concerned.[117]

This is the most common type of labelling disclosure that is required for genetically modified food.

Where a GM ingredient has been used in production, this must be stated in the ingredients list. The main exception to this relates to those products which are not obliged to produce a list of ingredients under the terms of the Framework Food Labelling Directive.[118] These products must have a clear presentation on the label informing the consumer that they have been 'genetically modified' or 'contains (name of ingredient) produced from genetically modified (name of organism)'.[119] Foods which contain trace amounts of GMOs are not subject to these additional labelling requirements. The Regulation states that there does not need to be disclosure about the presence of a GMO for

> foods containing material which contains, consists of or is produced from GMOs in a proportion no higher than 0.9% of the food ingredients … provided that this presence is adventitious or technically unavoidable.[120]

In order to be able to avail of this provision for the presence of very low levels of GMOs in foodstuffs, operators must provide evidence that they have taken appropriate measures to prevent the inclusion of genetically modified material in the finished product.[121] The 0.9 per cent maximum threshold can also be reduced by comitology.[122] While the GM Food and Feed Regulation does set out that there should be clear labelling indicating the presence of GMOs where appropriate, it goes further than this for those products which are deemed to be different from

---

[117] Art 13(1)(a).

[118] As set out in Art 6 of Directive 2000/13/EC of the European parliament and of the Council of 20 March 2000 on the approximation of the laws of the Member States relating to the labelling, presentation and advertising of foodstuffs [2000] OJ L 109/29. This provision is also contained in Art 19 of the Food Information Regulation 1169/2011 [2011] OJ L 304/18, effective from December 2014.

[119] Art 13(1)(c) of Reg 1829/2003, n 98 above.

[120] Art 12(2).

[121] Art 12(3).

[122] Art 12(4).

their conventional counterparts. There has to be a statement on the labelling where food produced from or containing a GMO varies from the original variety in relation to composition, nutritional value, usual use, health implications and/or where it may give rise to religious or ethical concerns.[123] There should be a statement like this on the label detailing the characteristics of the food even where no conventional counterpart exists.[124]

Similar requirements are set out in the Regulation for animal feed. There are general obligations to ensure, for example, that GM feed does not have adverse effects on humans, animals or the environment.[125] It should also be relatively similar to the feed that it is designed to replace, and its consumption should not therefore be nutritionally disadvantageous for animals or humans in any way. GM feed must first be authorised through the national competent authority,[126] then sent on to EFSA for its opinion[127] before responsibility passes over to the Commission, which, in consultation with the Standing Committee on the Food Chain and Animal Health, makes a final decision on authorisation.[128] As is the case for human food, any authorisation granted can be modified, suspended or revoked at any time.[129] The Commission can also consult with the European Group on Ethics in Science and New Technologies to obtain its opinion on any matter related to the genetic modification of food or feed.[130] Finally, emergency measures can be adopted where there is good reason to suspect that an authorised product constitutes a serious risk to humans, animals or the environment.[131] This should be done in accordance with the procedures set down in the General Food Law Regulation.[132]

Genetically Modified Food Labelling and Traceability

The GM Traceability and Labelling Regulation makes amendments to the Deliberate Release Directive, and consequently the Genetically Modified Organisms (Deliberate Release) Regulations 2002 as well. The 2003 EU Regulation is also designed to provide a framework for the traceability of products which consist of or contain GMOs in order to achieve more accurate labelling and better monitoring of the effects of these products on the environment and human health.[133] Most importantly, a proper system of traceability also assists in the

[123] Art 13(2).
[124] Art 13(3).
[125] Art 16(1).
[126] The Genetically Modified Animal Feed (England) Regulations 2004, n 101 above, provide in reg 3 that the national competent authority for these purposes is the Food Standards Agency.
[127] Art 17.
[128] Art 19.
[129] Art 22.
[130] Art 33.
[131] Art 34.
[132] Arts 53 and 54 of Reg 178/2002, n 111 above. The emergency procedures themselves have been discussed in more detail in ch 5.
[133] Art 1 of Reg 1830/2003, n 99 above.

taking of appropriate risk management measures should any safety concerns arise. The Regulation applies to all genetically modified foods as well as feed produced from GMOs.[134]

'Traceability' is defined in the Regulation as 'the ability to trace [GMOs] at all stages of their placing on the market through the production and distribution chains'.[135] This happens in the first instance through obliging all operators to ensure that full information on the presence of a GMO is transmitted to others receiving raw materials or product from them.[136] Each GMO is also to be assigned a unique identifier code, and details of this should be passed on though all stages of production and marketing as well.[137] The products should also be clearly labelled, with an indication on pre-packaged products that they contain genetically modified organisms.[138] This is subject to the exception, discussed above, for 'adventitious or technically unavoidable' trace amounts.[139] Under the Genetically Modified Organisms (Traceability and Labelling) (England) Regulations 2004, it is up to local authorities to ensure the enforcement of the provisions of the EU Regulation.[140] Inspectors can also be appointed by DEFRA where this is deemed to be necessary.[141] These inspectors have a range of powers that they can exercise in carrying out their duties, including the right to enter premises, carry out sampling and tests, seize equipment, retain records and question operators.[142] They can also serve notice on operators to desist from placing products on the market that have not been properly labelled in accordance with the terms of Regulation 1830/2003. This can include forcing the operator to withdraw products already on the market.[143]

There are a range of offences that can be committed under the terms of the Genetically Modified Organisms (Traceability and Labelling) (England) Regulations 2004. These include failing to comply with the relevant provisions of EU law, obstructing inspectors in the exercise of the powers conferred upon them, failure to comply with the terms of a notice served on any labelling matter or to knowingly furnishing false information to an inspector or under any of the EU requirements.[144] Regulation 1830/2003 provides that Member States must lay down rules on penalties applicable to infringements of the Regulation and they are to 'take all measures necessary to ensure that they are implemented.[145] It also states that the penalties provided must be effective, proportionate and

---

[134] Art 2.
[135] Art 3(3).
[136] Art 4(1) and Art 5.
[137] Art 4(1) and Art 8.
[138] Art 4(6).
[139] Art 4(7) and 4(8).
[140] SI No 2412/2004; reg 3.
[141] Regs 3 and 4.
[142] Reg 5.
[143] Reg 7.
[144] Reg 8.
[145] Art 11 of Reg 1830/2003, n 99 above.

dissuasive.[146] Those found guilty of any of these offences are liable to a fine of up to level 5 on the standard scale or imprisonment of three months, or both.[147]

Novel Foods Proposals, Cloning and Nanotechnology

It has been recognised for some time that the original Novel Foods Regulation is in need of updating.[148] Both the White Paper on Food Safety[149] and the initial proposal for new novel foods legislation identified that there was a broad consensus on the need for change.[150] One of the key changes already made to the Novel Foods Regulation was the removal of foods and ingredients containing or consisting of GMOs, and food and ingredients produced from but not containing GMOs, from the scope of its provisions.[151] The Preamble to the GM Food and Feed Regulation states that this was done 'to ensure clarity, transparency and a harmonised framework for authorisation of genetically modified food'.[152] The first proposal to have a significant overhaul of the Novel Foods Regulation, published in January 2008, was later abandoned. The Regulation was to be introduced via the ordinary legislative procedure, and much of the debate on it during this process surrounded the provisions on nanotechnology, animal cloning and risk analysis. The discussions reached an impasse, however, on the animal cloning issues in particular. Having reached the conciliation stage of the legislative process, the Committee failed to reach any agreement by its final meeting on the matter in March 2011. As a result, the second proposal for a new regulation on novel foods does not deal with the cloning issue. This is to be dealt with in a separate proposal.

More recent legislative developments at EU level have tended to be designed in a manner that corresponds with the broader aims of policy direction documentation, such as the Strategy for Better Regulation.[153] This proposal more specifically aims to pursue the objectives of the Communication on Smart Regulation in the EU[154] and the Europe 2020 Strategy.[155] The hope is that this will help to

---

[146] Member States are also obliged, under the terms of Art 11 of the Regulation, to notify the Commission about which penalties it imposes for breaches of the EU requirements.

[147] Reg 11.

[148] See also P Coppens, 'The revision of the novel foods regulation' (2013) 8 *European Food and Feed Law Review* 238 and C Jones, 'The novel food regulation: revision required?' (2012) 7 *European Food and Feed Law Review* 81.

[149] White Paper on Food Safety, COM (1999) 719.

[150] The Explanatory Memorandum to the Proposal for a Regulation of the European Parliament and of the Council on novel foods, COM (2007) 872, notes how a stakeholder consultation undertaken following a Commission discussion paper in 2002 highlighted the need to develop and update Reg 258/1997.

[151] Art 38(1) of Reg 1829/2003, n 98 above, deletes Art 1(2)(a) and (b) from Reg 258/1997.

[152] Recital 6 thereof.

[153] As now set out in the Communication from the Commission to the European Parliament, the Council, the European Economic and Social Committee and the Committee of the Regions on Regulatory Fitness, COM (2012) 746.

[154] COM (2010) 543.

[155] COM (2010) 2020.

simplify and streamline the regulatory process for novel foods, at a time when there is increased use, and the development of new technologies in production. Overall, new regulations, such as this, are being designed in a manner that should reduce regulatory burdens. This will consequently increase the competitiveness of the European food industry. Also, it will ensure the maintenance of food safety standards and public health protection, as well as providing that the EU, and the Member States, comply with their international obligations. As was discussed above, this has not always been the case when regulating for new technological processes being used in the food sector, most significantly when poor regulation led to findings of non-compliance with WTO obligations in relation to the application of the legislation on GMOs.

The Proposal provides for the simplification of the legislation and related administrative burdens for both public authorities and private parties by creating only one centralised procedure for the assessment and authorisation of novel foods. Applications would be made directly to the European Commission, who may then request a scientific opinion on the risk assessment from EFSA. The Commission will also continue to be assisted in its decision making by the Standing Committee on the Food Chain and Animal Health. If accepted, this should result in the removal of some national administrative procedures and duplication. The resulting authorisation procedure should also become more streamlined. This in turn would reduce the administrative burden and related costs for private parties. It should also be a quicker process. The need to be granted authorisations for individual foods is to be replaced with generic authorisations for a food type. This should significantly reduce the volume, and consequent costs, of applications. Authorisation should be automatically granted if it can be shown that there is no danger to human health or potential to deceive the consumer and that the 'novel' food is substantially equivalent to its conventional counterpart. It is also made very clear in this proposal that genetically modified food should no longer be subject to any of the novel foods legislation as they are now adequately accounted for elsewhere, most significantly in the provisions of the GM Food and Feed Regulation 1829/2003.

Finally, 'novel food' is defined in the Proposal as 'all food that was not used for human consumption to a significant degree ... before 15 May 1997'. This includes:

> food to which a new production process not used for food production ... is applied, where the production process gives rise to significant changes in the composition or structure of the food which affect its nutritional value, the way it is metabolised or the level of undesirable substances; food containing or consisting of engineered nanomaterials as defined in [the Food Information Regulation]; vitamins, minerals and other substances ... where a new production process has been applied [or] such substances contain or consist of engineered nanomaterials [or] food [previously] used exclusively in food supplements [which are now] to be used in foods other than food supplements.

This will, if accepted, expand the scope of the Novel Foods Regulation to account for new technologies, such as nanotechnology, and new uses for some edible substances, such as fortification materials. It will, quite deliberately, now exclude genetically modified foods and those which may be produced from cloned animals.

10.5 Protecting the Welfare of Food-producing Animals

English law and standards on the protection of farm animals are based on a range of domestic and EU policy documents, codes of practice and legislation. Minimum welfare requirements have traditionally been wide and varied across EU Member States. Many of the EU provisions are now set at a level which is either below that often applied in the UK, or which have been introduced at a time when British farmers were already meeting the requirements set by Union directives and regulations. But this has not always been the case.

There are two main types of legislation applicable to the welfare of food-producing animals. The first are the general requirements. These apply horizontally across all types of animals and methods or stages of production, including transportation and slaughter. The second type, which often link into the former, are animal-specific. We here focus on three food-producing animals: poultry, pigs and cattle, to provide examples of the level and type of requirement that has been set. All of these animal-specific requirements come directly from EU directives which have been transposed into English law.

10.5.1 European Union Animal Welfare Strategy

The general principles of EU policy on the protection of food-producing animals is set out in the Strategy for the Protection and Welfare of Animals 2012–2015.[156] This document, which followed on from the Community Action Plan on the Protection and Welfare of Animals 2006–2010,[157] is designed to set out a range of ways of both introducing and applying mechanisms to enforce the protection of the billions of animals which are kept for economic purposes in the EU. The Animal Welfare Strategy estimates that livestock farming is worth around €150 billion annually to the economies of the Member States. Approximately €16 billion (£12.5 billion) worth of this is attributable to the industry in Britain.[158]

---

[156] Communication from the Commission to the European Parliament, the Council and the European Economic and Social Committee on the European Union Strategy for the Protection and Welfare of Animals 2012–2015, COM (2012) 6.

[157] Communication from the Commission to the European Parliament and the Council on a Community Action Plan on the protection and Welfare of Animals 2006–2010, COM (2006) 13.

It is recognised in the Strategy Communication that although the animal welfare agenda has been advanced through the introduction of specific pieces of legislation, such as those which are discussed in more detail below, there are still areas which are not covered by any legislative requirements. The more general welfare requirements, which are also discussed below, can also be difficult to apply in some sectors. It is therefore proposed that a process of simplification of these broad stipulations could be undertaken to address common issues related to the welfare of animals. An evaluation of EU animal welfare policy has previously concluded that the imposition of standards has led to additional costs of around 2 per cent on the overall value of the livestock sector. It also found that at this level, this does not threaten economic sustainability in any way. The additional costs should also be lower in those States where higher welfare standards were already being applied. There is also recognition in the Strategy document that while the costs of improved welfare have tended to be low, the economic value added of this policy should be continually monitored to ensure that the competitiveness of the agricultural sector is maintained.

The Strategy for the Protection of the Welfare of Animals has recognised four key issues that affect the well-being of animals across the EU, and these will be used as the basis for any changes that are to be made to related legislation in the coming years. The first is that there remains a lack of enforcement by Member States across a number of areas. Second, studies show that consumer interest in welfare issues is significant, if not that high, but they also demonstrate that it is only one of a range of factors which affects consumer choice.[159] Poor understanding about production methods and the impact of these on animals also leads to purchasing decisions that do not necessarily relate to levels of concern about welfare. The Report suggested that the use of 'reserved terms' was a good way of informing purchasers and consumers about product characteristics and farming methods. Perhaps the best example of 'reserved terms' is the way in which they have been used in the marketing standards for eggs. Legislation has prescribed that eggs are labelled according to production method, be they 'eggs from caged hens' (since banned), 'barn eggs', 'free-range eggs' or, those which employ the highest welfare standards, 'organic eggs'.[160]

The Report notes that since this labelling system was introduced, the quantity of non-caged egg production increased significantly in nearly all EU Member

[158] DEFRA, 'Agriculture in the United Kingdom 2013', available at: www.gov.uk. This report fulfils the requirement set under the Agriculture Act 1993 for the publication of an annual report on the sector.

[159] A report was presented by the European Commission in 2009 entitled 'Options for animal welfare labelling and the establishment of a European Network of Reference Centres for the protection and welfare of animals', COM (2009) 584; available at: ec.europa.eu/food/animal/welfare. The surveys undertaken indicated that animal welfare was a significant issue for 64% of consumers across the EU.

[160] As set out in the Egg (Marketing Standards) Regulations 1995, SI No 1544/1995.

States. Similar 'reserved terms' are already also employed in the marketing of poultry. This is discussed in more detail below. The Report also stated that 'in addition to price, consumers' purchasing decisions are influenced by a number of "interpersonal" (culture, societal norms, social status, group and family influences) and "intrapersonal" (involvement, emotions, motives, attitudes, norms, personality) determinants'. While it was accepted that, in principle, more information provided by labels should facilitate consumers in making more informed choices, it was also recognised that they would need to have reliable knowledge about the value added of animal welfare-friendly products if expected to pay a higher price for these.

Labelling would therefore only have the desired effect if consumers are: (i) adequately informed on the meaning of the label; (ii) the information provided is readily understandable; and (iii) consumers, or their relevant sub-groups, are interested in having this information made available to them before making their purchasing decisions. It would not, therefore, be just about welfare labelling. Any efforts to encourage more ethical purchasing would also require proper information and education campaigns.

The results presented in the Report also show that animal welfare labelling could itself be used to raise consumer awareness and 'accelerate market penetration of animal welfare-friendly products that go beyond the minimum standards foreseen in EU legislation'. As a consequence, the development of new animal welfare practices would be more motivated by market demand. Additional specific communication and education initiatives could also contribute to further raising awareness amongst consumers on welfare issues, provided this is based on reputable scientific data.

A lack of understanding about the detriment that some production systems can have on animal welfare can itself be an impediment to calls for change, or the increased employment of more welfare-friendly practices. Any such information and/or education campaigns could also be used to address aspects of the third of the four key issues raised in the Strategy for the Protection of the Welfare of Animals. This is that many of the stakeholders in the sector lack sufficient knowledge about animal welfare. In particular, according to the Report, a common lack of awareness about alternative practices in food-production systems often leads to resistance to changes that could be brought in to improve welfare standards. Finally, it was recognised in the Report that there is a real need to develop clearer principles on animal welfare.

The framework directive on the protection of farm animals,[161] now transposed into English law by the Welfare of Farmed Animals (England) Regulations 2007,[162] was identified as containing provisions that are too general to have meaningful practical effects. An example was given of the provision contained in the

---

[161] Council Directive 1998/58/EC of 20 July 1998 concerning the protection of animals kept for farming purposes [1998] OJ L 221/23.
[162] SI No 2078/2007.

Annex to the directive which states that '[a]ll animals must have access to feed at intervals appropriate to their physiological needs'.

The Strategy is to be based on two complementary approaches. The first is to move away from the use of specific legislation designed to tackle specific problems. Instead, there should be a set of general principles established in a consolidated and revised EU legislative framework. This would also, it is hoped, facilitate better enforcement of animal welfare provisions. The second is the reinforcement or better use of actions which the Commission was already performing. Therefore, in addition to the envisaged simplified legislative framework, the Commission is also to develop tools to strengthen Member States' compliance; increase its support for more international co-operation in the field; provide consumers and the public with more appropriate information; optimise synergistic effects from the current Common Agricultural Policy; and carry out investigations into the welfare of farmed fish. However, all of this is to be done with regard for any impact that measures could have on fundamental rights, including those contained in Article 10 of the Charter of Fundamental Rights, Article 9 of the European Convention on Human Rights and Article 13 of the Human Rights Act 1998 on freedom of religion.

Taking all of this into consideration, it should also be noted at this stage that the issues related to the welfare of food-producing animals have taken on increased significance at EU level since relevant insertions on the matter were introduced into the Treaty on the Functioning of the European Union (TFEU), which came into effect in December 2009. Most significantly, Article 13 TFEU states that

> [i]n formulating and implementing the Union's agriculture, fisheries, transport, internal market, research and technological development and space policies, the Union and the Member States, since animals are sentient beings, pay full regard to the welfare requirements of animals, while respecting the legislative or administrative provisions and customs of the Member States relating in particular to religious rites, cultural traditions and regional heritage.

This is contained in Title II of the TFEU, which lists the key principles that should underpin Union activities, including policy, decision-making and legislative initiatives. Its inclusion here puts the protection of animal interests on a par with other such principles, including the promotion of gender equality, social protection, human health, eliminating discrimination, sustainable development, the protection of consumers and the protection of personal data.

New Legislative Initiatives on Animal Health

The Strategy for the Protection and Welfare of Animals suggests a number of ways in which EU law could be modified and reorganised in a manner that would offer better protection, increase consumer and other stakeholder awareness, and maximise compliance within the Member States. Coupled with other, more general, strategies developed by the EU,[163] a proposal for a new regulation on animal health was developed in 2013.[164] The Explanatory Memorandum to this proposal noted that there were almost 50 basic directives and regulations and around 400 pieces of secondary legislation within the EU animal health framework. Some of these dated back to 1964. A number of problems were identified. These included the overly complex existing animal health policy, a lack of overall strategy, an insufficient focus on disease prevention and issues related to intra-Union trade in live animals. This proposed Animal Health Law is designed to address these concerns by providing a legal framework for the priority issues identified in the Animal Health Strategy, published in 2007.[165] These issues included ensuring a high level of public health and food safety protection by minimising the incidence of biological and chemical risks to humans; promoting animal health by preventing or reducing the incidence of animal diseases; improving economic growth and competitiveness by the promotion of the free movement of goods and the proportionate movement of animals; and promoting farming practices and animal welfare standards which prevent animal health related threats and minimise environmental impacts in support of the EU Sustainable Development Strategy.[166] All of this is to be achieved by revising the legal framework in a manner which establishes

> a single, simplified, transparent and clear regulatory framework that sets out systemati-
> cally the objectives, scope and principles of regulatory intervention; based on good gov-
> ernance and compliant with international (eg the World Organisation for Animal Health
> (OIE)) standards; focusing on long-term preventative measures and working together
> with all relevant stakeholders.

With a clear link to the way in which previous animal health issues have been mismanaged in the past, most notably in the case of BSE, the proposal includes as specific objectives of this new Animal Health Law a commitment:

> [T]o introduce overarching general principles allowing a simplified legal framework in
> order to be prepared for the new challenges, ie to enable quick reaction in case of emerg-
> ing diseases; whilst ensuring the same quality of reaction as provided for in current
> legislation [and] to reduce the impact of animal diseases on animal and public health,
> animal welfare, economy and society as far as possible by enhancing disease awareness,
> preparedness, surveillance and emergency response systems at national and EU level.

---

[163] Such as the Communication from the Commission to the European Parliament, the Council, the European Economic and Social Committee and the Committee of the Regions on 'Smart Regulation in the European Union', COM (2010) 543; and the Communication from the Commission, 'Europe 2020: A strategy for smart, sustainable and inclusive growth', COM (2010) 2020.

[164] Proposal for a Regulation of the European Parliament and of the Council on Animal Health, COM (2013) 260.

[165] Communication from the Commission to the Council, the European Parliament, the European Economic and Social Committee and the Committee of the Regions on 'A new animal health strategy for the European Union (2007–2013) where prevention is better than cure', COM (2007) 539.

[166] As revised by the Council of the European Union, 'Review of the EU Sustainable Development Strategy', 15–16 June 2006.

To address all of this, the Proposal is divided into a number of parts which deal with, in particular, the control of, and reactions to, the incidence of animal disease.

The first part, which sets out the general rules of the Animal Health Law, provides for the prioritisation and listing of diseases which are the most likely to have a significant impact. It also sets out responsibilities for the key actors in the sector, including business operators and veterinarians.

The second part deals with notification, surveillance and the development of eradication programmes. It clarifies the roles for the business operators, national competent authorities and others in this regard.

The third part calls upon Member States to draw up contingency plans for dealing with certain diseases and to practise their implementation. Rules on control measures that are to be taken where the outbreak of a disease is suspected or confirmed are also laid down. These make little change to the already existing system, which is deemed to work well.

The fourth part sets out the requirements concerning traceability and the movement of animals. This includes introducing the potential for more animals to be registered and traced by electronic means, which it is hoped will promote better regulation and a reduction in administrative burdens through the increased use of technology.

While part five deals with dealings with third countries, the sixth part of the Proposal sets out further details on the adoption of emergency measures. These are seen to be a crucial part of animal disease management. The Proposal sets out the procedures to be followed in the case of an emergency to ensure that there is as rapid and consistent a response from the EU as possible. Again, few changes are made from existing legislative requirements in this regard as the system that has been developed since BSE is considered to function well.

10.5.2 Animal Welfare Requirements

While there are general strategies, and proposals for more general laws, on animal welfare and health, most of the legal requirements in this area come from specific provisions which set out the detail on how different animals are to be treated, and also how all animals are to be treated in different situations. There are, for example, specific provisions on the care of food-producing poultry, pigs and cattle. There are also general provisions applicable to all food-producing animals as regards their transportation and slaughter. These are all discussed in more detail below.

Welfare of Farmed Animals (England) Regulations 2007

The main framework legislation on the protection of animals in the UK is the Animal Welfare Act 2006. Subsequent to this, the Welfare of Farmed Animals

(England) Regulations 2007 were introduced to provide more specific detail on the conditions required for keeping food-producing animals. These also give effect to the main provisions of EU law in this area, first introduced through a series of directives in the 1990s. In the most general of senses, the welfare of farm animals is also guided by what are known as 'the five freedoms of animal welfare'.

These have been developed by the government advisory body, the Farm Animal Welfare Council (FAWC). They state that animal keepers must, at all times, ensure that the animals are (i) free from hunger and thirst—animals must have access to fresh water and a healthy diet; (ii) free from discomfort—an appropriate environment should be provided, including shelter and a comfortable resting area; (iii) free from pain, injury or disease—to include rapid diagnosis and treatment of illness; (iv) free to express normal behaviour—by ensuring that they have sufficient space, proper facilities and the company of animals of their own kind; and (v) free from fear and distress—by providing conditions and treatment which avoid mental suffering.

The 2007 Regulations are divided into two main parts. The first of these sets the definitions, scope, duties and offences which can be committed under the legislation. The main responsibilities are set for those who are either in charge of or own animals.[167] This includes taking all reasonable steps to ensure that the conditions under which an animal is being kept comply with the standards set out in the second part of the Regulations—the Schedules.[168] These schedules set out all of the specific requirements for different species of food-producing animals, including poultry, cattle and pigs. Those responsible for farmed animals must be acquainted with, and have access to, any relevant code of practice while attending to the animals.[169] This includes, for example, the Codes of Recommendation on meat chickens, laying hens and cattle. These Codes can be established under the terms of the Animal Welfare Act 2006.[170] They are not law, but failure to follow the Codes can be used as evidence in court when a prosecution is brought for causing unnecessary suffering to livestock. It is local authorities which are charged with bringing any such prosecutions under the Regulations.[171] Anyone found guilty of an offence under the legislation is liable to a term of imprisonment of up to 51 weeks or a fine up to level 4 on the standard scale,[172] or both.[173]

---

[167] 'Persons responsible for farmed animals' are as defined in section 3 of the Animal Welfare Act 2006. Under this provision, references to a person being responsible for an animal includes those who have this responsibility on either a permanent or on a temporary basis. It extends to those who are 'in charge' of animals, and for the purposes of the Act, a person who owns an animal shall always be regarded as being a person who is responsible for it. A person is also to be treated as being responsible for an animal where he has care and control over a person under 16 years of age who is looking after animals.

[168] Reg 4.

[169] Reg 6.

[170] Section 14 of the Animal Welfare Act 2006.

[171] Reg 8 of the Welfare of Farmed Animals (England) Regulations 2007.

[172] As set out in s 37 of the Criminal Justice Act 1982.

[173] Reg 9 of the 2007 Regulations, n 171 above.

It is really the schedules to the 2007 Regulations which provide the specific detail on how many of our food-producing animals are to be treated. These schedules transpose the original and amended key provisions of secondary EU law in this area into the domestic legal system. This includes, for example, the transposition of Directive 1991/630 on the protection of pigs,[174] Directive 1999/74 on the protection of egg-laying hens,[175] and Directive 1991/629 setting minimum standards for the protection of calves.[176]

Schedule 1 to the 2007 Regulations deals first with the general conditions under which all farmed animals should be kept. This includes requirements on staffing (sufficient numbers and competence), inspection systems (accessible and regular), record keeping (on health matters), freedom of movement (relatively unrestricted), accommodation (clean, safe and comfortable), protection from adverse weather, soundness of mechanical equipment, breeding procedures, feed and water (wholesome, appropriate, free from contamination) and a prohibition on the use of electrical currents for the immobilisation of animals. The requirements reflect those set out in EU Directive 1998/58. This Directive also contains provision for the recognition of the European Convention for the Protection of Animals, which is discussed in more detail below.

Welfare of Egg-laying and Meat-producing Poultry

Schedule 2 moves to deal with more specific requirements which are applicable to the keeping of egg-laying hens. This now deals with all such hens that are kept in unenriched cage systems. First flagged as a possibility in the EU Action Plan on Welfare,[177] the keeping of hens in conventional cages has been banned since January 2012. This prohibition, initially introduced by EU Directive 1999/74,[178] was later confirmed in Schedule 3 to the 2007 English Regulations. It represents one of the most significant advances made by EU intervention into unethical farming practices. Prior to the ban, which several EU Member States lobbied against for many years, egg-laying hens were categorised as being held in either enriched cages,[179] unenriched cages,[180] or, for the luckier ones, 'alternative' systems.[181] Those accommodated in the latter are provided with perching and nesting opportunities, as well as access to open runs. Enriched cages do include

---

[174] Council Directive 1991/630/EEC of 19 November 1991 laying down minimum standards for the protection of pigs [1991] OJ L 340/33. Later amended by Council Directive 2001/88/EC of 23 October 2001 [2001] OJ L 316/1.

[175] Council Directive 1999/74/EC of 19 July 1999 laying down minimum standards for the protection of laying hens [1999] OJ L 203/53.

[176] Council Directive 1991/629/EEC of 19 November 1991 laying down minimum standards for the protection of calves [1991] OJ L 340/28. This has since been amended by Directive 2008/119 [2008] OJ L 10/7.

[177] Note 157 above.

[178] Note 175 above.

[179] Art 6 of Directive 1999/74, n 175 above.

[180] ibid, Art 5.

[181] Art 4.

nests and perches, as well as a minimum requirement of 750 cm^2 of space per hen, although only 600 cm^2 of this must be 'usable'. This was reduced to 550 cm^2 for those held in unenriched cages, with no nesting or perch requirements. The requirements for meat-producing chickens are different. They are set out in EU Regulation 1538/1991,[182] combined with the Welfare of Farmed Animals (England) (Amendment) Regulations 2010.[183] This inserts a new Schedule 5a into the 2007 Regulations, which sets minimum standards for the training of animal keepers, stocking densities—which are set by kg per m^2, feeding, housing, inspecting and slaughter.

The 1991 EU Regulation covers a range of aspects related to the marketing of poultry, including welfare standards. It defines the different types of poultry (chickens, turkeys, ducks, geese, guinea fowl), the cuts of meat that can be taken from poultry (half, quarter, breast, leg, thigh, drumstick, wing), and there is special provision for the definition of 'foie gras'.[184] The Regulation sets out a range of definitions for the different kinds of farming methods that are employed in the production of poultry meat. This includes the setting of requirements that must be met before a producer can use descriptions such as 'free range', 'traditional free range', 'extensive indoor' and 'barn reared'. The highest welfare standards, which are those related to organic production methods, are not covered by this Regulation but are dealt with in Regulation 834/2007, as was discussed above. Annex IV to the 1991 Regulation provides that the term 'free range' can only be used for poultry where the following conditions are satisfied:

> [t]he stocking rate in the house … in accordance with the limits fixed [for barn reared but] the birds have had during at least half their lifetime continuous daytime access to open-air runs comprising an area mainly covered by vegetation of not less than 1 m^2 per chicken or guinea fowl, 2 m^2 per duck, 4 m^2 per turkey or goose [and] the feed formula used in the fattening stage contains at least 70% of cereals [and] the poultryhouse is provided with popholes of a combined length equal to or greater than that of a longer side of the house in the case of chickens.

The requirements for use of the term 'traditional free range' are slightly higher. So, for example, the open-air run size increases to 2 m^2 per chicken, 6 m^2 for turkeys and 10 m^2 for geese. Minimum slaughter ages are also increased for some poultry in this category, such as that for chickens which rises to a minimum life of 81 days, from 56 days, if the bird is to be labelled as 'traditional free range'. Finally, a description of 'free range—total freedom' can be used where the poultry have had continuous day-time access to open-air runs of an unlimited area.

---

[182] Commission Regulation (EEC) No 1538/1991 of 5 June 1991 introducing detailed rules for implementing Regulation (EEC) No 1906/1990 on certain marketing standards for poultry [1991] OJ L 143/11.

[183] SI No 3033/2010.

[184] Art 1 of Reg 1538/1991. 'Foie gras' is specified as being 'the livers of geese, or of ducks of [specified species] which have been fed in such a way as to produce hepatic fatty cellular hypertrophy'. 'Hypertrophy' is an abnormally large growth, in this case in the liver.

The 1991 Regulation was amended in 2008.[185] The same categories are set out as they were in 1991.[186] The 2008 Regulation does include a requirement that producers who use free-range systems must also keep records of the dates when birds were first given access to open-air runs.[187] Annex V to the 2008 amendments stipulates similar stocking rates, run sizes and feed requirements as were set out in its predecessor.

The standards for free-range are different for eggs. As noted above, one of the most significant legal developments related to the welfare of food-producing animals to have taken place at EU level has been the banning of egg production from hens housed in unenriched cages. Several different standards of welfare in egg production still remain. These are now set out in EU Regulation 589/2008,[188] which is given further effect at national level by the Eggs and Chicks (England) Regulations 2009.[189]

The 2008 Eggs Regulation provides a set of minimum requirements for the various egg farming methods. Annex II to the Regulation states that 'free range eggs'

> must be produced in systems of production which satisfy ... the following conditions: (a) hens must have continuous daytime access to open-air runs. However, this requirement does not prevent a producer from restricting access for a limited period of time in the morning hours in accordance with usual good farming practice, including good animal husbandry practice. In case of other restrictions, including veterinary restrictions, adopted under [EU] law to protect public and animal health, having the effect of restricting access of hens to open-air runs, eggs may continue to be marketed as 'free-range eggs' for the duration of the restriction, but under no circumstances for more than 12 weeks.

In a similar provision to that made for free-range poultrymeat, the Regulation further stipulates that the open air runs referred to

> must be mainly covered with vegetation and not be used for other purposes except for orchards, woodland and livestock grazing if the latter is authorised by the competent authorities; [they must also have a] maximum stocking density [not] greater than 2,500 hens per hectare of ground available to the hens or one hen per 4 m² at all times [and the] open-air runs must not extend beyond a radius of 150 m from the nearest pophole of the building.

The Regulation affords protection to both the poultry covered by its provisions, and consumers who are willing to pay extra for food produced according to higher welfare standards. It protects these purchasers by setting the minimum

---

[185] Commission Regulation (EC) No 543/2008 of 16 June 2008 laying down detailed rules for the application of Council Regulation 1234/2007 as regards the marketing standards for poultrymeat [2008] OJ L 157/46.

[186] ibid, Art 11.

[187] Art 12 thereof.

[188] Commission Regulation (EC) No 589/2008 of 23 June 2008 laying down detailed rules for implementing Council Regulation (EC) No 1234/2007 as regards marketing standards for eggs [2008] OJ L 163/6.

[189] SI No 2163/2009.

requirements that must be met before the stated sales descriptions can be used on the labelling of poultrymeat and eggs. The legislation also establishes a coding system, which must be used on all commercially produced eggs, which assists in the identification of the process used in production. The code includes details about the farming method, the Member State of production and the identification of the establishment where it was produced. Where a code starts with the number '0', this shows that the egg has been organically produced. The numbers '1', '2' and '3' are used to represent free-range, barn and caged production respectively. Thereafter there should be a country code, such as 'UK', followed by a unique number attached to the producing establishment. This is set out in the Annex to EU Directive 2002/4,[190] which was later transposed directly into English law by Regulation 589/2008.[191]

Welfare of Calves Used in the Production of Veal

The 2007 Regulations set out additional conditions for meat-producing calves. The production of calf meat, or veal, has been a controversial one in the UK for some time.[192] This has often been due to the conditions in which it has been reported that the calves are being kept, rather than concerns over the young age of the animal at slaughter. However, the Regulations clearly prohibit a number of the practices to which there have been objections in the past. For example, calves can not be confined in an individual stall or pen after the age of eight weeks, unless a veterinary surgeon has certified that this is necessary for its health or due to some behavioural issue.[193] Where the use of a stall or pen is permitted, they must meet a range of minimum size requirements. They must also have perforated walls that allow the animal to have visual and tactile contact.

Calves must have sufficient room to stand up, lie down, turn around, rest and groom without hindrance. They must also be able to see at least one other calf where they are kept on a holding of more than one animal. They should be inspected at least twice per day, reducing to once where they are kept outdoors. Schedule 6 also prohibits the use of tethering, with the exception of allowing this for up to one hour for the purposes of feeding. Calves may not be muzzled. A series of requirements are also set for the animals' housing, including stipulations

---

[190] Commission Directive 2002/4/EC of 30 January 2002 on the registration of establishments keeping laying hens, covered by Council Directive 1999/74/EC [2002] OJ L 30/44.

[191] Art 1(5) of Reg 589/2008, n 188 above.

[192] This includes the bringing of an action by the Royal Society for the Prevention of Cruelty to Animals (RSPCA) and Compassion in World Farming (CIWF) against the Minister of Agriculture, Fisheries and Food, challenging a refusal to restrict the export of veal calves to other EU Member States where they would be kept in veal crates. Case C-1/1996 *The Queen v Minister of Agriculture, Fisheries and Food, ex parte Compassion in World Farming Ltd* [1998] ECR I-1251. The Court held that the Art 36 TFEU exception to the Art 34 TFEU rule on the free movement of goods could not be used to justify such a restriction on exportation on the basis of the protection of public order or public morality. For further discussion on this see R Muñoz, 'Case C-1/96, *The Queen v Minister of Agriculture, Fisheries and Food, ex parte Compassion in World Farming Limited*' (1999) 36 *CML Rev* 831.

[193] Sch 6 to the Welfare of Farmed Animals (England) Regulations 2007.

related to the use of artificial light, sanitation, flooring and bedding. They should be fed at least twice per day. They should have sufficient quantities of fresh drinking water.

Welfare of Pigs

In addition to veal calves and caged egg-producing hens, the conditions in which many pigs are kept have given rise to most concern amongst welfare-conscious consumers. Minimum standards for the protection of pigs were initially set out in Directive 1991/630,[194] and are now transposed into English law by Schedule 8 to the Welfare of Farmed Animals (England) Regulations 2007. This provides that the pigs must be inspected daily, that they may not be tethered unless this is necessary for them to be examined by a vet, that they should be separated from aggressive or fighting pigs, and that they are given access to adequate amounts of food and water daily. Pigs must be free to turn around in their accommodation, without difficulty and at all times. Slatted floors can be used, but maximum widths for the openings between the slats are set depending on the degree to which the pig has matured and developed.

Farrowing crates are also permitted, but sow stalls are not. The two systems are quite different. Stalls have been banned across the EU since 2013. They have, however, been banned in the UK since 1999. The use of stalls and farrowing crates are amongst the more controversial elements of pig meat production. To look first at the provisions on farrowing, Schedule 8 to the 2007 Regulations provides that pens used for this purpose must incorporate some means of protecting the piglets from being smothered should their mother roll over on top of them. This is the key purpose behind the use of farrowing crates. It is designed to keep piglet mortality rates down. However, it is the design of some of the crates employed for this purpose that has given rise to some controversy. Many are deemed to be both uncomfortable and overly restrictive for the sow and on her ability to move freely. Stalls are different. They are often used to restrict the movement of the sow and to keep her separated from other animals during her gestation period due to concerns about fighting. As stated above, the UK has been ahead of the trend on the phasing out of the use of sow crates over welfare concerns. Their use has been prohibited in the UK since 1999. The EU followed, with its own ban coming into effect in 2013, although some Member States, notably Sweden, had also banned them prior to this (since 1988). The UK ban was introduced by the Welfare of Pigs Regulations 1991.[195]

A Report of the European Commission's Scientific Veterinary Committee on the Welfare of Intensively Kept Pigs, published in September 1997, carried the results of a comparative analysis of the figures for pig mortality in Sweden, where crates were banned, and Denmark, where they were not. Despite the arguments

---

[194] Council Directive 1991/630, n 174 above.
[195] SI No 1477/1991.

that have been made in favour of continuing with crating, the data showed that there was little difference between the mortality rates on those farms where crates were used (Denmark, average mortality 11.7 per cent) and many of those farms where they were not being used (Sweden, average mortality among best herds 12.9 per cent). The average overall was slightly higher for Sweden, but not significantly so. It also appeared from the studies examined that most of the threat to piglet mortality from the sow over-lying on, and crushing, them was in the few days immediately after birth.

The EU has now acted on the use of sow crates during and after gestation, introducing a prohibition on their use in the vast majority of Member States where this was not already the case. Directive 2008/120 states that

> [m]ember states shall ensure that sows and gilts are kept in groups during a period start-ing from four weeks after [gestation commences] to one week before the expected time of farrowing. The pen where the group is kept must have sides greater than 2.8 m in length. When fewer than six individuals are kept in a group the pen where the group is kept must have sides greater than 2.4 m in length. By way of derogation [from this] sows and gilts raised on holdings with fewer than 10 sows may be kept individually during the period mentioned [above] provided that they can turn around easily in their boxes.[196]

EU Member States were given 12 years to bring about this change, with the deci-sion to ban the use of individual sow stalls originally being taken in 2001.[197]

Despite the provision of this lengthy transitional period, nine Member States had to be served with a formal notice in February 2013 due to their failure to properly implement this important welfare provision. The list of non-conforming Member States included France, Germany, Denmark, Belgium, Ireland, Cyprus, Greece, Poland and Portugal. Failure to comply after this could lead to further enforcement action being taken, including the issuing of a reasoned opinion and ultimately action before the Court of Justice. Those Member States that do comply with EU obligations like this, including the UK, which has had this ban in place since 1999, would have an obvious grievance here, as would those hold-ings based in countries where the prohibition on stalls had yet to become fully operational. There is a clear competitive advantage for those operators who do not invest in higher welfare systems, both from a set-up cost and also possibly an ongoing operating cost perspective.

Transportation of Live Animals Provisions

The introduction of a new EU regulation in 2005 on the transportation of live animals marked a significant tightening-up of existing requirements on live

---

[196] Art 3(4) of Council Directive 2008/120/EC of 18 December 2008 laying down minimum stan-dards for the protection of pigs [2008] OJ L 47/5.
[197] Council Directive 2001/88/EC of 23 October 2001 amending Directive 1991/630/EEC laying down minimum standards for the protection of pigs [2001] OJ L 316/1.

animal transportation,[198] including the adoption of more stringent measures designed to prevent pain and suffering, as well as others designed to minimise the occurrence and spread of infectious diseases.[199] The European Parliament had previously called upon the Commission to draft proposals for amending these existing Union rules on the transportation of livestock. The use of a Regulation for this legislative initiative was specifically chosen after a series of difficulties were identified in the application of the earlier directives due to differences in transposition at national level. One of the key proposals put forward was to make transporters more accountable, and their activities more transparent. The Preamble to the 2005 Regulation noted that the welfare conditions of animals during transport results mainly from the daily conduct of the transporters. They would share the burden of the new regulations, along with the other relevant operators, such as farmers, traders and slaughterhouses. It was given full effect in English law by the Welfare of Animals (Transport) (England) Order 2006.[200] Under the terms of this Order, it is local authorities who are charged with the responsibility for enforcing the terms of the Regulation.

The Regulation sets out a number of general conditions for the transportation of live animals. The most general of these is that there is a prohibition on transporting in a way that is likely 'to cause injury or undue suffering'.[201] There are also a set of more specific conditions. These include ensuring that all necessary arrangements have been made in advance to minimise the length of, and to meet the animals' needs during, journeys.[202] The animals must be fit for the journey.[203] The means of transport and loading must be designed, constructed, maintained and operated so as to avoid injury and suffering, providing sufficient floor area and height for the animals appropriate to their size and journey.[204] Personnel should be properly trained and/or competent and must check the animals regularly, providing water, feed and rest at appropriate intervals.[205]

As stated above, the Regulation places a lot of responsibility on the transporters for the operation of the legislative requirements set out. More specifically, this includes carrying the appropriate documentation,[206] planning journeys

---

[198] As established by Council Directive 1991/628/EC of 19 November 1991 on the protection of animals during transport and amending Directives 1990/425/EEC and 1991/496/EEC [1991] OJ L 340/17. The two directives referred to here in the title of Directive 1991/628 were not transportation directives as such, but instead dealt more specifically with veterinary checks on animals entering the EU from third countries.

[199] Council Regulation (EC) No 1/2005 of 22 December 2004 on the protection of animals during transport and related operations and amending Directives 1964/432/EEC and 1993/119/EC and Regulation (EC) No 1255/1997 [2005] OJ L 3/1. The Regulation applied from January 2005, but most of its provisions came into effect during 2007 and 2008.

[200] SI No 3260/2006.

[201] Art 3.

[202] Art 3(a).

[203] Art 3(b).

[204] Art 3(c), (d) and (g).

[205] Art 3(e), (f) and (h).

[206] Art 4.

properly,[207] being in possession of authorisation from the national competent authority,[208] and ensuring that the means of transportation has been inspected and approved.[209]

As is the case for many of the welfare regulations, the real detail is set out in the Annex. This provides the more specific and practical requirements on how animals are to be treated before, during and after transportation. Annex I to Regulation 1/2005 sets out all of the technical rules about this. This includes a prohibition on the transportation of animals which are deemed unfit for their intended journey. More specifically, if an animal is unable to move or walk unassisted, has a severe open wound, is nearing the end of pregnancy or is a new-born mammal—including all journeys in excess of 100 km for pigs under three weeks, lambs under one week and calves under 10 days—it should not be transported. There are some exceptions to this, such as the transportation of an injured animal under veterinary supervision. Lactating females which are not accompanied by their offspring should be milked at least every 12 hours. Piglets, lambs and calves under a certain weight or age must be provided with appropriate bedding material.

One of the most significant progressions that has taken place in relation to welfare issues during animal transportation is the setting of more stringent requirements on watering, feeding and resting periods. Animals should be offered water, feed and the opportunity to rest, as appropriate to their species and age, at suitable intervals. Mammals and birds should be fed at least every 24 hours, and watered at least every 12 hours, unless specified otherwise. Clear requirements are set for different types of animals which are being transported by road. Unweaned calves, lambs, and piglets must all be given a rest period of at least one hour after nine hours of travel. Pigs can only be transported for a maximum period of 24 hours. They must be given continuous access to water for the duration of their journey. Most other animals must be given a rest of at least one hour after 14 hours of travel. They may then be transported for a further 14 hours after this. There are, of course, exceptions to all of these rules, depending on the type of animal, the mode of transportation, and the geographical location of the points of departure and arrival, especially for journeys by sea.

Some of the other stipulations contained in the Regulation include those related to the temperature and ventilation during transportation. The general rule is that it should not get hotter than 30 degrees Celsius, nor cooler than 5 degrees Celsius. Means of transportation should be fitted with alarms which indicate to the driver that maximum or minimum temperatures have been exceeded. All of the data related to this should be recorded. Similarly, road vehicles used for the transportation of animals should be fitted with navigation devices which record

---

[207] Art 5.

[208] Art 6 of Reg 1/2005, n 199 above. Section 20 of the Welfare of Animals (Transport) (England) Order 2006 provides that the Secretary of State is the competent authority for the purposes of granting or issuing transporters with authorisations.

[209] Art 7.

relevant information about journeys undertaken. Finally, all journeys involving animal transportation should be properly logged. Annex II to the Regulation provides that this should include verifiable set details on the route plan, which should be made available to the competent authorities in the Member State of departure.

Welfare at Time of Slaughter

In addition to the introduction of the ban on the use of unenriched cages in egg production, the EU Action Plan on Welfare also called for proposals to be brought forward on new legislation regulating the slaughtering process. This ultimately resulted in a new regulation being introduced on this matter in 2009.[210] This Regulation sets a series of both general and specific requirements for abattoirs, designed to make the slaughter process as free of stress and pain as possible for the animals. Amongst the general requirements is the provision that animals should be spared any avoidable pain or distress during slaughter.[211] This includes handling and housing the animals in a manner that has regard for their normal behaviour, as they await their fate at the abattoir. They should also be provided with feed and water if necessary and they should be provided with physical comfort and protection, in particular by being kept clean in adequate thermal conditions and prevented from falling or slipping.[212] The stunning of animals before slaughter is required under the legislation.

Animals can only be killed after stunning in a manner that is in accordance with the methods and specific requirements related to the application of those methods set out in Annex I to the Regulation. The loss of consciousness and sensibility of the animals has to be maintained until they are dead. The methods referred to in Annex I which do not result in an instantaneous death must be followed as quickly as possible by a procedure that does ensure death, such as bleeding, pithing, electrocution or prolonged exposure to anoxia.

The methods used in stunning can adapt over time, in particular where there are technological developments in this area. The Regulation can, and should, therefore be amended to take account of any such scientific and technical progress following an opinion of EFSA on the matter. Any such amendments must give full consideration to maintaining a level of animal welfare that is at least equivalent to that which was ensured by the already existing methods.

Animals which are subjected to particular methods of slaughter that are prescribed by religious rites are not subject to these stunning requirements, provided that the slaughter takes place in a slaughterhouse.[213] Similarly, stunning is not required for the private killing of poultry.[214] This is the first in a list of slaughter

---

[210] Council Regulation (EC) No 1099/2009 of 24 September 2009 on the protection of animals at the time of killing [2009] OJ L 303/1.

[211] Art 3.

[212] Art 3(a) and (e).

[213] Art 4.

[214] Art 10.

requirements which, although applying to most animals, are not required for poultry. This includes the suspending or hoisting of live animals and the tying of legs or feet or clamping.[215] Certificates of competence are required for all animal killing operations.[216] Welfare officers should be appointed for all slaughterhouses over a certain minimum size.[217] Finally, imports of meat into Britain, or any other part of the EU, from third countries must be certified as having been slaughtered to equivalent welfare standards to those set out in the 2009 Regulation.[218]

The Regulation, which replaces EU Directive 1993/119 and the transposing Welfare of Animals (Slaughter or Killing) Regulations 1995[219] came into effect in January 2013. All national approved slaughterhouses are supervised by official veterinary surgeons who were employed by the Meat Hygiene Service, which is a Government agency that is now part of the Food Standards Agency. These official vets must ensure that there is compliance by the food business operators with both the meat hygiene and the animal welfare rules. The vets themselves must follow DEFRA guidelines. Where they do not believe that the required standards are being met, the official vets can provide written or verbal advice or warnings or, where this is not sufficient, they can issue a recommendation for prosecution. The Animal Health and Veterinary Laboratories Agency (AHVLA) is charged with supervising killings on farms and at knackers' yards. This is not done on an ongoing basis, but instead takes place on AHVLA visits to farms. Those who are responsible for killing or slaughtering animals or birds on farms must hold a slaughter licence, unless it is being killed for disease control purposes, or it is suffering, or it is being killed for personal consumption or if it being killed by a qualified veterinary surgeon.

The slaughter of animals without stunning has been officially permitted in England since the Slaughter of Animals Act 1933, and then later by Schedule 12 to the Welfare of Animals (Slaughter or Killing) Regulations 1995. The Preamble to the present legislation on the matter, Regulation 1099/2009, states that

> [d]erogation from stunning in case of religious slaughter taking place in slaughterhouses was [originally] granted by Directive 93/119/EC. Since [Union] provisions applicable to religious slaughter have been transposed differently depending on national contexts and considering that national rules take into account dimensions that go beyond the purpose of this Regulation, it is important that derogation from stunning animals prior to slaughter should be maintained, leaving, however, a certain level of subsidiarity to each Member State. As a consequence, this Regulation respects the freedom of religion and the right to manifest religion or belief in worship, teaching, practice and observance, as enshrined in Article 10 of the Charter of Fundamental Rights of the European Union.[220]

---

[215] Art 15.
[216] Art 7.
[217] Art 17.
[218] Art 12.
[219] SI No 731/1995.
[220] Recital 18 of the Preamble to Reg 1099/2009, n 210 above.

Some stunning before slaughter is permitted under the Muslim rules for Halal meat production, and the evidence shows that the majority of animals killed this way were stunned first. This is outlined in more detail below. Shechita, the Jewish method of slaughtering animals and poultry for food, does not permit any pre-killing stunning. It is also forbidden to slaughter an animal in front of any other animals or to slaughter an animal and its offspring on the same day. While Shechita is normally performed when the animal is lying on its back, this is not permitted under English law. Where an animal is slaughtered without prior stunning, it must take place in a licensed abattoir, licensed poultry slaughterhouse under official veterinary supervision, or in another officially regulated poultry slaughterhouse. The shochet, who performs the Schechita, must be highly trained and licensed every 12 months by the Rabbinical Commission for the Licensing of Shochetim. The shochet must also be licensed by the local authority responsible for the place where the slaughter occurs.

A Food Standards Agency report, published in 2012, and based on a survey of slaughterhouses taken in September 2011, found that around 3 per cent of cattle were slaughtered by the Shechita method at four establishments, with 10 per cent of these stunned immediately after bleeding. Approximately 4 per cent of cattle were slaughtered by the Halal method at 16 establishments. Of these, 84 per cent were stunned before slaughter, and less than 1 per cent were stunned after bleeding. For sheep and goats, less than 1 per cent were slaughtered by the Jewish method, none of which were stunned. Around 50 per cent were slaughtered by the Muslim method, of which 81 per cent were stunned before slaughter. Again, around 1 per cent of all poultry slaughtered in the UK were by Shechita without stunning and around 30 per cent were slaughtered by the Halal method, almost all of which were stunned before slaughter. According to the Food Standards Agency, the results indicate that the number of animals not stunned prior to slaughter is relatively low, accounting for 3 per cent of cattle, 10 per cent of sheep and goats and 4 per cent of poultry.[221] They also show that the majority of animals destined for the Halal trade in both the red and white meat sectors are stunned before slaughter.[222]

European Convention for the Protection of Farmed Animals

Another significant influence on domestic animal welfare law has been the Council of Europe's Convention for the Protection of Animals Kept for Farming Purposes. Originally drafted in 1976, and amended in 1972, the Convention lays down a range of minimum standards to apply in the national laws across all Contracting Parties, including Britain. It is applicable to all animals kept for

---

[221] Whether these figures can offer comfort to those concerned with animal welfare is beyond the scope of this book.

[222] Food Standards Agency, 'Results of the 2011 FSA Animal Welfare Survey in Great Britain', 22 May 2012. Available at: http://multimedia.food.gov.uk/.

farming purposes, including food production, wool, skin or fur, and it also covers those animals which have been produced from genetic modification techniques. It is particularly concerned with animals reared and kept in intensive farming systems. Compliance with the Convention is deemed to demonstrate the implementation of an acceptable level of animal welfare protection.[223]

The main aims of the Convention are reflected in the key provisions of the framework EU and national legislation, most notably the objective of protecting farm animals from unnecessary injury or suffering. Article 1 broadly provides that

[t]his Convention shall apply to the keeping, care and housing of animals, and in particular to animals in modern intensive stock-farming systems [including] animals bred or kept for the production of food.

The key provisions, which should be given legal effect by each of the Contracting Parties to the Convention, are contained in Articles 3–7. This includes the requirement that

[a]nimals shall be housed and provided with food, water and care in a manner which, having regard to their species and to their degree of development … is appropriate to their physiological and ethological needs in accordance with established experience and scientific knowledge.[224]

The Convention identified at an earlier stage than the EU and many of its Member States that freedom of movement for animals was crucial to their welfare. This was later reflected in initiatives such as those introduced in the UK on the use of farrowing crates and stalls. Article 4 of the Convention states that

[t]he freedom of movement appropriate to an animal, having regard to its species and in accordance with established experience and scientific knowledge, shall not be restricted in such a manner as to cause it unnecessary suffering or injury.

Other provisions of the Convention include the condition that animals should not be provided with food or liquid, or provided with those substances in a way, that can cause unnecessary suffering or injury.[225] There are also requirements on the daily inspection of animals and farming equipment, especially in intensive stick-farming systems.[226] The relevance of, and the similarities between, the Convention and the content of EU and national law are obvious. The Convention has had a significant persuasive effect in shaping both European and domestic law in this area. The implementation and application of the Convention is overseen by a Standing Committee, which is made up of representatives of each of the Contracting Parties and observers.[227]

---

[223] Para 69 of Case C-1/1996, n 192 above.
[224] Art 3 of the Convention.
[225] Art 6.
[226] Art 7.
[227] Arts 8–13.

10.6 Future Challenges for Food Law

The way in which the food sector is regulated has the most significant impact on the well-being of society. It has obvious health, economic, environmental and ethical consequences. Being informed about, and protected from, risks to health has been recognised as an important human right, and its incorporation into policy making and law enforcement must be an integral part of all public-health decision making.[228] The application of this right must also be guaranteed through the corporate activities of food business operators.[229] Food law now needs to be rebalanced to give increased consideration to the promotion of consumer concerns.

It has been made clear that there is a public health crisis. It is largely related to a combination of the consumption of low-quality food and drink and low levels of physical activity, along with other medical factors. Levels of overweight, obesity and related illness and disease are at record highs. Food law has not been properly used to play a part in dealing with this crisis. The economic, physical, mental and societal consequences of this have all been outlined in this book. It is the most pressing concern for those responsible for the introduction and enforcement of food laws.

New technologies always give cause for concern, as do other food safety matters, be they real or anticipated. Nanotechnology, cloning, agricultural intensification and the importance of water regulation are all issues that must be properly addressed by regulation, designed to ensure that demand is satisfied in a way that does not compromise safety standards or ethical considerations. Campaigns for food autonomy have emphasised some of the positive consequences of altering production and marketing processes. The introduction of higher welfare standards for both egg-laying hens and pigs used for meat production have provided us with examples of the positive changes that can be made to the ways in which food is produced and consumed, where consumers are sufficiently motivated to ensure change.

---

[228] D Feldman, 'The contribution of human rights to improving public health' (2006) 120 *Public Health* 61.

[229] For further discussion on the way in which human rights impact on companies as well as on states and individuals see A Dignam and D Allen, *Company Law and the Human Rights Act 1998* (London, Butterworths, 2000).

INDEX